ESSENTIAL PSYCHOLOGY

Also in the HarperCollins Essential Series

Essential Government and Politics
Jim Cordell

Forthcoming titles

Essential Accountancy and Finance
Bijon Kar

Essential Business Studies
Stephen Barnes

Series Editor: Roger Gomm

ESSENTIAL
PSYCHOLOGY

G C Davenport

CollinsEducational

An imprint of HarperCollins*Publishers*

The author asserts the moral right to be
identified as the author of this work.

Published by
Collins Educational Ltd.
77–85 Fulham Palace Road
Hammersmith
London W6 8JB

First published in 1992

British Library Cataloguing in Publication Data

Davenport, G.C.
Essential psychology.
1 Psychology
I Title   Ii. Series
150

ISBN 0–00–3222667

Typeset by Ellis Associates; cover design by Ridgeway Associates
and printed in Great Britain at the University Press, Cambridge

Contents

PATRICK .

KEITH .

Foreword

Every book in the Essential Series is designed carefully to put you in control of your own learning.

When you use this book, you will not only cover the core elements of your course but you will also benefit from the author's use of modern teaching and learning techniques, with the result that you will make the best possible use of your time.

This book has:

- an introductory section at the beginning of each chapter, which focuses your attention on its contents and which tells you exactly what you should have learned by the end of the chapter. These are your 'learning objectives'

- periodic summaries and reviews which regularly remind you of the content you are covering and so reinforce your learning

- notes in the margin of the text, where the author takes the role of a tutor: picking out key facts, highlighting and explaining difficult concepts and guiding you to a better understanding of the main text

- a guide to making notes as you work through the book

- essay questions and other assignments which will give you exam practice and help you to develop your skills in presenting written work

- suggestions for further reading that you can fit in will help you to develop a broader understanding of your subject, and this is always worth extra marks in the exam, as well as being more satisfying

- a section on study skills which gives valuable advice and suggestions for making the best use of your study time and improving your learning. When you have developed these basic skills you will be much better equipped to direct and control your own learning.

Learning is not easy: nobody learns without effort. However, if you use this book effectively you will not only succeed in your course and in your exam but you will also enjoy the experience of learning.

Acknowledgements

I would like to thank the following people for their assistance in preparing this book.

My wife, Jane, for her constant support and encouragement, and for her patience and understanding.

My parents, Rosa and Dennis, upon whose unswerving love and help I have always relied.

Alison Wadeley, for her diligence, her wisdom and her humour when reviewing the manuscript for this book and Roger Gomm for his guidance as Series Editor and help in sub-editing this book.

And to countless students, past and present, who have provided such a rich source of inspiration.

The author and publisher would like to thank the following for permission to use material reproduced in this work: The Hulton-Deutsch Collection for photographs appearing on pages 33, 35, 38, 46, 55 and page 71; Mary Evans Picture Library for the photograph appearing on page 26; the Freud Museum for the photograph appearing on page 37; the estate of B.F. Skinner for the photograph appearing on page 41; Albert Bandura for the photograph appearing on page 45; the estate of Dr John Bowlby for the photograph appearing on page 52; and the American Psychological Association for the illustration redrawn on page 135.

① Introduction to psychology

Chapter objectives

By the end of this chapter you should:
■ be able to define psychology

■ be able to describe the kinds of occupation taken by psychologists and the agencies in which they work

■ be able to list the various ways in which psychologists gather data and the strengths and weaknesses of the different methods

■ be able to review the debate about whether psychology can or should be regarded as a science

■ be able to identify and discuss the ethical problems which sometimes arise in conducting psychological research.

Introduction

You are reading a book covering some topics and issues in psychology. You probably already have some notions about the nature of psychology. Is it the study of the mind and brain; or the study of how people think and reason? Or is it the study of people's behaviour and why they do things? Is it a comparison of human and animal behaviour; or the study of mental illness and disturbed behaviour? The answer is that it is all of these things – and many more.

Psychology probably began with the first human beings, as they started to think and plan ahead. We are all *amateur psychologists*. Every day we make predictions and assumptions about other people's behaviour. We see how other people treat us, and so form impressions of what we must be like. We change the image of ourselves we show to people depending on the circumstances we are in. You probably behave differently in the presence of an attractive member of the opposite sex at a social event than when you are at home with your family. We learn from past mistakes and thereby improve the accuracy of future predictions. This is essentially what science does. So we are also amateur scientists, looking at our environment to provide evidence for our expectations about it, and modifying our expectations when we do not find the evidence.

As an academic subject psychology isn't much more than a hundred years old. We have learned a lot and have many theories about human skills, and we have developed many techniques for investigating them. However, if you think that psychology has all the answers, you will be disappointed. Humans are a strange species. Their behaviour is affected by all kinds of things which we might find difficult to imagine. What might happen in one group may not be relevant to another.

► You have been an *amateur psychologist* since you were quite young. Did you ever try to manipulate your parents to get your own way over something? That's one facet of psychology!

Study skills

If you are reading this book as part of a course of study then you should realize that you not only have to learn psychology, but also to learn to *study* psychology. You can read as many psychology books as you like but if you don't master the skills of studying it won't do you any good at all. At this point it would be a good idea to turn to the appendix on study skills at the end of the book, read it and begin to put the advice there into action.

WHAT IS PSYCHOLOGY?

What is psychology is a much more difficult question to answer than you might realize. The *Penguin Dictionary of Psychology* says 'Psychology simply cannot be defined ... it really isn't a thing at all, it is about a thing, or many things'. The particular 'things' psychology is about include unconscious mental experiences (e.g. the unconscious mind), conscious mental experiences (e.g. deliberate thoughts, emotions, memory, etc.) and behaviour (i.e. those things that we actually do, which can be measured). Different psychologists have different views about each of these and about what psychology is. Some psychologists insist that because their area within psychology uses scientific principles and methods of investigation, psychology should be thought of as a science. Others do not.

It isn't fair to ask someone to begin a course of study of a subject which cannot really be defined so, for the purposes of this book, psychology will be defined as 'the study of human (and other animal) behaviour and human experience'.

The origin of psychology

During the seventeenth century several famous philosophers (Locke, Berkeley, Hume, Hartley) advanced the theory that the only way that we could ever really know anything is to experience it directly, through our own senses. We must see, feel, touch, smell, hear and, most of all, *experience* things in order to really understand their nature. They claimed that since knowledge can only ever be gained through experience, we must use all kinds of experiments and other ways of finding things out for ourselves. This theory and method became known as the *empirical tradition* or *empiricism*.

During the eighteenth and nineteenth centuries several sciences, such as biology, had been showing what could be discovered about the physical world by patient observation and careful experimentation. The invention of the microscope in 1609 had allowed investigation which revolutionized ideas about infection and disease. Discoveries concerning the circulation of the blood, the use of vaccination, the existence and eventual use of radium, among many others did much to improve human life at the time. By the early nineteenth century the achievements of science caused philosophers such as Auguste Comte to insist that the methods of the natural sciences should be applied to studying human interaction. This belief became known as *positivism*.

► Look up the definition of psychology in two or three different dictionaries. Are they able to agree on what psychology is?

REVIEW – Empiricism
Philosophers discuss the nature of human thought and existence. One British and Irish philosophical tradition was empiricism which saw personal experience as the key to all knowledge.

REVIEW – Positivism
Positivists believe that everything, including human thinking and behaviour, can be understood by applying the principles and methods of science, and that scientific methods are therefore the only means by which anything should be investigated.

The Founding Fathers of Psychology: William James and Wilhelm Wundt

William James came from a wealthy Irish American family, and took some time to decide on a career. He eventually qualified in medicine and became interested in the relationship between psychology and physiology. One of his main concerns was the nature of human consciousness, and how it is constantly changing. He is claimed to have set up the first psychology laboratory in America, at Harvard University, in 1875.

Wilhelm Wundt was also a doctor. He was a quiet, unassuming man, who spent most of his life researching and writing about psychology. He wrote many books on physiology and its relationship with human consciousness, and he also claimed to have set up the first psychological laboratory, in Leipzig, Germany, in 1879.

Whether Wundt or James actually set up the first psychological laboratory has become more a matter of national pride between American and European authors than a matter of historical accuracy! And it doesn't really matter.

Positivism rejects any explanations, such as theology (religious explanations), which are not supported by empirical evidence. Few psychologists today would accept all positivist views, although many *behaviourist* psychologists do accept the principle that psychology should be based on scientific evidence. Behaviourists argue that only things which can be observed and measured can be studied in a scientific fashion – and the only thing which can be observed and measured is human behaviour itself. Emotions, motivation, attraction, consciousness, personality, intelligence, etc., can only be observed through the effects they have on behaviour. Where such effects can't be observed or measured, the phenomena aren't worth studying.

In the late nineteenth century **William James** in America and **Wilhelm Wundt** in Germany started applying some of the principles of the natural sciences to aspects of human behaviour. These two men are usually considered to be the 'founding fathers' of psychology.

Since the late nineteenth century many theories have been offered to explain aspects of the ways humans function. There are explanations of the development and maintenance of personality, of the origin of the intellect, of how we learn, of how we become sociable, of why we behave aggressively, of how some behaviour becomes 'abnormal' and of how we define and treat people who we describe as 'mentally ill', etc. We will be studying these things in this book, particularly the explanations of personality and of 'learning', since these represent two of the major traditions in psychology.

Summary – what is psychology?

Psychology is that branch of knowledge concerned with studying human (and some other animal) behaviour and human experiences. It developed from the nineteenth-century philosophical view that it was appropriate to apply the methods and principles of the natural sciences to the study of human beings, and from the advances made in sciences such as biology. However not all psychologists today accept these positivistic views.

WHAT DO PSYCHOLOGISTS DO?

Psychologists are involved in many types of research. Some conduct *applied* research. This seeks answers to actual problems, such as finding ways of dealing with stress, or advising on the design of complicated equipment to make it as easy as possible for the operator to use it. *Basic* (or *pure*) research seeks knowledge about things which may not have an immediate and obvious application. Testing the effects of certain chemical compounds on various types of body tissue, or discovering what the digger wasp will do after it finds its sealed up honeycomb has been opened by a researcher's pin, have no immediate benefit to human beings. However, findings from basic research often provide the starting-point for applied research.

As well as being involved in research, psychologists work in teaching and education, in social work and the probation service, in the police and prison service, in clinical and counselling areas, in hospitals, in personnel and marketing, in design and manufacture, and many other fields. While they all have some aspects of their training in common, each will have specialist knowledge of their own particular field, and will be applying their knowledge for the benefit of the organization for whom they work, or for its members.

Some of the most notable areas of psychological research include the study of cognition, social psychology, comparative psychology, the biological bases of human behaviour, development and education, and psychopathology. We will look at these topics later.

Psychologists may be engaged in applying their knowledge in settings such as clinics, personnel departments, design and advertising agencies. They may be conducting further research, or pass on their knowledge through teaching.

▶ Basic research often provides valuable information for further research. However, it rarely makes money, and is often sacrificed to applied research in commercial or university research departments.

▶ *Developmental psychology* studies how we acquire our personalities and the various skills we have, such as language, or intelligence.

▶ *Social psychology* is concerned with how we learn about ourselves, how we interact with each other, how we acquire our attitudes, etc.

▶ *Clinical psychology* is concerned with the therapies and treatments which have been developed for dealing with people whose behaviour we might define as 'abnormal' in some way.

NM This logo marks points at which I give you some prompts about note making. Suggestions for note making are given throughout the book.

NM It would be a good idea to make notes on different methods of research used by psychologists. To help you focus your notes I will be asking you questions from time to time. You might want to make more extensive notes, but it is not a good idea to try copying out the book!

It is important for you to make notes in such a way that you will be able to refer to them later and understand what they mean. Your notes should be clearly headed. For example a note on 'cross-sectional research' should be headed something like 'Methods of psychological research; cross-sectional research'. If the notes answer a question, the notes should

---

Can we believe psychologists?

Some critics think that psychological research hasn't been conducted for long enough, and hasn't developed a sufficiently precise enough system of gathering data, for psychology to be called a science, or for its conclusions to be accepted. Laboratory-based psychological research began less than 150 years ago.

Some psychologists have made claims which have brought discredit to psychology. One claim was that our dreams show what we would really like to happen to us. Few people believe that now! We certainly should not believe any claim psychologists make until it has been thoroughly checked out.

It isn't possible to study human behaviour and experience (or however else we define psychology) in the same way as we can study plants, minerals or other inanimate objects. Most people don't volunteer to take part in psychological research, so those who do probably aren't typical, and people generally behave differently when they know they are being studied.

---

make clear what the question was. Cross referencing your notes to the pages of this book and others is useful. Notes should be properly stored: ringbinder files with thin card spacers are ideal.

HOW DO PSYCHOLOGISTS COLLECT THEIR DATA?

Many people think that psychologists are able to make predictions about other people's behaviour. To do this psychologists must have studied large numbers of people – and in a scientific way. Other people are more cautious about any such claim. There are a number of reasons for this caution, as you can see from the inset above.

Before we can discuss whether psychology can be thought of as a science, we ought to know about the types of research psychologists conduct and some of the methods they use.

Types of research

There are essentially three types of research: cross-sectional studies, longitudinal studies and cross-cultural studies.

Cross-sectional studies look at large numbers of people, all at the same time. They provide a 'snapshot' of the population being studied, and are often used in developmental psychology and social psychology. A 'cross-section' could include people of different ages, both sexes, different races, different cultures, and so on.

Longitudinal studies take one group of people and study them at several points during their lives. They are useful for seeing the effects of age, or changing environments, on people's attitudes and behaviour, and are used particularly in developmental and social psychology. For example, longitudinal studies measure the extent to which people from particular backgrounds, say those who have been orphaned, change after something intervenes in their lives, for example adoption. People from different social backgrounds could be studied at, say, 7, 14, 21 and 28 years of age.

Distinguish cross-sectional from longitudinal research. Suppose a cross-sectional study of 15 year olds showed that those who were more aggressive at 15 had watched more violent television in their earlier years. What doubts would you have about such a study, and how would they have been resolved if a longitudinal study had been used instead?

Cross-cultural research compares people from different cultural backgrounds to see how their experiences have shaped their attitudes and behaviour. Cross-cultural studies have been used in social psychology, for example, to compare the effects that different kinds of child-rearing have had. They are also used to investigate the influences of genetic inheritance, as opposed to social learning, on our behaviour. It is usually assumed that if human behaviour is similar, irrespective of the culture in which it develops, then it is due to genetic factors rather than learning.

 What is cross-cultural research? How could cross-cultural research help to decide whether human males were biologically more aggressive than human females?

Who will we study?

As well as deciding what type of research to conduct we must decide what kind of people we will study. People or animals used in scientific or other research are usually called *subjects*. The subjects we use will influence the methods we use to study them. For example, in research on adults' attitudes we could conduct formal interviews, stopping people in the street and asking them some pre-set questions. You can't use interviews if your subjects are newborn infants!

Psychologists study groups of subjects to find out what they have in common, and study individuals to find out what makes each of them the way they are. If we are studying individuals, trying to discover those things which make each person unique, then we are conducting *idiographic research*. We may study just one person, or one family, or even one small group so long as all the members are very similar. It isn't possible to apply the findings from idiographic research to anyone other than the subjects of the research. In order to be able to generalize from the group we are studying to others, we will have to investigate general aspects of behaviour or experience which are common to all people. This is known as *nomothetic research*, and such research does allow generalizations to be made.

 Distinguish between idiographic and nomothetic research. Which of the following would be idiographic and which nomothetic?

- A cross-cultural study of child rearing
- An in-depth study of a family experiencing psychological problems
- A cross-sectional study of people's attitudes to mental illness

---

► *Genetic inheritance* refers to the biological material we receive from our parents at conception. *Social learning* refers to the way we learn by observing and imitating people around us.

► *Idiographic* research studies what makes an individual, a group or a culture unique. *Nomothetic* research looks for generalisations which can be made about all people.

Whichever type of research we are doing we will need some subjects (Ss) to study. Imagine that we want to find out something about 'A level psychology students'. They would be called our *target population* because they are the group we are aiming our research at. Since several thousand people study A level psychology each year, we obviously couldn't study all of them, so we would need to take a *sample* of them.

A sample could be a few students chosen from each class in each school or college. It could be a 10 per cent sample, or a 20 per cent sample, or whatever percentage would give us the number of Ss that would be *representative* of the whole target population. Being representative means the sample must be identical to the target population in every important respect – except its size. For example, most A level students are aged between 16 and 19, but some are older. Our sample must represent them all, so most of the sample should be aged 16 to 19, with just a few being older. If most of the target population were female, then most of our sample should be female.

If the members of the target population are all very similar, i.e. they are *homogeneous*, then we may only need a small sample of them to maintain its representativeness. But if the members of the target population are all very different, i.e. they are *heterogeneous*, then we will need a larger sample. If the sample is representative of the target population then we may *generalize* (apply our findings) to all A level psychology students.

One other factor to consider is the number of subjects that we have the resources to study. It's no good studying a heterogeneous target population if we only have the time (and money) to study a few subjects. We could adapt to our limited resources by undertaking a less ambitious project attempting to study a target population of 16 to 19 year olds, or females only. In this case we should only make generalizations about the target population our more limited sample represented.

The process of applying conclusions drawn from a sample to a whole target population is called *induction*. Induction allows us to generalize our conclusions. The object of conducting research on particular cases is usually to allow inductions to be made.

 What is a sample? What is a target population? Why do psychologists study samples of people? What must be true of the sample before generalizations can be made from the characteristics of the sample to the characteristics of the target population?

Methods of data collection

There are many different methods of data collection available to the psychologist. These range from incidental, even accidental, observations to grand, controlled and detailed experiments. Idiographic and nomothetic researchers have their own preferences about the best method to suit their particular requirements. The following are some of the main methods employed by psychologists.

> **A sample**
> A *sample* is the group chosen for study from the target population. Samples must always be representative of their target populations.

► Generalizing from the conclusions about the subjects of one study to all similar subjects is a major purpose of science.

► *Induction* is a way of logical reasoning which allows general statements to be made from studies of particular cases.

► *Observation* is the starting-point of all research. It is also a method for collecting data.

► Just about anywhere where a psychologist conducts controlled observations can be thought of as a laboratory. A classroom would be a psychological laboratory if controlled research was being conducted there.

Observations

All research must begin with some observation. Otherwise how could the researcher know what to do research on? Observation can be acci-dental, some chance encounter that sets off a train of thought.

Observation is the starting-point of all research. It is also a method for collecting data.

We usually refer to observation used by psychologists as being either *naturalistic* or *controlled* in some way. Naturalistic observation is conducted in the subject's natural environment. For example, a study of industrial behaviour may involve naturalistic observation of some workers at work, or a naturalistic observation of children's play might take place in a playground at school. Controlled observation is deliberately set up by the researcher. A child may be left alone in a room full of toys and asked not to play with them, while a hidden camera films the child's behaviour.

In either case the researcher may become involved, as a part of the group being studied (*participant observation*), or may stay outside the group, possibly unobserved by its members (*non-participant observation*). Psychologists who support the idiographic view often prefer participant observation, while those supporting a nomothetic approach sometimes prefer non-participant observation. Both methods have certain problems. For example, researchers who become involved with the group might start to be influenced by the ideas of the other members. Their report of what went on may become biased by their feelings about the group. Or the behaviour of the group members may be affected by the presence of the observers, since knowing that you are being watched may make you behave differently. Non-participant observation overcomes some of these difficulties, but has the problem that because the researcher has to remain at a distance from the group important things may be missed.

Naturalistic observation is less formal than controlled observation, since subjects are observed in their own environment, for example, children at various ages playing in their homes, or at school. Naturalistic observation has one major advantage over some other methods. Because subjects are not manipulated in any way their behaviour is less likely to be unnatural or distorted. People often behave differently when they know they are being observed.

Controlled observation is more formal, and usually takes place in a psychological laboratory. We could decide beforehand exactly what we wanted to observe, find somewhere where that was to be seen, obtain the appropriate permissions, and set up our observation post. We might use a video camera to record the events for later analysis.

Observations are used for studying behaviour, for example, whether someone will respond to a call for help if they believe that there are others around who are better qualified to help. They are of less use for discovering motivation, i.e. why the subject behaved in that way. To put it simply, observations are good for describing *what* happens, they are less good for explaining *why* something occurs.

Distinguish between naturalistic and controlled observation. Suppose you wanted to study whether the presence of other people influenced whether people washed their hands after using the toilet. You have rigged up the washing area of a public toilet with a video camera. What would be the advantages of 'controlling' the observation by providing the on-lookers? Would there by any advantages instead in just recording what happened (naturalistic observation)? Think of other topics which might be studied by observation.

Draw up a list of the advantages and disadvantages of naturalistic and controlled observation respectively.

Ethology is the study of animal (including human) behaviour in its natural habitat. Ethologists have made extensive use of naturalistic observation. Ethologists look for the relative contributions made to the animal's behaviour by its genetic inheritance, and the environment it lives in. Having made some observations about what seems to be involved in certain behaviour, it may be possible to test some specific assumptions using controlled observations or experiments.

One of the best known ethologists was **Konrad Lorenz (1903–89)**. His observations led him to experiment on what he called *imprinting*. Imprinting is the special kind of learning that occurs in the hours following birth which allows an animal to form an attachment to its caregiver. This will increase the chances of the young animal's survival since the parent will feed and defend its young.

Case studies

Case studies are detailed studies of one individual, or a group of individuals, who all have similar backgrounds. Clinical psychologists may build up case studies of their 'patients' or 'clients'. When enough relevant facts are known about someone, some kind of treatment or therapy may be applied. While case studies are useful in understanding the individual concerned, most psychologists are hesitant about generalizing from sets of case studies. Sigmund Freud, the founder of psychoanalysis, developed his detailed theory of personality development from case studies of the many patients he treated. The fact that psychoanalytic theory is based on case studies is one reason why it is not regarded as scientific.

 Look at your notes on samples and the idea of representativeness. What is the shortcoming of a theory of human behaviour based on case studies of patients who presented themselves for treatment?

Surveys

Surveys are one of the quicker ways of gathering data. They consist of questionnaires, inventories, or interviews. *Questionnaires* are simply lists of questions which can be multiple choice or open-ended. *Inventories* are checklists of characteristics, behaviours, etc. *Interviews* may be verbal questionnaires or may be more loosely structured

► Observations, case studies, surveys, and correlational studies rely on the researcher's own choices and interpretations. While their findings may be interesting and useful, they are not usually thought able to provide scientifically acceptable evidence. The only method which allows such evidence to be gathered is the experimental method.

► *Variables* are those things which vary in the research situation.

conversations between interviewer and interviewee.

Surveys allow us to ask questions about things we might not be able to observe directly, or study in any other way. They are occasionally used by psychologists to gather large amounts of information about people. The information may be general, relating to people's opinions or beliefs, or more detailed and specific, relating to particular experiences. The data gathered can be oral, taped, filmed or written. Surveys are one of the (relatively) cheap methods to employ, although people often refuse to answer long lists of questions or to spend long periods being interviewed. Up to 75 per cent of questionnaires sent through the post may not be returned. Respondents may also not tell the truth, may misinterpret questions, or may be affected by the personality of the questioner.

Correlation studies

Correlation is a statistical method which shows whether two things, such as time of day and speed of reactions, are related to each other. If people's reactions are slower later at night, then we have found a correlation between the two *variables* – time of day and speed of reaction. A variable is literally anything which varies. Time, temperature, intelligence, and personality are all variables.

Variables which differ between subjects, such as sex, age, culture, intelligence, and personality, are called *subject variables*. Variables in the situation which could affect the subjects' behaviour, such as amount of noise, light, and distraction, are called *situational variables*.

Correlation is simply a statistical technique used to handle the results of observation, experiments, surveys or any other kind of research producing numerical data. *Correlation studies* are a way of collecting and handling data from naturally occurring situations. For example, a correlation study might take a number of cases of one variable, such as the number of children's books available in one hundred children's homes, and another, such as the children's scores on tests of verbal intelligence. The statistical procedure called correlation finds whether there is any relationship between the two variables. Do the children with the most books gain the highest scores? If so, we have found a *positive correlation*. Correlational statistics allow us to state the relationship between the two variables as a positive number somewhere between 0 and 1. If, when one variable increases, another variable increases proportionately, then we have a *perfect positive correlation* (expressed as +1). This rarely happens in psychology!

Sometimes the increase in one variable, for example the amount of overcrowding of living conditions, correlates with a decrease in the likelihood of another variable appearing, for example the amount of cooperative behaviour shown. Here we have a *negative correlation* which will be expressed as a number between –1 and 0, with *perfect negative correlation* (expressed as –1).

Correlational statistics simply predict the likelihood of two variables occurring together. They do not suggest that the appearance of one variable will *cause* the other to appear. *Correlation does not establish*

REVIEW – Correlation
Correlation is a statistical procedure for measuring the likelihood that two variables will change in relation to each other. It does not demonstrate that one variable has any influence on the other. Correlation studies are used where controlled experiments would be impossible.

cause. It could well be that the two things are causally related – children with a lot of books in their homes may do well in intelligence tests, and their books could well have helped them. But the finding could just as easily not be due to the books at all. Perhaps the kinds of parents who buy lots of books for their children are also more concerned with the children's general development and encourage them in many ways such as taking them on educational visits. Stimulation derived from the visits may have helped them do well.

 What is a correlation study? What are negative and positive correlations? Why do correlations not necessarily show cause and effect relationships between variables?

Experiments

All the methods of data collection described so far are rather *subjective*, i.e. they may be biased by the researcher's personal feelings about the topic or the subject they are studying. Researchers do the observing and interpreting in observational studies: they choose the questions to ask and what the answers to them mean in surveys; and they choose which variables to correlate. Clearly there is potential for bias to creep in. Also, observations, case studies, surveys, correlations, etc., do not necessarily show that one thing causes another thing to happen. They show only that certain things appear to occur together. To be objective means to adopt methods of research which are fully describable so that others can scrutinize the research and perhaps repeat it, and detect any faulty procedures, illogicalities or biases. Although surveys and correlation studies can achieve a high degree of objectivity, experimental research is usually more objective in this sense.

The method which can make the strongest claim to be objective is the experimental method.

Experiments use procedures derived from the *scientific method*. The scientific method involves defining the problem to be investigated, stating it in such a way as to show how it fits in with existing knowledge and theories. A testable hypothesis is stated. This means making a proposal that if some aspect of the theory is true then something else ought to be true. For example, if the theory holds that distractions impair the ability to memorize then the hypothesis could be that people will remember less when given a learning task accompanied by loud background music. The hypothesis must be investigated under rigorously controlled conditions, and the data analysed and communicated in ways that enable others to see how the results support or contradict existing knowledge.

There are different types of experiment depending on how some of the variables are controlled. Where the experimenter deliberately controls the variables (usually in the laboratory) they are called *laboratory experiments*. This isn't always possible. For example, we couldn't investigate the variables 'children's emotional health' and 'separation from their parents for various amounts of time'. It would be highly improper even to suggest it. Anyway, we'd never find

▶ *Laboratory experiments* are artificial situations created so that some variables can be controlled and manipulated to demonstrate their effects on other variables.

parents who would let us do this. Even if we did, what would we do with the children during the separation? There are obvious ethical and moral problems. There might well be legal ones too!

However, children do sometimes become separated from their parents. A mother may become seriously ill and have to go into hospital for some time. Or the child may have to go into hospital. The family may be split up temporarily if there are financial or social problems. The children may have to be fostered temporarily. Where the variables already exist in the subject's natural environment we may use *natural experiments*. Natural experiments and correlational studies are usually one and the same.

Sometimes the subjects may be tested in their natural environment, but the experimenter still controls some variables. For example, researchers may visit a child's home, where the child feels comfortable, and provide various materials for the child to manipulate, or create situations which the child must resolve in some way. This is known as a *field experiment*.

The reasoning behind conducting experiments is to enable us to study a small number of people and apply our findings to all similar people. This is sometimes called the *inductive method*. Every detail in any experiment must be carefully planned and precisely executed. The smallest error could affect the results and ruin the research. Let's say we're testing the ability of males and females to recognize certain shapes. We can only test the females in the morning and the males in the evening. We find that females are better than males. Are these findings valid? Are males poorer at shape recognition? Can you offer any other explanation?

Note that experiments vary in the degree to which they establish an artificial environment (i.e. are 'controlled'). They range from laboratory experiments, through field experiments to natural experiments (which are usually correlation studies). What are the advantages and disadvantages of a high degree of control and the corresponding advantages and disadvantages of a high degree of naturalness in experimentation (see your notes on controlled and naturalistic observation)

The main features of the experimental method

1 *Hypotheses*. Before we can conduct an experiment we must state quite clearly what we intend to study. This is our hypothesis. A hypothesis is a statement which proposes an explanation for some facts. For example, an *experimental hypothesis* might be that 'tired people have slow reaction times'. There are two variables here: 'reaction time' and 'being tired'. The hypothesis explains that subjects' slow reaction times depend on the other variable (tiredness). The 'reaction time' is called a *dependent variable* (DV). 'Being tired', which the experimenter could ensure by testing the subjects last thing at night, is an *independent variable* (IV).

'Tired people have slow reaction times' is a *one-tailed hypothesis*. This

► In a *natural experiment* the variables which would otherwise need to be controlled already exist. Natural experiments are particularly useful in psychology where there are so many ethical, moral, and legal problems in manipulating human behaviour.

► In a *field experiment* the experimenter tests the subjects in their own environment.

► *Two-tailed hypotheses* state that the IV will cause some change to occur in the DV, but do not state the direction in which that change will occur.

► *One-tailed hypotheses* state the direction of change in the DV which results from the IV.

Examples of one- and two-tailed hypotheses.

Two-tailed hypotheses
- Altering background noise levels will affect memory skills.
- Being observed by strangers alters a subject's ability to concentrate.
- Being rewarded for some behaviour leads to a change in the frequency of that behaviour occurring.

One-tailed hypotheses
- Practice at performing difficult motor skills increases the efficiency with which they are performed.
- Rearing a monkey in a dark environment will retard the development of its eyes.
- Giving subjects knowledge of their results as they complete each task improves overall performance in task completion.

 Identify exactly which words in the second group make them into one-tailed hypotheses.

means that it predicts that there will be some change in the DV, and also says the *direction* in which the change will occur, i.e. that reaction time is slow when the subject is tired. If the hypothesis said that there would be a change, but didn't predict what the change might be, it would be a *two-tailed hypothesis*. A two-tailed version of our hypothesis would be 'being tired affects time of reactions' i.e. reaction times could become faster or slower with increasing tiredness.

2 *Operationalizing.* Having stated the hypothesis we must carefully and precisely define what we mean by each of the terms, and how exactly we will measure any changes that might occur in the DV. What exactly do we mean by 'reaction times', and how will we measure them? What do we mean by 'tiredness', and how will we control exactly how tired our subjects are? Precisely defining our variables is called *operationalizing*.

3 *Confounding.* Even if some change in the DV does follow a change in the IV, this does not necessarily provide evidence that the IV is causing the change. It could occur by chance, or some third variable could be involved. So if tired subjects had slow reaction times this may still not confirm the hypothesis that being tired has caused the slow times. The tired subjects may have been tested under dim, artificial light. The type and level of light are variables which haven't been controlled and may have contributed to the results. If so they have become *confounding variables*.

4 *The null hypothesis.* We may not be certain that we have found that the state of one variable is causally linked to the state of another. Apart from confounding variables, which we should be able to avoid, there's still the risk that chance factors could explain correlation between two variables. What we can do is to statistically test the odds

 This logo marks points where I suggest an Activity for you to do. These are an important part of your learning process and should all be completed.

► *Operationalizing* is essential to all research. Only if other researchers know how each of the terms was operationalized can the validity of the research be assessed, and only then can others try to repeat it.

► *Confounding* occurs when researchers overlook the importance of a variable, not realizing that it is varying with the independent variable. The change in the DV appears to be the result of a change in the IV, but is actually caused by changes in the confounding variable.

► The *null hypothesis* states that any relationship between the IV and the DV occurs by chance, and there are several statistical tests to measure how likely this is.

► A *systematic sample* takes every nth subject from a collection of subjects. 'N' will be determined by the number of subjects we need in the sample to make it representative of the target population.

that the states could be explained by chance. The way to do this is to re-state the hypothesis, this time saying that the two states are not connected. For example, we could state that 'reaction time does not depend on being tired, and if tired subjects do have slow reactions they occur by chance'. This is a *null hypothesis*. The reason for making this converse statement is that there are statistical tests of probability which will help us to retain or reject the null hypothesis.

5 *Sampling.* Having stated our hypothesis we must gather a *sample* of subjects to test. The sample must represent the population from which it is drawn if results are to be generalized. There are several ways in which a sample can be drawn. In a *probability sample* subjects are chosen so that no particular member of the target population has any greater chance of being selected than any other. One way of probability sampling is *random sampling*. Subjects are chosen at random, by picking names from a hat, sticking a pin into an unseen list, or using specially designed random number tables.

Another method of probability sampling is *systematic sampling*. Here all the possible subjects are listed, and every nth subject is selected, where 'n' is the interval which will provide the number of subjects we need to ensure that the sample is representative. For example, every 10th, every 50th, or every other subject may be chosen in a systematic sample. If we want 25 subjects, and there are 100 in the target population, then every 4th subject will be selected.

Much psychological research goes on at universities in many countries. Inevitably, researchers use those subjects which they have the best opportunity to get hold of, i.e. their students. (It was estimated that in the States 90 per cent of psychology experiments are carried out on American college students.) These can be called *opportunity samples*. Such opportunity samples may be convenient, but are not necessarily representative of anyone except college students.

 Opportunity samples How representative do you think college students are of 'all people'? Explain your answer.

► An *experimental group* contains the subjects who are placed into each experimental condition.

6 *Designing the research.* The research may require that subjects are exposed to different *experimental conditions*, so may need to divide subjects into different *experimental groups*. For example we could have three experimental conditions: 'very tired', 'quite tired' and 'not tired at all'. We need three experimental groups. One third of the subjects must be made 'very tired', another third must be 'quite tired' and a further third 'not tired at all', in order to judge the effects of the various amounts of tiredness on the DV.

First we must divide the subjects into the three groups. There are three ways to do this. The subjects could be randomly allocated into each group. This is called *independent groups design*. It is probably the easiest method, although, as said earlier, we may need quite a large sample to be sure that each group is representative of the target population. Alternatively, all of the subjects could undergo each of the conditions on different occasions. This is called *repeated measures design*, and has the distinct advantage of providing far more scores than independent groups for the same number of subjects.

Finally the subjects could be matched so that similar subjects are placed into each group. For example, for every young person in the first group there is a young person in the second and third groups; for every old person in one group there must be an old person in each of the other groups, and so on. There must also be the same number of males and females in each group. This is called *matched subjects design*. It is rarely used since it isn't always possible to know what all the relevant variables are, much less be able to find subjects with identical variables to place in each group.

 Distinguish between independent groups design, repeated measures design and matched subjects design. What are the advantages and disadvantages of each?

Because the experiment has been carefully planned and executed, and the details made known to anyone who wants to know, the research can be repeated in an attempt to confirm or refute its findings. Each time the research is repeated there are further opportunities to improve or reject the hypothesis, thereby making any further hypothesis more accurate.

 Experimental Design Your experimental hypothesis is 'tired people have slow reaction times'.

a) How would you operationalize this hypothesis as a two-tailed hypothesis? What would your null hypothesis be?

b) Choose a target population for study. How would you select a sample to represent this target population adequately (i.e. so that you could generalize the findings relating to the sample to the target population as a whole)?

c) How would you divide the subjects into groups for study?

d) How would you test the experimental hypothesis by a laboratory experiment? How would you avoid confounding variables?

Summary – How do psychologists collect their data?

Psychologists can use natural or controlled observations, ethological studies, case studies, surveys, correlational studies, and experiments as part of cross-sectional, longitudinal, or cross-cultural research.

Those psychologists conducting nomothetic research require methods which produce results which can be generalized to large numbers of people and preferably to human beings as a whole. Methods such as case studies which gather information about individuals are preferred by those conducting idiographic research.

Experiments are the only method which allow support for or evidence opposing hypotheses to be discovered and great care must be exercised by those conducting them.

ACT Which would be the most appropriate method to investigate the following:

- Whether heavy smokers are more or less likely to suffer from stress.
- Whether the use of physical punishment teaches obedience.
- Whether people's reactions slow down as they become tired.

NM Look back through the previous pages and define the following terms:

Concepts	Null hypothesis
Subjective	Dependent variable
Objective	Independent variable
Induction	Independent groups design
Confounding	Repeated measures design
Positive correlation	Random sampling
Negative correlation	Systematic sampling
Natural experiments	Subject variables
Controlled experiments	Situational variables
Experimental hypothesis	

Some cautions in interpreting psychological data

There are four sets of problems involved in drawing conclusions from psychological research. The first involves the subjects used, the second concerns the situations in which the research takes place, and the third is to do with the tendency for researchers to see what they expect to see rather than what really happens. The fourth is to do with process of drawing conclusions.

Problems with subjects People behave differently if they know they are subjects of research. **Orne** asked people if they would perform a repetitive (and boring) task. Most refused, except when they were also told that it was part of research, in which case many of them performed the task enthusiastically. People develop certain *expectancy effects*, i.e. they have ideas about what they think the researcher wants to see or hear and so behave, not as they would normally, but as they think they ought to, or as they think that other people in the same situation would behave.

Where people are tested in the same room, the presence of the others often leads to an improvement in some of their skills. If people are asked to make their judgements known to others, who are also stating their judgements, the responses often become less extreme than when people are tested alone. These are called 'co-action' and 'audience' effects. We shall return to them in Chapter 9.

Problems with situations The responses people make in research will be affected by situational variables such as the time of day, the temperature in the room, the amount of distraction, the instructions

► People often behave differently in the company of others. Can you think of any reasons for this?

they hear, etc. Ideally, all subjects should be tested under the same conditions and should all hear the same instructions. Ensuring these similarities is called *standardizing*. If different conditions exist when groups of subjects are being tested, or if each group hears differences in the instructions, then any changes that might occur in their behaviour could be caused by these differences. The research is confounded.

Expectancy effects and researchers Researchers may sometimes interpret what they see as their findings to fit in with what they are looking for, rather than observing what is actually there. This may occur quite accidentally. **Rosenthal** asked two groups of his students to conduct some research using rats. He randomly divided the rats into two groups. He told one group of students that the rats they would be studying had been chosen because of their skill at learning to run mazes very quickly, making few mistakes. They were 'maze bright' rats. The other group were told that their rats were 'maze dull'. The students were asked to record the performance of their rats on maze-learning tests. (Remember the rats had been randomly allocated to the two groups, so there shouldn't have been any difference in their average maze-learning skill.) The students with the 'maze bright' rats reported far fewer errors than those with the 'maze dull' rats. It seems that they interpreted the behaviour of their rats according to what they 'knew' about them, i.e. that they were 'maze bright', or 'maze dull'.

 What is an expectancy effect? Give an example of an expectancy effect which is caused by the expectations of research subjects, and of an expectancy effect caused by the expectations of researchers themselves.

How might each be avoided in experimental design? Note that expectancy effects are special kinds of confounding variable.

What is meant by the standardization of the experimental situation? What problems might a lack of standardization give rise to? How would you standardize a laboratory experiment to test the relationship between tiredness and reaction times?

Problems with drawing conclusions All of the methods used by psychologists have some drawbacks and great care must be shown in applying the findings from studies of one group to others. Before accepting the conclusions of any psychological research we might ask the following questions.

1   Was the sample tested *representative* of the target population to whom the conclusions are being applied?

2   Was the research employed *reliable*? Research is said to be reliable if it would yield the same results if the same subjects took the test on subsequent occasions.

3   Were the tests *valid*? By valid we mean, does the test actually

measure what it claims to measure? For example, do intelligence tests actually measure intelligence? Is a laboratory a valid representation of real life?

4 Was the *hypothesis* properly *operationalized*? Were its terms clearly defined in ways that could be measured unambiguously?

5 Were the results produced by the interaction of the variables identified or were *confounding* variables at play?

6 Were the observations determined by what really happened or did *expectancy effects* distort observation?

Summary – Some cautions in interpreting psychological data

Many of the subjects used in psychological research may not be typical of all people, and they may not always behave 'normally' if they know they are being studied. Sometimes the conditions under which research is conducted are artificial and don't reflect 'real' life at all. Great care must be taken to ensure that all stages of the research are standardized, reliable and valid. Researchers may be tempted to interpret their observations to fit their hypotheses.

 Now take a sheet of notepaper and down one side make a list of all the methods of collecting data you have read about so far. Divide the page into two vertical columns headed advantages and disadvantages. From your reading so far, fill in the table you have created.

SCIENCE AND PSYCHOLOGY

Science claims to seek 'proof', or at least 'evidence', about the relationships between things, such as melting points, breaking points, chemical reactions, loads, stresses and strains, etc. This proof must have been gathered in an unbiased, reliable, systematic way, which has been checked by repeating the research many times. So can psychology claim to be a science? Before we can decide this question we must first define science.

What is science?

This is a much more difficult question to answer than it appears. A dictionary definition says that science is 'knowledge which has been derived from using the scientific method'. Experiments which have produced basic principles and laws used the scientific method. These principles and laws allow other hypotheses to be developed and tested.

Is psychology a science?

Some psychologists claim that psychology does qualify as a science since it does gather knowledge scientifically. However, there are some psychological theories which probably couldn't be tested scientifically. As we shall see in Chapter 2, Freud's psychoanalytic explanations for personality development, for example, were not

► The *scientific method is* a procedure which starts with some observations and speculations about which variables influence other variables. It ends with precise theories and laws concerning relationships between things.

derived from scientific methods but by rather subjective interpretation of case studies, despite Freud's claims that his was a scientific theory.

Other psychologists argue that the scientific method is inappropriate for psychology and that psychology is not, and should not try to be, a science (in the sense that this applies to the natural sciences). This opposition to the traditional view comes from two sources. One is from those psychologists who follow the *humanist* approach. For other reasons some philosophers of science have contested psychology's claim to be a science.

The humanist approach

Humanist psychologists say that it's impossible to test human beings and their behaviour in the same way that we could test what happens when chemicals are mixed or heated. Unlike chemicals, no two individuals can ever be completely alike; what applies to one person may not apply to another. Humanists, such as **Heather**, stress the uniqueness of people, and the way psychological research tends to dehumanize them. Simply calling someone a 'subject' in the research, rather than a human being, shows just what researchers think of the people they are researching. **Maslow** argues that psychology ought to be about helping people to make the most of themselves.

The philosophy of science

Not everyone agrees that it is even possible to conduct unbiased research. Since all research starts with observation, **Deese** argues that any researcher must have some ideas or biases about what they expect to see *before* formulating their hypothesis. The information which the original observations are supposed to collect cannot be unbiased since the researcher will already have decided on what she or he is looking for.

Philosophers such as **Karl Popper** and **Thomas Kuhn** believe that many sciences are not as unbiased or as scientific as they claim to be. While it is common for people to think of scientific knowledge as that which has been proved true, the philosopher Karl Popper argues that all scientific knowledge should be regarded as temporary and provisional. At any one time scientific knowledge is that which has been subjected to rigorous tests but has not been falsified. It is easy for a scientist to fall into the trap of finding evidence to support a hypothesis which he or she favours. Therefore Popper advises that scientists

▶ According to Deese, unbiased research is impossible since all researchers have expectations about the world which will influence their observations.

REVIEW – Humanism

Humanism has been called 'the third force in psychology', after the dominant behaviourist and psychoanalytic approaches. It promotes the pursuit of self-expression and self-fulfilment, of knowledge and achievement, and of understanding and appreciation. Humanism developed from the work of Alfred Adler, Abraham Maslow, and Carl Rogers. (Chapter 2 gives a fuller discussion of humanism, and Chapter 10 discusses its implications for therapy.)

should invest more effort in trying to disprove, or falsify their favoured theories.

According to Thomas Kuhn, knowledge passes through three distinct historical stages. The first is the stage of *pre-science*. In this stage there are untested hypotheses about what things are like which are shared by some people, but not everyone. For example, a few centuries ago some people believed that the world was flat, others that it was like a saucer, others that it was a globe. In pre-science there is no single view which unites a majority of scientists in the subject area. An overall view of what something is like is called a *paradigm*.

If enough people adopt a particular paradigm, and ways are found to test it, the second stage begins. This is the stage of *normal science* and employs the procedures of the scientific method. Many aspects of the paradigm are tested. However, over a period of time, more and more observations will accumulate which cannot be explained by the existing paradigm. Eventually some new idea will appear. If it gathers support it may eventually replace the previous paradigm. This is the stage of *revolution*. According to Kuhn, science does not grow through gradual additions of knowledge but through scientific revolutions.

According to many critics, psychology is still in the stage of pre-science. It has no dominant paradigm. Psychologists remain divided about exactly what psychology should be about. **Valentine** is a behaviourist psychologist (see Chapter 2) who believes that behaviourism is as near to a paradigm as any explanation is likely to become, since it has the three main requirements of a paradigm: clear *definitions* of the subject, fundamental *assumptions* about the nature of human learning and behaviour, and a clear and simple to understand *methodology*. However, even among behaviourists there are fundamental disagreements. The founder of modern behaviourism, **B.F. Skinner**, opposes the use of theory to explain behaviour, believing that psychology shouldn't be trying to explain behaviour at all, but rather to predict and control it.

► A *paradigm* is a point of view or perspective embodying a set of ideas, techniques and procedures which are held by a group of people at a particular time.

► A *scientific revolution* would have occurred when the majority of people became convinced that the world was a globe, that bacterial disease could be carried in the air, that injecting a small amount of a bacterium such as smallpox could build up the body's immune system.

Karl Popper's philosophy

Popper is a philosopher of science who believes that it is impossible to conduct scientific research without presupposing the results. He says:

> Observations ... and statements of experimental results are always interpretations of the facts observed ... they are interpretations in the light of theories. This is one of the main reasons why it is always deceptively easy to find verification of a theory and why we have to adopt a highly critical attitude towards our theories if we do not wish to argue in circles ...

He therefore advocates that scientists should invest more effort in falsifying theories than in attempting to prove them true.

(NM) What do humanists think that psychology should be about?
What do behaviourists think that psychology should be
about?

Summary – Science and psychology

It's not only difficult to define psychology, it's difficult to define
science itself. Some philosophers argue that science isn't a final state
of knowledge but is always in transition. As new paradigms are
advanced old ones will disappear. The process of data collection used
by all researchers may not always be objective. In view of these
difficulties it seems less important to ask whether psychology is a
science than to ask whether psychology can reveal important things
about people's behaviour and experience.

ETHICS IN RESEARCH

So far in this chapter we have discussed the problems associated with
particular methods of psychological research, and whether psychological findings should be considered scientifically acceptable. Now
let's look at some of the ethical difficulties psychologists face. As you
learn more about some of the actual research that psychologists have
conducted you will find examples of research that may have had
some effects on the person being studied. This is particularly true in
social psychological research and research on children.

Some methods are more likely to have ethical implications than
others. Naturalistic and controlled observations do not usually involve manipulating the subject's behaviour, although some aspects
of human behaviour can't or shouldn't be observed for reasons of
decency and privacy. Case studies are usually built up in order to
benefit the person being studied in some way. However, they must be
very strictly confidential and there could be problems if the psychologist discovers things of a sensitive nature. People have a choice as to
whether to participate in a survey, but we can never be certain that
some of the things we could ask will not give offence to someone.
Correlational studies manipulate statistical data that already exist, so
they don't have specific ethical problems associated with their use
apart from problems of confidentiality.

The main ethical problems are faced by psychologists conducting
experimental research which involves the deliberate manipulation of
other people's behaviour. Most countries where psychological research is conducted have departments or committees to oversee
experimental projects. In Britain the British Psychological Society
(BPS) and in America the American Psychological Association (APA)
are the governing bodies. Both have published guidelines stating
what kinds of research or activities are permissible and what are not.
In addition, many research institutions have ethical committees who
consider whether research projects should proceed. If a researcher is
in any doubt he or she can apply to the relevant authority, which can
then make a judgement. The following are some of the main problems.

►*Ethics* is a branch of philosophy
concerned with the judgement of
human behaviour as 'good' or
'bad'. In psychology ethical
problems are about whether the
search for knowledge justifies
lying to people, or altering their
lives through doing research.
Most of the methods which
psychologists use have ethical
implications.

What should subjects be told?

The first difficulty is whether to tell subjects that they are taking part in some research. If they are told, their behaviour may become distorted to fit in with what they think the researcher wants, or they may wish to do the opposite! (These are *expectancy effects*, or what Orne calls *demand characteristics*.) If they aren't told that they are being investigated, then the researcher is deliberately deceiving them. Is deceit acceptable? Is it ever acceptable for psychologists deliberately to use people, without their prior knowledge or consent, in psychological research?

The subjects' needs

Consideration must always be given to the subjects' needs, and they must not be exposed to excessive stress. Any stress which is involved must be short and mild, and the subjects must be reassured afterwards when the research is explained to them. Only if the gains in knowledge which result from the research are considered sufficiently great to justify putting people under stress will permission be given for the experiment to proceed. This itself poses an ethical problem: who should be able to say that the end justifies the means?

The needs of the subject must be put before the needs of the researcher at all times. Subjects must be reassured that they can withdraw from the research at any time, and that their contributions will be treated in the strictest confidence. Their identities must not be revealed and their privacy not invaded. Regrettably, this has not always been the case. There have been examples of research where the volunteers asked to be released from the experiment after it had started, and permission was refused.

If the subjects are not capable of speaking for themselves, then the permission of someone who is able to speak for them must be gained before they can take part. For example, if the research includes children their parents must be told exactly what the research entails, what its purpose is, and what possible risks might be involved. The research must not proceed if the parents or guardians object. Parents should be present, and have the right to withdraw their child as soon as they feel any anxiety about its welfare.

► The needs of the subject should always take priority over the needs of the researcher, and the subject should be free to withdraw from the experiment at any time.

Animal welfare

Some animal experiments have been conducted which have caused permanent severe problems for the animals including acute pain or death. These are unlikely to be repeated. There are now very strict guidelines on the use of animals in psychological research. Behaviourist (and other) psychologists have conducted countless experiments on animals to establish the principles that underlie learning (as we will see in Chapter 2). Generalizing from animal to human learning and behaviour has, however, been dismissed by many psychologists as invalid. There are some very fundamental differences between human and non-human animals, so that findings about one may not apply to the other. (We wouldn't expect greylag geese to learn to talk, so why should we imagine that human babies need to imprint?)

 Look back at your notes on expectancy effects. How does possibility of expectancy effects occurring encourage psychologists to lie to their research subjects? Do you think that lying is justified?

Look back at your notes on correlation studies and/or natural experiments. What ethical problems associated with experimental research do correlation studies/natural experiments avoid?

Summary – Ethics in research

If the subjects are animals, strict guidelines have to be followed which minimize the risk of pain. If our subjects are human the problems are obviously even greater. Whether or not to use someone without their knowledge, or to risk their knowledge confounding the study, is a problem faced by most researchers. Consideration of the needs of the subject, even at the risk of having to abandon the research, must always be put first. Where subjects can't give their own permission, the permission of someone in authority must be sought, and they then have the right to remove the subject from the research.

 Summarize the practical and ethical problems psychologists face in gathering their data.

Chapter summary

Psychology is that branch of knowledge which studies human and animal behaviour and experience. It developed from research in biology and philosophy during the nineteenth century. Modern psychologists are employed in both research and practical applications in areas such as industry, clinical practice, marketing, personnel and education.

Research psychologists use a variety of methods to collect their data as part of cross-cultural, cross-sectional, or longitudinal investigations. Observations, experiments, case studies and surveys are some of them. A sample of subjects to study can be drawn in several ways, depending on availability and what the research involves. Generalizations from their performance may be made to the whole target population if a properly representative sample is drawn.

Where it is not possible, for practical or ethical reasons, to conduct controlled investigations of the relationship between independent and dependent variables, statistical correlations may be sought from a naturally occurring situation.

Attempts to conduct value- and error-free research are not always successful and certain cautions must be observed in interpreting conclusions. People behave differently in groups and subject and situational variables can confound results. The research methodology may be unreliable or invalid, and may not have used standardized instructions or procedures.

In view of these cautions critics of psychology claim that it cannot be regarded as a legitimate science. However philosophers of science such as Popper and Kuhn argue that no science consistently lives up to scientific ideals, and in this sense psychology may be no less scientific than other sciences.

Conducting research on animals and humans has ethical, as well as practical implications. In always ensuring that the subject's needs are put before those of the researcher, the original intentions may become eroded, and the research weakened.

Exam Questions – 60 minutes each

1 From your understanding of the methods available to psychologists, discuss to what extent psychology might be regarded as a science.

2 Consider some of the ethical problems faced by psychologists who wish to conduct research.

3 Comment on the usefulness of the experimental method, as used by psychologists.

Now look back at the objectives listed on the first page of this chapter. Have you achieved them all?

Further Reading: Chapter 1

Easy to read and informative introductions to psychology, its methods and applications, are provided by

Gale A. 1985. *What is Psychology*. London: Edward Arnold.

Coleman A. 1988. *What is Psychology*. London: Hutchinson.

A readable and informative history of psychology is found in

Thomson R. 1968. *The Pelican History of Psychology*. Harmondsworth: Penguin.

For those who have a particular interest in the philosophy of science there is

Popper K. 1963. *Conjectures and Refutations*. London: Routledge & Kegan Paul.

Kuhn T.S. 1970. *The Structure of Scientific Revolutions*. Chicago: University of Chicago Press.

2 Influential psychological theories

Chapter objectives

By the end of this chapter you should:

■ be able to give an account of the psychodynamic theories of personality of Freud, Jung, Adler and Erikson

■ be able to give a critical review of the methods of research used by psychodynamic theorists and the conclusions they have drawn from their data

■ be able to give an account of the behaviourist theory of learning, including classical conditioning, and operant conditioning, and the research methods used by behaviourist psychologists

■ be able to write a critical review of behaviourism as an adequate theory of human behaviour

■ be able to give an account of social learning theory in relation to psychodynamic theory on the one hand and behaviourism on the other.

Introduction

Academic psychology is barely a century old and though we have had plenty of theories advanced to explain aspects of our behaviour and mental functioning, we are still a long way from understanding them completely. This chapter will review some of the more influential theories which have stimulated research in psychology during this century, in particular psychodynamic theories of personality development and behaviourist theories of how we learn. We will refer to these theories in several of the following chapters.

PSYCHODYNAMIC THEORIES OF PERSONALITY DEVELOPMENT

Psychodynamic simply means 'mental change', so psychodynamic theories emphasize reasons for mental change such as motivation and drive. According to psychodynamic theories, our personalities are the product of two forces which have acted on us. Firstly, all our childhood experiences have shaped the kind of person we are, and secondly, biological forces within us have pushed us in one way or another. One of the founding fathers of psychodynamic theory was **Sigmund Freud**, and we will start by describing his psychoanalytic model for personality development.

Sigmund Freud's psychoanalysis

Sigmund Freud was an Austrian doctor who spent most of his life, from the 1880s until his death in 1939, researching the part of the

► Personality is one of those annoying terms in psychology for which everyone knows the meaning, but no one can adequately define. Everyone emphasizes different qualities, depending upon their particular perspective.

► The psyche is the Greek word for 'soul' or 'mind' from which the word psychology is derived.

Sigmund Freud

► Freud believed the clinical situation had to be as unthreatening and undistracting as possible. He would listen to his patients, remembering all they said, and only make notes after they had left.

human psyche that he called the *unconscious mind*. Many of his patients behaved in strange, distorted ways for which Freud could find no physical cause. Some had severe headaches, rigidity of limbs, temporary blindness or deafness and temporary amnesia. Many had been turned away from other doctors since there appeared to be nothing physically wrong with them. Freud described these symptoms as hysteria. Because their cause was not *physical* or *conscious* Freud supposed that it had to be *mental* and *unconscious*.

As a doctor and researcher Freud believed that symptoms which are left untreated usually grow worse. Many illnesses and diseases result from some previous experience, such as being stung by an insect, eating something poisonous, or breathing in someone else's germs. Something similar, Freud reasoned, may be true of the 'illnesses' of his patients. Freud needed to know something of his patients' pasts.

Techniques for studying the unconscious

Freud and his colleague **Josef Breuer** used *clinical interviews* to find out about their patients' histories. The patient would relax and be encouraged to talk about his or her life and feelings. They would lie on a couch in Freud's consulting room, and he would sit behind their heads so that they couldn't see him. Occasionally Freud would need to prompt the patient with a question, or by applying a little pressure to their temples with his hands. Patients were encouraged to remember events that had happened during their childhood and the feelings that were associated with them. This technique is called *free association*.

This *free talk* technique seemed to help the patients, and Freud built up detailed *case studies* of their histories. Occasionally patients made a slip of the tongue, which Freud thought revealed something about what they truly meant. When some early patients told Freud about their dreams he believed he had stumbled onto 'the royal road to the unconscious'. (For a fuller discussion of Freud's methods, see Chapter 10.) Freud believed that the unconscious mind contains many primitive desires, wishes, urges and memories which are too upsetting to be conscious. Some of these urges will have been in the unconscious since we were born. Others will have been *repressed* there, because they produced too much anxiety at the time. These primitive urges drive us to behave in all kinds of ways, including the symptoms Freud had described as hysteria.

All activity needs an energy source. According to Freud the true unconscious mind is the isolated, primitive *id*, which is the source of all mental energy. Young babies who want to be fed or cleaned will feel some kind of discomfort, tension or pressure. The id will demand that this *excitation* be removed, so the baby will try to attract the attention of an adult to satisfy its needs. Id operates on the *pleasure principle*. Anything which gives the baby pleasure (and the removal of anything which does not or which causes pain) will be demanded by the baby driven by its irrational id.

Briefly explain what Freud meant by repression. What is the id, and what is its function?

The two instinctive urges

From countless hours of studying patients, and from his researches in human physiology, Freud eventually concluded that we are born with two essential urges. These are the *libido*, a force for life and sexuality, and the *death instinct*, which drives us towards danger and self-destruction. They both draw their energy from the id. Freud used the names of the Greek god *Eros* (the god of love) to describe the libido, and *Thanatos* (the god of death) to describe the death instincts. Throughout our lives the Eros and Thanatos urges will drive us to behave in different ways, until, at the moment of our death, Thanatos wins the struggle.

Name and briefly define the two primary instinctive urges in traditional psychoanalysis.

Parts of personality and stages of development

The child's main source of pleasure (*erogenous zone*) during the first year or two is its mouth, and the id obtains most of its satisfaction through the mouth. Freud called this period the *oral stage*. Parents are mainly responsible for satisfying the id's demands by giving the child what it appears to want. The id is a primitive and irrational force, and

► *Repression* means to hold back, to censor, to control some feeling which might otherwise produce anxiety that could impede personality development. Repression is an unconscious process.

► *Excitation* means physiological stimulation, i.e. activity in the nervous system.

► The *id* is the first of three parts of personality to occur. It is the source of all psychic energy and demands immediate satisfaction.

► *Libido*, or Eros, is the major life force which uses energy from id to drive us towards achievement. The *death instinct*, or Thanatos, opposes id and drives us towards our own destruction. Freud was fascinated by ancient Greek and Roman mythology and used ideas and names from them to symbolize some of the concepts he described.

► *Erogenous zones* are those parts of the body which produce sexual arousal when stimulated. Freud believed that the pleasure babies derive from feeding is in some sense sexual.

demands satisfaction immediately and at all costs. However, babies are not always fed on demand, and some may have too much oral stimulation. Either situation can create anxiety in a baby, who may not be able to deal with it. If feeding is withheld for too long, on too many occasions, the id will become frustrated and the resulting anxiety may be repressed into the unconscious. These frustrations could affect later personality development. Freud described the *oral character* as being either excessively optimistic, over generous, and constantly excited (if as a baby the person received too much stimulation), or pessimistic, frequently depressed, and aggressive (if as a baby the person received too little stimulation).

The oral stage, from birth to one or two years

Erogenous zone	Part of personality	Based on	Main characteristics	Tasks to achieve
Mouth	Id	Pleasure principle	Main pleasure from sucking, biting, licking, etc. Concerned with immediate gratification.	Weaning

From around two years the id's demands no longer automatically receive satisfaction and children must learn strategies such as asking and saying 'thank you' in order to gain what they want. The second part of personality, the *ego*, is needed. The ego is rational and tries to find more logical ways of satisfying id. It operates on the *reality principle*. Sometime around two years a second erogenous zone appears. Many patients could remember incidents concerning their potty training, and Freud concluded that the anus now became the source of the child's satisfaction since it could control the release or retention of its faeces. This is the *anal stage*. Parents who are too strict, or not strict enough, in potty training their children could allow frustrations and anxieties to build up which may be repressed into the unconscious giving rise to the *anal character*. Over-indulgent potty training leads to the *anal expulsive* character, who is untidy, over-generous, always gives in, and goes along with anyone else's ideas. Too strict training can create the *anal retentive* character, who is mean, obstinate, and obsessed by orderliness and hoarding.

► The *ego* is the second part of personality to appear. It's function is to find realistic ways of satisfying the id's demands.

The anal stage, from one or two to two or three years

Erogenous zone	Part of personality	Based on	Main characteristics	Tasks to achieve
Anus	Id	Reality principle	Controlling the bladder and bowels	Toilet training
	Ego			

 Outline the main features of personality development during the first two or three years, according to Freudian psychoanalysis.

From around three years children become able to follow instructions about what they should and shouldn't do. They will develop some limited sense of right and wrong from their parents. The id is still making demands which the ego is trying to satisfy. Some of the demands will contradict parental wishes. The child needs the third part of personality, the *superego*. The superego provides the basis for the child's sense of morality. According to Freud the superego develops because of the (pre-genital) sexual urges children are having about their parents. (Freud lost many supporters and gained many critics because of his notions about infantile sexuality, and he dropped many of them in his later writings.)

The superego consists of two parts, the *conscience*, and the *ego ideal*. Conscience refers to what we ought not to do and think. The ego ideal is a mental model of what good behaviour (which we learn from our parents) should be. The superego operates on the *morality principle*.

Freud claimed that the opposite sex parent becomes associated with pleasurable sexual feelings in the young child. Unconsciously the child is sexually drawn to its opposite sex parent. It begins to feel jealous of its same sex parent because she or he is favoured by the opposite sex parent. In boys this is called the *Oedipus complex*, and the feelings associated with it are called *Oedipal conflict*. The equivalent in girls is the *Electra complex*. If sexual urges become too great to bear, or if they are too strictly dealt with, then they too may become repressed into the unconscious, where they could cause disturbed behaviour in adulthood. Freud believed problems caused by inadequate resolution of Oedipal conflict were the major cause of adult *neuroses* in males.

The ego provides a solution to Oedipal conflict. If the son was more like his father, then his mother could well want him instead of his father. So the child begins to *identify* with his father. He will try to learn what it is like to be his father by copying him, helping him, repeating things he says and adopting his ideas and beliefs. He takes on his father's personality, as best he can. If the son is very much like his father, then his father surely will not hurt him because it would be like harming a part of himself. This is the *identification process*, and is central to Freud's understanding of the origins of personality.

Freud admitted that his views on girls' personality development

► The *superego* is the third part of personality to appear and provides the moral dimension to the id and the ego.

► Freud insisted that the id, ego and superego are not regarded as real biological structures. Rather they are hypothetical concepts which describe the actions that are associated with early personality development.

► Oedipus was the son of the king of Thebes in ancient Greek mythology who unwittingly fell in love with his own mother, and killed his father. Electra's father was murdered by his wife's lover, and Electra urged her brother to kill their mother in revenge.

► A *neurosis* is (usually) a fairly minor psychological disturbance.

► *Identification* is the process by which children take on the attitudes, beliefs and behaviour of their parents.

The phallic stage, from two to three to around five years

Erogenous zone	Part of personality	Based on	Main characteristics	Tasks to achieve
Phallus	Id	–	Gains pleasure playing with genitals. Associated with opposite sex parent	Successful resolution of Oedipal/ Electra conflict by identifying with same sex parent
	Ego	–		
	Superego	Morality principle		

and the Electra complex were rather speculative. He suggested that girls prefer the company of their father because he possesses a penis which they do not. By being close to him they might share his, or perhaps their own might grow back. Modern psychoanalysis pays little importance to some aspects of the Oedipus and Electra complexes.

 How does the Oedipus complex arise? How does the super-ego contribute?

By around five years the child should have sorted out many of its feelings about its parents, and should start channelling its energies into other relationships and activities. Games, sport, learning in school, and all kinds of adventures dominate personality development from about five until puberty. This is the latency period. It isn't a stage since major personality development has been temporarily suspended.

The latency period, from five to seven years to beginning of puberty

Erogenous zone	Part of personality	Based on	Main characteristics	Tasks to achieve
None	Id, ego and superego	–	Energies directed into non-sexual activities	None

► *Affective fixation* refers to the condition whereby the libido's energy has been so attached to one person or object that normal personality growth cannot proceed. While the person grows, their personality remains stuck in an earlier stage.

With puberty the major sex-linked hormones start to change body shape and body function, and the sex organs become biologically fertile. This is the genital stage, and lasts from puberty to old age. If the Oedipal or Electra conflicts have been resolved the young person's personality will start to become more sexually mature. They will have crushes on some familiar people, have their first serious boyfriend or girlfriend, and gradually emerge as sexually mature adults. If, on the other hand, some problems remain unresolved, the personality may become *fixated* on some person, such as the mother, or on an object, such as the mouth, from an earlier stage. This will frustrate making 'normal' relationships, and can contribute to various neuroses.

 What are the consequences of affective fixation?

The genital stage, from puberty to adulthood

Erogenous zone	Part of personality	Based on	Main characteristics	Tasks to achieve
Genitals	Id, ego and superego	–	Increasing interest in sexual matters with members of both sexes	Normal relationships

 What happens to personality development during the genital stage?

REVIEW – Freudian psychoanalysis
Freud's studies of many neurotic and other cases suggested to him that humans have an unconscious mind which contains irrational and primitive urges which find expression, as we grow, through bodily pleasure from the erogenous zones. The id is the source of all psychic energy, and demands immediate satisfaction. The ego seeks logical, realistic means of achieving the id's demands, and the superego provides the moral censor of the id and ego. Pre-genital 'phallic' pleasure results in identification with the same sex parent to resolve Oedipal or Electra conflicts, thus creating the child's superego. Stressful external influences can become fixated and repressed into the unconscious, where they will remain until they seek expression through some maladapted, neurotic behaviour later. Freudian psychoanalysis aimed to seek out the causes of these anxieties, and so relieve them.

REVIEW – The main features of Freud's psychodynamic model
Freud suggested that we have:
- two instinctive urges, the libido and the death instinct;
- three parts of personality, the id, ego and superego;
- four stages of personality development, the oral, anal, phallic and genital stages.

(ACT) Draw a diagram to show the relationship between the instinctive urges and other parts of the personality according to Freudian theory.

Defence mechanisms

Freud claimed that the ego uses some unconscious defence mechanisms which reduce the potential for conflict, and anxiety that might disrupt normal development. Repression is the ultimate defence mechanism. If we can't deal with the anxiety in any other way it may become repressed into the unconscious. Clearly this should be avoided wherever possible so as to avoid fixation and potential neuroses later. Identification is a defence mechanism whereby we incorporate aspects of someone else's personality into our own so that we become like them. *Projection* is the opposite defence mechanism to identification. We project our own unpleasant feelings onto someone else and blame them for having the thoughts that we really have.

Other defence mechanisms include *rationalization*, which means making something up which justifies your own (or someone else's) unjustifiable behaviour. For example a father might be annoyed by his son's behaviour, and hit the child harder than he might have intended. Feeling guilty he might say 'It was in your own interests, it was entirely your fault, sometimes one has to be cruel to be kind'. Each of these statements represent rationalization. *Displacement* occurs when we take out our frustrations on some innocent object (like hitting or kicking the furniture, the cat, a toy, etc.). *Sublimation* is a special and acceptable kind of displacement. Excess energy is expended through sport, or frustrations are expressed through doing something creative, such as painting a picture or carving something in wood. Sublimation is the only defence mechanism that is usually successful in coping with anxiety without causing further problems.

There are dozens of defence mechanisms which are used unconsciously to protect the ego and provide some time for the frustrations that prompted them to be absorbed into our consciousness and dealt

► *Defence mechanisms* are unconsciously directed processes or behaviours intended to protect the self (or ego) from anxiety-producing situations.

with in other ways. As such they are perfectly healthy, and to varying extents everyone uses them. However, danger could occur if they become over-used, and a substitute for recognizing reality.

 What are the functions of defence mechanisms in Freudian theory?

Evaluation of Freudian theory

Freud is accused of 'having an answer for everything'. It is impossible to prove or disprove the existence of the structures Freud identified. Driving forces for good and bad, primitive urges, the pursuit of rational solutions, and the emergence of conscience may all be seen in people's behaviour. This does not prove the existence of the libido and death instinct, the id, ego or superego, despite Freud's claims to have made a scientific breakthrough.

Freud's methods of free association, the interpretation of dreams, the interpretation of slips of the tongue, the interpretation of sense of humour, etc., all based on the clinical interview, are not scientific by the criteria raised in Chapter 1. Nor was Freud's sample in any way representative of the target population of all people. They were, by Freud's own definition, neurotic. A large number were middle class, and often Jewish, women living in Vienna between the 1880s and 1920s.

Thousands of studies have been conducted to test various aspects of

---

Comments on Freudian psychodynamic theory

Strengths	Criticisms
It provided the first detailed explanation for the development of personality.	Subsequent explanations may be improvements on Freud's original proposals.
Some of Freud's explanations appear quite plausible at first sight.	Some explanations such as the Oedipus complex seem impossible to believe.
It identified the major stages of personality development, and the most sensitive erogenous zones.	There is no evidence that personality development occurs in stages, or that erogenous zones are particularly important to personality growth.
It emphasized the importance of caregivers.	Psychoanalysis views the role of the child as being rather passive, merely responding to external forces.
Freud offers a number of useful concepts, such as the id, libido, identification, and defence mechanisms.	None of these entities can be proved to exist, so the whole theory lacks any scientific validity.
The theory offers explanations for several features of human society, such as aggression, the development of sex roles and moral development.	None of Freud's explanations has been proved, and other explanations may be more adequate.
Freudian psychoanalysis has stimulated a considerable amount of other research.	None of the other research has 'proved' any of Freud's major claims.

Freud's theory, and many have found evidence for the character types which Freud described, for example men who are over-concerned with cleanliness, orderliness, and meanness do exist. But this does not prove the existence of 'an anal character'. Such a man may simply have been socialized by people who behaved in just such ways themselves.

Yet despite these criticisms many people still find Freud's theories and explanations a source of inspiration, and at least in part, temptingly believable.

Carl Gustav Jung's analytical psychology

Carl Jung and Freud were colleagues until their disagreements about the nature of the libido, ego, and conscious and unconscious minds led them to part company in 1913. Jung, who had worked as a doctor in a mental hospital, was nearly 20 years younger than Freud. His father was a village pastor, as were most of his uncles, and his rather lonely childhood and his religious upbringing disposed him to be interested in such things as mysticism and magic. Freud, although a Jew by birth, was a convinced atheist, and had no time for anything to do with religion or mysticism.

Jung used similar techniques to Freud with his patients, but drew different conclusions from them. For example, Jung insisted that the personality should be seen as a whole, rather than as a combination of id, ego and superego, and that the potential for it to unfold existed

► *Carl Jung* was brought up in a Swiss village. His father seemed always to be busy, with pastoral duties, and his mother was ill and away for much of the time. His only sibling, a sister, was eight years younger than him, and he spent much time alone, reading widely.

Carl Gustav Jung

► *Individuation* refers to the process by which an individual becomes aware of his or her individuality.

Modern personality assessment makes considerable use of the dimensions of introversion and extraversion which Jung had identified.

► Jung's contribution to psychodynamic theory suggests that there are three parts to our personalities, one personal and conscious, and two unconscious. A balance must be maintained between them.

right from birth. He retained Freud's ideas about the existence of the personal unconscious, although he did not believe that sexual urges were much involved in its development. He also emphasized the role of the conscious mind much more than Freud. Children acquire a sense of their own consciousness as they become able to think and feel, to sense and to make reasoned guesses. This is the process of *individuation*.

Some children will become sociable and confident, and direct their libido (life force) outwards towards the world beyond themselves. These are *extraverts*. Other children will be more concerned with their own feelings and attitudes. These are *introverts*. Everyone is a mixture of introvert and extravert. For extraverts, many sources of stimulation will enter the conscious mind; for introverts, rather fewer will. The *ego* acts as a kind of guard, only allowing those things into consciousness which can be dealt with by the person.

 What did Jung mean by introvert and extravert?

In addition to this view of the nature of consciousness, Jung also proposed that the unconscious comprises two elements: a personal part, and a collective part. The *personal unconscious* contains all those repressed feelings and anxieties that Freud proposed, but also all those things that we have 'forgotten', or may be able to recall should it be necessary. We also have a *collective unconscious* which represents all of mankind's essential experiences. It results from our human (and pre-human) evolution and is genetically transmitted to each new generation. According to Jung our collective unconscious comprises a large number of *universal archetypes*. These are images that all people share, for example ideas about the 'Earth Mother', the 'fairy godmother', the 'evil brethren', the 'wise old man', the 'valiant hero', 'god', the 'trickster', the 'demon', etc. Encountering one of these archetypes in our daily lives triggers some unconscious reactions to it.

 What are universal archetypes and what is their role in Jungian psychoanalysis?

Jung identified very general stages of development towards individuation. These are Childhood, Youth and Young Adulthood, Middle Age, and Old Age. In each there has to be a balance between the conscious and unconscious parts of personality as they strive towards achieving future goals. Neuroses arise where the balance is unequal. The techniques of psychotherapy (particularly dream interpretation) can be employed to reintegrate the two parts and make the person aware of exactly what their goals are, so that more realistic ways of achieving them can be found.

Evaluation of Jungian theory

Like Freudian theory, it is impossible to test many of Jung's claims, and whether you believe them is more an act of faith than of science. Little empirical research has been generated by Jung's explanations,

REVIEW – Jungian psychoanalysis

Jung claimed a greater role for the conscious mind in shaping the personality than Freud. He also claimed that the unconscious mind has two components. One is personal and contains repressed and forgotten experiences, the other is collective and contains some images that all people share, genetically transmitted from our common ancestors.

largely because of its mystical references to the collective unconscious and universal archetypes. It would be impossible to test them. There have, however, been occasional revivals of interest in Jung's work, mainly by those associated with the more 'hippie' elements in psychiatry, and Jung's ideas are used as a basis for Jungian psychotherapy.

 List under the headings 'Freud' and 'Jung' some of the main points of difference between Freudian and Jungian explanations of the development of personality.

Alfred Adler's individual psychology

Like Jung, **Alfred Adler** (1870–1937) had been a student of Freud's, and like Jung he profoundly disagreed with Freud over the nature and role of sexuality in personality growth. He did accept that unconscious forces govern much of our behaviour, but argued that the most important force was quite simply a conscious desire for power. Power was to be seen in social situations, and the nature of social interaction is an important part of Adler's theory.

Adler believed that children, who are born weak and helpless, learn to envy the power that adults exert over them. For their first few years they need the care, protection and material comfort which adults provide. They develop what Adler called an *inferiority complex*. Adults appear to them to be powerful and happy. The child develops an urge to acquire power, become superior and to dominate.

Children (and adults) frequently find their desire to have power is frustrated. Someone who never seems able to exercise any power may develop a large inferiority complex and this may result in neuroses. The person cannot legally or reasonably gain power, so either avoids those situations where their inadequacies will be shown up, or resorts to whatever emotional blackmail they can in order to appear to have power.

Alfred Adler

Evaluation of Adler's theory

Adler's explanations are not a coherent and complete theory in the way that Freud's and Jung's theories can be described as complete. Inferiority and the desire to dominate are claimed to underlie all neuroses. But it is unlikely that many children will be sufficiently aware of feelings of inferiority to the extent that they will create anxieties which need to be repressed. Sensitive and loving parents will try to avoid a child feeling inferior, even in a bodily sense. However Adler's de-emphasis on unconscious and largely sexual forces, and his concentration on the role of social interaction and conscious forces, do mark a significant step towards a more modern understanding of the psychodynamics of personality.

► According to Adler an *inferiority complex* is a number of fears about one's own bodily inadequacies which become repressed into the unconscious. They can give rise to attitudes and feelings of general inferiority.

 What was Adler's principal objection to Freudian theory? How does his own theory overcome this objection?

► Erikson's *whole life* psychoanalysis is far removed from the traditional Freudian theory he studied in Vienna.

Erik Erikson's psychosocial theory

Erik Erikson studied at the Institute for Psychoanalysis in Vienna after being encouraged by Sigmund Freud and his daughter, Anna Freud. He left in 1933 for America where he spent many years developing his *whole life* theory of personality development. His first and most influential book is *Childhood and Society*, published in 1950. superego, but he shifts the emphasis from psychosexual development to psychosocial development, extending Freud's four principal stages of childhood into eight stages, lasting the whole of one's life. Erikson accepts that sexual urges do exist. (He talks of the *organ stages* to refer to Freud's early stages.) However, other features are also important. Erikson studied people from different cultures, both children and

Erikson's main stages of psycho-social development

Stage	Approx. age	Crisis to resolve	Meaning
1	0–1	Trust vs mistrust	A trusting relationship develops with parents. If mistrust dominates it can have serious consequences for the rest of personality development.
2	1–3	Autonomy vs shame and doubt	The child's experiences must give it a sense of freedom and not the shame of self-consciousness.
3	3–6	Initiative vs guilt	The child needs to be given opportunities for active and enthusiastic explorations, not feel guilt over what it intends to do.
4	7–12	Industry vs inferiority	The child needs to gain recognition through hard work and avoid inferiority through failure.
5	12–18	Identity vs role confusion	The youth learns 'who' he or she is, and what is to be expected of them (occupationally), avoiding the distorted behaviour of confused roles.
6	20+	Intimacy vs isolation	Confidence to enter intimate relationships as opposed to the need to isolate oneself from others.
7	30–50	Generativity vs stagnation	The person socializes and guides the next generation, assuming their upbringing hasn't 'stagnated' these pleasures and skills.
8	50+	Ego integrity vs despair	Successful completion of the 7 stages leads to ego integration. An unsuccessful passage results in despair.

Erik Erikson

adults. In order to reach maturity he claims we have to resolve certain 'crises' or 'dilemmas' in each stage. The extent to which each of these crises is resolved before passing to the next stage will determine the adult's personality.

Evaluation of Erikson's theory

Erikson's theory is a much more realistic attempt at explaining personality development, seeing the whole life stages posing various dilemmas to be resolved. Feeling that one has achieved a satisfactory mastery of the various skills involved in each stage will produce a satisfactory self-image. Failing to do so can lead to various kinds of neurotic or behavioural disorder.

► Erikson extends rather than rejects much of Freudian theory. He is happy to be described as 'a Freudian'.

 Take the main features of Erikson's stages of personality development and from your own personal knowledge try to identify behaviour corresponding to each stage, for yourself, people you know, or fictional characters.

On the whole, psychoanalytic theory has had a powerful influence on clinical practice with disturbed people, as well as on how childhood is regarded. Many other researchers have been influenced by psychoanalysis, which has become both a model for the acquisition of personality, and a system of applied therapies. Understandably we will discuss psychoanalysis again.

BEHAVIOURISM AND LEARNING

What is learning?

Learning has been defined as 'a relatively permanent change in behaviour that occurs as a result of previous experience'. The first systematic attempts to study the acquisition of associations (the simplest form of learning) were conducted by a Russian Nobel-prize-

► Learning is 'a relatively permanent change in behaviour that occurs as a result of previous experience' according to behaviourist psychologists.

Ivan Pavlov

► Around the turn of this century, when Pavlov was conducting his research, psychology was very fragmented. Pavlov was not remotely interested in it, and threatened to dismiss any of his assistants if they used any psychological terms to describe his work.

winning physiologist, **Ivan Pavlov** (1849–1936). He was investigating the digestive system, using dogs as his subjects, and he developed the principles of classical conditioning.

Classical conditioning

Pavlov noticed that some of his older laboratory dogs were starting to salivate when his laboratory assistants were approaching with the dogs' food. They appeared to have learned that the sight or sound of the assistants meant that they were about to be fed. The *stimulus* of food should trigger the *response* of salivation. That was perfectly normal. But here the assistants were the stimulus which elicited the response. Pavlov decided to investigate.

The stimulus which naturally elicits a response Pavlov called an *unconditional stimulus* (US) and the response it triggers is an *unconditional response* (UR). So the US (food) elicits the UR (salivation).

Pavlov paired the sound of a buzzer with the presentation of the food every time the animals were to be fed. Each time such a *pairing* is made is called a *trial*. The buzzer is a *conditioned stimulus* (CS), i.e. any salivation response to it will only occur on condition that the animal has learned an association between it and food. So the US and the CS together elicit the UR.

After just a few trials the animals did start to salivate to the sound of the buzzer. By the tenth trial the animals had been *classically conditioned* to salivate to the sound of a buzzer. So the CS elicited the CR.

Classical Conditioning		
Stage 1	US » UR	(food » salivation)
Stage 2	CS + US » UR	(buzzer and food » salivation)
until		
Stage 3	CS » CR	(buzzer » salivation)

Note: The response stays the same – salivation. What elicits it is determined by whether or not it is conditioned.

 How would you condition a dog to salivate at the sight of a blue circle painted on a white card? Identify the various stimuli and responses.

Pavlov conditioned a number of dogs to salivate at the sound of buzzers, bells and metronomes. On average the response was fully conditioned in 10 trials. He altered the original stimulus in a number of ways and measured the response. From these experiments he derived several principles of learning.

Principles of learning in higher conditioning

1 *Higher order conditioning.* If an animal is fully conditioned to salivate to one CS (e.g. a bell tuned to the musical note, middle C), then if another CS (e.g. a buzzer) is associated with it, the animal will

learn to salivate to some extent when it hears the buzzer. The animal might salivate to a stimulus which is of a *higher order* than the original CS.

2 *Stimulus generalization.* If the CS is a bell tuned to the musical note C, then presenting a similar response stimulus (a bell tuned to B) will elicit a small response (perhaps just a few drops of saliva). The stimulus (the bell) can be *generalized* to some extent.

3 *Discrimination.* Since the bell tuned to B wasn't followed by food, the animals soon learned not to salivate to it. They learned to *discriminate* between those stimuli which preceded food and those which did not.

► In classical conditioning an organism learns that two stimuli go together. In Pavlov's experiments, for example, dogs learned to associate the ringing of a bell or buzzer (one stimulus) with the presentation of food (another stimulus).

4 *Extinction.* Pavlov conditioned an animal to salivate to a particular CS. He then stopped presenting the food afterwards. The animal soon learned that the particular CS no longer meant the arrival of food, so the salivation response was *extinguished*.

5 *Spontaneous recovery.* Even after a CR had been extinguished, an animal would occasionally salivate after hearing the old CS. The response would immediately extinguish again. Presumably this *spontaneous recovery* occurs because the response wasn't completely extinguished. Rather it was inhibited.

Little Albert

Classical conditioning has been used on humans too, even quite young ones. In their 1919 experiment **John B. Watson** and **Rosalie Rayner** found that a nine-month-old infant (called 'Little Albert') did not show a fear response to white furry animals such as monkeys, rats and rabbits, masks with and without hair, cotton wool, etc. However he did show fear when a steel bar was hit by a hammer just behind his head! The noise was the US, and the fear was the UR. When Albert was just over eleven months old a white furry rat (CS) was paired with the hammer striking the bar (US). There were seven pairings, and by the last one the sight of the furry animal was enough to elicit the fear response. The fear response was also generalized to a fur coat, Santa Claus masks, and even Watson's hair. The response persisted (possibly for the rest of Albert's life, since the child was removed from the hospital before any deconditioning began!).

► Watson and Rayner's research may have been revolutionary at the time, but certainly wouldn't be allowed now!

Evaluation of classical conditioning

Classical conditioning does explain how some human (and other animal) reflexive behaviours are acquired. It does not explain the majority of human learning which is not reflexive. Only a few reflex responses can be conditioned, and generalizations can only be made to other reflexive responses. Several therapies have been developed to deal with such reflexive behaviours as phobias, increased blood pressure, and sexual deviations, as we shall see in Chapter 10.

> **REVIEW – Classical conditioning**
> Classical conditioning shows how a reflexive response can be triggered by a stimulus which has become associated with it in the organism's mind. The response can be generalized and discriminated, and may extinguish if the stimulus is not followed by some benefit. Classical conditioning has been successfully used in the treatment of a number of human conditions.

Operant or instrumental conditioning

Modern operant conditioning developed from the pioneering work of Ivan Pavlov and J. B. Watson. It is more concerned with how voluntary behaviour can be evoked than with reflexive behaviour. It started as *instrumental conditioning* where an animal has to use some part of the experimental apparatus in order to gain some reward. *Operant conditioning* includes this, but also refers to any freely chosen behaviours in 'real life'.

Thorndike and early operant conditioning

Edward L. Thorndike applied some of the principles Pavlov had discovered to learned, non-reflexive behaviour. He put a series of cats into a puzzle box which he had made. Performing some operation (an *operant*), such as pulling a string or pressing a treadle, would open the box, allowing the cat to escape. Food outside the box, or the satisfaction of gaining freedom, were the reward for performing the operation. Eventually most of the animals accidentally pulled the string or pressed the treadle and escaped. Having eaten their fish (their reward), they were returned to the box for another trial. Figure 2.1 shows Thorndike's results.

► In *operant* conditioning an organism learns to associate some behaviour of its own with some result.

► Thorndike conducted carefully controlled experiments to discover the rate at which cats would perform an operant in order to gain some reward. What started as trial and error soon became intentional behaviour.

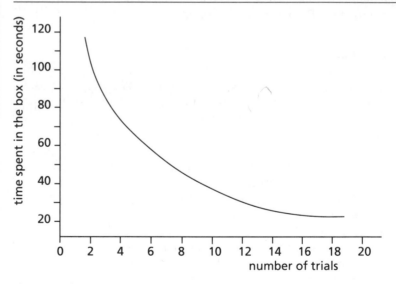

Figure 2.1 Simplified graph of Thorndike's results.

The graph shows the time cats spent in the puzzle box before pressing the treadle and escaping

Thorndike claimed that the cats' learning is essentially by *trial and error*. They have no understanding of what they're doing, but the more times they do it and gain their reward, the fewer errors they'll make before repeating the response on the next trial. The animals are learning some association between a stimulus (the string or treadle) and a response (their pulling or pressing it) and the result of their response (a reward).

In 1904 Thorndike first stated his *Law of Effect* from which modern operant conditioning developed. It stated that a response will follow

> ### The main differences between classical and operant conditioning
>
> In Thorndike's experiments the animal has to learn to perform an operant (a learned response such as string pulling) before receiving any reward. In Pavlov's research the animal doesn't learn to perform anything, its response was reflexive.
>
> In Pavlov's research the salivation response came after the presentation of the stimulus. In operant conditioning the animal's response occurs before any reinforcement is presented.

a stimulus if it is associated in the organism's mind with 'a satisfying state of affairs'. Thus any behaviour that leads to something 'good' will be repeated, and any behaviour that results in something 'bad' will be avoided (and become extinguished). Early research into conditioning is sometimes called *stimulus response* (or S-R) psychology.

 What are the main differences between classical and operant conditioning?

B.F. Skinner

Skinner and modern operant conditioning

Over the last half a century **Burrhus Frederic Skinner** (1904–90) investigated, refined, and generalized the principles and applications of operant conditioning. He used strict scientific principles to test animal behaviour and learning, and applied some of his conclusions to humans. (Operant conditioning has been called *behaviourism*, *Skinnerian psychology*, and *learning theory*.) Skinner was less concerned with explaining *why* we behave than in predicting and controlling *how* we will behave. This has led to much criticism of him and his theories.

Skinner believed that 'satisfying states of affairs' and 'rewards' are insufficiently precise to be of use to science. How could we observe or measure the satisfaction of a laboratory rat? What would be a reward for it? He preferred the terms *reinforcement* and *reinforcer* because they are precise and can be measured. A reinforcer is anything which increases or maintains the likelihood of some behaviour recurring. We aren't concerned about why or how it works, only that it does. If you ask some people why they go to work most will say something like, 'Because I need the money'. Money is a reinforcer. It maintains our going to work behaviour. We do not need to know what someone does with their money, what they spend it on, how much they save, etc., to know that money is a reinforcer. Reinforcement is simply the process or consequence of being reinforced, e.g. getting paid, spending the money, etc.

Skinner tested a number of animals in various puzzle boxes which have become known as *Skinner boxes*. They were often similar to Thorndike's puzzle boxes. Animals had to perform some behaviour in order to obtain a reinforcer. Food was the usual reinforcer for hungry animals. Skinner helped rats to learn to press levers, pigeons to turn full circle on their perches, various birds to peck at differently

---

Free will

Various religious groups, philosophers and psychologists, among others, have claimed that people have free will, i.e. the ability to make up our own minds about what we believe to be right and wrong, and how to behave accordingly.

Skinner is accused of taking a me*chanistic* and *reductionist* view of human beings. This means that he seemed to believe that all human functioning can be ultimately explained in simple, mechanical terms, just as the functioning of a motor car engine can, and can be reduced to the basic principles of physics and physiology.

Skinner's view is also criticized for being *deterministic*, i.e. that everything has a cause or reason, and that it is possible to discover the cause or reason. Many psychologists disagree about whether we could ever know the cause of all human behaviour, or that we should want to!

► Most early behaviourist research was conducted on animals since they were convenient subjects to use. Behaviourists assume that the principles of learning which describe the way lower order animals learn will also describe the way humans learn.

► Reinforcement increases the likelihood that a given response will be repeated when relevant or possible, in the future, in order to gain a similar beneficial or desirable response. Punishment increases the likelihood that some response will not be repeated. Punishment therefore is not a reinforcer.

coloured disks, and even some pigeons to play a version of ping pong!

Types of reinforcement

A number of different types of reinforcer were identified by Skinner. There are *positive* and *negative* reinforcers. Positive reinforcers can be *primary* and *secondary*. Primary reinforcers satisfy some physiological need, something we may find it difficult to live without, e.g. food, water, rest, warmth, shelter, or sexual expression. Secondary reinforcers have to be learned, by association with primary reinforcers. Often secondary reinforcers can be exchanged for primary reinforcers, for example money can be exchanged for food.

Negative reinforcers are unpleasant, and we learn to avoid or escape from them. If we find the taste of avocado pear to be unpleasant, then we will try to avoid eating it. This is *avoidance learning*. If we are given an avocado pear at a party we may have to find a way to escape from eating it, perhaps by hiding it in our handkerchief! This is *escape learning*. It is important to distinguish between negative reinforcement and punishment. A negative reinforcer is something unpleasant which ceases when the animal makes the desired response, i.e., the animal is rewarded by the cessation of pain or some other discomfort. Punishment by contrast is something administered because the animal makes an undesired response. Punishment is not a reinforcer because it does not teach someone how to behave. It teaches them how not to. Administering punishment has proved very ineffectual in promoting learning.

One other feature of the learning process is *punishment*. Punishment is not a reinforcer because it does not teach someone how to behave. It teaches them how not to. Skinner believed that punishment is largely irrelevant since we should be able to predict and control people's behaviour by the appropriate distribution of reinforcements so that punishment should never be necessary.

What are the main kinds of reinforcers? Give an example of each one.

Skinner experimented with *how* and *when* he gave reinforcers, since it isn't necessary to reinforce after every correct response – continuous reinforcement. He identified five other *schedules of reinforcement* which are outlined in the following summary box. If learning is being maintained by continuous or *fixed schedules*, it will also extinguish quite quickly when the reinforcement stops. When learning occurs as a result of *variable schedules*, it will be slow to extinguish.

► *Extinction resistance* refers to the probability that the organism will continue to show the learned behaviour.

► The best way to condition an operant response is to reinforce continuously at first, then to switch to a fixed schedule, then to a variable schedule.

Schedules of reinforcement

Schedule	When reinforcer applied	Extinction resistance
1 Continuous	Every correct response	Low
2 Fixed ratio	Every so many correct responses, e.g. every third	Low – medium
3 Variable ratio	The number varies	High
4 Fixed interval	Every so much time, e.g. every 30 seconds as long as one correct response has occurred	Low – medium
5 Variable interval	The amount of time between reinforcements is varied	High

 Why does the kind of schedule used affect the ease or difficulty with which the learning will extinguish?

Reinforcement can be used to 'shape' quite complex behaviour in both animals and humans. Skinner taught two pigeons to play ping pong using the technique called behaviour shaping by successive *approximations*. The complex task of hitting a ball in a particular direction has to be broken down into its smallest parts. Each part is reinforced until finally the animal can perform the whole task.

Evaluation of operant conditioning

Operant learning techniques work well enough with animals, and some of the principles might apply to some human situations. For example, autistic (emotionally withdrawn) children have been taught to dress themselves, to use a knife and fork, and other life skills in this way. Mentally or behaviourally disturbed adults have also been 'trained' to behave more normally (as we shall see in Chapter 11.) But not all human learning is the result of previously reinforced responses. Some is totally novel (new), and nothing similar has ever been reinforced before. Some learning is accidental, some is spontaneous, and some occurs for no apparent reason at all.

Behaviour shaping

A pigeon is to be taught to play table tennis. The animal must learn to approach a bouncing ball, then to hit the ball, to hit it hard enough to make it travel some distance, and to hit it in the right direction.

Task	Teaching
1 The pigeon is to allow itself to be struck by a table tennis ball.	The pigeon is reinforced every time it is struck by the ball.
When this task is fully conditioned the reinforcement stops.	
2 The pigeon is to seek a bouncing ball, and hit it with any part of its body.	A reinforcer is applied whenever the pigeon seeks and strikes a bouncing ball.
When this task is fully conditioned the reinforcement stops.	
3 Now the pigeon must hit the ball only with its upper body.	Only strikes with the head and upper body are reinforced.
When this task is fully conditioned the reinforcement stops.	
4 The pigeon must hit the ball with its beak.	Only strikes with the beak are reinforced.
When this task is fully conditioned the reinforcement stops.	
5 The ball must be hit by the beak in a given direction.	Only strikes towards the position of the other pigeon are reinforced.
When this task is fully conditioned the reinforcement stops.	
6 The beak must strike the ball hard enough in the required direction to make it travel to the other side of the 'court'.	Reinforcement is given to the pigeon only for those strikes which send the ball hard enough in the right direction.
Repeat this procedure with another pigeon, and watch them play!	

ACT Draw up a plan to teach a child with some learning difficulties to put his own jumper on.

REVIEW – Operant conditioning

Skinner argued that most behaviour, whether 'good', 'normal', 'bad' or 'disturbed', is learned by reinforcement. Reinforcement increases the chances that some particular behaviour is more likely to occur with a given stimulus than any other behaviour. Reinforcement can be positive or negative, and quite complex behaviours can be shaped by systematically and selectively applying reinforcers.

Types of reinforcement

Positive ⟨ Primary (necessary for survival)
Secondary (associated with primary)

Negative ⟨ Escape learning
Avoidance learning

Stages in negative reinforcement have been demonstrated in the laboratory.

Escape learning
1   The floor of a rat's cage has a mild electrical current passed through it which the rat appears to finds unpleasant.
2   Pressing a lever in the cage will turn the current off. The rat hits the lever, by accident, whilst trying to escape from the electricity. The current is turned off.
3   After a time the current is turned on again. The rat again accidentally presses the lever and so turns off the current.
4   After a few trials the animal learns to press the lever as soon as the current is switched on.

Avoidance learning
1   A buzzer is sounded just before the current is switched on.
2   The rat learns to associate the buzzer and the current.
3   The rat presses the lever when it hears the buzzer.

 How could you teach a circus elephant to walk around the ring with its front feet on the back of the animal in front?

SOCIAL LEARNING THEORY

During the last forty years, interest in Freudian psychoanalytic theory has declined, partly because it can't be validated, partly because its applications do not always work, and partly because Freud's references to infantile sexuality in his early writing are now seen by many as rather scandalous and ridiculous. However, as was said earlier, some of Freud's ideas seem reasonable. For example, children do imitate their parents' behaviour, including saying things they've heard their parents say and applying, as best they can, principles they have learned from their parents. Freud's concept of identification appeared to deserve further study.

Meanwhile competition to be the new paradigm came from B.F. Skinner's new behaviourism, and his application of scientific techniques to the mechanisms of learning. People do learn by being reinforced, and sometimes bad behaviour can be learned by being accidentally associated with something pleasant.

► Social learning theorists have tried to combine the psychoanalytic type of identification with the behaviourists' laboratory approach to learning.

Albert Bandura

▶ Albert Bandura uses the term *observational learning* to describe learning which does not rely on reinforcement or shaping, but merely on some behaviour being observed.

▶ *Modelling* is one of the fundamental processes in socialization. Models are seen as very influential people, who children may feel they need to imitate.

Social learning theorists have tried to combine aspects of behaviourism with psychoanalysis by applying laboratory techniques to the study of identification. One of the most notable theorists is **Albert Bandura** who has been developing social learning theory since the 1950s. Social learning theorists do not deny the value of reinforcement but they do not believe that reinforcement alone can explain all learning. Certain cognitive (mental events to do with 'knowing') factors are involved between stimulus and response.

Children, and adults too, often learn by simply *observing* and then imitating someone who they consider to be a powerful or attractive or important person. The cognitive influence concerns why someone thinks that one person is more worthy of imitation than another. For children the most important models are parents. Parents need not deliberately try to influence the child, or apply a reinforcer for *observational learning* to occur.

 What is meant by observational learning in social learning theory?

Summary – Major features in observational learning

1 *Paying attention* to those parts of the model's behaviour which are important to the observer, and not misinterpreting or becoming distracted by other environmental events.

2 *Accurately remembering* what has been observed. Older children can model events from some time ago; younger children do not have such cognitive skills.

3 *Accurately reproducing* the observed behaviour. Younger children may need several observations and trials before successfully modelling some observed behaviour.

4 *Motivation*, being the desire to imitate one model rather than another.

 How does Albert Bandura's social learning theory compare with the behaviourist approach of B. F. Skinner?

Abraham Maslow

HUMANISM, THE 'THIRD FORCE' IN PSYCHOLOGY

Abraham Maslow was a revolutionary psychologist who, over forty years ago, rejected psychology's preoccupation with psychoanalytic treatments for neuroses, and simplistic behaviourist explanations for behaviour and its mechanistic view of humanity. Instead he proposed that psychology should be about maximizing each individual person's full human potential. Psychology should be about showing everyone how they can fully achieve the highest motives, the greatest knowledge, the fullest understanding, and the finest control and appreciation of the emotions of which they were capable. (Maslow himself was an intensely shy person who possibly might have benefited from the goal he set for psychology.) The result of this ultimate self-knowledge Maslow called *self-actualization*.

Humanist psychologists do not believe that psychology can deal with generalizations but must apply itself to each unique individual. It must be idiographic. It cannot be scientific since it is concerned with individuals and doesn't seek similarities between people which can be generalized. Rather, it is involved with helping each person to maximize their individual talents. A major figure in the humanist approach is **Carl Rogers**, whose work will be discussed in Chapter 10.

Early psychological theories, such as Freud's psychoanalysis, were dominated by ideas about 'the mind'. They were most influential during the first few decades of this century. Behaviourists reject such ideas since they did not believe that 'the mind' could be investigated using scientific methods. This view was widely held after the 1940s. Humanism does accept the relevance of 'the mind' as a topic in psychology. It is in 'the mind' that we attend, perceive, reason, remember, form ideas, plan, dream, hope, think and 'know'. Such mental activities are called cognition and interest in cognitive psychology has grown dramatically during the last forty years.

Cognitive psychology doesn't, as yet, have a single, unifying theory. Nor does it have one particular spokesperson. It isn't thought of as a major force in the way that the others are. Nevertheless cognitive psychologists have made great contributions to our understanding of the way humans think, as we shall see in the following chapters.

▶ *Self-actualization* is both a process and a final state of human consciousness when one can think independently, can resist outside temptations and pressures, and generally 'know' oneself.

Chapter summary – Influential psychological theories

Modern psychology has several themes and perspectives which are constantly developing as new insights are gained. However, two influential theories have dominated psychology for most of this century.

Psychodynamic theory was originally conceived and developed by Sigmund Freud in Vienna, and concerns the development of personality. Freud hypothesized the existence of two instinctive forces, the libido and the death instinct, deriving their energy from the unconscious part of our mind, the id. Irrational demands are modified by a consciousness represented by one's increasing self knowledge (the ego), and our growing sense of morality (the superego). Personality finds expression through the erogenous zones of the mouth and the anus, until some sexual feelings are awakened during the phallic stage, which have to be met by a successful resolution of Oedipal or Electra conflicts. Anything less may produce anxiety which may become repressed into the unconscious during the remainder of childhood, and may emerge as hysterical neurosis later in life.

Other psychoanalysts have been unable to agree with Freud. Jung sees a mystical collective unconscious resulting from early evolution joining the personal unconscious. Adler diminishes the importance of both sexual and unconscious forces. He argues that power and dominance are important conscious goals which influence our personality. Erikson sees personality growth continuing throughout life as we attempt to resolve certain dilemmas associated with each major developmental stage.

The other major theory (behaviourism) concerns the development of learned behaviour. Pavlov's pioneering work on association learning in dogs demonstrated how the principles of learning trigger reflexive responses. Generalization, discrimination, extinction and spontaneous recovery were demonstrated in the laboratory. Watson showed that something similar could be applied to humans. Skinner contributed the notion of reinforcement as the key to understanding all learned behaviour. The consequences of an act thus become more important than what happened before it in determining the chances that it will recur in the future.

Social learning theory is an attempt to combine some of the aspects of psychodynamic theory with those of behaviourism. Social learning theorists argue that learning appropriate responses is also influenced by observing and modelling the behaviour of those people (whether real or fictional) that the learner sees as important or attractive in some way. Reinforcement and punishment are important too.

Although more influenced by psychodynamic theory than by behaviourism humanist psychologists represent a third force in psychology. Humanists reject the idea that people can or should be observed and measured, and claim rather that psychology should attempt to help individuals to fulfil themselves.

Exam Questions – 60 minutes each

1   Describe and evaluate Freud's explanation of the growth of personality.

2   Contrast two psychoanalytic theories of the development of personality.

3   How do children learn?

Further Reading: Chapter 2

For those who like original sources these books may be of particular interest

Freud S. 1978. *New Introductory Lectures*. Harmondsworth: Penguin.

Freud S. 1986. *Essential Psychoanalysis*. Harmondsworth: Penguin.

Skinner B. 1974. *About Behaviourism*. London: Jonathan Cape.

Bandura A. 1977. *Social Learning*. London: Prentice-Hall.

Kline P. 1984. *Psychology and Freudian Theory: an Introduction*. London: Methuen.

Medcoff J. & Roth J. 1979. *Approaches to Psychology*. Milton Keynes: Open University Press.

Hearnshaw L. 1987. *The Shaping of Modern Psychology: an Historical Introduction*. London: Routledge & Kegan Paul.

Developmental psychology: sociability and attachment

Introduction

Some early philosophers and psychologists argued that humans are genetically 'programmed' to behave and think in certain ways. Freud, for example, claimed that we inherit various instinctive urges that will condition our personalities. The idea that much of our behaviour and thought is genetically determined is known as the *nature* view, and those who support it are called *nativists*.

During this century there has been a steady movement in psychology away from this idea. Behaviourists, for example Skinner, argue that most of our behaviour is learned and influenced by social experiences. This is known as the *nurture* view, and those who support it are called *nurturists*. The *nature–nurture debate* has influenced a great deal of psychological research and theory, particularly in the area of child development.

Nowadays we accept that the capacity to develop human skills and abilities is genetically inherited from our parents, though whether we develop some of them depends on how we are brought up.

This is the first of three chapters on developmental psychology. It deals with the development of the child as a social being and especially the young child's need for emotional and social experiences and the role of the mother and others in supplying them. Chapter 4 deals with the development of thought, and Chapter 5 with moral development. Chapter 2 introduced some of the most influential theories in psychology. In these three chapters you will see how they have been applied to child development.

> ### The biology of reproduction
> After sexual intercourse between a biologically fertile male and female, millions of sperm may be released into the female vagina. If a (tadpole-like) sperm survives swimming its way up the vagina and into the fallopian tube, it may find an ovum – a female egg – capable of being fertilized. If the sperm penetrates the wall of the ovum its chromosomes will combine with the chromosomes in the ovum.
>
> Chromosomes in the nuclei of cells carry the genetic material called DNA. Each species has a fixed number of chromosomes in its males and females. Human female chromosomes are shaped rather like an X, while male chromosomes are shaped like a Y. Each chromosome carries about 20,000 genes, and each person is the result of about a million genes.

EARLY SOCIALIZATION

Genetic influences

At the moment of conception 23 pairs of *chromosomes* in the male sperm combine with 23 pairs from the female ovum or egg, and this fertilized egg becomes the start of a new human life. Each chromosome carries thousands of tiny packages of information called *genes* which convey information about the parent whose chromosome it is. The combination of the chromosomes will determine what the new life should be like. What sex it is, what size it will be, what hair, eye and skin colour it will have, are all determined by the genes. This fertilized egg carries the new life's *genotype*.

Since the mix of the genes is unique in each individual, so each new life will be quite different. The exception is the case of identical twins, where the fertilized egg divides into two identical halves which then develop separately in the womb. If the new life survives the next nine months, it will have grown into a baby. Obviously each baby is going to be very different.

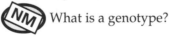 What is a genotype?

► A *genotype* is the name of the unique mixture of characteristics inherited from both parents. The shape of the family nose or the family chin can be inherited genetically, as well as some disorders such as Down's syndrome.

What must children learn?

Each unique baby is born into a society with its own particular culture, language, style of dress and behaviour, and set of acceptable attitudes, all of which the baby will have to learn. The baby will start on this huge learning task just a few months after birth. Different societies have different standards of behaviour which are typical of, and acceptable to, most of its people. These are *norms*. Norms are not simple rules which can easily be written down as instructions for correct behaviour. Appropriate behaviour varies from time to time, place to place and social group to social group. What is appropriate eating behaviour at home, would not necessarily be appropriate in a restaurant and what is appropriate behaviour at the end of a party

► *Norms* are socially acceptable or appropriate standards of behaviour which are typical, or representative of, members of each social group.

► *Values* are general moral principles which we use in making judgements about right and wrong.

> ### REVIEW – Socialization
>
> Socialization is the name of the process by which people learn the ways of behaving and thinking – norms and values – which are thought appropriate by other people. Social groups have norms and values representing acceptable standards of behaviour and thought. Each new member of society has to learn these standards if they are to fit in with the other members.

would not necessarily be appropriate at the beginning. So not only do people have to learn norms, they also have to learn when, where and by whom they are appropriate. Learning the rules of social life and how to apply them is a very complicated business.

 (ACT) Write some reasons for why socialization is so important for humans and not for other animals.

THE DEVELOPMENT OF SOCIABILITY

The beginning of any discussion about babies and children must be to say that they are all different. No two babies are alike, and many do not do the same things at the same time. They all have different *temperaments*. Some are happy and sleep well, some are irritable and cry a lot. There are probably some genetically inherited reasons for this, so even the most devoted mother may have a 'difficult baby'. **Helen Bee** estimates that about ten per cent of babies might have difficult temperaments; most babies are easier to handle. The times mentioned in the following text when certain 'developmental milestones' are achieved refer only to when the majority of children have achieved those skills. Nor does early achievement of one skill mean that the child will stay advanced in that skill, or be advanced in achieving any other.

► *Temperament* refers to the aspect of an individual's personality concerning changes in moods, level of emotionality, and level of general sensitivity.

According to **Rudi Schaffer** *neonates* prefer humans to inanimate objects. They reach and smile and cry and wave and do whatever they can to attract someone's attention. It takes a month or so before they can clearly distinguish between different people. From that time the face and voice of their main caregiver should elicit a smile from the infant. By showing babies combinations of their mother's face and a stranger's face, and presenting them with their mother's voice and a stranger's voice, **Genevieve Carpenter** found that babies of just a few weeks could tell the difference between their mother and a stranger.

► *Neonate* means new born.

► For the first few months of life babies have a great deal to experience. They aren't very aware of anyone else until they start to recognize and respond to some of the people around them. This often takes up to two or three months.

After a few more months the infant will start to show distinct preferences between the people who care for it and others. The baby of 6 to 12 months is capable of making a firm emotional relationship. This is an *attachment*. Once a child has an attachment it starts to be wary of strangers and becomes upset if separated from the person or persons to whom it is attached. This wariness and upset are the two ways in which we can tell to whom babies are attached.

Mary Ainsworth devised 'the strange situation' to show who babies are attached to. The child and its caregivers are placed in a room, then mother, father or a stranger leave and re-enter the room, and the

► An *attachment* is an emotional bond that develops between a baby of 6 to 12 months old and the person or people who are closest to it.

► *Bonding* is an alternative word for attachment.

► A child is said to be attached to someone if it shows distress when that person leaves it, or when a stranger approaches it.

child's reaction to each event is recorded. If the child shows no distress when the mother leaves the room, but does when father leaves, then we could say the child is attached to its father. If it shows distress when approached by a stranger when father is present, but not when mother is, then this could confirm the child's preference for its father.

Summary – Temperament and preference

All babies are born with different genetic inheritances, and will have different predispositions to mature in different ways. They all have different temperaments too. By temperament we mean emotions and moods which affect babies' reactions to stimuli such as being touched, cuddled, left alone, approached by strangers and so forth. Differences exist in very young babies, and are probably genetic in origin. Regardless of temperament most babies gradually learn to recognize their own mothers or main caregivers, and begin to prefer them to the company of others.

 What is an attachment? Name three examples of behaviour which would aid attachment formation between an infant and its mother.

How did Mary Ainsworth operationalize attachment and use this operationalization in her 'strange situation' study.

Why might babies of differing temperaments have different patterns of attachment? **?**

► Any behaviour which has *survival value* could contribute to preserving the organism's life. If there is some threat, a baby who is grasping its mother's hair while she seeks shelter is more likely to survive than one who doesn't grasp, and is dropped!

Bowlby and babies' need for attachment

John Bowlby became an authority on early social experiences after his research into motherless children in the late 1940s. He believed that infants are born with a range of abilities, such as sucking, smiling, reaching and grasping, which are likely to attract and keep an adult caregiver's attention. Such skills would certainly have *survival value* since they might convince the caregiver that the baby was content and happy to be with them. This might reinforce the belief that they are effective caregivers, and make them even more pleased to care for their infant.

Bowlby claimed that making successful attachments is essential for future emotional, social and intellectual development. He is not saying that children who have unsuccessful attachment bonding will automatically suffer later. Their adult personalities and intellectual skills will be influenced by all kinds of other factors. However, inadequate bonding is certainly a contributing factor. He suggests that about 40 per cent of children whose attachments were inadequately formed in childhood will have problems as adults. Children between six months and five years of age should not be separated from their mothers for a prolonged period, according to Bowlby. A separation of just two weeks could be disastrous for a young child's future development.

One way to investigate the function of attachments is to compare those children whose attachments have not been normal with those

John Bowlby

> **REVIEW – Bowlby's views**
> John Bowlby was a leading and influential child psychiatrist who claimed that humans have evolved a need for a special, close emotional bond with their primary caregivers – their mother or mother substitute. This need is associated with feeding since mothers have always fed their babies. Any disruption of the attachment bond could have adverse effects on personality development. According to Bowlby our future mental health is influenced by the success of our bonding with our mother or mother surrogate during the first year of life, and by the bond not being broken thereafter in childhood.

for whom they have. If the two groups show dramatic differences in their emotions or personality then those differences may be explained by their different attachment experiences. There are two possibilities for distorted attachment. One is where attachments never formed in the first place, the second is where they existed, but were broken by a separation.

Where 'normal' attachments were never formed

Barbara Tizard, **Judith Rees** and **Jill Hodges** studied 65 children who had been placed in a residential nursery before they were four months old. Many of their mothers were unmarried, and were unable to cope. Two to three years later some of the children were adopted, some returned to their natural mothers, and some remained in the nursery. The adopted children were emotionally disturbed, often very demanding, dependent on their parents, and difficult with their peers. They nevertheless coped better than those children who remained in the nursery. However the group who seemed least emotionally secure were those who returned to their natural mothers. The mothers still had difficulties in coping, and the children appeared to suffer. Bowlby claimed that 'even the worst mother is better than the best institution' for childrearing. Tizard *et al*'s research does not support this claim. It seems that making a child's environment better (enrichment) will assist in emotional development. Making an environment worse (impoverishment) will hinder normal progress.

Wayne and **Marsena Dennis** measured the intelligence of some teenage orphans from an unstimulating Lebanese orphanage. They were well below average. Wayne Dennis followed up a group who had been adopted at various ages 15 years afterwards. He found that the longer they stayed in the orphanage after the age of two years, the further below average they remained. This suggests that enriching a deprived environment has benefits for intellectual development.

We obviously can't conduct controlled experiments on humans to investigate the effects of non-existent attachments, but such research has been conducted on animals. **Harry Harlow** removed some rhesus monkeys from their mothers just after birth and reared them in isolation. Their cages contained a blanket and the animals spent many hours cuddling up to it. When the blanket was removed they

▶ Tizard's study is a longitudinal natural experiment. The researchers had no say in which children were adopted, etc. The samples and experimental conditions were chosen by the authorities.

▶ Tizard *et al*'s study concentrated on the effects of emotional development, while the Dennis' study concentrated on intellectual development. Both studies show that enrichment and impoverishment have their effects.

▶ Rhesus monkeys are small animals (about 18 inches long) and were easy to obtain and keep. Harlow *privated* some of them, i.e. denied them any social contact with other monkeys.

►Some time between three and six months seems to be a cut-off point after which privated monkeys appeared unable to adjust to normal life.

►A *surrogate* is a substitute or stand in, usually for a parent. Primary school teachers are often used as surrogate parents by the children in their classes. Harlow's wire and cloth-covered dolls were surrogate mothers.

►Harlow and Bowlby rejected the central importance of feeding for infants. Instead they saw *contact comfort* as far more important. Bowlby claimed that contact comfort would help in the bonding process as well as in survival.

showed violent emotional reactions that lasted for several days. This suggests that young animals need something constant, dependable and comfortable in their lives.

When some of the rhesus monkeys were released into the company of normally reared monkeys at the age of three months they were seemingly shy and withdrawn, but they gradually learned to adapt and became accepted by the other monkeys. Those released after six months' isolation were severely withdrawn and never fully adapted. They were attacked by the others, had little idea about play or establishing their place in the group. The males had little success at attracting a mate, and the females that did mate had little idea of motherhood and neglected their offspring.

To test whether comfort was more important than food Harlow removed eight rhesus monkeys from their mothers just after birth and raised them in total isolation from other monkeys. Four were in cages with a wooden model *surrogate* mother covered in terry towelling; the model contained a feeding bottle. There was also a wire-mesh, uncovered surrogate model. The other four monkeys' cages had similar surrogates but were fed by the wire-mesh surrogate. Regardless of which surrogate had the feeding bottle, all the monkeys spent most of their days clinging on to the terry-covered substitute. This *contact comfort* was clearly as important for these monkeys, as it had appeared to be for the earlier group with their blankets.

When the monkeys were frightened (by Harlow putting strange toys, such as a mechanical teddy bear or large wooden spider, into their cage), they all clung to the towelling-covered mother. Eventually they would leave the model briefly to go and explore, then rush back to it for comfort again. The terry-covered surrogate served as a safe base from which to explore.

At first sight it seems that Harlow's research supports Bowlby's predictions that maternal deprivation leads to unsatisfactory development. However, these animals weren't just being deprived of their mothers (maternal deprivation), but of all social contact (social privation). It could be this privation from all contact with other monkeys, rather than just with their mothers, that explains their disturbed behaviour.

In later experiments by Harry Harlow and **Steven Suomi** three-month-old 'normally reared' females were gradually introduced into the isolates' cages. The behaviour of the isolated monkeys gradually improved as they played with their 'therapists', and when released later they seemed better able to cope. This suggests that young rhesus monkeys need other monkeys around to learn from, and not just their mothers.

►Harlow's early research points to the need for contact comfort, and its role in the animal's independence. The later research shows that animals other than the mother can provide the stimulation for making normal relationships with others.

(NM) Summarize Harlow's experiments with monkeys. How far can the results of these experiments be applied to human development? (You should note that Harlow's monkeys were socially privated rather than maternally deprived as such, and that there are problems about generalizing from animal studies to human behaviour.)

Konrad Lorenz

Konrad Lorenz was an ethologist who observed the events he called *imprinting*. Ethologists study the interaction of genetic and social forces on animal behaviour in their natural habitat. They make detailed observations and construct hypotheses which may then be tested experimentally. Lorenz observed that some newborn animals tend to follow the first moving thing they see after they are born. Presumably they have some genetic instinct for following. Usually the first thing a newborn will see is its mother. Of course they do not know what their mother looks like, so they learn that the first thing they see will be their mother.

Lorenz hatched some greylag goslings away from their mothers, and had them following all kinds of things, including himself, a matchbox tied to string, and a yellow rubber glove. Lorenz claimed that imprinting also had some important implications for later mating behaviour. Animals who had imprinted on an unusual object often tried to mate with it later. It has been suggested that human attachments are a kind of imprinting (without the implications for mating!).

According to Lorenz, there was a *critical period* during which imprinting must occur, otherwise it wouldn't occur at all. The length of this time varies depending on the animal species in question. For ducks and geese it was about 24 hours following birth. According to Lorenz for humans it could start after a few months, and might last a few years. Later researchers have challenged Lorenz's ideas of a critical period, preferring instead a *sensitive period* when animals and people may be particularly receptive to certain stimuli.

Lorenz's findings about the period immediately following the hatching of goslings and ducks seem far removed from a discussion of the needs of humans for attachment. Much animal behaviour is governed by primitive instincts and reflexes, whereas humans have much greater capacities for learning. We have intelligence, a *cognitive system* and a more highly developed brain than other animals. At best the animal research suggests that humans may have a need for social

► *Imprinting* is a special form of learning that occurs soon after birth in some animal species. Konrad Lorenz found that many animals imprinted on their caregivers during the few hours following birth. Why can't we test for it in humans?

► Having an instinctive urge to follow the first thing one sees would contribute to one's survival. In the wild the first thing one sees is likely to be the mother, who will feed and protect the newborn.

► A *sensitive period* is a period of time after birth when some animals are particularly sensitive to certain stimuli, such as the sight of their caregiver. The idea of a sensitive period is a weak form of the idea of a critical period.

Bowlby's study of 44 juvenile thieves

There are certain problems with Bowlby's study. He found two variables, 'maternal separation' and 'delinquency', and assumed that one causes the other. A third variable, e.g. poverty, could have caused both. Bowlby didn't take a control group of non-thieves to see how many of them had been separated from their mothers.

► Traditional psychoanalysis sees feeding and the erogenous zone during the oral stage being central to a child's personality. Bowlby believes attachment formation to be even more important.

contact in order to build emotional relationships. It does not define the mother's role in this process.

 Summarize Lorenz's work on imprinting. Say why the 'following response' might have survival value. How far can Lorenz's work on animals be applied to human development?

Summary – Where 'normal' attachments were never formed

Tizard *et al*'s study showed that mothers weren't necessarily the best people to bring up their children unless they had the ability and adequate material conditions. Those reared by adopting parents did overcome most of their problems later. The Dennis' study claimed a sensitive period of two years for intellectual development.

Harlow's privation studies found that monkeys can recover from the loss of their mother if they have other social contact. Lorenz found that certain species have an instinctive need to form a relationship with the first thing they see. For similar reasons humans might have evolved something similar, but this is debatable.

Where attachments had been broken

John Bowlby and his colleagues **James** and **Joyce Robertson** adopted a psychoanalytic perspective which encourages the belief that the early relationship of a child with its parents can have long term effects on personality development. Over the last forty years Bowlby, in many books, and the Robertsons, in a powerful series of documentary films, have pointed to the dangers in separating a child from its mother during the first few years of life.

Bowlby observed the cases of a number of adolescents who had been referred to a child guidance clinic in which he worked in the 1930s. He selected 44 of them who had been convicted after stealing and noted that almost 40 per cent had been separated from their mother for six months or more before they were five years old. Fourteen were described as having a clinical condition which Bowlby described as 'affectionless psychopathy'. They showed no guilt for their crime, or concern for their victims. In his paper *44 Juvenile Thieves* Bowlby claims that maternal separation could have contributed to this condition. He wrote: 'There is a very strong case indeed for believing that separation of a child from his mother (or mother substitute) during the first five years of life stands foremost among the causes of delinquent character development.' Delinquency wouldn't be the only consequence of maternal deprivation. Bowlby claims that emotional disturbance, social maladjustment and retarded intellectual growth could also result from being separated from one's mother.

 Take Bowlby's study of 44 juvenile thieves (inset). How could this study have been improved?

Other research on institutionalized children was turned to by Bowlby for further evidence to support his hypothesis that maternal deprivation leads to social, emotional and intellectual problems. In 1943

William Goldfarb published the results of his longitudinal study of two groups of 15 teenagers. One group had been fostered before they were 12 months old, the other group had spent at least the first three and a half years of their lives in an understaffed and unstimulating institution. The two groups were similar in their ages, numbers of each sex, and social background of their parents. The children were studied at three and a half, six and a half, eight and a half, and twelve years. Those in the institution for three years or more scored lower on tests of intelligence, were more dependent on adults, had problems with language and speech, had more temper tantrums and were socially immature. They were more likely to become aggressive if frustrated, some were hyperactive, and most were more likely to try to deceive their parents. They spent much time alone and didn't make or keep friends because they seemed emotionally insecure. Goldfarb claimed that all these difficulties were because of the time spent in the orphanage.

Goldfarb's study seems to show that children who have an unstimulating early social experience will find it difficult to catch up later compared to those whose environments are more stimulating. However, this doesn't prove that the best source of such stimulation is a mother in a family. Other people, even within the institution, could have provided the stimulation. It appears that they *did not*, not that they *could not*. (And it is possible that those children who were adopted earlier were more intelligent and sociable to begin with.)

In 1946 **Rene Spitz** and **Katharine Wolf** published their study of 123 babies during their first year of life who were being looked after by their unmarried mothers in an American penal institution. At one point the mothers were moved to another part of the institution and the babies were cared for by the other mothers or pregnant girls. The 123 babies were between six and nine months old at the time. During the separation 'the child either didn't see its mother at all, or at best, once a week'. Spitz and Wolf noted that the children cried more than they had before. They lost their appetites, and failed to gain weight. When their mothers returned the babies' conditions returned to what they had been before the separation.

Bowlby claimed that this study, and other research on institutional children conducted by Spitz and Wolf, supported his hypothesis that babies need their mothers. However, it could equally well be argued that what this study shows is that babies whose routines are disrupted become distressed. We do not know about the quality of the alternative care offered to the babies during their mothers' absence. It may not have been the same as that provided by their mothers, and this could account for some of their distress.

During the 1950s and 1960s **James** and **Joyce Robertson** drew attention to the distress suffered by children in Britain who were temporarily separated from their mothers when they or the mother went into hospital. The usual medical procedure was not to encourage children and mothers to see much of each other if one of them was in hospital. The Robertsons were convinced this practice was wrong. Attempts to convince the medical profession failed so James Robertson

> ### Goldfarb's study
> Goldfarb found evidence that late adoption leads to retarded development where early adoption does not. His study, like Bowlby's, takes two variables, 'maternal deprivation', and 'retarded development', and sees a relationship between them, assuming it to be causal.

►Spitz and Wolf suggest that separating young babies from their mothers has physical effects on the child, but again there are other variables which could equally well explain these effects.

► James Robertson's claim that babies suffered as a result of being removed from their mothers was ridiculed by some members of the medical profession, but he determined to prove them wrong.

► Even after viewing the Robertsons' films many members of the medical profession were still hostile to their warnings. Some said that the films were an untypical and distorted record. They claimed that the children suffered because of inappropriate care, not because they were being separated from their mothers.

bought a cine-camera to film some children during their separation, and show the results to other doctors. The Robertsons made a series of powerful films of children aged between 17 months and 29 months.

One child, John, was 17 months old when he was placed in a residential nursery while his mother was in hospital having a second child. The film showed how John's condition deteriorated as the separation continued. For the first few days John showed *distress*. He tried to make attachments with the nurses, but the system of group care meant that they had to tend to the most demanding children, and John was unable to compete with the other children who'd been in the nursery for a long time. The nightly visits of his father, who was at work all day, did little to comfort the child.

John's condition passed from distress to *despair*. He cried constantly and was more demanding of attention. He started to refuse food, and had difficulties sleeping. The nurses were worried about him and tried to comfort him. While he was being held by a nurse he quietened, but the other children demanded attention too and he had to be put down. His condition changed again. He seemed to give up trying to attract attention and appeared less interested in the nurses or his father. This is *detachment*. When his mother finally came to collect him he ignored her and wouldn't allow her to comfort him.

► In separation the usual pattern of *distress, despair, detachment* is called the *syndrome of distress*.

John's experiences appeared to have some long-term effects. His personality seemed to have changed. He had more temper tantrums, sometimes refused to walk, and was occasionally hostile and uncaring. Some of these mood changes could have resulted from the separation. However remember that there was now another baby who would demand much of his mother's attention, and first-born children often have problems when they are no longer the exclusive centre of attention. Also, more happened to John than just being separated from his mother. The alternative care provided simply wasn't appropriate to his needs.

To show the importance of the mother, or mother substitute, the Robertsons themselves temporarily fostered four children while their mothers were unavailable. The children stayed with the Robertsons between 10 and 27 days. Two were under two years old, the other two were around two and a half. Joyce Robertson provided very high-quality care for each child. The younger ones adapted to their substitute mother, and coped well. The two older ones had more problems, but fewer compared with John.

 What are Bowlby's conclusions about the relationships between babies and their mothers?

Ethical considerations prevent experiments like Harlow's being conducted on human infants. What are the shortcomings of a natural experimental approach such as that of Tizard, Rees and Hodges, Bowlby or the Robertsons, by comparison with an experimental approach?

► Most of the studies described above do not necessarily show that there will be any effects of maternal separation. It depends very much on what happens to the child during the separation. We may distinguish short-term effects (the syndrome of distress) from long-term effects (developmental retardation). However many other factors are involved.

Evaluation of John Bowlby's claims

On the basis of the research on children separated from their mothers, Bowlby claims that humans have a sensitive period of 6 to 60 months for the development of attachment bonds with the mother. Failure to form satisfactory bonds will limit normal emotional, social and intellectual development, and produce someone who may have 'affectionless psychopathy', who will have retarded intellectual development, and who will be more likely to need medical attention for their mental state.

To assess Bowlby's claim it is necessary to distinguish possible short-term effects from long-term effects of separation from familiar people and routines. In the short term, distress, despair and possibly detachment may occur. The other possible effects include the slowing down of normal development, physically, emotionally, socially or intellectually. However all children are different and numerous factors influence the extent of any effects, including the child's age, temperament, relationships with the person from whom it is being separated, previous experiences of separation, and the alternative care being provided. Nor is separation from one's mother necessarily more harmful than separation from other people such as one's father.

Michael Rutter's correlational studies of groups of adolescent boys in London and the Isle of Wight found that conflict in the home was more likely to lead to disturbed behaviour, including delinquency, than was maternal separation. Children who lose their mothers completely, through death for example, are not necessarily going to have a disturbed personality if the alternative care is good. Rutter concludes that long-term damage may result from failure to form any attachments.

Ann and **Alan Clarke** also reject Bowlby's claims. They do not see the first few years of life as being all important for future development. They name several studies which do not support Bowlby's claims. For example, **Anna Freud** and **Sophie Dann's** case study of six Jewish war orphans at the Bulldogs Bank children's home in the late 1940s found them totally attached to each other. They had never known their mothers, who had been killed by the Nazis in concentration camps. However, the children gradually adjusted to life in the home, and appeared to make good progress, although we do not know what these children became like as adults.

Jarmila Koluchova studied identical twin Czechoslovakian boys who had been kept isolated from anyone else, often locked in the cellar, and treated very cruelly by their stepmother for five years. She would beat them if they cried. When discovered at the age of seven they had severe rickets, were covered in scar tissue from the beatings, couldn't speak, and were frightened of humans. Their intelligence was too low to be measured. They received intensive medical attention, and educational stimulation. They were successfully adopted and appeared to make a full recovery.

(ACT) Construct a table of brief notes showing studies which support Bowlby's ideas and studies which challenge his ideas.

► According to Michael Rutter conflict and tension in the home can make a child feel insecure, and this insecurity may lead to disturbed behaviour such as delinquency.

► The Clarkes see infancy and childhood as the first stages in development. Problems we experience during the first few years can be overcome later as we become more able to understand what has happened to us.

► The Bulldogs Bank children had probably never made attachments to any adults, but had attached to each other.

Summary – Babies' need for attachment
Attachments are special bonds which develop in early childhood between babies and their caregivers. Several animal experiments such as those of Harlow and Lorenz have demonstrated the need animals have for early experience with other members of their species. However we must be careful of generalizing from animal to human behaviour. John Bowlby claims we need to attach to our mother, otherwise development will be disrupted, although not everyone agrees.

MAKING SUCCESSFUL ATTACHMENTS

The important factors in attachment formation

Since attachments are two-way processes, we can distinguish factors which are important from the caregiver's point of view and those which are important from the infant's point of view. According to **Marshall Klaus** and **John Kennel** 'intimacy' and 'timing' are the major contribution caregivers make. They conducted a natural experiment on premature and full-term babies, and found that those who had the most 'skin to skin' contact immediately after birth with their caregivers were most likely to develop close attachments with them. Klaus and Kennel's longitudinal study of 28 infant and mother pairs for the first year of the babies' lives found that very early social contact is beneficial.

They studied a group of new mothers. Half of their sample underwent the normal maternity hospital routines, with the infant being removed from the mother after birth for the usual tests, then seeing its parents for between 6 and 12 hours a day while the mother stayed in hospital. The other half of the sample were allowed extra contact with the baby. They had an extra hour of skin to skin contact within three hours of birth, then an extra five hours a day while their mothers stayed in hospital. Klaus and Kennel claim there is a sensitive period of 6 to 12 hours following birth for establishing an early bond. They suggest that there are various hormones associated with giving birth that focus the mother's attention on the baby. Allowing this early contact encourages the mother to express the emotions associated with these hormones.

Klaus and Kennel visited the mother–infant pairs a month after leaving hospital, recording their general activities together. They interviewed the mothers, asking about their feelings towards their babies; they examined the infants, and filmed the mothers feeding them. They reported that the 'extended contact' group were closer and more loving towards their babies. They held them closer during feeding, and seemed generally more involved with them. When the babies were a year old they were visited again, and the researchers concluded that the early effects were still noticeable. Compared to the 'normal routine' control group, the extended contact experimental

► Klaus and Kennel suggest that emotional bonds will be strengthened with the right kind of contact at the right time in the infant's life.

► Klaus and Kennel conducted a longitudinal natural experiment of 28 mother–infant pairs. What are the independent variables used in this research? What are the dependent variables?

►Klaus and Kennel's studies of the caregiver suggest that timing and frequency of interaction are the most important factors in establishing close emotional ties in early childhood.

group were still more deeply involved with their babies.

However, other research has failed to confirm the benefits of early extended contact, or the existence of any sensitive period for emotional bonding in humans. For example, parents of babies who are kept in intensive care until long after any 'sensitive period' might exist still develop close emotional bonds with them, and Michael Rutter has shown how parents who adopt children develop very close bonds with them even if they are adopted weeks and months after birth. So, not everyone agrees that extended skin to skin contact is essential for close attachments, although the practice shouldn't be discouraged if both partners find it pleasant.

 Make notes on Klaus and Kennel's study as an example of longitudinal research. What did this method allow them to study which a cross-sectional study of mothers and babies would not have?

Apart from timing and amount of contact, other factors in successful bonding can be inferred from studying the behaviour of infant rather than the behaviour of caregiver. **Mary Ainsworth** and **Silvia Bell** naturalistically observed 26 mother–baby pairs in their homes for four hours at a time, every three weeks, during the infant's first 12 months of life. They particularly noted the mothers' reactions to their babies crying. It soon became apparent that young babies cried most when separated from their mothers, and least when being held by them. It seemed that some mothers were very sensitive to their babies' needs and responded quickly by picking the baby up. Others let the baby cry for some time before responding. The mothers who appeared to be more sensitive had babies who cried less and seemed generally more content.

► Crying is a sign that something is wrong with the baby, and babies use different kinds of cry for different kinds of distress. Parents soon learn to recognize whether the particular cry indicates hunger, pain, boredom or tiredness.

The sensitive mother

According to Mary Ainsworth a sensitive mother is

... able to see things from her baby's point of view. She is tuned in to receive her baby's signals: she interprets them correctly, and she responds to them promptly and appropriately. Although she nearly always gives the baby what he seems to want, when she does not she is tactful in acknowledging his communication... The sensitive mother, by implication, can not be rejecting, interfering or ignoring.

 What does Mary Ainsworth mean by the 'sensitive mother'? Name three factors that caregivers provide which have been claimed to aid attachment formation.

The relationship between parents and babies isn't all one way. Babies are active in the exchange too. **Daniel Stern** maintains that babies are good at communicating their needs and thus regulating the amount of social contact they receive. They can start some contact by arm

► Daniel Stern has applied his psychoanalytic training to the study of babies and concludes that they are much more advanced than was previously thought in the way they regulate social contact.

> **An observation by Daniel Stern**
> A mother is feeding her three-month-old infant. While talking and looking at me the mother turned her head and gazed at the infant's face. He was gazing at the ceiling, but out of the corner of his eye he saw her head turn towards him, and he turned to gaze back at her... he stopped sucking. He let go of the nipple .... The mother abruptly stopped talking... her eyes opened a little wider and her eyebrows raised a bit. His eyes locked onto hers, and together they held motionless for an instant. This silent and almost motionless instant continued to hang until the mother suddenly shattered it by saying 'Hey!' and simultaneously opened her eyes wider, raising her eyebrows further, and throwing her head up toward the infant. Almost simultaneously the baby's eyes widened. His head tilted up, and, as his smile broadened, the nipple fell out of his mouth. 'Well, Hello! ... Heello ... Heeelloo' so that her pitch rose and the 'Hellos' became longer and more emphatic on each successive repetition. With each phrase the baby expressed more pleasure, and his body resonated almost like a balloon ... filling a little more with each breath. They watched each other expectantly for a moment ... then the baby took the initiative ... his head lurched forward, his hands jerked up, and a fuller smile blossomed.

► Daniel Stern, Mary Ainsworth, and Trevarthen and Richards are all claiming that even quite young babies are capable of making social exchanges, and having some control over their exchanges.

waving, gazing and smiling. Smiles are very powerful social signals inviting someone to pay the baby some attention. Babies make and break eye contact as they 'hold conversations' with their caregivers. They stop the interaction by frowning, stiffening and even crying. By three months of age babies are using similar kinds of social signals as adults use.

Stern believes that babies are genetically predisposed to be sociable and to regulate their communication. The actual social contact, and what they derive from it, is purely socially learned, and some is simply for fun.

Colwyn Trevarthen and **Martin Richards** filmed five babies, (sometimes playing alone, sometimes with their mothers) for one hour a week each, over their first six months. The infants behaved quite differently when alone than when with their mothers. The researchers noted how babies move their bodies during interaction with an adult. From around two months, as the adult speaks, the child remains quiet and still. Two months later, if the infant wants to butt in it will raise its arms and babble more loudly. When the adult stops talking the infant begins to make noises and move its body in the way Daniel Stern observed in the background reading. Trevarthen and Richards describe this as *interactional synchrony*.

► The way in which adults and babies co-ordinate their interaction is called *interactional synchrony*, or *mutual reciprocity*.

Rudi Schaffer also stresses the importance for both partners to be equally involved. He calls it *mutual reciprocity*.

► According to Trevarthen and Richards babies are not the passive, helpless creatures that Bowlby and others believe. Rather they interact actively in their social contact.

What is meant by 'interactional synchrony' or 'mutual reciprocity'?

What is the evidence in the quote from Daniel Stern's observation for interactional synchrony or mutual reciprocity?

Summary – The baby–adult social interaction

The baby	The adult
Looks, gazes, stares at caregiver, uses reflexive and social smiles.	Returns gaze, is sensitive to baby's needs.
Exchanges 'conversations'.	Participates in 'exchange games'.
Expresses physical needs, through crying, etc.	Responds to them quickly.

Most of the evidence for the (supposed) social skills of young babies comes from observational studies. Inevitably observations are not completely *objective* because the observer may already have some idea of what to expect and may interpret the observations accordingly.

Taking turns

Kenneth Kaye claims that

... mother-infant interaction is characterised by turn taking right from the first, but the roles of mother and infant in managing the turns is highly asymmetrical. The mother's role is a matter of fitting in to those rhythms so as to produce a semblance of dialogue for which she alone is really responsible. Gradually the roles become more symmetrical but adults continue to manage and lead dialogue with children until the children themselves become adults.

Kenneth Kaye has made extensive studies of the young baby's cognitive development. While he accepts that babies are born with some ability to take turns in their social exchanges, he claims that most of what is seen as being 'social' is probably merely innately driven responses which have some 'survival value'. He doesn't believe that some of the social skills claimed for very young babies would actually be acquired until they were many months old.

Summary – The research on attachment formation

See also Bowlby pages 52–3, 56–60, Tizard et al page 53, Harlow pages 53–4, Lorenz pages 55–6, the Robertsons pages 56–8, Goldfarb page 57, Spitz & Wolf page 57, Rutter pages 59.

Researchers	Main Conclusion	Status
Klaus & Kennel	Early contact is beneficial for making attachments	Unsupported
Ainsworth & Bell	Mother's sensitivity facilitates attachment	Probably true
Stern	Babies regulate contact	Possibly true
Trevarthen & Richards	Ability to participate in interactional synchrony is socially learned	Possibly true
Kaye	Little early learning of social skills	Possibly true

Whether babies have early social skills to assist them and their caregivers in attachment formation isn't known for sure. No doubt sensitive, stimulating company is much better than uncaring, unstimulating company, no matter what the baby makes of it.

Making more than one attachment

Bowlby originally claimed that babies make one essential attachment to their mothers, or mother substitute. Later he admitted that a hierarchy of attachments is possible, with the mother figure at the top. In 1964 Rudi Schaffer and Peggy Emerson published the findings of their longitudinal survey of 60 Glasgow babies from their birth until they were 18 months old. Every month for the first year the mothers were interviewed and asked about how the baby behaved with the various people with whom it came into regular contact. A final interview occurred when the babies were 18 months old. As their definition of an attachment Schaffer and Emerson used *separation distress*. If the baby showed distress when separated from someone, then it could be said to be attached to that person.

Schaffer and Emerson identified four stages in the development of attachments. For the first six weeks the babies had no particular preference about who they were with. Between six weeks and six months they became increasingly more sociable with anyone who wanted to interact with them. Over the next month or so nearly 30 per cent formed attachments to several people (ten per cent had as many as five attachments by seven months). The rest started to prefer to be near their main caregiver, and to show signs of distress if approached by a stranger. This is the beginning of their first attachment. From around eight months the final stage was reached with the babies being content to attach to several people. By 10 months nearly 60 per cent had more than one attachment. By 18 months 87 per cent had more than one attachment, and over 30 per cent had five or more.

► There are two ways of measuring if a baby is attached to someone. They are *separation distress* and *stranger fear*.

► Schaffer and Emerson used 'separation distress' as their main method of measuring whether an attachment had formed. Can you think of any limitations this might pose for the validity of their research?

Only a half were primarily attached to their mothers. A third were mainly attached to their fathers.

In contrast to Bowlby's claim, Schaffer and Emerson found that the quality of each attachment was much the same. The babies did not always want their mothers and seemed to use different adults for different things. When frightened they preferred to be close to their mother. When they wanted more robust play, they seemed to prefer their father.

Bowlby claimed that the bond that grows between a mother (or mother substitute) and her baby is special. It has evolved in us, and plays an important role in survival. Schaffer and Emerson disagree. They did not find significant differences in the relationships that the babies developed with each of the people they became attached to. As Schaffer says, 'being attached to several people does not imply a shallower feeling for each one, for an infant's capacity for attachment is not like a cake that has to be shared out. Love, even in babies, has no limits.'

Not all children are reared by their own parents. Some people choose to live in communes and collectives, where the children tend to be brought up by the whole community, or by particular people other than their parents. There is no evidence that this pattern of childrearing causes emotional disturbance. In Israel a small percentage of the population choose to live in kibbutzim (agricultural communes). The success of the group depends on all of its members contributing, so new mothers gradually return to work during the child's first year, and a children's nurse takes over childcare. Eventually the child will be brought up with all the other children in the Children's House, although most of them will see their parents every day. They usually form attachments with their parents, and with others in the Children's House. Bowlby would fear that most of these children will experience mental disturbance in later life, but there is no evidence for this.

The kibbutz allows us to make a cross-cultural study of attachment bonding. In the kibbutz children are reared with all the other children by a special children's nurse, and by their parents. They make attachments with other people as well as their parents.

Summarize the evidence that babies can make multiple attachments

Make notes on the use of evidence from the Kibbutz as cross-cultural research

Summary – Multiple attachments

In many families it simply isn't possible for one or more of the adults to provide continuous care for the offspring. Increasing numbers of mothers work outside the home, while fathers may stay at home and look after the child, or often a baby-minder or older siblings will be entrusted with the care of the baby. Not surprisingly the babies are quite likely to form strong attachment bonds with these various caregivers. Schaffer and Emerson found that babies of between 6 and 18 months could form several attachments to different people (see pages 64–5), and that each attachment was of the same quality.

▶ Older babies seem to be able to recognize different people, associate each of them with different activities or qualities, and prefer the individual that possesses the skill the baby wants at the time. Schaffer and Emerson claim that 'Love, even in babies, has no limits'.

►Harlow's monkeys used their surrogates as a safe base from which to explore their environment and frightening things in it. Could anything similar occur in humans?

► According to Freud children identify with their same sex parent. Bandura claims they identify with more attractive or important models. The more people the child is attached to the more experiences it can have, and the more of the adults' experiences it can draw on.

► Attachments are important to children up to the age of about five. As they become more independent and able to understand the reasons for the absence of their caregiver, they are more able to be left with someone to whom they are not attached.

Children reared in kibbutzim also usually attach to more than one adult.

If a baby is securely attached it will develop some ideas about security and trust. It will feel safe and protected, and more able to explore away from its caregivers. It may be able to treat them as some kind of safe base to which it can return in case of worry, rather as some of Harlow's privated monkeys treated the towelling-covered surrogates (see pages 53–4). Knowing that there is this safe base could encourage a child to be more adventurous, and possibly more independent too. This could be beneficial to cognitive development, as we'll see later.

There are several benefits for the child. As it grows it will have a variety of people to identify with. Its personality will be shaped by the personalities of the people it is closest to. It will also have a variety of role models to model behaviour on. ·

There are also benefits to the adults. If a child is attached to one person, that person must be constantly available to comfort and stimulate the child as necessary. Knowing that the baby is content to be with someone while its primary caregiver is away could encourage many caregivers to return to outside work, or to take up social or other activities, at least for part of the time. If the parent has to enter hospital, then the presence of others to whom the child is attached can help it cope with the separation. James and Joyce Robertson tried to establish some kind of attachment with the children they fostered to minimize the ill effects of the separation. Patient, high-quality care and love did help these children (see page 58).

 What would be the benefits to a parent of having its child attached to several people?

What kind of differences would you expect to find in the behaviour of securely and insecurely attached children?

Outline the conclusions of the following researchers:
1 Colwyn Trevarthen and Martin Richards; 2 Genevieve Carpenter; 3 Daniel Stern; 4 Mary Ainsworth and Silvia Bell; 5 Marshall Klaus and John Kennel; 6 Rudi Schaffer and Peggy Emerson.

 What kind of advice would you give to someone adopting a child from an orphanage? The next time you see parents relating to their baby, observe any particular activities which might contribute to bonding.

CHILD ABUSE

► It is impossible to estimate the true extent of child abuse since we can only know the statistics of cases known to childcare professionals or to the police. Higher statistics do not necessarily mean more abuse.

Abuse takes many forms, and increasing numbers of cases of it are being reported in the media. This does not necessarily mean that the incidence of abuse is increasing. Increased vigilance on the part of teachers, health visitors, paediatricians and social workers may simply have brought more cases to light. However, it needs pointing out that child abuse is probably not common, and that the vast majority of parents are kind, loving and protective towards their children.

Psychologists are continuing to investigate which children are most at risk of becoming a victim, and which adults are most likely to become abusers. They have found some social factors which correlate with higher than average numbers of cases of abuse. Children with families living in high stress conditions are most 'at risk'. High *stress* conditions are caused by inadequate housing, low paid work, a small circle of friends, or insufficient money to become a well integrated member of the community. That is not to say that only poorer people abuse their children. Some well-off and well integrated adults also abuse their children.

The abused tend to be children with some appearance, attitude or habit which triggers an aggressive urge in an adult. Even infants can contribute to their own abuse by being irritable, unresponsive, poor sleepers, hyperactive, or generally less pleasant to be with than infants who are easy and rewarding to care for. Children do vary widely, and although no one can blame a child for being unresponsive, irritable, etc., it does seem that such children are more at risk than others.

The highest at risk group of infants are premature babies who are most likely to be irritable, etc. As they grow, children who are disobedient, who refuse to cooperate or to show self-discipline, who defy or ignore their caregivers, are most at risk. The reasons for such behaviour may have some links with genetically inherited hormone balances. Or again for genetic reasons it may be that those parts of the brain which are involved with arousal or aggression may be more sensitive in some children than others.

However, such behaviour is more likely to be socially learned than genetically inherited. A child might observe and model the aggressive behaviour of its parents. Or it might be repeating behaviour that had been effective in achieving its goals previously. If ignoring an adult who told the child to do something one day seems to work, because the adult doesn't insist, then we can't entirely blame the child for ignoring another request from that adult on another day.

Child abusers come from both sexes, all races, cultures, classes and communities. This might imply some physiological basis to abusing. Research by **Ann Frodi** and **Michael Lamb** suggests that abusers have heightened physiological reactions to both smiles and cries from infants, and are less keen to interact with the child, even when it is smiling. Some people may simply be more quick-tempered than others, particularly when the social conditions mentioned previously also apply.

There seems to be a correlation between those who were abused when they were a child and those who abuse their own children. Some of Harlow's female isolated monkeys described earlier abused their offspring by pushing them away, biting them badly, and showing no interest in protecting them. However, there is nothing automatic about this. Children who are abused often develop loving relationships with others when they are older, including with their own children. But where other stress-inducing conditions also apply,

► *Stress* is the result of factors which are beyond the immediate control of the individual suffering from it. It is an effect caused by those factors, but can become a contributory cause to other effects, e.g. child abuse.

► No one knows why some babies are simply less responsive or worse adapted than others. Some just are and they are most likely to provoke an abusing reaction in their parents.

► There are no sexual, racial or cultural correlates to the likelihood of abuse, although there may be a physiological factor common to abusers.

► Correlations cannot prove cause and there may well be other reasons why people who were abused as children are statistically more likely to abuse their own children than people who were not abused.

► Attachments are warm, loving bonds which include protective feelings towards the infant and from which the baby learns trust and security. Where such bonds fail to form the potential for abuse increases.

the chances of them abusing their own children will increase.

Failure to form a successful attachment may also contribute to abuse. Attachments between parents and children are two-way. Babies who are handicapped in some way may not be able to participate in the interactions that lead to attachment formation (see Trevarthen and Richards, Stern and Ainsworth, page 62, among others). Parents may feel rejected by their blind infants, who can't return their gazes, or deaf infants, who do not turn their heads because they can't hear their parents approach, and they may therefore not attach to them so closely. Some parents may put their own needs before those of their children. They may not know what is involved in attachment bonding, and they may feel that there are too many other pressures in their lives. Or they may not have wanted the baby in the first place. Those who have such attitudes are more likely to abuse their children.

When a 'difficult' baby, an 'inadequate' parent and 'high stress' living conditions combine, the chances of abuse occurring are greatest.

 Make notes on the circumstances under which children are most likely to become the victims of abuse.

Chapter summary

Early research by John Bowlby into human emotional development claimed that babies develop a strong emotional bond, preferably with their mothers, during their first year of life. The evidence for this came from Bowlby's study of *44 Juvenile Thieves*, and from studies of babies and children in institutional care such as those of Goldfarb, and Spitz and Wolf. Experimental data came from Harlow's rhesus monkey experiments and Lorenz's ethological studies. However, each piece of research is capable of being interpreted in other ways. The case for the need for *maternal* attachment was not proven. Schaffer and Emerson found babies successfully attaching to several people, and sometimes hardly attaching to the mother at all.

Bowlby predicted that breaking the bond could have serious consequences for emotional, social and intellectual development. Others have not found evidence to support this. Michael Rutter argues that there are other factors more important than maternal deprivation for explaining disturbed development. The atmosphere in the home is one major influence. The Clarkes quote several studies of children whose early lives were disturbed but who made a recovery. They see the early years as just the first stage in development, and no more important than any other stage.

Finally we mentioned some of the factors involved in child abuse. We do not really understand the psychology of it, except for our appreciation of the need for attachments. We have a better idea of the social correlates of those most at risk than of the psychological ones.

Exam Questions – 60 minutes each

1 Discuss the evidence for the formation of attachments in early childhood.

2 What evidence is there that deprivation of attachment in early childhood could affect future development?

Further Reading: Chapter 3

Three readable and informative original sources are

Bowlby J. 1953. *Child Care and the Growth of Love*. Harmondsworth: Penguin.

Bowlby J. 1971. *Attachment and Loss (volume 1)*. Harmondsworth: Penguin.

Bowlby J. 1975. *Separation: Anxiety and Anger, Attachment and Loss (volume 2)*. Harmondsworth: Penguin.

Alternative views which provide information and a source of evaluation are

Schaffer H.R. 1982. 'Social Development in early childhood' in A. Chapman & A. Gale *(eds)*. *Psychology and People: A Tutorial Text*. London: British Psychological Society & Macmillan Press.

and

Clarke A. & A. 1976. *Early Experience: Myth & Evidence*. Wells: Open Books.

General texts
An excellent American general text covering most aspects of child development is provided by

Shaffer D.R. 1985. *Developmental Psychology*. Brooks-Cole.

An excellent British text is

Meadows S. 1986. *Understanding Child Development*. London: Hutchinson.

and a much more modest summary is found in

Davenport G.C. 1987. *An Introduction to Child Development*. London: HarperCollins.

4 Cognitive development

Chapter objectives

By the end of this chapter you should:

▌ be able to describe and evaluate Piaget's contribution to our understanding of how cognitive development occurs and discuss the implications of his theory for early education

▌ be able to describe and evaluate Bruner's explanation of cognitive development and discuss the implications of his theory for education

▌ be able to describe, contrast and evaluate the major theories of language acquisition

▌ be able to describe the nature and function of play, the ways in which play develops in early childhood and its impact on social and cognitive growth.

Introduction

One of the major differences between humans and other animals concerns our greater capacity to make sense of and use the large amounts of sensory data that we can take in. Humans are especially good at mentally manipulating ideas, this allows us to think and plan ahead. We can recognize and correct errors in our thinking and improve our performance in the future. We can adapt our environments to suit our needs. We are an adaptive species and, unlike most other animals, can create rather than merely respond to, our environment.

In this chapter we will summarize some of the major contributions to our understanding of the development of the cognitive processes that separate humans from other animals.

WHAT IS COGNITION?

► Cognition refers to activities such as thinking, knowing, symbolizing, reasoning and problem-solving.

The *Penguin Dictionary of Psychology* defines cognition as a '... broad term which has been traditionally used to refer to such activities as thinking, conceiving, reasoning ... symbolising, insight, expectancy, complex rule use, imagery, belief, intentionality, problem solving and so forth'. In Chapter 2 we noted some research which suggested that children of just a few months may be able to behave socially, to smile and babble in response to their caregiver's signals (see pages 62–3). This would involve cognition. **Kenneth Kaye** (page 63) and others are more sceptical about the existence of such early cognitive skills. This illustrates one of the major problems in developmental psychology: we do not know the precise relationship between physical and mental development.

Early psychology owed much to biology and to the evolutionary theories of **Charles Darwin**. Evolution places great emphasis on genetic inheritance. Early psychologists believed that many of our cognitive skills were genetically, innately acquired. This is called 'the nature approach' and its supporters are called 'nativists'. Nativists believe that many human skills or capacities will appear when the organism is maturationally ready.

As more research during this century has been conducted into children's mental development, more psychologists have rejected the nature view in favour of the idea that we learn to develop our skills. This is the nurture approach and its supporters are nurturists or empiricists. The nature–nurture debate about the relative influence of learning and maturation is important in as much as if we know what skills will develop at what age, and the circumstances under which those skills will flourish, then we can help children to develop their maximum potential.

 Describe in your own words what is meant by the nature–nurture debate. How might cross-cultural evidence (see pages 115–18) be used in this debate?

► *Innate* means inborn or genetically determined.

► *Maturation* is the process of physical growth which is genetically determined. Thus growing bigger and heavier is a maturational process, although how big and heavy we become and at what speed will be influenced by environmental factors.

► *Nurture* refers to the influence of the environment on development.

Jean Piaget's contribution

In 1920 a young Swiss researcher named **Jean Piaget** was helping to standardize an English intelligence test for use with French schoolchildren at Alfred Binet's laboratory in Paris. Piaget was working in Paris to pay for his other studies at the Sorbonne. He was a trained biologist and had little interest in children. However he noticed that many of the children were giving the same wrong answer to certain questions and decided that he should investigate further.

Piaget's researches convinced him that children aren't 'little adults' simply waiting to grow up, which was the popular idea at the time. Rather they seemed to have ways of viewing things which were quite different from those of an adult. This chance observation has led to one of the major contributions to our understanding of how children think. Piaget spent over 50 years studying children's thinking, until his death in 1980.

Piaget's methods

Piaget had learned the *clinical interview* technique while studying Freudian psychoanalysis, and applied aspects of it when talking to hundreds of children (including his own three) to discover their views on rules, relationships between things, the appearance of objects, etc. The clinical interview method was used firstly by doctors and therapists to gather data about a patient, and then to apply a form of therapy. There are no set questions, nor any particular sequence in which questions should be asked. The answers are interpreted by the interviewer, and used as a basis for further questioning. The whole procedure is regarded as rather *subjective by psychologists* who prefer more scientific methods.

An added difficulty for Piaget was that his subjects were children,

Jean Piaget

► Jean Piaget can be fairly described as the founding father of developmental cognitive psychology. His countless hours of detailed study have produced a theory which has had enormous impact on child-rearing and educational practices in the West.

► Piaget used the *clinical interview* technique to gather information from children about why they thought they did things.

► Piaget used clinical interviews, observations, story-telling and experiments to discover similarities in the thinking of children of the same age, and how and when this changed.

many of whom were likely to be reluctant to answer his questions, even if their knowledge of language was advanced enough to allow them to do so. In fact much of Piaget's research and understanding was inspired by the three children of his own for whom this questioning was not a problem: Jacqueline, Lucienne and Laurent Piaget.

Piaget also *naturalistically observed* children playing alone, and together, to see how they responded to each other and to the structure of their games. He was looking for similarities in the thinking and behaviour of children of the same age. Naturalistic observation leads to insights which can be investigated further by questioning. Similarities in play might suggest that the children share the same ways of perceiving the game, and this might reveal more about their general cognitive development.

 What are the two main methods of data collection employed by Piaget, and what are the advantages and disadvantages of each?

Piaget told children of different ages *stories* he made up about other people, asking them to make judgements about the intentions of the people involved, or the consequences of what they had done. Similarities here could reveal the ways in which childhood reasoning differs from adult reasoning. Piaget also used *experiments* to test certain of children's reasoning abilities.

Over a period of years he constructed a theory, largely influenced by his knowledge of biological structures, which attempted to provide a model for how children think, and for intelligence.

Basic cognitive processes

► Piaget uses the term *schemas* to refer to strategies or mental structures which children use to handle information. The first schemas are involuntary, reflexive responses, many of which increase the infant's chances of survival. These are *action schemas*. Action schemas are joined by *symbolic schemas* from around the age of two years.

Piaget believed that babies are born with a few basic strategies or ideas for receiving information and dealing with it. They build up ideas or 'mental structures' about what they experience. These mental structures are called *schemas*. There are three types of schema which appear as the child matures. The first, *action schemas*, are the 50 or so reflexes which we have at birth. Breathing, sucking, grasping and crying are fairly obvious examples. Many reflexes involve actions or behaviour (since the young baby isn't mature enough for any other kind) which promote survival value.

By around the age of two the child learns to communicate. The word 'doll' can be used to stand for the object, and two-year-old children will know what you mean if you ask them 'Is that your doll?' They also learn to let one thing, such as a doll, stand for another, such as a 'mummy' or a 'baby'. These are *symbolic schemas*.

After another five years or so the child's thinking becomes more logical. It begins to realize that it can influence objects and events in its environment in a deliberate and meaningful way. It learns that performing some operation produces a predictable outcome. *Operational schemas* allow the child mentally to reverse some process and predict what the outcome will be. The child will realize that rules can be changed, that things aren't always what they seem, and that they

Cognition and intelligence

The nature and definition of intelligence has been one of the most widely discussed and researched issues in psychology. Early views saw it as a group of 'abilities' which each of us are born with, and which could be measured to see who had more or less of it. Alfred Binet believed that intelligence could be seen in an individual's ability to reason, have insight, make judgements and be adaptable. L.L. Thurstone saw two factors: 'general' intelligence, which we apply to most things we do, and 'specific' intelligence, which is applied to particular situations. Hebb and Vernon argued there were three components: 'Intelligence A', which is innate potential; 'Intelligence B', which we develop during our lives; and 'Intelligence C', which is what intelligence tests measure.

Piaget rejected all such notions. For him intelligence was a dynamic process which each child undergoes through direct and personal experience, especially during the first ten years or so. It results in flexible adaptations to the environment. Each child constructs its own interpretations of what the world is like from its own experiences. This intelligence cannot be measured since it would be impossible to invent any means of measuring such a process.

can solve problems by thinking about them. Piaget described schemas and operations as 'variant mental structures', because everyone's cognition is different.

What does Piaget mean by 'intelligence'? *– child goes through direct*

What do you understand by the concept 'schema'? Name the types of schema identified by Piaget. *– mental*

Why does Piaget call schemas and operations 'variant mental structures'?

Apart from the predisposition to develop schemas Piaget also claims we inherit the unconscious capacity mentally to *organize* them so that new experiences build on old ones. An infant who has learned that it can 'hold and shake' a rattle will combine this with the 'reach and grasp' schema. Now the sight of the rattle will trigger the 'reach and

► An *operation* is a mental routine for transposing information. An operation is reversible. Cutting a cake in half, really or in the imagination, is an operation because we can reverse the procedure and put it back together again.

► Everyone is born with three unconscious capacities; firstly to develop schemas and secondly to organize them for dealing with our world. Everyone has different experiences so each person's particular schemas will be different. Thirdly we have the capacity to adapt our knowledge according to experience.

REVIEW – Schemas (alternative plural 'schemata')

Schemas are basic concepts or mental representations of how to deal with something. Some schemas are fairly simple, such as eating with a knife and fork. Some are more complex, such as playing various games. Others are more complex still, such as playing a musical instrument or driving a car. Operations are more logical ways of combining schemas and do not appear until middle childhood.

grasp, hold and shake' schema. The inborn capacity to combine schemas is called *organization*.

There is one other inborn tendency which Piaget identified. This is the capacity to adapt our knowledge (and possibly our future behaviour) based on our previous relevant experiences. *Adaptation* consists of two interdependent processes, *assimilation* and *accommodation*.

Imagine a two-year-old girl who has the symbolic schema 'dada'. In the child's mind the schema consists of her concepts of 'big', 'deep voice', 'dark clothes', 'dark hair', 'dark beard', 'gentle', 'funny' and so on. One day while out shopping with her mother the local vicar stops to have a chat. The vicar is fair-haired and has no beard, but he still has enough similarities, such as dark clothes and deep voice, to be greeted with 'dada' by the child.

► *Adaptation*: consists of two independent processes *assimilation* and *accommodation*.

Her mother will probably correct the child who will have to make a mental *adaptation* to her 'dada' schema to exclude vicars! She will also start a new 'vicar schema'. First she must take in through her perceptual senses (*assimilate*) those characteristics which differentiate 'dada' people from 'vicar people'. Then she must alter (*accommodate*) the existing 'dada schema' to exclude certain categories of similar creature, e.g. those wearing clerical collars.

► The process of adaptation is central to Piaget's theory. The nature of intelligence itself is the result of this process.

When the child has learned from some adaptation it has made, its knowledge is said to be in a state of *equilibrium* or *cognitive balance*. It has assimilated and accommodated, and now it 'knows'. For example, a two-year-old might know that 'doggies' have four legs, a head at one end and a tail at the other. Then she sees a cat, and logically calls it 'doggie'. Mother explains that it is a cat. Now there is new information to be assimilated and accommodated, and the appropriate mental adaptation to be made. The child was in a state of equilibrium, knowing that all four-legged creatures with heads and tails were called 'doggie'. Then new information about four-legged creatures has to be dealt with, and the child's mental processing is in a state of *equilibration*. A new state of equilibrium has to be achieved after assimilating and adapting the new knowledge. Cognitive growth is a constant shift between states of equilibrium and equilibration.

► For Piaget 'knowing' or 'having cognition' is as a *state of equilibrium* between assimilation and accommodation. When a new adaptation needs to be made we are in a state of *equilibration*.

(NM) Describe Piaget's concept of adaptation.

REVIEW – Piaget's assumptions

Each child develops a unique set of insights gained from its particular experiences of its world. The child constructs increasingly complex schemas through the process of organization. Each schema is subject to adaptation as new information is assimilated and accommodated.

Piaget's stages of cognitive development

Piaget found that we do not acquire new schemas in a simple continuous sequence. Children's ways of thinking change as they mature. Every child passes through the same sequence of stages, although the ages at which they enter and leave each one vary widely. Progress through them cannot be speeded up since it is a maturational process controlled by genetic forces.

Piaget identified four broad stages, each with a number of substages. At each stage the child is able to make increasingly complex adaptations.

1 *The sensory motor stage, 0–2 years*

The young child develops action schemas, is preoccupied with itself and involves itself in solitary pastimes. Its thinking is dominated by its direct sensory experiences of the immediate environment, and what it can do with objects in its environment.

The following is a summary of the substages of development in the sensory motor stage:

i For the first month the child concentrates on instinctive behaviour such as grasping and sucking. The child gradually begins deliberately to repeat actions that are directly satisfying.

ii By four or five months actions are performed on objects which will not directly satisfy the child's basic needs, but are stimulating in some way. Waving its hands around in front of its eyes may be satisfying so the child deliberately waves its hands.

iii By eight months the child is developing some idea about objects in the environment being 'real' and still being present even though they are no longer visible. If the rattle is thrown to the floor the child will know that it still exists, although it is temporarily out of sight.

iv By 12 to 18 months the child will follow the movement of an object as it disappears from view, and look for it in the place where it was last seen.

v Between about 18 and 24 months the child first shows signs of insight, the ability to solve problems in its head, i.e. *symbolically*.

2 *The pre-operational stage, 2–7 years*

This stage was extensively studied by Piaget, yet somehow seems rather negative, with Piaget concentrating on what children can't do. The title *pre-operational* tells us that children in this stage can't think in an operational – logical – way. Between two and seven years children are improving their symbolic skills, and language is a particularly useful asset to developing intelligence. The child asks questions and makes what sense it can of the answers. It might imitate solutions, and apply experiences from one situation to another. Yet most of the child's thinking is dominated by a number of limitations imposed by its lack of maturity. Mostly the child cannot learn from being taught, and has difficulty using someone else's knowledge to solve its problems. The child must learn for itself.

During the *preconceptual thought* substage the child uses objects and words as symbols in its fantasy, or make-believe play. Between two and four children's thinking is preconceptual because it is dominated by unrealistic ideas, such as *animism*. Animism is the child's idea that,

▶ The four stages of cognitive development are *invariant*, that is they always occur in the same sequence since they are dependent on the child's state of maturation which is genetically controlled. The four stages are:

0–2 yrs sensory motor stage
2–7 yrs pre-operational stage
7–11 yrs concrete operations stage
11 yrs onwards formal operations stage

▶ Between two and seven children's thinking is illogical and inconsistent, and yet they seem to learn a colossal amount, without appearing to have been taught very much.

Object permanence

For the very young child things only exist if they can be perceived. *Object permanence* is the knowledge that something still exists even when hidden from view. It was said by Piaget to develop at around eight months.

Not everyone agrees. **Tom Bower** has conducted experiments with babies of between one and four months in which they were shown an interesting object placed in front of them. When their attention had been caught the object was hidden by a sliding screen. The object was removed while unseen by the baby. The screen was then retracted and the babies' reactions were observed. If they showed surprise that the object was no longer visible, then they could be said to have some idea of object permanence. Many did. Bower also showed them an object which they might try to take. When they started to reach for it the lights were turned off. Observations with an infra-red camera showed the babies continued to try and reach for the object, despite not being able to see it.

Mundy-Castle and **Anglin** sat some four-month-old infants in front of an apparatus that had two portholes (A and B). An object travelled behind the apparatus so that it appeared at the bottom of porthole A travelling upwards, and at the top of porthole B travelling downwards. The researchers watched the infants' eyes. After a few revolutions the babies started to anticipate the movement of the object by switching their attention to the next point where it would appear. These infants had *object permanence* long before the eight months that Piaget predicted it would occur.

 Outline the first stage in Piaget's theory of cognitive development.

Comment on the role of object permanence in Piagetian theory.

▶ *Egocentrism* means being able to conceive of the world only from one's own position. Considerable maturation and experience are necessary before the child can put itself mentally into someone else's place and imagine what things look like from there. This is *decentring*.

▶ A major problem in conducting research that needs the child's participation is trying to discover things which children find interesting or involving enough to make them cooperate.

since it has feelings, motives and intentions then everything must have them, including inanimate things. 'Smacking the naughty table' for hurting the child who bumped into it, or 'scolding the naughty dolly' for getting itself lost are examples of a four-year-old's preconceptual thinking.

Another characteristic of preconceptual thinking is *egocentrism*. This is the inability to take anyone else's needs into account, or to see things from their point of view. The egocentric child will answer questions from its viewpoint. Ask a four-year-old if she has a sister and (assuming that she does) the child will say 'yes'. But ask her if her sister has a sister and she may say 'no'. She can't always imagine what it would be like to see family relationships from her sister's point of view, only her own. Sit a four-year-old facing someone, and ask the child what the other can see. The child will probably tell you what he himself can see. Children learn to *decentre* sometime after seven years.

Piaget conducted a rather complicated experiment to demonstrate egocentrism. He constructed three model mountains from papier mâché, each in a different shape and each with something different on the top. A doll was moved to different positions around the mountains and the child was asked to choose one of 10 photographs which corresponded to what the doll would be able to see from its position. Children under eight were unable to do this, often choosing the picture corresponding to its own viewpoint. This experiment has been criticized for being unnecessarily elaborate. Perhaps the child would have had more chance if the experiment were more comprehensible and more involving.

What does Piaget mean by egocentrism? What are the criticisms of the 'three mountains' experiment in which Piaget investigated egocentrism?

What does Piaget mean by decentring?

The second substage of the pre-operational stage is that of *intuitive thought*. Thinking is less dominated by egocentrism and animism and more concerned with the most obvious feature of any object – what it looks like. The best known examples of intuitive thought are *conservation* tasks. Between the ages of four and seven children rarely understand that an object can be transformed in its appearance without necessarily changing in any other way. Show the child two identical balls of Plasticine and ask them to agree that they contain the same amount of Plasticine. Roll one into a sausage shape and ask if the balls still contain the same amount of Plasticine. The intuitive, pre-operational child will often say that the sausage shape has more. This is because it looks bigger. Or try showing the child two identically spaced rows of five buttons. The child will agree that both rows have the same number of buttons. Spread the buttons in one row out, and the child will probably say that there are more buttons in that row.

There are two reasons why children under about seven years cannot conserve. One is their inability to hold all the features of the situation in their head, and be able to think about them being reversed. (The ability to do this is called *reversibility*.) One of Piaget's most famous conservation tasks involves two identical tall thin jugs containing the same amount of liquid. The contents of one of the jugs is emptied into a shorter, wider jug, and the child is asked which jug has the most liquid. The pre-operational child will say the tall thin jug contains more. It cannot imagine what the liquid level in the first jug would be if the liquid was poured back into it. Piaget claimed that mental reversibility will not appear until the child is around eight years old.

The other reason why children under about seven cannot conserve is *centration*. This is the tendency to concentrate on only one aspect of a situation at a time, while ignoring all others which are necessary for the child to solve the problem. The child concentrates on either the height of the jug or the width of the jug, but not both. Centration does not disappear until the child is able to compensate for the effects of one feature with reference to the others.

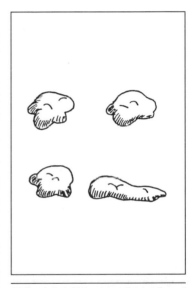

Figure 4.1 Conservation of Plasticine

► *Conservation* means the ability to maintain a mental image of what something is truly like when its appearance is transformed.

► *Reversibility* is a mental process whereby someone thinks about the consequences of a series of actions if performed in reverse.

► *Centration*, as in concentration, is the fixing on only one aspect of a situation at a time, and ignoring others which could have an important bearing on a solution.

What is conservation?

Name the two substages in pre-operational thinking, and give examples of the thinking in each substage.

Summary – Main features of pre-operational stage

Preconceptual Thought
Animism: everything has consciousness, therefore has feelings, motives, etc.
Egocentrism: one's own needs dominate one's thinking.

Intuitive Thought
Inability to conserve an object's appearance dominates one's thinking about what it 'is like'.
Centration: one feature of an object or situation dominates one's thinking about it.

Piaget's research

Piaget's work was revolutionary. No one had made such detailed observations of children or conducted such experiments, and no one had imagined that cognitive development would be so complex. Not only was Piaget discovering the essential features of cognition, but he was also providing a detailed description of the stages and substages of its development.

Whenever scientists reveal their findings, others try to reproduce them. The original findings are either supported, refined or refuted. Not everyone agreed with Piaget's judgements about the ages at which certain things occur, as we saw earlier with object permanence. The ages at which children stop being egocentric, and can conserve and decentre were two points of disagreement. Although later research has refined and modified Piaget's original claims (most of which refinements he accepted), this should take nothing away from the 'founding father of developmental cognitive psychology'.

Figure 4.2 Hughes' experiment

Challenges to some of Piaget's claims

Later research has tested Piaget's ideas, and there has been some refinement of the age for egocentrism as put forward by Piaget.

In the 1970s **Martin Hughes** constructed an experiment which comprised two intersecting model walls and some dolls which could be moved, by the experimenter or the child, into various places behind or in front of the four walls. There was a policeman doll and a boy doll, and the game was to place the boy in various positions and ask the child if he could be seen by the policeman. The child too placed the boy so that he was hiding. Hughes found that children as young as three and four years had little difficulty in decentring to the boy and the policeman. Even when more walls were introduced, and more dolls, over 90 per cent of the children could still decentre.

John Flavell showed three-year-olds some cards with a drawing of a cat on one side and a dog on the other. Holding the card vertically between himself and the child, so that the child could see the dog, he asked them what he could see. These three-year-olds had no difficulty in saying that he could see the cat. In another experiment children between two and a half and five were seated on the opposite side of a table to a researcher. On the table was a Snoopy doll. The children were asked to close their eyes, and then answered questions like 'Can I see you?', 'Can I see your head?', 'Can I see your arm?', and 'Can I see Snoopy?' The youngest children weren't sure whether the researcher could see them, although most said she could see their arm or head. Yet all said she could see Snoopy. Clearly these children aren't egocentric.

Other research was conducted into the age for conservation. **McGarrigle** and **Donaldson** devised a game to test conservation of number in which two identical rows of sweets were placed in front of the child, and a glove puppet called 'Naughty Teddy' then spread the sweets in one of the rows while not moving the others. Of the 80 four and five-year-olds tested 50 said that the number of sweets remained the same, and so could conserve number. However when the adult researchers moved the sweets, only 13 out of 80 said there were the same number. It is possible that the children responded more accurately with 'Naughty Teddy' because the experiment was more like an enjoyable game. But it is also possible that some of the children were actually being distracted by the puppet and weren't really concentrating on the conservation task at all, so some may have given the correct answers without being able to conserve.

(ACT) Conduct a conservation experiment on any children you know. State your hypothesis in null and alternate form (see page 13). Describe your sample and your method and identify any confounding variables. Do your findings support Piaget's view?

Reconstruct Martin Hughes experimental procedure with your own sample of children. Do your findings support Piaget's view on decentring?

► Hughes' experiment was probably more interesting for a young child than Piaget's model mountains and a selection of photographs. It is more like a 'real game' in which the child can become involved.

► The experiments by Hughes and Flavell do not imply that two- to four-year-olds can decentre to other viewpoints over more complex issues. The tasks being tested were rather simple. Things requiring abstract thought would be impossible for such young children.

► Conservation of number probably occurs at a younger age than Piaget predicted since his experiments may not have involved the child's interest and cooperation.

Figure 4.3 'Naughty Teddy'

REVIEW – Egocentrism and conservation
Piaget's observations and experiments led him to conclude that children below the age of seven years weren't maturationally ready to decentre or conserve. Their cognitive development relies on both a state of maturation and a state of experience. When both are present, decentring and conservation occur. More recent research has suggested that Piaget is too pessimistic. Some of his experiments may have been inappropriate for testing children below seven years. When the test is made more relevant or when training and practice are given, children of only three or four years show that they can conserve.

Numerous experiments have shown that children of three or four can conserve when they have been taught about how number, mass, length, weight, volume, speed, etc. do not change just because appearances do. If they can practise the knowledge they have been taught, they can solve conservation problems. It appears that conservation isn't dependent on the degree of cognitive maturation which Piaget predicted doesn't occur until later childhood. Whatever maturation is necessary has occurred by four or five years. What seems to be needed is training and practice, and these are socially acquired. **Dorothy Field** trained some four-year-olds in one conservation task and later found that they could apply their new skill to other conservation tasks in which they weren't trained.

Further research took up the question of whether conservation and decentring are cognitive milestones anyway. **Olivera Petrovich** of Oxford University has asked many children questions designed to test if they do think in the ways which Piaget identified. She claims that four- and five-year-olds can speculate answers to questions such as 'If you were a bird flying above us what could you see?', 'Where does water come from?', 'Where did the first rabbit come from?', 'What is the sky?', 'Who made the clouds?', 'Where do grapes come from?' In most cases children give thought out and reasoned answers, and not the stereotyped responses Piaget would predict that pre-operational children would give. She claims that children do think competently, they show genuine interest and curiosity, and that their styles of thinking aren't much different from those of adults.

 To what extent were Piaget's views about egocentrism and conservation correct?

3 *The concrete operations stage, 7–11 years*

By this age many children will be in school. They will be competing and cooperating in play, and must be able to decentre in order to understand the benefits of having mutually agreed sets of rules, or of negotiating other rules. They are rapidly acquiring and practising cognitive skills, and performing mental operations. Objects and events which they have experienced, or at least imagined, will be acted upon through play and manipulation. This is what Piaget means by 'concrete' operations. For example, arithmetic has formal rules which must be learned in a logically progressive way. One of the first things to be learned is 'adding up'. A child who is about to learn to add will want to know *what* we are adding up. Children can see the point of adding three apples to two apples to see how many apples there are now. It makes sense. They have schemas for apples. It doesn't make sense just to add up. This need for concrete, real objects to manipulate is what Piaget means by concrete operations.

During the concrete operations stage children's conservation skills expand. Most words ending in 'er' will be 'relative' words, i.e. comparing one state with another. Old*er*–young*er*, fast*er*–slow*er*, long*er*–short*er*, thick*er*–thinn*er*, etc., are all relative words, and will all need to be conserved. Some things are easier to understand and conserve than others, and these will be learned first. Conservation of number, for example, only requires the child to consider one thing when making the judgement about whether there are 'more' or 'less' of something. Piaget claimed that six- and seven-year-olds could conserve number. Mass requires the child to consider both size and shape when making conservation. This will take longer. Weight requires size and mass to be considered, while volume requires an understanding of shape, size and mass. Children will need to be 10 or more before they achieve this, according to Piaget.

4 *Formal operations stage, 11 years on*

During the previous stage children were able to learn to mentally manipulate objects or events so long as they had some direct experience of them. Formal operational thinking does not require this direct experience. Adding up and taking away can now be performed in the person's head, without the aid of apples. The youngster can also now answer hypothetical questions, and concepts such as justice, freedom and conscience can be considered. (Questions like 'Who am I?', 'What will I become?' are part of what Erikson calls every adolescent's 'identity crisis', see pages 35–7.)

Formal operational thinking takes several years to achieve, and not everyone fully achieves it. It's quite possible to think formally for some propositions, but not others. Most people think irrationally about some things sometimes, particularly if they are especially sensitive to that issue, or are tired, 'in a mood' etc. Nor does everyone agree that formal logic, which Piaget thought would be more or less achieved (in some areas anyway) by 15 or 20 years, is the last stage of development. It could be that there are stages above that which only certain, gifted people, like Piaget himself, would reach.

Not all people use what by Western scientists is understood by formal logic anyway. Some societies have their own forms of logic, and reason in ways which are logical but follow a logic different from that of Western scientists.

 Outline the main differences in the thinking of children above and below the age of seven, according to Piaget.

There's more to human mental processing than solving conservation tasks and the ability to decentre. There are wide individual differences between children in their development of operational thought and adults sometimes think operationally and sometimes do not. Therefore to talk about 'operational thought' as if it were a single entity is misleading.

> ► A formal operational thinker could answer the following question: 'If you go to town to buy a T-shirt during lunchtime, will you be able to get back to college before the first afternoon lesson, and if not, what will the teacher say to you?'

> ► Formal operational thinking is flexible, rational and systematic. It is like mental hypothesis testing involving rapid solutions to 'what would happen if?', and 'if this, then that' type questions.

> ► Physical and mental maturity coincide after puberty. However the formal operational type of thinking which Piaget described as rational and flexible is not shared by everyone.

REVIEW - *Operational thought*

Piaget believed that children acquire operational thought some time after the age of seven. Piaget's methods have been criticized as inadequate, and others have found the kind of thinking Piaget described developing rather earlier. Not everyone acquires fully operational thought in the Western sense of the logical rules of Western science or philosophy.

Evaluation of Piaget's theory

Theory	Comment
For the first 10 years children are incapable of logical, operational thought.	Modern research shows that Piaget underestimated the cognitive abilities of younger children.
Operational thought develops from puberty.	Many adolescents and adults do not think formally at all.
Cognitive skills change at 2, 7 and 11.	The changes probably occur before these ages.
Piaget gave children particular tasks and asked them specific questions which he assumed allowed them to demonstrate their cognitive skills.	The tasks may have been too difficult, or lacking interest or relevance to the child thus producing an underestimation of their abilities.
Piaget claimed that cognition develops through four distinct stages.	Piaget is unclear about why one stage ends and another begins.
Piaget describes what the average or typical child of a given age can do.	There are wide variations in individual children's abilities.
Piaget emphasized the importance of the child's relationship with the environment for cognitive development.	The child's relationship with other people may be very important too.

 Using your earlier notes on Piaget outline his thinking on cognitive development, the methods he used to investigate it, and the criticisms which have been made of his idea.

Piaget on education

Piaget did not specifically apply his theory of how children think to classroom education, but he highlighted the interaction between maturation and experience, and this has clear implications for schooling until puberty. Many educationalists have drawn on Piaget's ideas think pre-operationally and in concrete operational ways learn by manipulating real objects. They investigate the object's forms – size, shape, weight, mass, colour and functions – what it can be made to do, and what the child can do with it. They often try to transform one object into something else. Egg boxes become the surface of a planet, the sandpit becomes a race track, and the sink becomes the high seas. These transformations excite the child's imagination. All this is an active process of discovery, of finding out about things, in which the child is very actively involved. The application of Piaget's work to education is referred to as *Discovery Learning*.

▶ Piaget always emphasizes the active nature of learning, and the central role the child plays in shaping its own learning. Other theorists do not see the child playing such an active role. *Discovery learning* is a common way of describing Piaget's ideas when applied in education.

The first schoolteacher's role

i To provide a safe, warm, secure environment in which the child can feel comfortable.

ii To provide the kind of materials which are appropriate to the children's age group.

iii To encourage the children to explore and to think about what they are doing with the materials, and how else they can be used. This assists assimilation (see page 74).

iv To encourage a variety of activities which both complement and contrast with each other, thus maintaining variety and novelty. This assists accommodation (see page 74).

v To provide new materials when the properties of previous ones have been explored as fully as seems appropriate. This assists adaptation (see page 74). The child must be encouraged, but not pushed, since the child may not be able to learn from things for which it is not maturationally ready.

vi To allow children to discover things for themselves by observing, or competing with others. The teacher may arrange pairs or small groups of children to work together.

vii To know exactly what stage of development each child is in, what skills a child in that stage is capable of, and what skills will be mastered in the next stage. The child must be helped towards its transition into the next stage. This is called the 'readiness approach'.

viii Always to be ready to show the child an alternative strategy for achieving whatever the child is attempting if the strategy being used has no chance of success. Achieving its success is important to a child.

The role of the first schoolteacher in discovery learning
Children are naturally curious and active. This provides the primary schoolteacher with an excellent opportunity to help them to learn. As the child progresses from stage to stage so the kind of experiences they are offered should be altered to suit their cognitive needs. It would be inappropriate to 'teach' young children in the formal sense since they do not think operationally until they are about seven, and even then the operations they are capable of are specific and immediate according to Piaget.

► The role of the primary schoolteacher is to give children practise in the skills relevant to the stage they are in, and to prepare them for the skills of the next stage. The role of the child is to be enthusiastic. The role of the parent is to encourage enthusiasm.

The role of the child in discovery learning
The child should be enthusiastic, active, curious and adventurous. It should regard school as a fun place, because learning should be fun to young children. It should see school as a place of adventure and stimulation. The role of the parent is to encourage the child to adopt these ideas about school.

 What are the implications of Piaget's theory for how schooling should be organized?

Cognitive factors and reading
From around six or seven years (according to Piaget, and younger according to other writers) children are beginning to decentre (see pages 76–7). This allows them to realize that language can be written as well as spoken. The child will have learned that an object stays the same regardless of the angle from which it is viewed. (This is called

► By about seven children can speak about 4000 words and read about 600. Over the next year practise and consolidation of previous knowledge should increase this to about 9000 and 3000 words respectively.

► If you view a cup from the top or bottom or side you still recognize it as a cup. This is 'shape constancy'. There are several other constancies too, including size, distance and colour. Alphabetical letters lay a trap for children because a's and b's show shape constancy but change their meanings!

shape constancy.) As children start to look at printed letters this knowledge has to be challenged since d and b or p and q are not the same. They will need to understand the relationship between upper and lower case letters, and to become aware of the relationship between sound, shape and the meaning of words and sentences. Children will need to use insight to make reasoned guesses about pronunciation. These tasks would be impossible for an egocentric child.

Concrete operational children need hands-on experience of written language materials. Attractive books with big, simple words accompanying colourful drawings are most likely to hold a child's attention and encourage it to want to read. Being read an interesting story will also encourage a child to want to read for itself.

Problems with reading

Piaget sees cognitive development as being based on inborn biological processes which unfold as the child matures. If cognitive development is biologically based then it is logical to assume that failures in cognitive development may be due to biological malfunctions.

Some children will have some problems involving the organization and workings of their brain which will inhibit their learning to read. A much larger group will have some *specific learning disability* – what is also called *dyslexia.* Since several skills are involved in reading, a problem in any one of them could account for reading difficulties. The main skills are visual, visual and auditory, auditory, memory, and language. There may be a problem in the visual system which makes it difficult for the child to recognize or 'decode' the letters and words. Or the child may not be able to link the sight of a word with the sound that it makes. Most young children read 'out loud'. Children may have difficulties in hearing the separated sounds that new words comprise, or find it difficult to remember a word even though it has been encountered previously. A child who is having difficulties with spoken language is likely to have problems with reading too.

Jerome Bruner's view

► Bruner suggests that the ways in which children are able to organize their experiences change as they mature. He describes these as *modes* of thinking or *modes of representation.*

Jerome Bruner shares Piaget's view that the development of cognition is the result of continuous, dynamic interactions between maturational and environmental forces: between nature and nurture. Children are naturally curious so there must be some genetic force driving us to find out about our world. This force seems to be present from birth. As the higher brain centres develop throughout childhood so the form the child's enquiries take, and what it makes of its findings, will change.

► Jerome Bruner was greatly impressed by Piaget's ideas and his theory shouldn't be seen as radically different from Piaget's. It differs in emphasis rather than being a rejection of Piaget.

Where Piaget was concerned mostly with the stages of cognitive development, Bruner is more concerned with the form that knowledge takes. Piaget thought that we pass through the stages of cognitive development in an *invariant sequence,* each stage replacing the previous one. Bruner believes that each mode of thought is added to the previous one(s). Essentially he sees knowledge gained throughout childhood being represented mentally in one or more of three possible forms or 'modes'.

Enactive representation

According to Bruner for the first couple of years babies' knowledge of the world is derived through their own actions and movements. The child's ideas about an object or event are based on what it can do with it. This knowledge is a series of *enactive representations*. Enactive means acting upon. Given a particular stimulus, such as the sight of a caregiver, the baby responds with reaching and smiling. These responses are the result of its enactive representation of that caregiver. The baby knows what caregivers can do. Enactive representation is a fairly primitive type of knowledge. The young child cannot distinguish between a perception of an object or an event, and its own reaction to it.

By adolescence many things concerning action and movement will have been learned enactively. Swimming, running and hiding are things that we have ideas about which do not need to involve words or images. They are simply things that we can do. For adults some aspects of driving a car are fairly automatic. Fluently playing musical instruments or being skilled at a sport have aspects of enactive representation. We don't think about what we are doing, we just do it.

►*Enactive representations* are ideas the baby has, based on its experience of what objects such as people can do with the baby. As we grow older enactive representations are our fairly simple ideas about things which do not need to be thought about in other ways. Knowledge about how to ride a bicycle is in terms of an enactive representation.

Iconic representation

Iconic representations are forms of knowledge derived from our senses. They result from visual, auditory, smell, touch or taste images. (They are exclusively perceptual.) Several experiences will build up to form an iconic representation. For example seeing a cup of coffee, smelling it and tasting it result in an iconic representation which we don't generally think about in words.

Iconic representations are rather more complicated than enactive forms of knowledge. The 18-month-old child starts to be able to put together ideas about its own behaviour, and what it can do with various toys and people it has experienced previously. The seven-year-old child will have iconic knowledge of Plasticine and shapes, mass and size, but has difficulties in making connections between them, so cannot solve the conservation problem.

► *Iconic representations* are ideas derived from combinations of sensory information.

Symbolic representation

From around the age of seven children add the third, *symbolic mode of representation*. Bruner was particularly interested in the addition of the symbolic mode, which marks the move to a more logical, systematic type of thinking that comes about through the child's ability to use language and to think in linguistic *symbols*. Thinking in words is of enormous benefit to the pursuit of logic and the ability to solve problems (which is, after all, what intelligence is all about.) To demonstrate this Bruner and **Kenny** devised an experimental apparatus comprising a board divided into nine equal squares, plus nine tumblers which would stand on the squares.

► A *symbol* is something which stands in the place of something else. Words are symbols which stand for the objects they represent.

Children from five to seven, i.e. both younger ones who used only enactive and iconic imagery, and older ones who would have some symbolic imagery too, were shown the board with the tumblers arranged on it in a certain way. The tumblers were then scrambled and the children were asked to put them back where they had been before. This was the *reproduction test*.

Bruner and Kenny then moved all of the tumblers from the board, and put the tumbler which had been in the bottom right-hand corner in the bottom left-hand corner. The children had to rebuild the pattern in a mirror image, using the same principles as before. This was the *transpositional test*. Children with a symbolic mode of representing the original board should be able to solve this. Those relying on iconic imagery should not. The results are set out in the table which show the percentage of successes.

Age of child	Type of test	
	Reproduction %	Transposition %
5 years	60	0
6 years	72	27
7 years	80	79

These results suggest that the younger children have an inflexible visual representation (icon or image) of the way the matrix looks, and can't do anything to change it since they lack the ability to transform symbolically. Older children who have symbolic thought can imagine, and apply the rules they have perceived.

 Name and briefly describe the three modes of representation in Bruner's theory of cognitive growth.

Summary – A comparison of Piaget and Bruner's approaches

Piaget	Bruner
Piaget identifies a series of stages of cognitive development each with its characteristic mode of thought. When one stage has been completed the child moves on to the next stage.	Bruner identifies a series of modes of representation. While these appear in a distinct order, each new mode is added to the next rather than replacing it.

Bruner and Kenny's results

 Summarize the main difference between Piaget's and Bruner's view of developing cognition.

THE DEVELOPMENT OF LANGUAGE

What is language?

Everyone knows what *language* is, until they attempt to define it. The following statements describe some characteristics which most people would probably agree about. Language is a system of communication used by humans. It is capable of expressing very complex ideas. It is spoken, written and represented by signs. Language acquisition starts some time towards the end of the first year of life. It consists of words (vocabulary) and grammar (how to combine words.)

The study of language is called *linguistics*. One of its main topics is *grammar*. This is the set of rules which each language has for combining words into understandable, 'correct' sentences. 'The cat sat on the mat' is grammatically correct. 'Mat, the sat cat on' is not.

Each language consists of sounds, *phonemes*. Each letter of the alphabet is a phoneme, and some letters can be pronounced differently in different words. For example the 'o' varies in sound when used in the weapon that fires an arrow, the 'bow', and in what you do to royalty, 'bow', and also when used in 'bother' and 'mother', so it is a different phoneme depending on how it is pronounced. Altogether the English language has 45 phonemes.

Phonemes are combined to produce units of meaning, called *morphemes*. All words are morphemes. But single letters when added to the beginning or end of a word can also change the word's meaning, e.g. 'pen' is a morpheme, but adding an 's' to the end makes it plural, which changes the meaning of 'pen'. 'S' is thus a morpheme when added to the end of many words. So is 'ed' when making a verb such as 'learn' into the past tense, 'learned'.

Morphemes are usually combined into sentences, and there are rules which dictate how sentences will be structured. These rules are called the *syntax* of a language. 'The cat sat on the mat on Tuesday' is correct. The subject of the sentence comes at the beginning, followed by what the subject did, followed by where it did it, and finally when the action occurred. So subject, action, place and time are customary in English. In German the rule is time, manner, place. So 'we are going to London by train today' would become 'heute fahren wir mit der Eisenbahn nach London', or 'today we travel with the train to London'.

Sentences must convey meaning. The study of meaning is called *semantics*. 'The cat sat on the mat' is both syntactically correct and semantically correct. We know exactly what the subject was up to concerning its sitting behaviour. 'The mat sat on the cat' is syntactically correct – we have a subject doing something to an object – but it is semantically wrong since it makes no sense at all.

(NM) What are the main features in the production of grammar?

▶ Different languages have different words for things which are exclusive to that culture, and which cannot directly translate into other cultures. Language is learned from about the end of the first year.

▶ *Grammar* is the set of rules that each language uses to govern how words are to be combined to make sense to other language users.

▶ *Phonemes* are basic units of sound.

▶ There are thousands of *morphemes* in the English language. English dictionaries are full of them!

▶ *Syntax* is the set of rules which determines how words (morphemes) are combined into sentences.

▶ *Semantics* are the rules which make sense out of syntax. An utterance may be syntactically correct but may make no sense at all.

> ### REVIEW – What is language?
> Language is the system of spoken, written and signed symbols used by humans to communicate with each other. Its study is called *psycholinguistics*, including grammar. Grammar consists of the study of phonemes, morphemes, syntax and semantics.

► Neonates are only capable of producing certain sounds since the nerves and muscles which are involved in producing other sounds are immature.

► The nature–nurture debate has tried to separate the contributions of genetic and social forces in language development.

► By six months or so babies start to use babbles deliberately to attract adult attention, and babbling may have some significance in social exchanges between them.

► For the first 12 months or so maturational forces are influential in an infant's verbal behaviour. After 12 months learning takes over.

► Children learn the language they hear around them by a combination of observation, modelling and conditioning.

Stages of language development

Most children speak their first words towards the end of their first year. They acquire phonemes and morphemes increasingly quickly over the next four years. By their second birthday children are learning syntax and semantics too. All this learning seems to require no effort at all. We don't generally teach our children to use language, they seem to acquire it for themselves.

Psychologists are interested in how children manage to acquire it so rapidly. Do they learn it in the same way as they learn to eat with a knife and fork, or dress themselves? Some children learn the basics of language very quickly while others take many years. This might suggest that language is learned. Or are there biological forces pre-conditioning us to produce language when maturationally ready? The sequence of language acquisition is *universal*, i.e. all children are acquiring the same skills at about the same ages, in all cultures. This suggests that biological forces are involved.

Psychologists refer to three broad stages of language acquisition.

1 *Pre-linguistic stage, 0–1 year*

For the first year or so babies are linguistically immature. They can only produce the sounds which their mouths, muscle control and nervous systems allow. For the first few weeks babies have reflexive crying and other random noises. They use different kinds of cry to communicate their different wants or needs. As we saw in Chapter 2, by about six weeks they start to make more controlled 'cooing' noises which have been described as having some social significance.

By about six months the baby's range of sounds is described as *babbling*. Babbles consist of combinations of phonemes. 'Ba', 'ma', 'da' are common. They also comprise phonemes which occur in all human languages, not just the language the infant hears around it. Deaf babies babble, and all children start babbling at about the same age. This suggests a genetic origin for babbling. Babbling seems to provide some satisfaction since babies will babble away to themselves quite contentedly without adult intervention. Babbling also seems to vary in response to adult behaviour, as well as being used to attract adult attention.

Over the next few months phonemes start being repeated. At six months the infant isn't able to control its breathing and facial muscles well enough to produce the sound 'mamamama'. At 12 months it is. By the end of the first year phonemes which do not occur in the language of the baby's own culture begin to disappear. *Learning* is taking over from the forces of maturation which have dominated the first 12 months.

Parents will be encouraging their babies to make some particular sounds, e.g. 'mama' or 'dada', rather than others. Until about 10 months of age babies of profoundly deaf and dumb parents have the same patterns of vocal behaviour as babies brought up by hearing and talking parents, but after 10 months their babbling begins to decrease. This suggests that learning is becoming important, and that babies of about 10 months need something stimulating, such as adult speech, to learn from.

What must children learn to be good communicators?

Before they can be considered as good communicators children must learn several practical lessons. They must learn how to attract the attention of those around them. Pre-linguistic children (before they understand language) use gazing, reaching and crying to attract attention. As the child grows it must learn to use language to begin, and then maintain, a communication. They will have to learn how to make their meanings clear when they do not know the correct word or grammar to express it. This is often accomplished in the same way as adults, with gestures and postures. And they must, of course, be good listeners so that they can be sure their messages have been received and understood, or so that they can repeat or try to clarify anything which was not understood.

2 *Holophrastic, or one-word stage, 12–18 months*

Some time between about 10 and 18 months the amount of babbling decreases and the number of single words increases. At first some of the 'words' may only be understood by the child's parents, and may not be real words at all. If a sound such as 'moo' is used whenever the child sees a plate, then 'moo' is a 'word' as far as the baby's parents are concerned. Some theorists argue that babies often use a word to convey a more complex meaning, e.g. 'mil' might actually mean 'I want some more milk'. The word 'mil' would be a *holophrase*. Not everyone agrees that the baby is capable of having the idea 'I want some more milk', although most parents and older siblings are often able to interpret correctly the baby's needs.

Right from the time the baby uses its first words it will have some understanding of much more complex meanings. By 18 months it will have a vocabulary of about 50 words, but will be able to respond appropriately to many more which it cannot use. Most of the child's own speech will be nouns to describe familiar objects, and verbs to describe what they do. In a study of how 18 infants acquired their first 50 words **Katherine Nelson** found that 'they do not learn the names of objects which are simply "there", such as tables, plates, towels, grass, or stones. With few exceptions all the terms listed are terms applying to manipulable or movable objects.' Those objects which the child could act upon in some way, such as a ball or shoes, were quickly learned, as were those which did something themselves, such as truck, dog and clock. It appears that manipulation of objects has a role in early cognitive and language development.

Inevitably children make mistakes. Pronunciation errors and errors in applying words correctly are common. Some sounds are quite difficult for the child to make, so words containing them will be simplified. 'Spoon' becomes 'poon' because the 's' sound requires complicated movements of the tongue. Some sounds might be more fun to make too, so those will be used in place of the difficult ones. Adults, for example, often teach children to call cows 'moomoos', or dogs 'bow wows'.

► A *holophrase* is a single word which conveys the meaning of a whole sentence.

► How do you make the 'k' phoneme in 'kitten'? What are you doing with your mouth? How about the 'g' sound in 'go', or the 'q' sound in 'question'? They require quite difficult control of the mouth and breathing, compared to 'front of mouth' sounds such as 'b', 'd', 'p' etc.

> ### Why do children make mistakes?
> To explain why children make mistakes, Eve Clark suggests the *semantic features hypothesis* whereby the child identifies one or two of the main features of an object, e.g. its colour, shape, size, smell, etc. Anything which has similar features will be assumed to have the same name. The result of this is overextension.
> Katherine Nelson suggests the *functional similarities* hypothesis whereby the child learns what something does, or what the child can do with it. Anything which acts, or can be used, in the same way will be called by the same name.

Errors in applying words include *overextension* and *underextension*. Overextension occurs where the child applies a word whose meaning it knows, e.g. 'dog', to anything with similar features, such as four legs, a head and a tail, so a horse, or a cow may be called 'a big doggie'.

Underextension occurs when the child uses the word too narrowly. Having learned that Mummy has a car, and it is red and has four wheels, the child might only apply the word 'car' to those vehicles which have the same characteristics as Mummy's car, i.e. four wheels and red. Three-wheelers and other coloured vehicles can't be cars.

Herbert and **Eve Clark** suggest that children pass through several stages in learning word usage. These are underextension, appropriate usage (without really knowing the word's correct meaning), overextension and finally correct usage.

3 Early sentences, from about 18 months

During this stage vocabulary increases rapidly, and the rules of grammar begin to be learned. Some children are using 'two-word sentences' long before 18 months, while others do not use them until they are well over two years old. It is virtually impossible to describe the speech of a 'typical' two-year-old or an 'average' three-year-old. Meanwhile they all continue to use single words to express those ideas which can be expressed in a single word. When asked if it is tired, a 15-month-old might say 'no'. This means 'No, I'm not tired yet'. 'No' is a holophrase. By two years the child might say 'Not tired'. This is a two-word sentence.

Early 'sentences' are examples of what **Roger Brown** calls *telegraphic speech*. Since children vary so widely in their speed of language acquisition he invented the 'mean length of utterance' (MLU) as a measure of a child's progress. Brown conducted a 10-year longitudinal naturalistic observation study of three children 'Adam', 'Eve' and 'Sarah'. He listed 14 of the most commonly used morphemes, and studied the children's speech to discover when and how they acquired them. He recorded an average of one hour of each child's speech per week.

Brown found that children's early telegraphic speech concerned several main themes. They learn to name objects, e.g. 'ball', 'shoe'; to demand things, e.g. 'more milk'; to indicate non-existence, e.g. 'milk all gone now'; to show possession, e.g. 'my ball'; to locate things, e.g. 'sweater chair'; to modify descriptions, e.g. 'big train'; and to initiate action, e.g. 'Eve read'.

► *Telegraphic speech* derives its name from the way in which people used to write telegrams, for which they paid by the word.

► Early speech is largely concerned with naming, demanding, non existence,

The children were asked to repeat particular stimulus sentences to see which words they would repeat, and which they would leave out. 'I will read the book', for example, would be repeated as something like 'I read book' by a two-year-old, 'I read the book' by a child of two years six months, and would probably be correct by the age of three. There are two or three possible explanations for why certain words are said and others left out. The most obvious one is that the spoken words carry the message, while the ones which are left out have the function of making the sentence grammatically correct, but do not necessarily add anything to its meaning. The child does not understand grammar, and so does not appreciate the need for what Brown calls *functor words*. Another possibility is that adults put more stress on the important words. A mother might say 'NO, you may NOT GO out' and this may be repeated 'No, not go'. Or the child may simply not have sufficient memory to remember the whole sentence, so just remembers the message.

► Until 18-24 months children have some vocabulary, but no understanding of grammar.

► *Functor* words are the words we use to make our utterances grammatically correct. The meaning of 'I go shops' is perfectly clear, but we add the morphemes 'am, ing, to, the' to make it grammatically correct.

Roger Brown's five stages of sentence production

Brown suggested that sentence production proceeds through five stages.

Stage 1   Simple two or three word sentences to describe actions, e.g. 'hit ball'.

Stage 2   Naming objects and events, e.g. 'Eve sleeped', 'that a pencil'.

Stage 3   Questions of what, why, where, e.g. 'where Eve gone?'.

Stage 4   Joining short sentences, e.g. 'who that ... that there?'.

Stage 5   Complex sentences with more than one subject can be joined, e.g. 'Eve and Adam are going to play'.

(NM) Outline the main stages of language development.

Summary – Stages of linguistic development

For the first year of life a baby's nervous system, motor control and state of cognition need to mature. The baby needs direct experience, including actual manipulation, to stimulate its interest in objects and events around it. Before five months it makes various noises which may serve some function in making relationships. This is replaced by babbling which becomes selectively reinforced by caregivers. By 12 months the infant will be able to make some sounds which it associates with those things with which it has become familiar. These are the first words. Continued maturation, experience and encouragement result in words being combined into two word sentences from around 18 months.

ea of psychological
...will find alternative
...t the origin, nature
and functioning of human
abilities. The development of
language is no exception.

► Operant conditioning explains
almost all learning as the result of
the organism being reinforced. A
reinforcer is anything which
increases the likelihood of some
response occurring again.

► If a response does not result in
some beneficial reinforcer then it
is said to extinguish (disappear).

► Parents often respond to
incorrect grammar, thus reinforcing
it.

The main theories of language acquisition

There are two views on the origins and development of language.
One view sees language as something which is primarily learned. For
example in 1957 B.F. Skinner outlined his operant conditioning
theory, which says that language is learned in the same way that
everything else is learned, through 'selective reinforcement' and
'behaviour shaping', see pages 40–3. An extension of this is offered by
social learning theorists who say that children learn language through
imitation and 'modelling' their linguistic behaviour on those people
whom they see as most worth imitating. A contrasting view was
advanced in response to these theories by **Noam Chomsky**. Chomsky argues that we are born with the potential to develop language.
These views represent each side of the nature–nurture debate which
we discussed at the beginning of this chapter.

Skinner's operant conditioning theory

In Chapter 2 we described how Skinner saw most behaviour being
acquired through selective reinforcement. The same process accounts
for verbal behaviour. Those babbles that most resemble the language
the child is to learn will be reinforced by parental stimulation such as
smiles, soothing words, cuddles, etc. Soon only those babbles which
have been reinforced will continue, the rest will extinguish.

Next, those combinations of babbles that represent words will be
most reinforced by parents, particularly 'naming words' such as
'mama' or 'dada'. By 18 months the child will have been sufficiently
reinforced in the use of single words, while others are still being
reinforced, to combine some of them into 'sentences'. Skinner claims
that if the sentence makes sense it will be reinforced. If it doesn't it will
either be corrected or ignored, so that it will extinguish. In the same
way longer sentences will be reinforced if they are correct, and if they
are wrong and thus do not achieve the desired goal, they will
extinguish. In this way correct grammar is learned.

On the whole there is little evidence to support some of these claims.
Babies probably do learn words by reinforcement, or by imitation,
but they probably do not learn their grammar in the same way. Most
of the studies suggest that parents do not *shape* their children's
grammar by correcting or ignoring it. Parents correct their children
only if what they are saying is untrue or hurtful. So long as it is
truthful a young child's speech which is grammatically incorrect is
not usually corrected.

Indeed there is some evidence that children whose grammar is
corrected do not acquire correct grammar more quickly than others,
and might actually be slower to learn it. It appears that children learn
the rules of grammar regardless of their parents. Contrary to what
Skinner would predict, parents will reinforce their child's incorrect
grammar (by responding appropriately). It would also be wrong to
assume that parents themselves always know and use correct grammar.

Criticisms of Skinner's explanation for language acquisition

If language is learned through reinforcement, how do children combine the words they have learned into original sentences which they have never heard before, and couldn't possibly have been reinforced for using previously?

Skinner's theory only explains how children talk, but doesn't explain all the mental events, such as perceiving, understanding, knowing and therefore wanting to communicate, which underlie it. Children may learn words by reinforcement, but not the complex meaning of sentences.

Further, why do children make mistakes such as 'sleeped' instead of slept, or 'Weetabik' to mean one Weetabix? They can't have heard these words, and wouldn't have been reinforced for using them. Rather they are *applying* the rules of grammar which they are learning. They can use these rules as they mature and have experiences, but all children pass through the same sequence in language acquisition. If it relied on reinforcement alone then children's speech development would vary enormously.

Learning language by reinforcement alone would probably be impossible, or at least would take several lifetimes. Yet most children have mastered the rules of their language's grammar by the time they are about five years old.

Chomsky's 'Language Acquisition Device'

Noam Chomsky disputed many of Skinner's claims about the role of learning and reinforcement in language acquisition. He argued that all languages have certain sounds in common, as well as such categories as nouns and verbs. There is also a number of ways in which they can be combined into language. These are what Chomsky identifies as a *Language Acquisition Device* (LAD), or *Language Acquisition System* (LAS), a genetically inherited predisposition to learn language. As children hear the particular language of the community in which they grow up so the LAD prepares them to use that language.

▶ Chomsky claims that we are born with a *Language Acquisition Device* (LAD), a genetic predisposition to learn language.

Chomsky also suggests we acquire the ability to communicate meanings by combining sounds and words into messages. This is called *deep structure*. It may exist in all people. The actual sounds, words, phrases etc. are learned and are called *surface structure*.

What evidence is there for genetic involvement in language acquisition? We said earlier that all children pass through the same stages of language learning at about the same time. This suggests that it is linked to maturation and genetics. Our vocal equipment, breathing control and brain centres are all affected by maturation too.

▶ *Surface structure* is learned. The ability to combine units of it into words *(transformational grammar)*, and the desire to communicate our ideas (*deep structure*) is innate.

E.H. Lenneberg found that in both 'normal' and Down's syndrome children there was a positive correlation between motor development and language development. Babies start to babble when they start to crawl, they say their first words when they take their first steps, and are producing simple sentences when they begin to walk. Motor skills are obviously determined by maturation, perhaps speech is too.

▶ There is evidence that linguistic skills are influenced by genetically determined maturational factors.

Language is acquired through a combination of genetic and environmental factors. Children are probably genetically programmed to use language and the particular language they use depends on which one they hear around them, which they imitate and which they are reinforced for using.

▶ There are many problems for supporters of the view that language is innate, such as why it takes so long to acquire, why children make so many mistakes, and why there are such wide differences between children's linguistic abilities?

Compare and contrast Skinner's behaviourist theory of language acquisition with Chomsky's theory of language acquisition.

> **REVIEW – Theories of language development**
> Operant conditioning theory says that language is learned through selective reinforcement. However, children combine words to produce sentences for which they could never have been reinforced. Chomsky hypothesizes the existence of an innate Language Acquisition Device comprising transformational grammar and deep structure which are genetically determined, and surface structure which is learned.

PLAY

What is play, and what is it for?

Valentine: 'The very essence of play is that it is an activity carried out entirely for its own sake – for the mere enjoyment of the activity.'

Lowe: 'Children take play seriously, so seriously that it has been described as the work of children.'

If we can't agree about what play is, then let's agree about what it accomplishes

Gardner: Play leads to 'greater mastery of the world, more adequate coping with problems and fears, superior understanding of oneself and one's relationship to the rest of the world, an initial exploration of the relation between reality and fantasy, an arena in which intuitive, semi-logical forms of thought can be freely tested.'

> **Some early views of play**
> **Herbert Spencer**, in the mid 19th century, saw play as an outlet for surplus energy, thus reducing the potential for tension that would otherwise build up. No reasons were given for why children have surplus energy, why they continue to play when they're tired, why there are different forms of play, or why any surplus energy couldn't be used up in other ways, such as work.
>
> **Karl Groos**, around 1900, considered play as a biologically necessary preparation for activities in adult life. This is probably true of animals – Groos mainly studied animal behaviour – but the evidence for it in humans is unclear.
>
> **Stanley Hall**, also around 1900, put forward the 'recapitulation theory' – each individual is considered to evolve through all the stages that the whole species has passed through. There is no evidence for this idea and this theory has little support today.

► The further up the evolutionary scale one looks, the more the members of that species play. Fish and insects play very little, monkeys and chimps play quite a lot.

Play is a normal part of the development of many animal species. It occupies most of the child's time, much of the adolescent's and some of the adult's. Play consists of three elements: *curiosity*, *exploration* and *manipulation* of objects. There may be a genetically inherited basis for play but psychologists have concentrated on how play contributes to social relationships and intellectual development rather than on how or where it originates.

During childhood, play is for fun, for practice, for discovery, for developing our knowledge about properties of various things, for discovering what effect we can have on the environment, for playing out our feelings, for expressing ideas and experimenting with them, for developing muscles and co-ordination, for learning about how other people behave, and much more. Play prevents boredom and promotes happiness, and can also help relieve stress. As well as being fun, play can be a very serious business. Children can concentrate for quite a long time on their Lego and Meccano constructions, or completing their jigsaws. In a word, play is for *stimulation*.

There are different kinds of play activities which children enjoy. Each offers different kinds of stimulation, and the child will switch from one to another during the day. These different kinds of play emphasise different skills. There is *discovery play*, where the child finds out what things are like, and what they can be used for. In *physical play* the child is active and develops muscles and co-ordination. In *creative play* the child expresses its own ideas, tests things out, and sees what can be achieved with things. During *social play* the child is learning about itself and other people.

How play changes as we grow

If you observe children's play you will notice that it seems to develop through four stages.

1 *Solitary play*

For the first few months of life a child's play is largely *solitary*. Infants are unable to take very much in, so anything requiring them to concentrate or cooperate will be impossible. At best they can join in interactional synchrony and exchange games. Some psychologists claim that we shouldn't allow a child to be over-stimulated since this can lead to frustration. The child might try to take in more than it can reasonably be expected to understand. Over-stimulation can be as bad as under-stimulation.

During the second year children's motor skills enable them to start making choices about the things they reach for or put down. Manipulative skills lead to more exploration and experimentation with objects. Play may involve someone else to some extent, but the child is still playing its own game.

2 *Parallel play*

By two to three years of age children start to take some notice of others, and will play alongside other children. Two girls might be playing with toy cars in the sandpit, building roads and bridges in the sand for their cars. But they do not play together. Each has its own

► Play has many functions such as soothing emotions, gaining practical experience, promoting social relationships, developing physical skills and advancing intellectual development.

► Children's play allows them to be curious, to explore and to manipulate. Humans have higher cognitive centres in their brains which demand these things. Discovery, physical, creative and social play all contribute to the stimulation that humans need.

► Stages of play
1 Solitary play   0 – 2 years
2 Parallel play   2 – 3 years
3 Associative play   3 – 4 years
4 Cooperative play 3 – 4+ years

► For the first year or so children aren't able to understand a great deal. Solitary play allows them to experience aspects of their environment which will contribute to their understanding as they mature.

roads and cars. One child might try to take over another's game, or sneak onto their roads, or take the other's car, but mostly they merely tolerate each other's presence, and ignore each other. Piaget calls this *parallel play*, and it is an extension of solitary play.

3 Associative play

Within a few months of parallel play appearing the next stage appears. The children begin to share a toy, or play in each other's area, or agree to some limited cooperation. The sandpit roads may be joined so that one child's car can drive on the other child's roads. The cars might be allowed to crash, or they may be swapped. This is *associative play*. The children are still playing their own game, and wouldn't welcome too much interference from other children.

4 Cooperative play

Most children reach the final stage some time between three and five years of age. Now children are able to join in with each other's games, or agree to play 'your' game now so long as we play 'my' game later. Piaget calls this *cooperative play*. Cooperative play usually involves just two children to begin with, but can include more children over the next year or so. Simple cooperative play involves two or three children working together, perhaps to build a tower from building blocks. Complex cooperative play features several children taking part in more adventurous games, including imaginative games involving role play.

Summary – Stages of play

Age (years)	Stage	Features
0 – 2	Solitary play	Simple, repetitive activities helping mastery of skills
2 – 3	Parallel play	Playing the same game alongside each other, but not playing together
3	Associative play	Acceptance of other child, occasional sharing of toys
3 – 4	Cooperative play	Increasing acceptance of benefits of sharing; taking different roles to make role play games work

 Outline the major stages in the development of play.

(ACT) If you have access to children between one and five note examples of their play. See if these could fit the description of solitary, parallel, associative or cooperative play.

Sex differences in play

One very noticeable thing about the development of play in most Western societies is that boys and girls tend not to play together. Very few boys include girls in their group, and few girls play in the same way as boys.

From around three years of age children know whether they are a boy or a girl, and this will influence some of the ways they will play. Boys tend to play with noisier, more active toys, like balls, drums, bikes and scooters. They are more independent, do not often seek advice or assistance, and frequently play at some distance from an adult. Girls tend to play with the quieter, more gentle toys, often in 'pretend games'. They will often seek to involve an adult in their game, or obtain assistance from one, so will tend to play near to an adult.

From around three children seek out the company of others of the same sex as themselves. By school age sex differences in play will be firmly established, and any boy who appears to want to play with a girl's toy, or become involved in a girl's game, will quickly be discouraged by other boys. **Michael Lamb** studied three- to five-year-old boys and girls playing with toys that are traditionally 'girls' toys' and 'boys' toys', and with 'neutral sex' toys. When the children played with the toys in a 'sex appropriate' way the games were inventive and involving. Being involved seems to increase the enjoyment, and make the children want to play the game again. If a child started to play with the opposite sex's toys, or in a an 'opposite sex way', they were soon 'told off' by their same sex peers. Lamb noted that the child who was behaving in a 'cross sex' way would be back playing with its same sex peers within one minute.

> ► Most children are treated differently by parents, and different expectations are made of them, according to their sex. They learn that boys and girls are different and so acquire their gender roles.

> ► There are sex differences in the toys children choose, the ways they play with them, and the extent to which they involve adults.

> ► Sex differences in play are quite marked by about five years old, although there are always exceptions. A younger brother with several sisters may seek out 'girls' toys' by choice. According to Lamb this tendency will soon be changed by the other boys.

Review – Sex differences in play

There are genetic differences between boys and girls. For example on average, boys grow bigger and heavier, and girls develop language skills earlier. Girls may be better able to play games requiring verbal communication earlier than boys. These genetic differences probably do not account for all the differences in the ways the two sexes play. We expect different kinds of play activities from our sons and daughters. We dress them differently, speak to them differently, handle them differently, offer them different things to play with, offer them different kinds of discipline. Traditionally boys have been encouraged to be more robust than girls. By about four years old each sex knows what kind of play is expected of it, and will ridicule or isolate anyone playing in a 'cross sex way'. These differences continue until beyond puberty.

Some theories of play

Freud's psychodynamic theory

As children grow they will inevitably face certain problems. With sensitive handling parents should be able to help their children through most of them. But sometimes parents aren't sensitive or the circumstances are so difficult that the child becomes anxious. This anxiety can build up until it becomes almost too much for the child to bear. The defence mechanisms such as sublimation and displacement may reduce some of the anxieties (see page 31). Freud sees play as

> ► Piaget believes play is essential to cognitive development during the first 10 years or so, since children learn best through direct manipulation of concrete objects.

another way for children to relieve their worries. They 'act out' their problems on toys and games. This helps to minimize the risk of fixation which would otherwise contribute to their personalities becoming distorted.

Piaget's cognitive theory

As we said earlier (pages 71–84), Jean Piaget was one of the most influential researchers into child development and proposed that the way children think passes through four stages until it finally becomes more logical at around puberty. The child's level of thinking will obviously reflect its play activities, especially during the first three stages.

Mastery or *practice play* is the earliest stage. According to Piaget, for the first two years of life play is mostly concerned with practising motor and interpersonal skills. Babies start by reaching and grasping things. Shaking a rattle produces interesting noises and the baby is learning that it can control certain noises. Throwing the rattle out of the buggy, and having Dad pick it up and return it with a mild complaint, can be an interesting game to a young baby. It is learning that it can influence other people too. By two years of age most children are mobile and can move around and manipulate objects. They should also have developed enough language to promote their relationships with others. Learning what a ball is called by asking 'What dat?' will give the child the ability to ask for the ball the next time it wants it.

In *symbolic play*, the next stage, the child's ability to use words and ideas as *symbols* should stimulate their imagination. (A symbol is anything which stands for something else.) Dressing-up games and make-believe play allow the child to experience what it must feel like to be the person who they are imitating. Fantasy will stretch the young child's imagination.

Play with rules is the third stage. By about seven years the child should be able to share toys and materials, and play cooperatively. Team games are common. The child starts to realize that other people have needs and can contribute too. They begin to appreciate the need for and benefits of having some rules about which they all agree, although children often change the rules (usually to suit themselves) as they play.

Bruner's cognitive theory

Jerome Bruner has spent many years studying children of all ages in all kinds of situations (see pages 84–6). Like Piaget he believes that the way in which children can understand alters as they grow. Babies' intellects respond to active exploration and direct perception. Babies can only '*know* about' things from what they can *do* with them. Their mental representation of what the world around them is like is *enactive*, i.e. it results only from the way they personally have acted upon it. Younger children play with small objects, often repeating their actions. In this way they build up their enactive representation of that object.

In older children thinking doesn't result only from direct enactive manipulation but can rely on what things look like. This leads to *iconic representation.*

Play materials and activities should promote this development of knowledge if they are used in constructive ways. Simply leaving children to play with materials, no matter how stimulating the materials could be, is not of great educational value. Children need structure, purpose and achievement.

Vygotsky's rules of play view

Vygotsky is especially interested in how children view, use and change the rules of play. They use play to help reduce stress, to help understand what is happening. If something happens which causes stress the child will use everyday objects such as a doll or a toy soldier in a game whose rules the child makes up. The rules will allow the child to play the game, which will help it to come to terms with its feelings, or arrive at some manageable understanding of the problem.

(NM) What is the main function of play according to

a Freud; b Piaget; c Bruner; d Vygotsky?

Some studies of play

Corinne Hutt investigated the relationship between curiosity, exploration and manipulation in 30 pre-school children. She invented a toy which was a red metal rectangular box on four brass legs. On the top was a lever which could be moved to different positions. Sometimes moving the stick had no consequences, sometimes it made pictures appear on one side of the box, sometimes it made a bell and a buzzer sound and sometimes it made both the pictures (visual feedback) and the sounds (auditory feedback) occur at the same time.

In the experimental playroom there were also five ordinary toys. Most of the children explored the novel toy, particularly when they discovered the noises it made. This is exploratory behaviour, and according to Hutt isn't quite the same thing as play. Many tried to use the new toy in their games with the usual toys. This is play. Some of the children didn't play with the novel toy at all, while others explored it but didn't incorporate it into their games.

Five years later **Hutt** and **Bhavrani** revisited the children who hadn't explored the toy and found that the boys were generally lacking in curiosity and any spirit of adventure, while the girls seemed to be socially withdrawn and had personality difficulties. The children who had actively explored and used the novel toy were more likely to be seen as curious and creative.

(NM) What is 'exploratory behaviour', and how does it differ from play?

Kathy Sylva, **Carolyn Roy** and **Marjorie Painter** naturalistically observed 120 pre-schoolers in Oxfordshire as part of the Oxfordshire Pre-school Research Project. They distinguished *complex play*, which is involving and stimulating (and which Bruner claims would promote intellectual and educational achievements), from *simple play*, which is unstructured and simply passes time. Complex or elaborated play

---

REVIEW – Theories of play

Freud sees play as aiding personality growth by helping the child to reduce its anxieties by playing them through.

Piaget offers a comprehensive theory where play mirrors the stages through which cognition develops.

Bruner sees constructive play as part of a continuous process of cognitive growth. Vygotsky emphasizes the role of play in the comprehension of rules, since children's lives are dominated by rules.

▶ Exploring and investigating a new toy isn't quite the same thing as using it in an inventive way by including it in a game.

▶ Curious children tend to remain curious and are most likely to benefit cognitively.

▶ Sylva, Roy and Painter found that completing or creating something made the greatest contribution to cognitive development.

has two essential features: a clear and achievable goal and some means of letting the child become aware of its progress. Sylva and her colleagues found that the complex play most likely to promote cognitive development involved completing or creating something such as a construction, a jigsaw or a drawing or painting. The next best activities for promoting cognition are playing with small toys and with sand. 'Messing around' games were only useful for using up energy and making social contact. Children like an adult to be present, for security and to provide occasional authority, but not for organizing them. Children can learn from each other, so work well in pairs.

 What evidence is there that play contributes to cognitive development?

Chapter summary

Piaget sees the growth of cognition passing through four identifiable, biologically controlled stages which can be grouped into two: pre-operational and operational. Pre-operational thinking is immediate, illogical, and uses appearance as the basis for other judgement. Operational thought is logical and appears from about the age of seven. Bruner argues that there are different ways in which people can think: enactive, iconic and symbolic representation.

Language is a system of communication that we acquire from when the early social babbles start to resemble human speech. Both learning and genetic factors are involved in producing language.

Play is a complex business which changes as we grow, and has different forms and functions at each age. It can contribute constructively to cognitive development if stimulating materials are used in creative ways.

Exam questions – 60 minutes each

1 Evaluate Piaget's theory of cognitive development.

2 What kinds of factors are thought to affect the acquisition of language?

3 'Children possess an innate capacity to develop language.' Discuss.

4 Discuss the nature and purpose of play in childhood.

acquire our sense of what our society believes is 'right' and 'wrong', or 'good' and 'bad'. Different societies and different groups within a society have different norms and values reflecting that society's traditions of desirable and undesirable behaviour. Some moral principles may even be universal to all societies. Psychologists are less interested in the actual norms and values or moral principles than in how they are acquired. The result of moral development is that we acquire a *conscience* which psychologists see as developing through the individual incorporating ideas of right and wrong into his or her personality: a process known as *internalization*.

Just because we have internalized a conscience does not necessarily imply that we always, or even often, live by it. We may have desires to do something which is against the 'rules' and beliefs that form our conscience. The consequence may be guilt or shame, pride or vanity. This *affective* component of moral development was studied by Sigmund Freud. We may actually do something which opposes our own system of ideals. This *behavioural* component was studied by B.F. Skinner and Albert Bandura and others. Our ideas about what constitutes right and wrong, and how we should react, will change with age and experience. This *cognitive* component was studied by Jean Piaget and Lawrence Kohlberg.

► A *conscience* is a set of ethical and moral principles that allows us to evaluate actions and events, which are either real or contemplated.

► To *internalize* means to take in some set of principles or standards of behaviour and thought which then become a part of our own motives.

► *Affective* refers to human emotions, moods or feelings.

 What is moral development?

Freud's psychodynamic theory of moral development

(For a fuller discussion of Freud's psychoanalytic theory see Chapter 2, pages 25–33.)

Freud once claimed that one of the hardest tasks of parenthood was the moral development of the children. By the age of about three children are mastering their motor skills, they can communicate quite well, and they can understand much more than they may choose to say. The irrational source of their psychic energy, the *id*, is still making demands for their logical *ego* to find satisfaction. For males during the *phallic stage* the main demand will be to experience and enjoy the erotic stimulation felt by the 'all important' phallus. Since this stimulation will be provided (inadvertently but naturally) by the mother (at bath time, when dressing, etc.), the id will drive the male to want to be near to his mother. His mother becomes a sexual object of the child's love. His father is seen as a threat since he shares the mother's time and affections, and since he already 'possesses' the mother. The id will energize the *death instinct* to make the boy feel hostile and jealous towards his father.

At least three major sources of unconscious anxiety combine in the phallic stage. First, feelings of hostility and jealousy towards someone who is bigger and more powerful than you lead to frustration. These negative emotions will be one source of anxiety in the male child. Second, wanting your rival out of the way while loving him at

► The *id* and the *ego* are the first two parts of personality development in traditional Freudian theory. The third part, the *superego*, emerges during the phallic stage (3–7). The *death instinct* and *libido* are the two instinctive urges which prompt particular behaviour.

► By *identification* Freud means the way we (mostly unconsciously) transfer ideas which we have about someone else to ourself. The boy adopts his father's attitudes, sex roles, moral values, etc., and so develops his own superego by identifying with his father.

> ### Review – The Oedipus complex
> Perhaps Freud's most controversial ideas are expressed in his early writings and concern the relationship between childhood sexual feelings and personality growth. The id is demanding that pre-genital sexual feelings must be satisfied. The ego provides the only way to achieve this, which is for the boy to replace his father as the object of his mother's love. He must possess his mother and eliminate his father. At the same time as boys are feeling sexually drawn towards their mothers they feel guilty and fearful of their fathers. Ultimately they fear their father might castrate them for their desires. Freud described this mass of love, desire, guilt, worry and fear as *Oedipus conflict*. It was derived largely from interpreting the spoken memories of disturbed adult patients.

► One of the major criticisms of Freudian theory of personality development during childhood is that it was not derived from studying many children but rather from the dreams and spoken memories of some 'hysterical' patients. Freud wasn't studying Little Hans 'first hand' either.

► Phobias are irrational fears towards people, objects or events. Children usually grow out of their fear of the dark, fear of strangers, fear of open spaces or closed in spaces.

► Freud and Hans' father were not examining the child's symptoms in an unbiased way. As Deese points out (see Chapter 1, page 19) there is no such thing as unbiased observation. They had already decided what the child's problem was, and were simply fitting the facts to the theory!

the same time will add further anxiety. Third, anxiety comes from the fear the male child has that his father will find out about his desires, and punish him for them. The ultimate punishment will be to have the source of his erotic pleasure, his penis, cut off. This fear of castration would provide a further source of anxiety. These unconscious anxieties combine into what has been called the *Oedipus complex*. They can only be overcome by the child *repressing* his feelings about his mother, which he does by *identifying* with his father.

Apart from his own children, Freud really studied only one other child, and that was mostly by correspondence. 'Little Hans' was the son of an admirer of Freud. Hans' father told Freud of his five-year-old son's phobia about horses. The family lived opposite a coaching inn during the first decade of this century, and the streets were full of horses. One day Hans had seen a large horse fall down in the street, and thought it was dead. His father said that ever since then the boy had been afraid of horses. The child imagined they might fall over, make a frightening noise, or bite him. Freud, and Hans' father, interpreted the horse phobia quite differently, claiming that the boy was suffering the anxieties of the Oedipus complex. Freud told Hans' father to explain to his son what was happening, that he wouldn't be angry with his son for the boy's feelings about him and his mother, and that he was not going to punish Hans. The phobia would then disappear. Hans' father did explain, and the phobia did eventually disappear.

Freud claimed that the case of little Hans proved the truth of Oedipal conflict. Clearly it does no such thing. There are several explanations for why Hans developed his phobia, the most obvious one being that he had seen a large horse fall over and he was afraid that another might fall and hurt him. He had a younger sister and the phobia may also have served to attract his mother's attention away from his sister and back to Hans. It may even have been an expression of resentment at having to share his mother's affections with his sister. Most children develop phobias towards something or other during childhood. Surely they can't all be related to unconscious anxieties about parents?

> ### The Electra complex
>
> Freud felt quite satisfied with his explanations of why and how boys acquire their moral codes, but he admitted being much less certain about why girls come to identify with their mothers. Girls are supposed to envy their fathers for having a phallus, which they themselves don't have, and hope that by choosing him as their partner they could share his. Perhaps their own might even grow again. They supposedly imagine that their mother has already castrated them for some wrongdoing, and they harbour thoughts of hate and revenge towards her. These feelings are supposed to be repressed by identifying with their mothers.
>
> Girls would have less strong reason to identify with their mothers than boys with their fathers, and so are supposed to develop weaker superegos. There is no evidence for this at all. The concept of the Electra complex has been severely criticized, not least by female psychoanalysts, who point out that it's not a penis that girls envy, but the power that men exert over women, and everything else in society!

There are also reasons why Hans's phobia may have disappeared that have nothing to do with his father promising not to castrate him. (In fact his mother, not his father, had actually threatened to castrate him if he played with his 'widdler'.) One explanation for the phobia disappearing is *habituation*. If you were forced to be exposed to something you had a phobic reaction to for several hours, the fear would eventually subside. This is called habituation. Hans could not have avoided seeing or hearing horses every day of his life. (See Chapter 10 for a discussion of habituation and *desensitization*.)

 What 'evidence' from the case of Little Hans could Freud claim supported his theory? What are the shortcomings of this evidence?

Freud's explanation for how girls acquire their personalities has always seemed bizarre, and hardly anyone takes it at all seriously now. It's called the *Electra complex*. Little girls are supposed to imagine that their penis has already been cut off by their mothers. They become afraid that their mothers may mutilate them further. They are supposed to suffer 'penis envy' (since the male phallus is supposed to be all important during the phallic stage). This unconsciously draws the girl to their father who has a penis. By associating with her father the girl is supposed to imagine that her penis will grow again. This causes conflict with her mother, and anxiety follows. In order to overcome this anxiety the girl represses her sexual feelings toward her father by identifying with her mother. The girl also fears that her mother will lose even more affection towards her, and this increases the need for identification.

 Explain what Freud meant by the Oedipus and Electra complexes.

► *Ego ideal* says what we should do, *conscience* says what we should not do.

The consequence of all this identification is that the child learns to think, act, and feel like his or her same sex parent. Each child will internalize the values that this parent holds. It will develop a superego. The superego comprises a *conscience* and an *ego ideal*. Conscience is a set of moral principles held by each of us which will punish us with feelings of guilt, shame and remorse for our wrongdoings. Conscience refers to those things we *should not do*. Ego ideal says what we *should do*. It is a mental image of what the parent with whom we identified would do or think under the same circumstances.

The superego is concerned with ideal behaviour. At first the parents are mainly responsible for showing the child what is ideal and what is not. Other important people such as teachers become involved later, until eventually the child has self-discipline and can control its own behaviour, regardless of what its parents would think. The superego monitors the behaviour of the ego, and orders it to pursue certain behaviour and avoid other kinds. In fact it behaves just like the parent, whose job it has taken over.

Summary – Identification

Identification is at the heart of Freud's theory of personality development. It explains how children acquire one of the most important parts of their personalities, their superego.

1 The child experiences (pre-genital) sexual feelings towards its opposite sex parent.

2 The child feels angry about the power its father/mother holds over its life. (Fathers/mothers are powerful, and they possess the object of the child's love, its opposite sex parent.)

3 The ego 'reasons' that if the child becomes more like its same sex parent its same sex parent will want to be with it.

4 Partly to overcome the feelings of guilt about its feelings towards its father/mother, and partly to appear more desirable to its opposite sex parent, the child will want to become like its same sex parent.

5 The child identifies with its father/mother, taking on (internalizing) the same sex parent's ideas, beliefs, attitudes, etc., i.e. their personality.

► *Child-rearing style* refers to the general approach parents have towards rearing their children. Some parents are more authoritarian and use more punishment than others.

6 One aspect of its same sex parent's personality will be that parent's ideas about moral conduct. The child acquires its superego (conscience and ego ideal) from its same sex parent.

Children do develop consciences, but whether they do so as a result of identification used for repressing sexual feelings is far from accepted. Children do learn by identification (among a number of other strategies), but probably not through any association with their genitals.

A number of studies of differing *child-rearing styles* have found that children whose parents use excessive punishment become very careful about what they do; they will try to avoid the punishment. They might be described as having a strong superego. Freud argued that a strong superego was the result of a strong identification. A threatening parent might arouse a great fear of castration, and thus a great pressure to identify strongly. But do children of authoritarian, punishment-centred parents strongly identify with them? A father who uses excessive punishment is more likely to be avoided by the child than identified with. A child cannot identify strongly with someone he tries to avoid!

 What is the superego and how does it come into existence according to Freud?

The behaviourist explanation of moral development

Generally behaviourists are sceptical about the usefulness of punishment in childrearing. **Hans Eysenck** is an exception to this however. Eysenck is a British behaviourist psychologist. He believes that conscience is a set of classically *conditioned emotional responses* (CERs). If a child is punished for some wicked act on a few occasions (trials), the pain or discomfort received from the punishment will become associated with the wicked act that elicited the punishment. The next time the child thinks about performing the wicked act he will also remember the pain and discomfort which the punishment provoked. This should be sufficient to stop the wicked behaviour.

▶ According to Eysenck, CERs are the reflexive, emotional parts of moral behaviour.

Clearly the best time to administer punishment would be just before the child performs the undesirable act, since the anxiety elicited then will be remembered just before the act could occur the next time. Also, any pleasure or reinforcement the child could have gained from its wickedness will be denied, so cannot become associated with the act and encourage the child to repeat it.

▶ In an ideal world we might know when a child is about to commit a wicked act. Unfortunately we often only find out after the act has occurred, if we ever find out at all!

But there is more to moral behaviour than just its reflexive emotional components. Operant learning theory says that children learn their moral behaviour in the same way as they learn anything else – by a process of reinforcement. Any number of studies of child-rearing styles have shown how children who are reinforced for behaving in a compassionate, generous way are more likely to behave in that way again. If children are reinforced for behaving in an anti-social way, they are probably more likely to behave in that way again too.

▶ A reinforcer is anything the actor finds beneficial in some way, which then increases the chances of that behaviour recurring when the opportunity for it occurs again.

Behaviourists do not generally favour the use of punishment, since it really only teaches someone what they should not do, not what they should do. If wicked behaviour goes unreinforced it is likely to extinguish anyway. Unfortunately, the rewards of wicked behaviour may be extremely reinforcing!

▶ Behaviourist psychologists do not advocate the use of punishment since it does not reinforce appropriate behaviour.

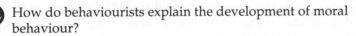 How do behaviourists explain the development of moral behaviour?

Reinforcement and punishment

Reinforcement increases some behaviour.	Punishment decreases some behaviour.
Consistent reinforcement good behaviour contributes to well-being and a positive self-image.	Punishment contributes to for misery and a lowered self-image.
Reinforcement for good behaviour provides positive models with whom to identify.	Punishment provides a system of discipline that children need in order to curb excessively bad behaviour.

The social learning theory of Albert Bandura

In Chapter 2 (pages 25–48) we noted how Albert Bandura and others attempted to reinterpret Freud's concept of identification in behaviourist terms. Identification relies on *observational learning* which consists essentially of observation, imitation and modelling. Children learn appropriate behaviour from the important people they see around them. Perhaps the best known laboratory-based research on observational learning was conducted by Bandura in the 1960s. Bandura has concentrated on aggressive behaviour, but his research also throws light on the modelling of *prosocial* behaviour.

In one experiment a sample of nursery-school children were divided into three groups. Each child in the three groups watched a film of someone behaving in an aggressive way towards a large inflatable rubber doll called a Bobo doll. The adult in the film was seen hitting, kicking, throwing, punching and generally behaving aggressively towards the doll. But each film had a rather different outcome. The first group of children saw another adult approach the aggressor and give him some sweets in return for such a 'good performance'. The second group saw the aggressive adult being smacked for his wickedness. The third (control) group didn't see any reward or punishment being offered.

After observing these performances the children were individually given a Bobo doll of their own to play with. The first group and the control group were equally aggressive towards the Bobo doll. The group who had seen the model being punished were less aggressive. This finding suggests that children are more likely to model behaviour which they see being either reinforced or at least not punished. They are less likely to model behaviour which they see being punished.

Aggression may of course be influenced by factors other than modelling. **Dollard** and **Miller's** 'frustration aggression hypothesis' suggests that frustration leads to aggression. In another experiment by Bandura and his colleagues two groups of nursery-school children were told that they would be allowed to play in a room which was full of attractive toys. One group had seen a film in which an adult was

► *Prosocial* behaviour refers to any behaviour which encourages cooperation and caring.

► Bandura's Bobo doll experiment is an elaborate, highly controlled experiment. The only differences between the children in each group were the outcomes they saw to each film.

► Children will often model behaviour they see around them if it is performed by someone who is attractive or important to them, or who receives some reward for their behaviour.

► *Frustration* refers to stopping or blocking some behaviour which gives rise to those emotional responses which we also call frustration. The emotional response may inspire some further response which will help achieve the goal which is being blocked. Some further responses will be aggressive.

> **Why is observational learning important in socialization?**
> * Learning by watching someone else's achievements is much more efficient than learning by trial and error, or waiting for some reinforcement.
> * Many skills could probably never be learned without observing and imitating. Learning to speak one's language, or to play a musical instrument, or to learn many sports, probably could not be achieved without observational learning.

behaving aggressively towards the Bobo doll. The other group had not. All the children were then told that they couldn't play with the toys after all, the experimenter had changed his mind, and another group of children were to play with the toys instead. The children were shown into a room full of unattractive toys, and a Bobo doll. Those who had seen the film behaved in a much more aggressive way than those who had not. From this finding it seems that it isn't just frustration which causes aggression, observational learning does too.

A number of criticisms have been made of Bandura's research. The experiments are rather artificial. In real life people do not often give grandstand performances of their aggressive behaviour towards inanimate objects and then receive some reward for their aggressive behaviour. People are more likely to be punished for aggression. The children were probably unfamiliar with Bobo dolls, and so may have thought that the adult's behaviour was what you were supposed to do with such dolls. If so they were not behaving aggressively but appropriately. (When a child kicks a ball is it behaving aggressively or appropriately?) But despite the criticisms, Bandura's experiments have been taken to indicate the importance of observational learning in children and adults.

► Showing children films of people doing things with a strange object is rather artificial since the child may not associate the action on the screen with 'real life' at all.

 Explain how Bandura's experiments illustrate the principles of social, observational learning.

 Evaluate Bandura's claims by listing the points which you find convincing and the points which you find unconvincing about his Bobo doll research.

COGNITIVE THEORIES OF MORAL DEVELOPMENT

Piaget's cognitive view of moral development
(For a fuller discussion of Piaget's theory of cognitive development, see Chapter 4, pages 74–8.)

According to Piaget, for the first seven to ten years of its life the child's state of maturation does not permit it to use abstract rules and principles to guide its behaviour. He described this type of thinking as *pre-operational*. The child's thinking is dominated by what things look like, and by externally imposed instructions (from adults). Children of this age can't really 'think for themselves'.

► Below the age of seven Piaget described children's thinking as *pre-operational*, i.e. illogical (at least according to adult rules of logic!).

► Telling stories, asking questions and playing games, are invaluable tools for investigating children's ideas. But children may become shy, or say things that aren't necessarily what they really mean.

► *Heteronymous* means governed from the outside.

► *Autonomous* means controlled from within.

Review – Piaget's explanation for moral development

Moral thinking comes about in the same way as cognitive development generally. Pre-operational children have heteronymous morality, believing that all rules are imposed by an all-powerful authority who determines what is right and wrong, and who will severely punish anyone who transgresses. Children who can think operationally use *autonomous morality* and realize that rules can be changed by negotiation.

Piaget investigated children's responses to moral issues in several ways. He told them stories which involved an issue that could be interpreted in several ways. He played games such as marbles, which had rules that everyone knew, and asked about where the rules came from, and what would happen if we tried to change them. Generally pre-operational children are egocentric and obey rules without question. Children in the *concrete* operations stage are more willing to invent new rules and negotiate changes in existing ones.

Piaget identified two stages in the development of moral reasoning. The stage of *heteronymous morality* (or the stage of *moral realism*) coincides with the pre-operational stage (two to seven years). The child accepts that all rules are fixed by some external authority such as parents, or even God, and that breaking them will lead to immediate and severe punishment. Rules cannot be changed, and have always been the same as they are now. The child believes that all behaviour will be judged by its consequences, regardless of the intentions or reasons for that behaviour. When told a story about two boys, one of whom quite accidentally broke 15 cups, and the other of whom broke one cup while doing something he knew was wrong, the children in this stage judged the first child to be the more wicked since he broke more cups.

From seven to ten years children start to learn that rules can be changed by agreement, or by trial and error. Punishment for wickedness is not automatic since a child who can *decentre* can take other intentions and circumstances into account when making moral judgements. Piaget calls this the stage of *autonomous morality* (or *moral independence*).

Piaget's theory of moral development

Advantages	Criticisms
Children's moral thinking appears to change with age.	Piaget's methods for investigating moral issues are open to question.
Distinct stages correspond to a wider theory of cognitive development.	The wider cognitive theory has been criticised for under-estimating about the ages at which the stages occur.
A link is made between cognitive growth and the adherence to moral rules.	There are different kinds of rules and children respond to them differently at different ages.
A link is made between cognitive development and the ability to make judgements.	Other research shows that children as young as three can take motives into account if the motives are explained to them.

(NM) Outline Piaget's explanation for moral development.

Lawrence Kohlberg's cognitive view of moral development

Piaget's main findings were set out in his book *The Moral Judgements of the Child* published in 1932. Twenty years later **Lawrence Kohlberg** set out to retest, refine and extend Piaget's ideas. Kohlberg told children and adults stories involving moral dilemmas.

In each story there is a choice to be made between some authority and some 'deserving' individual who is being unfairly treated. Possibly the best known example concerns a man whose wife was very close to death from a particular type of cancer. A new kind of radium had been discovered by a local chemist and the husband tried desperately to buy some, but the chemist was charging much more than the husband could afford. The husband explained that his wife was dying and asked if he could have the drug now and pay the rest of the money later. The chemist refused, replying 'I discovered the drug, and I'm going to make money from it.' The man was desperate to save his wife, so later that night he broke into the chemist's laboratory and stole the drug.

Kohlberg then asked a series of questions such as 'Should the husband have stolen the drug?', 'Why?', 'What should happen to him?', 'Would it have been different if the woman had been a very important person?', 'Should the chemist have refused to sell the drug?', 'Should the police arrest the chemist for murder if the woman died?' Some of the children and adults said that theft is wrong, and that the husband should be punished severely. Others said that theft is wrong, but that the man should receive a moderate punishment since he was trying to care for his wife.

► A dilemma is a problem which has two or more possible solutions, neither of which is totally satisfactory.

► In this story there is a clear dilemma between not doing something illegal, and possibly letting someone die, and doing something illegal, and saving a loved one's life.

Kohlberg's levels of moral development

After asking many subjects questions from a series of similar moral dilemmas such as that just described, Kohlberg identified three distinct levels in the development of moral reasoning, with each level comprising two stages. People generally progress through these levels in the order in which they are presented here. However, the stage or level each person reaches can vary greatly according to when they reach it or whether they reach it at all.

Level One

The level of preconventional morality (up to teens approximately):

Stage 1   Younger children are only concerned with the outcome of behaviour and are unable to take motives into account. Their main preoccupation is avoiding physical discomfort, i.e. punishment.

Stage 2   Older children make judgements according to what gives them, or their favourite people, pleasure.

Level Two

The level of conventional morality (13–16 years approximately):

Stage 3   Young teenagers are keen to win approval from others (some kind of 'psychological reward'), so their judgements take into account what they think will make them popular.

Stage 4   Many rules exist which must not be disobeyed or punishment will certainly follow. Others can be negotiated. The young person will often be 'good' in order to avoid psychological discomfort such as guilt.

Level Three

The level of post-conventional morality (16–20 years approximately):

Stage 5   The interests of the wider community are becoming recognized, and sometimes may have to be put before the interests of the individual. The principle of 'the greatest good for the greatest number' may be employed in reasoning moral issues. Ideas about justice and fairness, democracy and what should happen become more usual.

Stage 6   The deepest religious and philosophical reasoning occurs here, and few people ever reach this stage. The individual conscience develops from a conviction that one must be true to oneself and one's own standards.

It is quite likely that some people will be reasoning at the third level by the time they are 20 years old. Some 60-year-olds may never progress beyond level two.

Further researches into moral reasoning, including some by Kohlberg himself, have found little evidence for stage 6 among the general population. It may not be a general stage at all, but accessible only to certain great thinkers. There may even be special stages beyond stage 6.

Criticisms of Kohlberg's view

Kohlberg is accused of telling rather unrealistic dilemma stories which have little to do with his subjects' real lives and have no personal consequences for them. Perhaps if the children could actually be involved in the stories their reasoning might be quite different. It is quite likely that being exposed to people who reason at higher levels might contribute to cognitive structures needed to reason at that level oneself.

Nor do these stages necessarily exist in all societies. And there may be differences between the sexes in any one society, since boys and girls are often socialized to have different expectations.

► Kohlberg's methods are criticized for being too distant from the listeners' own experiences for them to give thought out answers. Anyway, what people say and what they actually do aren't always the same. There may be cultural bias in the research too, because what is a morally correct resolution in one culture will not be so in another.

 How does Kohlberg's explanation of moral development differ from Piaget's?

 Devise a story which poses a moral dilemma. Use it as Kohlberg used his story with some children, or repeat Kohlberg's research.

Summary – Moral development

Freud sees moral feelings resulting from identification with our same sex parent as a part of the resolution of Oedipal or Electral conflict. Eysenck believes moral behaviour is learned in exactly the same way as all other kinds of behaviour, through the process of reinforcement.

In an attempt to combine the best parts of psychoanalysis and operant theory, Bandura sees a role for observational learning from influential models in explaining children's moral behaviour and attitudes. Piaget identified heteronymous morality coinciding with the pre-operational stage, and autonomous morality emerging from the formal operational stage. Kohlberg identified six stages in three levels of reasoning which develop throughout life.

DEVELOPMENT OF SELF AND SELF-ESTEEM

Self, or *self-concept*, is a psychological term which loosely refers to what we know about ourselves. Our sex, age, height, personality, and our likes and dislikes are all part of our self-concept. **Michael Lewis** and **Jeanne Brooks-Gunn** distinguish the *existential self* – the sense of knowing about being different and separate from others – from the *categorical self* – knowing our age, sex, height, personality, likes and dislikes, etc. Young babies have no idea about either of these 'selves'.

During the first couple of years babies have to learn that they are separate from all the other people and objects around them. By about two years of age children can refer to themselves by name, and soon start using 'my', 'mine', 'yours', etc. They learn about their bodies, and what they look and feel like. They are learning their existential self. They will also learn to talk about their categorical self, describing themselves as 'a girl', or 'a child'.

By three years most children have some ideas of categorical and existential self and can identify themselves in photographs, will refer to themselves and their possessions accurately, and will know what other familiar people are called, and something about them.

One ingenious technique for investigating the emergence of existential self involves letting a baby watch its own image in a mirror. At first the baby will try to touch, smile at, and generally interact with the image. After a while the investigator distracts the child long enough to place a dab of cosmetic make-up such as lipstick on its nose. The image the baby sees now is clearly different from the previous one. If the child does not show surprise at the new mirror image then it can't know that either of the images was itself. It hasn't developed existential self. If the child looks surprised, and perhaps reaches to touch its own nose, then it must recognize itself as the image in the mirror, and must have some idea of existential self. Up to about 15 months of age very few babies show surprise at the changed image or attempt to touch their nose. By 20 months about 25 per cent do. Between 20 and 24 months this rises to 75 per cent. Lewis and Brooks-Gunn found that during the last few months before their second birthday children pay more attention to any sources of information about themselves, such as video tapes and photographs, and are generally more interested in themselves!

During their third year, and as they acquire language, children begin comparing themselves to others, and enjoy talking about the categorical differences they observe. In this way, they develop their categorical self. Sex and size are two easy points of comparison. Big

▶ *Self-concept* is the general idea that we each have about the kind of person we are. Write down ten statements answering the question 'Who am I?', and you'll have described your self-concept.

▶ *Existential self* and *categorical self* are two aspects of the self-concept which develop during the first few years.

▶ An ingenious experiment using a mirror for testing for existential self in babies shows that self-recognition and interest in oneself occurs from around two years.

▶ Self-esteem refers to our judgement of our own worth. Are we truthful, honest, trustworthy, reliable, etc.? Self-esteem appears to be the result of socialization.

people are seen as having power over small people. Age is also used, although as Piaget has shown, children judge age by appearances, so mistakes occasionally occur. The earliest distinctions are between 'children' and 'adults'. Given the choice, children prefer the company of adults.

Apart from their existential and categorical selves we also know that children develop evaluations of their own worth – self-esteem – which they at times prefer to keep private. Parents sometimes refer to their children positively (as 'clever girl' or 'kind boy') and sometimes negatively (as 'wicked boy' or 'stupid girl'). These evaluations will influence the child's self-esteem. High self-esteem (a positive self-concept) will increase a child's confidence and desire to interact socially, to become inquisitive and develop its cognitive skills, and to become independent. Low self-esteem can inhibit the child's confidence and willingness to participate socially. Between the ages of three and five children develop a private as well as a public sense of themselves that other people do not see. Freudians see a potential source for anxiety and repression here that could seriously inhibit personality growth

As children grow their ability to categorize themselves by what they do, as well as what they are, increases. Asking a four-year-old 'Who is the little girl who goes to playgroup?' may elicit the answer 'Me'. Asking the same child 'Who is the little girl who goes to school?' may confuse the child. Since she does not go to school she can't be 'the little girl' referred to in the question. She is unlikely to be able to say, 'It can't be me because I don't go to school.' As the child passes through school a third system of categories, what we like and dislike, is added. 'Who is the girl who goes to school and likes Jonathan Calvert, but dislikes apples?' could be answered differently by two 10-year-olds, depending on their feelings about the young man and apples!

Categories of self

Early categorization depended on observable physical features such as age, size and sex. As we move towards adulthood the categories of self become more complex and include feelings, likes and dislikes,

---

REVIEW – Self

Our ideas about our 'self' start with a knowledge of our own existence, develop into a knowledge of who and what we are publicly, and finally include a knowledge of what we are like. This knowledge may be essentially private, although it is greatly influenced by how our parents have socialized us. The level of self-esteem can affect children's performance in many things.

Self-esteem

In the 1950s and 1960s **Stanley Coopersmith** conducted a longitudinal study of children from 10 years to early adult life. He tested them several times, using questionnaires about how they felt about themselves, about their family, their work, etc. He found some who had high levels of self-esteem, and others with less liking for themselves and their relationships. Those with lots of friends who were doing well at school were more likely to describe themselves as having high self-esteem.

He also found a positive relationship between children who had high self-esteem and children whose parents also felt good about themselves. The parents were warm and supportive towards their children and treated them as responsible individuals who were rewarded for their successes and encouraged not to fail. The parents with high self-esteem were genuinely interested in their children and encouraged them to have and share their opinions with others. The moral is, if you want to have children with high self-esteem, start improving how you feel about yourself!

hopes and fears, and ambitions and expectations. This conforms to Piaget's predictions that younger children need concrete features which they can observe, while older children use more abstract ideas.

Children's public and private thinking about themselves reflects these changes too. Younger children who have the highest self-esteem think they are doing well in school and have a large number of friends. The modern psychoanalyst Erik Erikson described the achievements of this stage as 'industry versus inferiority' (see pages 35–7). Those who were doing well would feel that they measured up well against their friends, and so their self-concept and self-esteem improve. This would prepare them well for the potential identity crises of adolescence.

▶ Piaget's view of the stages of cognitive development are outlined in Chapter 4, pages 74–80.

Summary – Emergence of self

Age	Sense of self
0–1	None
1–2	Existential
2–3	Existential and categorical
3–5	Existential, categorical and private

 How does the child's self-concept change as it grows?

DEVELOPMENT OF GENDER ROLES

One aspect of self is one's sex identity. This is the knowledge that children acquire about what sex they are. Young children are not cognitively mature enough to realize that their sex has certain biological implications about their future behaviour, or that their sex won't change as they grow. Learning the appropriate *gender role* will take a few years. One's sex is a biological fact, a consequence of the mix of X and Y chromosomes received from each parent at the moment of conception. One's gender is a product of *socialization*. Historically in the West boys have been seen as the future 'breadwinners' who should behave in an authoritative, logical and emotionless way. Girls have been seen as weak, indecisive and dependent upon others.

Supporters of each side of the nature–nurture debate have looked for evidence for their view from studies of males and females from many cultures. We review evidence for the two claims below.

 List four things about yourself which you have acquired through socialization, and four which result from genetic inheritance.

The nature claim: instincts and genes

During pregnancy, and with post-natal maturation, various hormones are released which affect male and female body and brain structures. The *androgens* affect males by controlling the onset of puberty, the growth spurt, biological fertility and so on. The *oestrogens* are important female hormones which control the timing of

▶ Hormones are chemical messengers which are released into the bloodstream by some of our glands to instruct various body organs to function in some way.

biological maturity and menstruation. It could be that these, and other hormones, also affect psychological development. Both sexes have androgens and oestrogens, males usually having more androgens and females more oestrogen.

Some studies by **John Money** and his colleagues have been made of girls whose mothers received excessive amounts of androgens during pregnancy (to reduce the likelihood of miscarriage). The babies developed androgenital syndrome. As they grew they tended to be more aggressive and 'tomboyish', and less feminine. They preferred male activities with male company, and expressed more interest in a career than in having a family.

Bowlby claimed that females have a maternal instinct to have, and care for, their young. In most societies childcare roles are mainly performed by females. If gender roles are genetically transmitted then it seems reasonable to imagine that any differences between the sexes would appear soon after birth, they would be the same in all societies, and they would probably appear in the higher primates such as gorillas and chimps too.

► Male babies are generally heavier, more active, more irritable, less easy to manage, and more susceptible to illness and disease than girl babies. They are also slightly less likely to survive into middle childhood.

There are differences between male and female infants. On average boys are heavier, more active, more irritable, more demanding, less hardy, sleep less well and are less easy to comfort than girls. On average girls are walking and talking before boys. Over the next few years these differences largely disappear and there's no evidence that these early differences explain future gender role behaviour. Also there are wide individual differences within these group averages. Some boys will be more intellectually and socially advanced and easier to raise than some girls. On balance, by puberty, the two sexes are equally sociable, have similar levels of self-esteem, and are similarly motivated towards achievement.

► Most lower order animals rely on instinct and simple association learning (see Chapter 2). Humans may also have instincts and learn by association, but rely much more on their perceptions, cognition, prediction of outcome, etc.

In all societies sex differences in behaviour can be seen by about two years. However, humans aren't simply the prisoners of their hormones. We have cognition and can make predictions. If you have something that I want, and I know that you are bigger, stronger and more aggressive than I am, then fighting you does not make good sense to me. An animal in this position might leave and try its chances elsewhere. However, being human, I might try to think of some way to outwit you, or may have a position whereby I can outrank you, or I may be able to appeal to your sense of fairness or justice. Because I have knowledge and understanding, intelligence and communication skills I can control my own behaviour. My gender-related behaviour will be determined by my higher cognitive brain centres too, and not by simple responses to biological urges. Studying animals is of limited value to understanding the psychology of human gender role behaviour.

► Testosterone is one of the main androgens. Altering the amounts of the opposite sex's hormones will cause changes in an animal's behaviour. Hormones are concerned in sex-linked behaviour.

The influence of sex hormones on animal behaviour is considerable, and has been demonstrated several times. **W.C. Young** experimentally demonstrated the effects of hormones. Every day from the 42nd to the 122nd day of the pregnancy he injected a pregnant monkey carrying a female foetus with the male hormone testosterone. After birth and during its life the female acted more like a male monkey acts. It was more assertive, challenging others for a place in the group, and it was more independent. When mature it even tried to mount another female for mating. Numerous experiments with lower order animals have shown that altering the androgen and oestrogen levels affects the extent of sex-linked behaviour. Increasing oestrogen levels in males produces behaviour more typical of females, while increasing testosterone in females produces more 'male like' behaviour.

Evidence links sex hormones to certain kinds of aggression, and aggression is a predominantly male phenomenon. (The androgenous females in the experiments mentioned above usually started fights with their non-androgenous sisters.) This is not to say that females aren't capable of acts of aggression too, for example in defence of their young. However, the environment also influences the amount of hormones released. Monkeys who won their battles against challengers seemed to produce more testosterone than they had before, while the levels of hormones in those who lost their fights went down.

► The level of hormones can affect an animal's behaviour, but the consequences of its behaviour can also affect its hormone levels.

(NM) Summarize the nativist explanation for gender role behaviour.

The nurture claim: socialization

Differences in socialization
Each culture has evolved roles which it expects its members to play. Children learn their roles from the influential models they observe around them, particularly parents. If the two sexes are treated differently, and have different expectations made of their behaviour, then they will learn to behave differently. Parents do treat their daughters differently from their sons, and differences in the children's behaviour can be seen from a very young age. Boys may be regarded by parents as more robust than girls, and so are more likely to be offered rough and tumble type play. Girls are more likely to receive cuddles and gentle treatment.

► As societies change, the roles expected of its male and female members will also change. Changes in the role of women during this century in the West, for example, have been dramatic.

In 1978 **Beverley Fagot** studied 24 American families, each with a child between 20 and 24 months old. She visited each family five times, observing parents interacting with their child for an hour on each visit. She was looking for examples of the kind of behaviour parents encouraged and discouraged in their sons and daughters.

► Fagot's study is a naturalistic observation study since it took place in the children's home environment.

Girls were encouraged to ask for help when it was needed, to follow and stay near to a parent, to dance, to take an interest in girls' clothes, and to play with dolls. They were usually discouraged from running around, jumping, climbing, and generally being too active, being aggressive and playing 'rough' games, and generally manipulating and exploring objects.

Boys were encouraged to play with and explore toys such as trucks and building blocks in an active, manipulative way which would help build strong muscles. They were firmly discouraged from playing with dolls, from asking for assistance and from anything the parents considered 'feminine'.

► Fagot observed clear differences in the expectations parents have of their boys and girls. Boys are encouraged to be independent and assertive. Girls were encouraged to be passive and dependent.

The two sexes were not treated equally in what they were discouraged from doing. Boys who started any 'female' activities were more

► Goldberg and Lewis's study is an example of controlled observation. They found that 13-month-old toddlers have ideas about what they prefer to play with, and these represent sex role stereotypes.

severely criticized than girls who played in a 'masculine' way. It seems that parents will tolerate their daughters being independent and assertive occasionally. They will not tolerate their sons being passive and dependent.

Goldberg and **Lewis** interviewed the mothers of 32 male and 32 female six-month-old babies to discover any differences in how the boys and girls were treated. When they were 13 months, and toddling, the babies and their mothers attended a laboratory containing a chair for the mother, and nine toys. Some of the toys, like drums, encouraged active or noisy play. Others, like dolls, encouraged more passive and quiet play. When the child had settled in the play room it was put onto the floor where it could investigate the toys. The mothers were to behave 'normally'. Their and their babies' activities were recorded for 15 minutes. Girls tended to choose quieter toys and play nearer their mothers, involving her in their games. Boys tended to choose more active toys and appeared more independent.

Summary – Goldberg and Lewis' observations

	Reactions to play	Reactions to mother
Girls	Preferred quieter toys which were played with or near to mother.	Seemed more dependent, enjoying involvement and conversation.
Boys	Preferred bigger, noisier toys or those which could be investigated in detail.	Generally more independent or less socially skilled. Played away from their mothers.

► Goldberg and Lewis' 'frustration response' study is a controlled experiment. An independent variable, the barrier, is being manipulated, and the children's reactions to it (the dependent variable) are being observed.

► Goldberg and Lewis claim that socialization, not genetic factors, is more involved in explaining their results.

In another play session Goldberg and Lewis tested the children's responses to frustration. They waited until each child was separated from its mother, and quickly raised a see-through barrier between them. The mothers were instructed not to go to their child immediately, but to wait and see what it would do. The girls generally approached the barrier, looked at their mothers through it and, presumably realizing their way was blocked, started to cry. The boys tended to approach the barrier, explore it to see if there was any way through or around, and only then begin to cry.

Combining their earlier interviews and observations with the observations that were used during the experiment at 13 months, Goldberg and Lewis were able to draw some conclusions about the effects of child-rearing on gender role behaviour. Girls had been treated more gently than boys. They were more likely to have been breast fed when younger. They were more likely to be picked up and cuddled, and the amount of time they were held was longer than for boys too. They were spoken to in a softer tone of voice. Boys were generally treated more robustly. Goldberg and Lewis felt that these differences would have explained some of the differences in the boys' and girls' behaviour at 13 months.

Cross cultural evidence
If gender roles were biological in origin then we would expect that males and females everywhere would have similar roles and

Margaret Mead's anthropological studies for gender roles

The Arapesh were a poor, gentle, cooperative people. All jobs, including childcare, were shared equally by husband and wife. The children too were treated with respect. Aggression was virtually unknown in either sex. They were a humble, caring, loving people.

Among the Tchambuli, women socialized their male children to be artistic, creative and sentimental. The adult males would sit around the village gossiping, making themselves look pretty, and arranging entertainment for the women. The women took the lead in all matters. They were competitive, efficient and conducted all the tribe's trade and commerce. The men's lives revolved around the women except in times of war.

Among the Mundugumor tribe's males and females, both adults and youngsters, were aggressive, argumentative and suspicious of everyone else. They were forever spying on each other, making alliances and truces, and fighting. Children were not welcomed since they might form alliances against one of their parents. The wives tended to rear their sons, and the fathers their daughters. Both parents gave as little attention as possible to their children, and the children learned that they had to fight for everything they wanted.

expectations. In the 1920s and 1930s Margaret Mead conducted some anthropological research among various peoples living in the Pacific region. She found dramatic differences in the ways boys and girls were treated, and in the personalities and behaviour of the adults which appeared to result. In one society there were no gender differences in the behaviour of the two sexes, in another the most usual sex roles were reversed, with women being dominant. Although Mead's research has been criticized for sometimes relying on second-hand reports which may have been exaggerated, she does provide some evidence that gender roles result from childhood social experiences.

▶ Anthropologists study the group behaviour of societies or cultures of people.

Children socialize children

It's not just adults who provide their children with models for appropriate gender role behaviour. Other children do too. **Michael Lamb** studied three- to five-year-old boys and girls playing with a variety of toys. When the children played with their toys in a 'sex appropriate way' the games were inventive and enjoyable. If a child picked up a toy which its same sex peers thought was a 'cross sex' toy (e.g. if a boy started to play with a doll) then they would be very critical and the doll would soon be rejected as the child rejoined its same sex peers.

▶ Lamb's observational study shows that same sex peers are a source of approval and disapproval for children as young as three and four.

Androgenital syndrome

One final item of evidence to support the view that gender roles are learned comes from studies of a small number of androgenital syndrome (AGS) females who were mistakenly identified as boys when they were born, and the mistake went undiscovered for some time. (The infant female's genital organs looked like those of an infant male.) John Money found that if the error was realized before the child was about 18 months old, then appropriate surgery and changing the way the child was being socialized produced no major

▶ AGS (androgenital syndrome) can result in the wrong decision about the girl's sex being made. Some girls have been raised as boys for the first few years of life before the error is realized.

► A child whose genotype is female will always be female. She will obviously not be able to function sexually as a male.

► Gender roles are the roles that people in society expect of us. Money's study suggests strongly that these roles are the result of socialization. However the children studied were having hormone treatments as well as changed socialization.

problems for the girl. If the error wasn't discovered until the child was three years or over, then there could be serious problems.

Money reported the case of one girl who was thought to be a boy until she was three and a half years old. The parents decided that the risk to the child's personality of changing its sex and gender back to female was simply too great, and the decision was taken to continue to raise the child as a boy. With appropriate surgery and hormone treatment the 'boy' continued to behave like a boy, joining in with the other boys' active play, and taking a sexual interest in girls, etc.

Money also reports the case of a seven-month-old identical twin boy whose penis was damaged by faulty equipment during circumcision. Since he wouldn't be able to function as a male it was decided to make him into a girl. At 17 months he had surgery, and a course of hormone treatment began. With 'female' socialization the child soon started behaving like most other girls in Western society. By the age of five the differences between the twins was considerable. The 'daughter' enjoyed feminine things such as playing with dolls, having her hair brushed and her face washed. She disliked being dirty, moved carefully and gently, and spoke softly. If gender roles were determined by innate forces then such a change in behaviour would not have been possible since this child was genetically male.

 Take your notes on the nativist explanation for general role behaviour and write a corresponding set for the nurturist explanation.

Summary – Gender roles

Nativists claim that hormones and instincts are largely responsible for gender role behaviour. Maturation leads to sex differences in the way children behave appearing by about two years. However, we have higher cognitive centres which influence our voluntary behaviour.

According to nurturists socialization is vital to acquiring gender behaviour. In our own society parents tend to treat their sons and daughters differently, and have different expectations of them, from a very early age. Mead's cross-cultural studies show clear evidence of each sex being treated differently from the Western norm, and their adult personalities being very different from Western ones. Studies of children whose sex has been changed after a few years also show that a new personality can develop as a result of changed socialization and hormone treatment.

ACHIEVEMENT, APPROVAL AND AFFILIATION

In many societies parents would like their children to become independent, hard working and self-reliant. Piaget argued that children appear to be innately prepared to want to master their environment, since most actively explore and manipulate it without needing much adult encouragement. Social learning theorists see learning by observation as a major feature of childhood. If children model their behaviour on competent adults then they are likely to become self-reliant and independent, and inspired to work hard and achieve their goals.

Achievement and approval

Any observer of children will confirm that some are more 'achievement oriented' than others. Some ask more questions, appear more studious, try to do well in lessons, take a lead in suggesting and organizing activities etc. Psychologists are interested in measuring the extent of achievement motivation in children, and in discovering any conditions which make one child try to acquire and make good use of information, while another will be more passive and unimaginative.

The first attempts to measure achievement motivation were made by **Henry Murray** and his colleagues during the 1930s and 1940s. They developed the Thematic Apperception Test (TAT), which comprised 30 black and white pictures, each showing some action or event which subjects could interpreted in one of several ways. The subjects were asked to study each picture and to write a short story which explains what is happening. They were to use their imaginations and write a dramatic and exciting tale. These stories were then interpreted by several 'judges' to see if they agreed on whether the subject was excessively aggressive, timid, optimistic, had a need for achievement or showed other aspects of personality.

A decade later **McLelland** and his colleagues attempted to improve Murray's methods by providing a score from TAT reports that is supposed to reflect each person's need for achievement and success. Inevitably such methods are highly subjective, and their conclusions cannot be accepted as entirely valid.

> ► *Achievement motivation* or 'need for achievement' is a personality variable which describes the extent to which each person feels the need to meet some inner and outer standards of excellence.

> ► One TAT picture showed a young man in a check shirt resting his head on his hand and looking slightly worried. One subject said he was taking an examination and couldn't remember a particular point. If he can't recall it he would be angry. Another said he was thinking about a career as a doctor and he could see himself as a great surgeon performing an operation.

Projective Testing

Projective tests usually involve stimuli which the subject has to describe and thereby supposedly reveal their attitudes, beliefs and desires. Sometimes these are otherwise meaningless shapes, and sometimes scenes of social activities. The Thematic Apperception Test (TAT) is type of projective test of 30 black and white pictures each showing some event or situation. Subjects are asked to study each picture and write a short story to say what is happening. Users of TAT believed that interpretations revealed the subjects' psychosocial make up. Few people now accept that the TAT is a valid measure of personality.

 What is meant by achievement motivation?

Susan Harter developed a 28-point self-rating scale which allows children to assess their cognitive, social and physical competence, as well as their general worth. She gave this scale to over 2000 American schoolchildren and found that different levels of self-esteem were established by the time the child was eight years old. She also found

> ► According to Harter's American study, by the time children are eight they have some clear idea about how competent they think they are in several areas of their lives.

► Parental involvement in their young child's socialization can have tremendous influences on the child's self-confidence and self-esteem, which are closely linked to the need to achieve.

► *Intrinsic* refers to motivation (motivation literally means 'to move') which comes from within us.

► *Extrinsic* motivation refers to those 'movers' which come from outside us.

► Our socialization and maturation combine to create in each child the extent of its internal or external orientation.

► *Learned helplessness* refers to an unpleasant state from which there appears to be no chance of escape, e.g. you may be convinced that you will not be able to answer some test questions. Once learned, the response will be given every time the situation in which it was first learned appears, so you will think yourself unable to answer questions in subsequent tests.

that the degree of self-esteem varied according to what area of competence was involved. Children could have a high self-esteem in social activities and a low one in academic or cognitive competencies. She also found that the children's assessments of themselves were fairly accurate, or at least they were shared by their teachers and friends.

Harter suggests that children's need to achieve could be caused by either, or both, of two factors. One is because they feel a personal need for mastery of some skill or other. They have a sense of achievement which they find pleasing. Children who have these personal needs are said to have an *intrinsic orientation*. The other factor is to achieve some external reward such as praise or money, or a special treat. Mastering a skill will result in something pleasant happening. This is called *extrinsic orientation*. Harter claims that those who are more intrinsically motivated will achieve more, because they enjoy challenges and see themselves as competent at meeting and overcoming them. So where do high levels of intrinsic motivation come from? The evidence suggests that the state of maturation is important during the early stages, but social experiences soon take over.

A child who crawls, walks and talks early, who is more alert and has well-developed senses, will have more opportunities to explore and manipulate its world. And parents who are responsive to the child's needs, who put the infant's needs first, and who offer a warm and secure attachment to their baby, will have children who are more confident in exploring their environment and less dependent on adult intervention. The home itself must involve objects and events which will stimulate the child and offer it opportunities for investigation and experimentation. There's no point in having parents who encourage exploration if there's little new to investigate. Several longitudinal studies have found positive correlations between the variables 'stimulating homes' and 'academic and social success in later schooling'.

Weiner argues that people tend to explain the consequences of their behaviour with reference to 'internal' or 'external orientations'. Those who have a high need to achieve tend to see success as being achieved by them personally, through their own efforts. They are *internally oriented*. Those who are *externally oriented* tend to hold the situation responsible for whatever happens. Such people are described as having high levels of *learned helplessness*.

Dweck identified two groups of children, one being 'mastery oriented', the other having high levels of learned helplessness. The first group took responsibility for both their successes and their failures, each being explained by their own effort. If they failed they were determined to do better next time. The learned helplessness group blamed the situation, the tasks, bad luck, or anything other than themselves for their failures. They were more apathetic and didn't see the point of trying harder, since the 'tasks were too difficult', or 'luck was against them'. Some studies have encouraged children to blame their own lack of effort, and not external factors, for their failures, and this has led to improvements in effort and success among those children who possess the intelligence or skill to do the tasks.

Children seek adult approval. Parents who approve of achievement encourage their children to want to achieve. The desire to succeed appears to be even more important to success in school than intelligence. Most of the early work on achievement was conducted on boys since they were imagined to have higher needs for achievement than girls. The pictures in the TAT were mostly of males doing things such as a boy playing a violin, or two men working a machine. Now we know that there are only slight differences between boys and girls. Girls tend to do better than boys in most primary school activities, but boys catch up by about puberty. Girls then consistently underestimate their abilities while boys consistently overestimate theirs. The result is that girls do not always achieve their intellectual potential because they are taught to see achievement in certain subjects, such as science and maths, as less attainable, and possibly even of less value to them.

What sort of parental behaviour is likely to affect the child's need to achieve?

What is learned helplessness?

How might parents and teachers use the findings from studies of learned helplessness to improve a child's performance in particular subjects?

Affiliation

Most people live in groups. We can achieve more by cooperation with others, particularly with people we like. We are born into a family group, we have friendship groups and work groups, we create a new group when we raise a family. Affiliation refers to this process of grouping.

Some of the first groups we choose to make are friendship groups. For the first few years children, whose thinking is egocentric, have very little understanding of what 'groups' or 'friendship' mean, or the feelings and cognitions that accompany them. They 'make friends' and call people 'their friend', but 'friend' is being used more as a description of someone who the child interacts with, rather than as someone with whom they have a more special relationship. Only as children's thinking changes, from around five to ten years, does their understanding and use of 'friend' change. Piaget might have said, they learn to conserve friendship (see pages 78–9).

One of the main researchers into the ways children perceive others is **Robert Selman.** He identified a series of stages through which an understanding of friendships develops:

Stage 0   No understanding. 'Close friends' are the people the child is playing with at the time.

Stage 1   Friends are seen as useful as playmates, serving some self-interest for the child as 'someone to play with'.

Stage 2   Friends serve functions for pleasing each other and will stop being friends when their mutual satisfaction ceases.

▶ In male-dominated societies females have been discriminated against by being denied the opportunities to compete on equal terms with males. The idea that females aren't as good at certain subjects becomes part of that culture's popular consciousness and a stereotype of female inferiority.

▶ Affiliation is defined as 'forming associations involving cooperation, friendship, even love'. For a discussion of affiliation in adulthood see Chapter 8.

▶ *Conservation* is a mental skill which allows someone to know that an object has not changed its true nature simply because some aspects of its appearance have changed.

> ### *Studying friendship using dilemma stories*
> Several techniques have been used for studying how children regard friends, based on Piaget's early 'clinical interviews' and 'dilemma stories'. The following is an example used by Robert Selman:
>
> 'Holly is an eight-year-old girl who likes to climb trees. She is the best tree climber in the neighbourhood. One day, while climbing down from a tall tree, she falls off the bottom branch, but does not hurt herself. Her father sees her fall. He is upset and asks her to promise not to climb trees any more. Holly promises.
>
> 'Later that day Holly and her friends meet Shawn. Shawn's kitten is caught up in a tree and can't get down. Something has to be done right away or the kitten may fall. Holly is the only one who climbs trees well enough to reach the kitten and get it down, but she remembers her promise to her father.'
>
> Children are asked questions such as what the girl in the story should do, who their friends are, why that person is their friend, how long they have had their friend, and who was their best friend before, what should friends do when they disagree, can people have arguments and still be friends, who their enemies are, and why those people are enemies and not friends?

Stage 3   Friends share secrets and confidences, and their friend ship becomes all important.

Stage 4   Friendships are maintained, change or end as new relationships which offer different satisfactions are discovered.

► Circumstantial factors are more important in determining friendships than psychological ones until around puberty.

Up until somewhere between puberty and adolescence most friendships are based on circumstantial rather than psychological factors. Living near to someone who is a similar age to you, who speaks the same language, and is probably the same sex, are the main factors. Friendships are usually made between people of the same age, social group, race and sex.

During later childhood 'psychological' factors become more important. Friends are more likely to be chosen for having similar values. Boys stress the needs for competitiveness and individual achievement, often in activities such as team games requiring skill and physical exercise. Members of the same team often develop close friendships and will close ranks on competitors. Girls emphasize cooperation, sharing and intimacy. While often willing to participate in 'boys' games', their presence is rarely welcomed by the boys, and where it is the girls are used in a lowly capacity, such as 'look out', or 'minding the boys' equipment', or to 'make up the numbers'. Girls' attitudes towards boys are generally more mature than boys' attitudes towards girls.

► Early friendships are based on living close by, being the same age, etc. Later psychological dimensions such as having similar attitudes and values become important.

Kandel conducted a longitudinal study of friendships during adolescence. She assessed the friendship choices, social attitudes and personality characteristics of a sample of American High School students at the beginning of their academic year, and again at the end. She was interested in three categories for each student: who they had stayed friends with, who they had stopped being friends with, and who had become their friend during the year. Those who stayed friends, and the new friends that were added, were found to have similar values, personality characteristics and behaviour as the student being questioned. Among those whose friendships had ended, one or both of them had changed and they were no longer similar. Kandel concluded that similarities in attitudes, behaviour and personality are important in choosing and maintaining friendships, and that friendships are important in socialization. Children who remain friends tend to grow increasingly alike.

 Outline and evaluate Selman's methods for studying children's friendships.

What factors influence the likelihood that children will stay friends?

How are friends important to the socialization process?

ACT Ask some children who their friends are and why each one is their friend. Do any of the factors discussed in this chapter apply?

Chapter summary

Freud claims that moral feelings are learned from our parents through identification. The behaviourists see moral behaviour resulting from reinforcement. Piaget and Kohlberg stress cognitive factors in the growth of moral reasoning in children.

Ideas of existential and categorical self emerge between the ages of one and three years. Self-esteem, which can determine how children perform in many areas of their lives, develops from around five to eight years.

Controversy exists between those who emphasize the importance of biological forces and those who emphasize the importance of socialization in the acquisition of gender roles, each finding supporting evidence. No doubt both are involved.

Achievement motivation is developed as a result of the amount of approval a child receives and the degree of success he or she achieves.

In early childhood, friendships are based on the circumstantial factors which throw children together. Later friends choose each other for the similarities in their beliefs and attitudes. Friends also influence each other so that their beliefs and attitudes are likely to stay similar.

Essay questions – 60 minutes each

1 Contrast Freudian and social learning explanations for the development of a sense of morality in the child.

2 Discuss the cognitive approach to understanding moral development.

3 'Boys and girls are made, not born.' Discuss.

4 Identify some of the main factors in the self-concept and describe their origins.

Further Reading: Chapter 5

For those who like original sources

Piaget J. 1932. *The Moral Judgement of the Child*. London: Routledge & Kegan Paul.

Kohlberg L. 1981. *Essays on Moral Development*. New York: Harper & Row.

Bandura A., Ross, P. & Ross S. 1961. 'Transmission of aggression through imitation of aggressive models', *Journal of Abnormal and Social Psychology* Vol. X Pages 375–82.

Kopp C. & Krakow J., Lewis M. & Brooks Gunn J. (eds) 1982. 'The Development of Self Knowledge' in *The Child: Development in a Social Context*. Addison-Wesley.

Mead M. 1962. *Male and Female*. Harmondsworth: Penguin.

Other useful references include

Run Z. 1980. *Children's Friendships*. London: Fontana.

Schaffer H. 1977. *Mothering*. London: Fontana.

6 _Attention, perception and memory_

Chapter objectives

By the end of this chapter you should:

■ be able to give a review of the major theories of selective attention and the experimental evidence associated with them

■ be able to give an account of perception as a process of organizing information

■ be able to outline, compare and contrast and evaluate the two major psychological models of memory

■ be able to describe and evaluate the major psychological explanations for why we forget.

Introduction

In an instant you can see or hear something, recognize it, and respond to it. This requires cognition. Cognition is the name of the mental process by which we come to know and understand things.

Before any organism can deal with any aspect of its environment it must first become aware of that thing's existence. Humans probably have the most highly sophisticated mental processing system of any animal, but even we can't become aware of everything that surrounds us all the time. We have to pay attention to something before we can fully deal with it. Paying selective attention is the first activity in the _cognitive process_.

Having selectively attended to some stimulus we must take information about it into our perceptual system. We have several sensory or perceptual systems which can provide information about an object, such as what it looks like, sounds like, feels like, etc.

All this information from our perceptual systems may be interpreted according to our memories of previous experiences to help us make sense of the object.

SELECTIVE ATTENTION

No matter how acute our perception is, we cannot pay equal attention to many things at the same time. You may be able to sing and play a keyboard at the same time, you may be able to knit and watch _Neighbours_ on TV. With practice these skills become fairly automatic and don't require great attention. But could you watch two basketball games play at the same time, paying equal attention to both? Or add up your shopping list at the same time as completing a jigsaw? Or do your homework competently whilst plugged into a personal stereo? (If you think you can, you're wrong!) The way humans pay attention

► Human perception has been thought of as a _low capacity_ (can't handle very much), _single channel_ (can only concentrate on one thing at a time) operation by several 'filter theorists'.

has been described as a *single channel* system. Moreover we can't handle too much information in that single channel. We may have a *low capacity* system.

 What is meant by 'a low capacity, single channel' model of attention?

As you are reading these words many things are going on around you. People may be talking, cars may be passing, phones may be ringing, birds may be singing, etc. If you're 'paying attention' to your reading you should be unaware of most of them. That's not to say that you can't hear them, just that you are not attending to them. You can often choose what to pay attention to and what to ignore. Attention must be selective.

Inevitably some stimuli are more likely to be attended to than others. Things which are different from what we know to be the usual level of stimulation are more likely to attract you, so, for example, an unexpected loud noise or flash of light will certainly attract your attention away from your studies. Sudden movement will also attract you, at least until you find out whether it is threatening. Things which you are expecting to see will be quickly perceived, compared to the time it takes to perceive something unexpected. This is an example of *perceptual set*. Even as you are studying your book, other information about your physical condition is being processed in your brain. Are you hungry, warm, comfortable, tired and so on? If you are concentrating you shouldn't be aware of any of them. Only when you stop concentrating, or one of them becomes acute, will your attention switch.

 Describe what is meant by perceptual set.

▶ *Selective attention* refers to the ability many living things have to switch their attention from one stimulus to another.

▶ *Perceptual set* is a term which refers to a state of readiness to respond in a particular way. If you are meeting a friend from a train your perceptual set will make you particularly receptive to the sight of people who look like, and could be, your friend.

▶ A *physiological filter* is a hypothetical idea that some stimuli are decoded sufficiently for their importance to be assessed, and then rejected or 'filtered out', whilst other are 'filtered in'.

Most of the explanations for how selective attention works refer to some kind of a *physiological filter* which allows one source of information through into consciousness, while not allowing other sources through. The theories differ in where and how they see that filter occurring.

The cocktail party effect

The earliest research on selective attention was conducted in the 1950s by **Colin Cherry**. He was interested in what he called the 'cocktail party effect' (which just shows how psychologists pass their leisure time!). If you're at a party where several conversations are happening, and you hear someone mention your name in one of them, you instantly switch your attention from the conversation you are having to the other one. This is the 'cocktail party effect'. But if you are focusing your attention on your own conversation, how did you know someone elsewhere mentioned your name? Cherry wished to investigate the nature of human attention further.

ACT Recall any incidents when you overheard your name being used. Did you 'listen in'? How did what you heard effect your behaviour towards the speakers?

In order to investigate how and why we switch attention Cherry played back tape-recorded material to his subjects, through earphones. Some heard two stories at the same time, through both ears. This is called *binaural presentation*. They found it very difficult to understand either story, even after hearing the tapes twenty times. Others heard two stories, but one story in each ear. This is called *dichotomous presentation*. If asked to concentrate on the story in one ear, this presents no great problem to most people, who were able to describe the story afterwards. Cherry's subjects had to repeat the story they were hearing in one ear as they heard it. This is called *speech shadowing* and has been widely used.

If you are shadowing a story in an 'attended ear', you can't be paying much conscious attention to what's being played in the 'unattended ear'. When both stories were read by the same speaker, subjects could shadow the attended one perfectly, even at considerable speed, but had very little knowledge of the story being played in the other ear. They knew what was being presented was speech, but couldn't even be sure whether it was in English or any other language.

► *Speech shadowing* was used as a measure that the subjects really were attending to the stimuli in one ear rather than the other ear.

► This kind of selective attention research could only be conducted after the invention of the tape recorder and the ability to separate channels through stereoscopic headphones.

NM Explain what is meant by binaural and dichotomous presentation.

Other researchers have modified Cherry's experimental procedures. **Anne Triesman** had the language spoken in the unattended ear changed from English to German, and found that the subjects didn't notice. **Neville Moray** had the same word repeated up to 35 times in the unattended ear while the subjects were shadowing the other ear's message, and the subjects later said they hadn't heard the word at all. But if the voice speaking the unattended ear was of the opposite sex to that heard speaking in the attended ear, or if other sounds than speech were played, then subjects could tell that something different was happening in the unattended ear. This suggests that the subjects could detect the *physical* properties of the unattended sound – its pitch or tone – although they could not process it very deeply for *meaning*. However when Moray presented the subject's name in the unattended ear about one third of the subjects switched attention, i.e. the cocktail party effect operated.

► Early research which claimed that unattended messages aren't heard at all are probably wrong. They are processed for any obvious significance they may have. If they have no significance the message will be lost.

NM Summarize the evidence for our ability to attend to different messages at the same time.

Cherry concluded that the likelihood of the cocktail party effect occurring depends on three main factors: first, how predictable the rest of an utterance was, which was called *redundancy* because if it's highly predictable then we don't need to hear it in order to make sense of the message. Attention could be switched without losing

► Take the sentence 'It's raining, if you're going out, put your ...' The rest can be guessed without being heard. This is an example of *redundancy*.

track of what was being said. Secondly, where the speaker is in relation to the listener is important. If the conversation wasn't too distant it would be easier to eavesdrop. Thirdly, the tone of the speaker's voice is significant. Voices which were muffled or unclear were harder to follow than clear voices.

Some theories of selective attention

Donald Broadbent's early filter theory (1958)

Broadbent's was the first theory to propose the idea of a filter to explain why some stimuli are made conscious while others are not. He suggests the existence of two related systems. The *sensory system* includes each of the senses – sight, hearing, taste, touch, smell, etc. – and exists at the level of the particular sense organ. The sensory system interprets the simple physical characteristics of a stimulus, such as its volume, brightness, temperature, pressure, etc. It can hold many different kinds of stimuli, but for a very short time. The *perceptual system*, which is what we mean by 'consciousness', 'attention' or 'short term memory', is aware of the individual's current state of attention. It 'scans' the sensory system, allowing information relevant to current needs to pass, while anything which is irrelevant is filtered out. Hence Broadbent's is an *early filter* and *single channel model*.

► The *sensory system* is made up of a network of nerves throughout our bodies that carry information to the brain about the state of our sense organs, where information will be decoded and acted upon by the *perceptual system*.

► Broadbent proposed that the 'filter' for deciding which information is to be processed more deeply is based early in the perceptual process. But how can the filter 'know' whether something is important or not until the information has been processed?

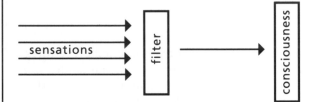

Figure 6.1 Broadbent's early filter model

Unfortunately Broadbent's model cannot explain some aspects of the cocktail party effect, as shown by Moray. If your current needs are for information being shared with the group with whom you are having a conversation, why does attention switch when hearing your name elsewhere in the room? The sound of it should have been filtered out.

Anne Triesman's attenuator model (1963)

If you are concentrating on watching a film or listening to music, you might become quite oblivious to other things going on around you. Your mother may be talking to you, but you may not be aware of what she is saying. Your visual system or auditory system will be dominating your attention. **Anne Triesman** proposed that everything picked up by your senses, including your mother's speech, will be analysed by a filter. If the sounds you are hearing (mother's words) are relevant to your state of awareness (watching a film on TV), then they will pass through the filter for further analysis to see if they are important enough to be paid attention.

► According to Triesman's model everything detected by your sensory system will be decoded for relevance before being accepted or rejected.

By 'relevant' Triesman means that the sounds are of the right pitch and volume, coming from the right place, etc., i.e. the signals are

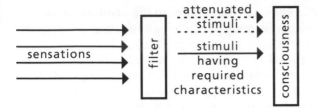

Figure 6.2 Triesman's attenuator model

analysed for their gross physical *characteristics*. Your mother's words may not pass into your consciousness because they are from the wrong direction or of the wrong volume to be coming from the film. Signals which do not pass the first 'channel filter' are *attenuated* (reduced in strength), but are still available for further analysis.

Triesman has conducted numerous experiments to investigate the level at which processing occurs. In one experiment some subjects heard simultaneous messages, one in each ear. They had to shadow the message in the attended ear. The messages had their last few words switched to the other ear. For example, '*Richard and Steven rode their bikes from Devon to Dorset in search of tastes sweeter than all the rest to me.*' might be played in one ear, and '*Marmalade, jam and blackcurrant jelly are all favourites of mine, although I know that honey the camp where they stayed last year.*' If Broadbent's 'early filter' is correct, then the message shadowed will be just as stated, making no sense. If Triesman is correct, and messages are processed for meaning, then the subjects will switch ears in order for their utterances to make

▶ *Attenuation* is the process of reducing the strength of an unwanted signal. The signal is not eliminated altogether.

▶ Most of the research into selective attention has used *dichotomous presentation* (different messages in each ear).

▶ *Binaural presentation* (different messages in both ears) leads to confusion.

The attenuator model and the cocktail party effect

Triesman's proposal	*The cocktail party effect*
Triesman hypothesized that all stimuli received by the sensory system are decoded by the appropriate channel filter for their gross physical characteristics, according to the person's current awarenes	All words which are heard will be filtered to see if they fit the discussion. Those which are coming from the right place, etc., will pass into consciousness.
Those signals which do not pass the 'gross physical characteristics' test may still be important, and are attenuated.	Hearing one's own name being mentioned elsewhere in the room goes for further processing.
Analysis of the contents of words in the secondary filter (the attenuator) for meaning allows important messages to pass into consciousness, thus altering the sensitivity of the first filter.	One's name has special meaning and will become the centre of our attention. The first filter will be set to pass those signals from the place where your name was spoken and all others will be attenuated.

sense. They did. This shows that messages in the unattended ear are still being processed for meaning, even though the subjects are quite unaware of it.

There are two problems with Triesman's attenuation model. First, why bother to have two systems of filter? If messages can still pass into consciousness after first being attenuated, why bother filtering them in the first place? Second, each channel filter must have access to very complex sensory processes in order to decide which signals are relevant and which are to be filtered out, and the attenuator must have access to very high levels of cognitive processing to decide what is relevant to current needs. Quite simply, the attenuator doesn't seem to be very necessary.

 Contrast Broadbent and Triesman's models of selective attention.

Deutsch and Deutsch's pertinence model (1963)

Anthony and **Diana Deutsch** also suggest an attenuator model, but one in which the attenuation is very late in the filtering process. Unlike Broadbent and Triesman who suggest 'early filter theories', Deutsch and Deutsch propose a *late filter theory.* They suggest that all sensations are processed in the brain to quite a high degree. Visual stimuli are recognized as people, houses, etc. Auditory stimuli are recognized as words or other sounds. Further analysis for meaning will only occur if they are *pertinent* (relevant) to whatever you were doing at the time of perception. For example, while engrossed in watching some film, you hear, and possibly recognize, your mother's voice. (The verbal stimulus has been decoded as 'mother's speech'.) Since her voice is not pertinent to your film watching activity, what she is saying is unlikely to be decoded further for its meaning.

▶ A *late filter theory* sees the decision about what to process fully and bring into consciousness as taken quite late in the perceptual process. The sensory stimulus has been decoded for its physical properties and meaning before the decision is made.

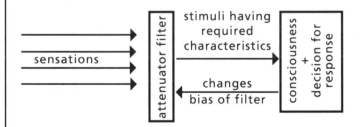

Figure 6.3 Deutsch and Deutsch's pertinence model

There are two main problems with this theory. First, it would seem a rather inefficient use of our cognitive system to have to take in and analyse every item of information which we are capable of perceiving. Evolution has usually provided us with the most efficient way of achieving most things which we can reasonably hope to have. The second problem is more important. There doesn't appear to be any experimental evidence to support the theory! (This is possibly because it would be extremely difficult to operationally define 'pertinence'!)

 How does the pertinence model differ from the other models of selective attention?

Comments on studies of selective attention

There have been numerous experimental studies of selective attention. Most have concentrated on the auditory channel. The reasons for this are that there is a tradition of studying hearing, dating back to Cherry's work, so the techniques are tried and tested. Tape recorders and other experimental apparatus are widely available and inexpensive to operate. And separating the two ears (under headphones) is much easier than separating signals sent to the two eyes, or different parts of the tongue, or different organs in the sense of balance. In any discussion of selective attention, we know more about auditory attention than any other kind.

Review – Selective attention

Selective attention refers to our ability to focus our attention on one source of stimulation, and studies have tried to discover the circumstances under which attention will switch to other sources of information. The first theories saw some filter operating early in the perceptual process, removing all stimuli which were irrelevant to what the organism was doing at the time. Theories which claim that a filter operates later during perception claim that all stimuli are decoded at quite a high level. Both ideas have serious flaws, and the concept of a simple filter operating at a given point in the process of perception and decoding only for physical properties or for meaning is probably far too simple.

PERCEPTION

Perception is simply the name of those processes which take in, and makes some sense of, all the things we see, hear, touch, taste, or are aware of, i.e. our *sensations*. Perception is essential to survival for if we aren't aware that an enemy is approaching to attack us, we have little chance of escaping from it. If we can't recognize our own food, we are not going to be able to eat it!

One fairly recent school of thought within cognitive psychology is known as the *information processing approach*. 'Information' is anything you pay attention to and become aware of, or any idea or knowledge you already have. Information processing means moving towards the goal of being able to make an appropriate response through a series of stages such as perception (seeing something), coding (recognizing it as a source of sensory stimulation), memory storage (searching for whether we have some previous experience of it), retrieval (recognizing it as a known object), and response (taking the appropriate action). The information processing approach is the latest in a long line of analogies that have been used to illustrate how we come to know things.

NM What is perception?
How does the information processing approach regard perception?

► There are said to be five main perceptual senses: sight, hearing, smell, touch and taste. There are also the body senses such as the vestibular sense (sense of head position, speed of movement, and balance) and the kinaesthetic sense (which tells us about the position of the parts of our body in space).

► Although what we perceive is outside us, perception is a mental process that occurs within us. Since we are all slightly different we are all likely to have rather different perceptions.

► The specialized photoreceptors on the retina can only respond to light. They provide us with the sensations of light, shape, pattern and colour.

► Sense receptors pick up a source of physical energy (light, sound, etc.) and transduce (convert) it into an electro-chemical code which can be carried to and decoded by the appropriate specialized area of the brain, such as the visual and auditory cortices.

► *Bottom up* theories say that our perceptual system responds to simple stimuli which need cognitive processing in order to make sense, whereas *top down* theorists claim that we already have the basic principles, such as the ability to recognize depth and distance, required to interpret what we perceive.

► Some of the factors which affect the way we perceive things include: what we want or expect to perceive, how we are feeling generally and especially how we feel about the particular object or event, our age, sex, intelligence and personality, and the likelihood of anything pleasant or unpleasant occurring as a consequence. These factors also influence our memories.

Of the perceptual senses the eyes and ears are undoubtedly the most important since they probably provide the vast majority of all the things we will come to know. Each perceptual sense contains *receptor cells* which respond to a particular, specialized source of stimulation, e.g. the retina of the eye comprises millions of photoreceptor cells called *rods* and *cones* which respond to particular kinds of light. The information received by the receptor cells is decoded by the visual system into our impression of sight.

In the cochlea of the inner ear millions of *hair cells* respond to vibrations caused by movements in the air around us. These air movements are caused by anything which makes a noise, and are decoded into what we 'hear'. So long as a light is bright enough to stimulate enough retinal cells to respond, then we will 'see' something. Similarly, there must be a certain level of sound for us to be able to hear it. The minimum levels of stimulation which we need in order to perceive are called *absolute thresholds*. Most dogs have a higher threshold for sound than people do, i.e. they can hear noises of a much higher frequency than humans.

Organization in perception

There is some disagreement between psychologists about the nature of perception. Some psychologists, such as **James Gibson,** claim that we start off with simple sensations, such as light triggering cells on the retina into action, or sounds causing hair cells in the cochlea to vibrate. This produces 'raw' stimulation, such as shapes and sounds, which need deeper and deeper processing until we finally arrive at an understanding of what the stimuli means to us, e.g. a photograph of a friend or a piece of music. These are *bottom up* theories. Those who support *top down* theories, such as **R.L. Gregory**, claim that we already have some ideas about the nature of the stimuli being perceived, and these ideas or principles influence how we perceive things.

Top down theorists claim that perception is an *active* process. We must interpret and make reasoned guesses about the things we experience. Most of the time our interpretations are correct. Sometimes we may think we've seen or heard something when we actually saw or heard something else. We can be misled into thinking we have perceived something which we have not. In a classic study conducted over fifty years ago, **Carmichael, Hogan** and **Walter** showed two groups of subjects the same set of 12 simple, ambiguous line drawings (see Figure 6.4). Each group was shown different labels for the drawings. For example, group one was told an object was a bottle, the other that it was a stirrup. A crescent moon was also labelled as the letter 'C', while a beehive was also described as a hat. Some time later the two groups were asked to draw the objects they'd seen. In each case their drawing resembled the object described by the label rather than the original drawing they'd seen. This suggests that either our perception of an object is influenced by what we are told it is, or that our memory is influenced by the description when we recall the object later.

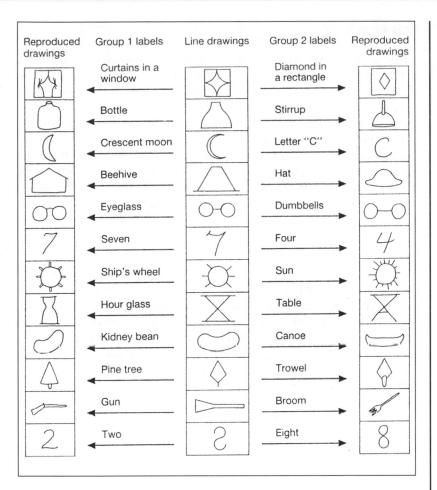

Reproduced drawings	Group 1 labels	Line drawings	Group 2 labels	Reproduced drawings
	Curtains in a window		Diamond in a rectangle	
	Bottle		Stirrup	
	Crescent moon		Letter "C"	
	Beehive		Hat	
	Eyeglass		Dumbbells	
	Seven		Four	
	Ship's wheel		Sun	
	Hour glass		Table	
	Kidney bean		Canoe	
	Pine tree		Trowel	
	Gun		Broom	
	Two		Eight	

Figure 6.4 Carmichael, Hogan and Walter's line drawings study

Some definitions of perception

R. L. Gregory: 'A dynamic searching for the best interpretation of the available data.'

Coon: 'The process of assembling information into a usable mental representation of the world.'

NM Explain how the following factors could affect your perception of your holiday hotel as you arrive after a long journey: your expectations, how you are feeling, your age.

Review – Perception
Perception is the active process of interpreting our experiences so that they make sense to us. Sensations are received by the sense organs, and decoded by the appropriate brain centres. How we interpret those sensations is affected by subject variables such as our expectations, feelings, state of health and fitness, age, abilities, etc.

▶ *Memory* is an essential part of intelligence. Well adapted people with good memories will be able to search their memories in order to make sensible adaptations to their environments.

▶ Amnesia refers to a loss of memory, either due to an inability to process and store information, or to a failure to retrieve previously known information. It can be caused by physiological factors, including old age, accidents, or substance abuse. Or it can be caused by some psychological problem which blocks recall.

MEMORY

Most animals are capable of some kind of association learning. Pavlov and Skinner and countless sheepdog and circus trainers have demonstrated this many times. Human memory is rather more complex. We are able to store information for use at some later date which enables us to make sensible adaptations to our environment and to pass on our knowledge to the next generation.

The term *memory* has three variations of meaning. It can refer to the mental function of processing and storing information which can be recalled later. It is used to mean the storage system which we actually use, and which has been experimentally investigated. And it can mean the actual information which is remembered.

Early studies

Early studies of memory tended to see it as being the result of numerous conditioned responses. Just over 100 years ago **Hermann Ebbinghaus** applied the tools of science to measure his own memory capacity by learning lists of nonsense syllables. Unfortunately, knowing the capacity one scientist had for memorizing meaningless verbal material tells us little about 'normal' human memory concerning things which do have meaning for us.

During the early part of this century most of the research on memory was performed on laboratory animals, patients with *amnesia* – memory loss – or people in specialized occupations such as air traffic control. Some studies identified the physiological existence of a *short term memory store* where attention was paid to various kinds of stimuli (visual, auditory, etc.) for a few moments. Other studies were explaining *long term memory storage* in terms of simple associations between stimuli and responses.

Hermann Ebbinghaus

Ebbinghaus was a German philosopher who decided to apply the principles of experimental psychology being developed by Fechner and Wundt to the cognitive function of memory. He decided to investigate the learning of new information, so he devised lists which altogether comprised 2300 'nonsense syllables', for example, mib, jev, vaf, koj, tuq, sov, roh, pag, lun. He quickly read through the lists on several occasions, always at the same time of day. Each time he recorded exactly how many 'syllables' he could recall. He then measured how long the list took him to learn 'to criterion'. (This means to reach the standard whereby he could recall all the items.) His performance was analysed statistically, comparing it to the previous occasion, and identifying the amount of time 'saved' until he could remember the whole list.

Such an effort shows an enormous dedication to science. After two years of highly original research Ebbinghaus published a book outlining the basic principles of memory, and went on to study other things.

Modern approaches

We now believe that memory is a much more dynamic process. It involves three distinct stages. First, we *perceive* something which is encoded into neural activity. Second, the coded information is *stored* in some way. (The type and duration of different stores will be discussed later.) Third, memory requires *retrieval*; there's no point in storing something unless we can recall it later. However, breakdowns may occur in each of these stages. We may misperceive, and hence store and recall wrong information. Or we may perceive accurately, but the coding process is inadequate so we store the information in the wrong place, or in a mistaken form, so that later recall is confused. Or we may perceive and code the scene correctly, but still fail to recall because of some 'retrieval failure'.

 What are the stages in the dynamic process called memory?

Even this summary sounds as though the job of memory could be performed by a mechanical device such as a computer. Each of the stages is in fact more complex than it seems, and psychologists have hypothesized about what kind of activities are occurring in them. We shall describe in the following pages two of the best known information processing theories: the *two process model* first suggested by **Richard Atkinson** and **Richard Shiffrin** in the 1960s, and the *levels of processing approach* proposed by **Fergus Craik** and **Robert Lockhart** in the early 1970s.

 What is consciousness?

The sensory register

Before we can process information we must first receive it. Cognitive psychologists refer to a *sensory register* where this process occurs.

Humans have many senses which provide them with information about their world. The main ones include the visual sense, the auditory sense, several aspects of the sense of touch, the sense of smell, the taste senses and the senses of balance and body position. Each probably has its own sensory register, although only the visual and auditory senses have been studied in any detail. The sensory register may lie in the system of nerves which links the sense organ with the brain. Broadbent proposed that the first stage in selective attention would be a filter for deciding what should be evaluated and what should be lost, and he called this 'the S (sensory) system'. This would perform similar functions to those performed by the sensory register.

Since information can only be held in the sensory registers for a few moments, new information coming in will displace any already there. Imagine we arrange that you see a photograph of a street scene with people and traffic projected onto a screen for a fraction of a second. Then we keep you in the dark while we ask you some questions about the picture. You should be able to hold the image in

> ▶ *Dynamic* means constantly in a state of change.

> ▶ Regarding memory as a dynamic processor of information is another aspect of the information processing approach.

> ▶ The *sensory register* is a filter for decoding information from the environment, and is the first stage towards achieving consciousness.

> ▶ The sensory register is another way of describing the early filters in Broadbent's and Triesman's models of selective attention.

> ▶ The sensory register decodes incoming information and passes it on for further analysis. It doesn't filter information according to its meaning. Information will be filtered out by being overwritten by new incoming information.

sensory register for long enough for most of it to pass to the short term store and long term store, and so allow you to answer our questions. If we showed you other pictures immediately following the first, then the first picture would be 'overwritten', and wouldn't pass to the other stores. You wouldn't be able to answer many questions about it.

(NM) What is the sensory register?

The first major research into visual sensory decoding was conducted in the late 1950s by **George Sperling**. Sperling had a difficult experimental problem to solve. If people remember some things for only very short periods, how can you find out what they remember if they forget it more quickly than it takes them to tell you about it? Sperling came up with an ingenious solution.

His experiment used an apparatus called a *tachistoscope* to show subjects visual stimuli for one twentieth of a second. He showed them twelve letters in three rows of four. He only asked them to recall four of them. He did this by sounding a tone to indicate which four letters out of the twelve they should announce. A high tone indicated that they should recall the top row, a middle tone the middle row and a low tone the bottom row. He reasoned that if subjects could announce any row of four letters out of twelve then there was a brief period when they could remember all twelve, although that period might be shorter than it would take to say all twelve letters.

The inset shows Sperling's experimental procedure and Figure 6.5 shows some of his results. He found that if the tone was sounded immediately after the presentation of the letters, subjects on average could remember between 3 and 4 of their four letters: the average score was 3.3 letters. He took this to mean that subjects on average could actually remember 9.9 letters out of 12 on the sounding of the tone, but would have forgotten some of them had they had to announce them all. This is shown as a recall of 82.5 per cent on the bar chart in Figure 6.5.

Sperling concluded that his subjects had an afterimage of the display in their minds which they used to recall the letters. The afterimage would quickly fade so that the longer after the tachistoscope presentation the tone was sounded, the fewer of the letters subjects could recall. This is confirmed by the results in Figure 6.5. With a half a second delay between presentation and the sounding of the tone, subjects on average could only remember just over two letters from a row of four, equivalent to an afterimage of just over 6 letters out of twelve, and with a delay of one second they could only remember the equivalent of 5 letters out of twelve. The results in the bar diagram as a whole show the speed at which the afterimage fades.

Sperling's procedure is outlined below, together with a diagram of his results in figure 6.5.

► *Tachistoscopes* are machines which allow people to see particular objects or words, possibly superimposed on various backgrounds, for precisely timed periods from one millisecond (one thousandth of a second). They are widely used by psychologists to test the thresholds of human perception.

► According to George Sperling's research visual sensory registration lasts for about half a second in ideal laboratory conditions, using very simple stimuli which the subjects were told to expect. In 'real life' the duration of sensory registration will be affected by all kind of things including its intensity, importance, novelty, duration, etc.

► The timing of the tone in Sperling's experiment could be changed. It could be sounded just before the presentation, during it, or just afterwards. What differences would you expect this to make?

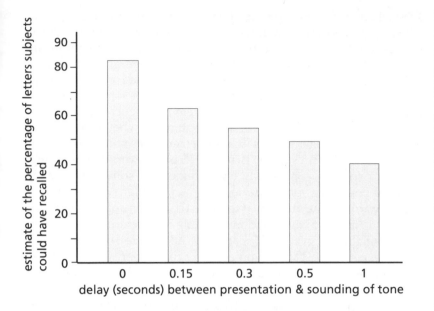

Figure 6.5 Bar chart of Sperling's results

Note: The bar chart shows that the number of letters recalled declines as the delay between presentation and recall increases. Sperling took this to represent the fading of an afterimage of the presentation.

Stage 1	Stage 2	Stage 3	Stage 4
Becoming accustomed to looking into the tachistoscope	Presentation for one twentieth of a second	Sounding of tone §	Recall
	Q F H T Z M K E C B V R	High Medium Low	Q F ...

Sperling's experimental procedure

§ the tone could sound before, during or after the presentation

Atkinson's and Shiffrin's two process model

Short Term Store (STS) for Short Term Memory (STM)

According to the two process model selective attention is paid to some feature in the environment. For example, the fire bell rings while you are concentrating on preparing an essay in the library. The feature will be held for a few moments in a *sensory register* or *store* while decoding, and possibly rehearsal (paying special attention to it), takes place. You recognize it within a second as the fire bell. This sensory register is more a filter for selective attention than an actual process of memory.

Information about the feature which is recognized will be passed on to a *short term store* (STS). This process is the first of the two processes in Atkinson and Shiffrin's *model* and is more or less what we mean when we talk of 'consciousness'. In the STS the coded information about the feature will be further processed for up to 20 or 30 seconds. Its importance may be evaluated in some way. You may ponder, 'Is it a real fire, or is it a drill?'

If it is valuable the information may then pass into *long term store*

► Short term memory (STM) is the memory we use for dealing with everyday experiences. It is what we mean by 'consciousness'.

► A *model* is a hypothetical description of a pattern of relationships observed in nature. It is an untested theory about what something is like from which predictions can be made, which can then be tested. A theory is a more specific attempt to explain the relationship between a limited number of events.

► A *control process* is a strategy we use for directing our knowledge in some way to achieve some greater understanding.

► Retrieval strategies search for information in long term memory to enable interpretation or evaluation of the present contents of STS.

► Memory had not been widely studied since Ebbinghaus's early work. Behaviourist explanations for learning were adapted to explain forgetting.

► Rehearsal is said to be necessary for STS to encode information for storage in LTS. The retention interval for this is only a few seconds. Blocking rehearsal during the retention interval should make recall impossible.

(LTS) where it may last for years. If it doesn't appear to have value, it will simply be lost as new information enters the short term store. Although we talk of two stores, Atkinson and Shiffrin do not mean that they will be in two different locations in the brain. This is only a *model* to characterize the memory process, not a guide to the functions of parts of the brain. Information entering our sensory register depends entirely on what is going on in our environment at the time. We have no conscious control over what enters, or whether it will be processed to any extent. The same is not true of the short term store. Atkinson and Shiffrin suggest that the STS is our everyday 'working memory'. You can consciously try to remember something which will help you solve some puzzle, such as using landmarks to find your way around the unfamiliar town on the first day of your holiday abroad. Listening to conversations, reading an article, playing games or following the story in a TV soap opera all require you to use your *short term memory* (STM). If you couldn't remember what had happened in the last few seconds you would not be able to follow any activity very well!

Atkinson and Shiffrin say the STS contains some *control processes* which enable us to exercise some control. For example, we may choose to *rehearse* some information so that it will be transferred to long term memory. After parking in the multi-storey car park you may say to yourself, 'The car is on Level Four, by the Market Street entrance, down the alley with the café and bridal gowns shop.' This is verbal rehearsal. If you take a look over your shoulder at the alley when you're some distance from it, this is visual rehearsal. Both should help you find your car later. Rehearsal is a *control process*.

Another example of control processes are the *retrieval strategies* we employ to find relevant information in our long term stores (LTS) which will help us decide the importance of the information currently in STS. When all the processing and 'coding' are finished, decisions are made in STS about any action which may be required. After your shopping trip you look down the left-hand parade in the precinct, and see a bridal gown shop. Is this the way to the car? STS searches LTS for other clues which might confirm or reject the possibility. You might look down the right-hand parade to see if there's more than one bridal gown shop. In almost conscious consultation with LTS, our STS makes a decision, and we behave accordingly.

 Describe the role of the STS in Atkinson and Shiffrin's two process model of memory.

STS can process information very quickly, but it can only process a few items of information at a time. This was confirmed independently in the late 1950s by **J.M. Brown** in England and **Lloyd** and **Margaret Peterson** in America. They were actually investigating forgetting rather than memory and the technique they devised demonstrated, really for the first time, that short and long term storage could be seen as two processes within memory. Until then researchers investigating the process of forgetting were either behaviourists

---

The duration of sensory registration

Things which we look at, e.g. objects around us, exist *in space* and can always be looked at again if we need more information about them. We've all had something 'catch our eye', and paused to 'have a second look'. We take in so much through our eyes it wouldn't be efficient to have a long period of visual sensory registration. We need to take in things very quickly and move onto the next object or event.

However things we hear, e.g. people talking, a car horn telling us to move, exist *in time*. If we miss it the message may not be repeated. (Try asking the TV weather forecaster to tell you again what the weather will be like tomorrow because you missed it the first time!) Research into auditory memory suggests that it has a slightly longer duration than visual memory. Numerous experiments have shown that things which are said out loud are remembered longer than things which are read silently. If you need to look up a telephone number in the phone book, read it out loud before closing the book and reaching for the receiver. You have a better chance of remembering the spoken words than the visual image.

The visual sensory register can hold up to about 15 items for somewhere between a half and one second. Research into auditory sensory registration suggests that it can hold a few items for up to four or five seconds.

---

who believed that learning occurred by association, and therefore forgetting results from a breakdown in these associations. Or they were clinical psychologists studying problems of short term memory loss in patients suffering from various kinds of amnesia.

The *Brown Peterson method* tachistoscopically flashed a stimulus – a three-letter nonsense syllable such as those used by Ebbinghaus – and a three-digit number, e.g. 486, simultaneously. The subject had to look at the number and nonsense syllable, and immediately start to count backwards from the number seen, in multiples of four or three, e.g. 486, 483, 480, 477, 474, etc., to ensure that no rehearsal of the letters could occur. After a delay of several seconds, the *retention interval*, the subjects were to stop counting and try to recall the letters. The Petersons found the duration of the STS for this kind of material was about 18 seconds. If the retention interval was longer than 18 seconds, recall was impossible.

The amount of information that can be held in STS can also be made to vary. **George Miller** argues that the maximum capacity of STS is about seven items of meaning, plus or minus two, depending on the nature of the information. However an 'item' of meaning can be a combination of smaller units of meaning. A letter of the alphabet has some meaning, so one letter could be one item. 'C', 'A' and 'T' are thus three items, but they can be *chunked* together to make a 'one word item' – 'CAT'. Since 'CAT' is also a unit of meaning for us, so 'CAT' is an item of meaning. Miller says that STS capacity is determined by

▶ *Chunking* and *chaining* refer to combining individual bits of information into a larger item.

the number of chunks of meaning, rather than the amount of information taken to establish that meaning. Words can be *chained* into sentences. A coherent sentence also has meaning for us. So 'The cat sat on the mat' could count as 17 'letter items', 6 'word items', or a 'one sentence' item. Chunking and chaining are useful techniques for expanding memory.

 What is the duration and capacity of short term storage?

Long term store (LTS) *for long term memory* (LTM)

The long term store can hold information for any period of time up to one lifetime. As far as we know, there is no limit to the amount it can hold. It contains all our knowledge (and misunderstandings) of physical objects – their use, size, colour, weight, etc., social relationships – where each person stands in relation to others, locations and how to move from one to another, perceptions of objects and events, and understanding of communication between each other, among many other things.

One interesting finding from studies of long term memory is that what is recalled after a period of time isn't necessarily exactly what was perceived in the first place. Our long term memories are *dynamic*. They tend to 'reconstruct' past events in terms of our present understanding. **Frederic Bartlett** demonstrated this over fifty years ago by telling people stories which were from another culture, and which weren't always easily understood. At various intervals afterwards he asked his subjects to recite the story back to him. The best known example of Bartlett's stories is probably 'The War of the Ghosts'.

The versions Bartlett's subjects gave of 'The War of the Ghosts' were different from the original in several respects. They were generally shorter, since details, and aspects which did not conform to the subject's own culture, were usually omitted. Details were also added to make sense of, or *rationalize,* the parts of the story which were difficult to understand. Some parts, usually the death scene, were taken to be more important than others, and much more detail was provided about them. Some of the words were changed and events were taken out of sequence to make more sense.

Bartlett concluded that all learning is based on previously existing *schemas*. His subjects would try to understand the story in terms of what was normal in their culture and experience. When they tried to remember it they reconstructed it according to their existing knowledge about the world. What they recalled was reconstructed from what they thought they knew.

 Try Bartlett's experiment on your friends. Get them to read 'The War of the Ghosts' and test their recall in a weeks' time.

Marcia Johnson suggests that what we remember is what we 'reconstruct' from the meanings we have stored in our memories. She presented subjects with a series of sentences. One was: 'John was trying to fix the birdhouse. He was pounding the nail when his father

> ► LTS can last for one's whole life, and seems to have no limit to its capacity.

> ► Although psychologists talk of long and short term memory as though they were 'real' and known to exist, the evidence for the distinction is not conclusive.

The War of the Ghosts

One night two young men from Egulac went down to the river to hunt seals, and while they were there it became foggy and calm. Then they heard war cries and they thought, 'Maybe this is a war party.' They escaped to the shore and hid behind a log. Now canoes came up and they heard the noise of paddles and saw one canoe coming up to them. There were five men in the canoe and they said: 'What do you think? We wish to take you along. We are going up the river to make war on the people.'
One of the young men said, 'I have no arrows.'
'Arrows are in the canoe,' they said.
'I will not go along. I might be killed. My relatives do not know where I have gone. But you,' he said, turning to the other, 'may go with them.'

So one of the young men went and the other returned home. And the warriors went up the river to a town on the other side of Kalama. The people came down to the water and they began to fight, and many were killed. But presently the young man heard one of the warriors say: 'Quick, let us go home: that Indian has been hit.' Now he thought, 'Oh they are ghosts.' He did not feel sick but they said he had been shot.

So the canoes went back to Egulac and the young man went ashore to his house and made a fire. And he told everybody and said, 'Behold I accompanied the ghosts and we went to a fight. Many of our fellows were killed, and many of those who attacked us were killed. They said I was hit and I did not feel sick.'
He told it all, and then he became quiet. When the sun rose he fell down. Something black came out of his mouth. His face became contorted. The people jumped up and cried. He was dead.

> ► 'The War of the Ghosts' is an American Indian folk story, and would make sense to the Indians. Their ideas about death and spirits are quite different from ours.

came out to watch him and to help him do the work.' Later she presented the subjects with several sentences. They included the original sentence, and all had similar meanings. She asked them to pick out the one they had heard originally. Most chose the following sentence: 'John was using the hammer to fix the birdhouse when his father came out to watch and help him do the work.' The original sentence doesn't mention a hammer, but that was the meaning the subjects remembered. If the subjects were given the choice immediately after hearing the original sentence, then they would probably have chosen correctly. However the passage of time leads to meanings rather than actual details being stored for later recall.

 What is meant by 'reconstructive memory'?

Some researchers, such as **Endel Tulving**, suggest there are at least two types of long term storage. These are the *semantic store*, where events are stored by the meaning they had for us at the time, and the *episodic store*, where memories of particular episodes in our lives are stored. The two types of store will inevitably be interlinked.

> ► Suggesting two types of long term storage does not mean there are necessarily two different parts of the brain where these different stores are found. It is a model that is being proposed, a hypothetical way of understanding memory processes, and not a guide around the brain.

Life without long term memory

Without long term memory life would consist only of immediate impressions of where we are at the moment with no understanding of ourselves, our personality, our family or our background. We would have very little knowledge of the world and wouldn't know anything about the people we were with, apart from what they had said and done in the previous 20 seconds. Meaningful conversation would be impossible. We couldn't play any games because we'd have no understanding of rules. In fact life would be altogether meaningless. This is why the study of memory is important in psychology and why memory is regarded as one of the central cognitive processes.

► A hierarchy is any group of items that are placed in rank order, from the most general to the most specific, or from the highest to the lowest, e.g. 'Animal, vertebrate, mammal, feline, cat', or '90 per cent, 78 per cent, 45 per cent, 30 per cent, 23 per cent'.

► If items are stored hierarchically, and items in each hierarchy are 'cross referenced' to other relevant items in other hierarchies, could 'intelligence' be the physiological efficiency with which these hierarchies are made, maintained and accessed?

► Tulving's distinction between episodic and semantic long term storage is not shared by all cognitive psychologists. Perhaps we only remember episodes in our lives in terms of the meaning they had for us at the time.

During the 1960s **Allan Collins** and **Ross Quillian** concluded that meaningful information was stored in a hierarchical way, with ideas which 'go together' being stored together. For example there would be a hierarchy for 'people'. Below 'all people' might be knowledge about different races, each divided by knowledge about men, women and children. Further down would come sets of ideas about family members. Figure 6.6 shows one of Collins and Quillian's best known hierarchies. Each hierarchy starts with some general categories, and becomes more specific as we move through it. Having our knowledge stored in hierarchies allows easier access to appropriate information.

Collins and Quillian tested their model by asking subjects to say whether a series of statements they were shown were true or false. If the theory is correct, then statements that are closely related in where they are stored will be processed, and a response made, more quickly than statements which are from different parts of the hierarchy. Thus the statement 'Canaries are yellow' involves very little processing time, since the information about the colour of canaries is very close in the hierarchy. The statement 'Canaries have skin' involves several levels of processing, and the response should take longer. Collins and Quillian tested the response time, and found that it did increase with the number of levels which would have to be processed.

Apart from information being stored according to its meaning, it is also stored according to the relevance it has for us personally. We can each remember stories about things that happened to us or things that we were involved in. This is *episodic storage* and does not require hierarchies for retrieval. (This might explain why some items stored in episodic memory are more likely to be forgotten than semantically stored information.) Not everyone agrees with Tulving's semantic/episodic distinction since it would be impossible to recall incidents from our lives (episodic memory) without the meaning (semantic memory) they had for us at the time.

We could not hope to remember everything that goes on around us. One of the factors that influences the likelihood of something being remembered is how it is organized. **Gordon Bower** and his colleagues showed that when verbal items were organized into meaningful hierarchies they could be learned and recalled more quickly

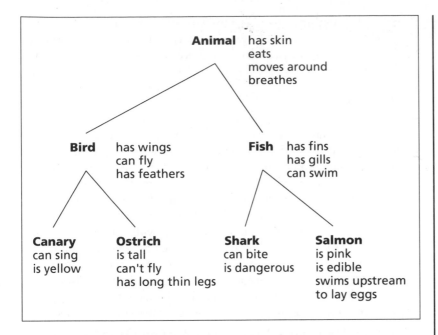

Figure 6.6 Example of Collins and Quillian's semantic hierarchies

and accurately than when the same material was not organized. An example of their organized hierarchies is shown in Figure 6.7.

One group of subjects (the 'organized' group) saw the words to be recalled set out in hierarchies, like the one in Figure 6.7. Another group (the 'randomized' group) saw the same words in lists which only appeared to have some structure. Altogether there were 112 words to be remembered. When tested later the 'organized' group could remember 65 per cent of the words in the hierarchies, while the 'randomized' group could recall only 19 per cent.

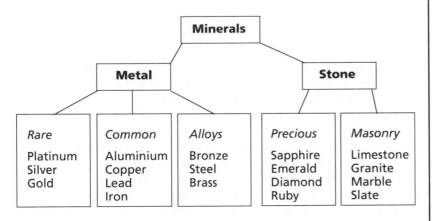

Figure 6.7 Example of Bower et al's organized hierarchies

Compare Collins and Quillian's conclusions about the nature of long term storage with those of Gordon Bower.

► Most of the experiments in memory research have been conducted to test the duration, capacity or speed of processing of various kinds of material. This psychometric approach may be useful for explaining how some system works in theory, but it doesn't necessarily help psychologists explain real life memory in real life situations.

► The technique of making a 'mental map' is called the method of loci and can be extremely effective. If you have a good imagination you could use each room in your house for different topics.

► A *mnemonic device* is anything which aids the memory such as a silly question featuring the initial letters of what we want to remember.

► If we do not know very much about something, the first information we have is likely to have the greatest effect on us. This is the *primacy effect*. If we already have some knowledge, but are uncertain, the last information we receive is likely to have most influence. This is the *recency effect*.

Regrettably the things we have to learn during our lives are rarely possible to organize in such ways as Bower's material. We could try to impose some organization on things we want to remember, such as information for an exam. One way is to imagine that you are in a familiar place, your room at home perhaps. Take the first things you need to know and imagine them to be on, in or near the first thing you see when you enter your room. The theories of selective attention could be on a chair, just inside the door perhaps. The next items are to be imagined around the next feature of your room. Maybe the sensory register can be imagined on the mantelshelf above the fireplace. Information on STS and LTS could be on your pillow and the end of the bed. Organization in memory might lie near the waste bin. Eventually you will have arranged all the material around the room. To recall it, just mentally open the door and walk round the room!

Or we could make a silly sentence out of the first letters of important words in the order we need to recall them. For example, the first major schools of thought in psychology were structuralism, functionalism, associationism, psychoanalysis, behaviourism, cognitive theory and humanism. One student's sentence for remembering this was

'**S**cience **F**iction **A**nnoys **P**sychologists **B**ut **C**an't **H**urt.'

Evidence for the two process model

Earlier we discussed the Brown Peterson technique which seems to indicate the existence of a short term store. Information in it will be overwritten by new information coming in if rehearsal and further processing are frustrated by a task such as counting backwards. The Brown Peterson method is taken to support the view that memory comprises two (hypothetically) distinct types or levels of processing.

Other research has asked people to read aloud a list of words. Immediately afterwards they are asked to recall as many of the words as they can. Most people can recall the first few and the last few, but rarely many from the middle of the list. This is taken as further evidence for the two process model. The first words which are read are supposed to have been processed into LTS, from where they can be recalled later. The last words read are supposed to be recalled from the STS. This demonstrates what psychologists call the *primacy* and *recency* effects. Primacy refers to what we experience first, and recency to what we experience last.

None of the evidence actually *proves* a distinction between a short and long term memory store. There is no particular need for any distinction to exist. Why should the primacy effect suggest a separate, long term mode of storage from the recency effect? Perhaps we are simply more receptive to the novelty of the words at the beginning, so they are remembered. And the words we heard last can be recalled simply because we heard them last. Why should they be being remembered from a different (short term) type of store? Further, why aren't the words in the middle of the list remembered well at all? If we have a long term store, why aren't they being stored there along with the first ones we hear? At the very least we have to accept that the case is not proven.

> **The two process model of memory**
> Short term memory provides our conscious awareness of the world around us. Control processes allow us to rehearse information or effect decisions. Brown and Peterson found that information in STS can't last for more than 18 to 20 seconds without rehearsal. Miller claims that up to seven items can be chunked and chained for meaning to increase STS capacity. LTS has unlimited capacity and is reconstructive in nature, and it is more effective if the information to be stored is organized.

► The primacy and recency effects are taken as support for the STS/LTS distinction. However there are alternative views.

Other 'evidence' against the two process model comes from studies of brain-damaged patients. Some patients with amnesia have been found to have very limited short term storage abilities, yet their long term memories are perfect. If STS is a 'working memory' supplying LTS with rehearsed and coded information, then why could these patients continue to learn new things, which they could subsequently remember, while apparently having no short term memory at all?

Atkinson and Shiffrin have presented a neat and attractive model of two, separate memory storage systems, each with its own functions. There may indeed be two systems, but the case is far from proven.

► Studies of people with different types of brain disorder do not support any single explanation for memory function. The human brain seems to be extremely adaptable, and when some dysfunction occurs in one part, other parts appear to try to compensate for them.

The levels of processing approach to memory

As Bower and others have shown, new items are stored in memory in terms of some association they have with existing memories. For example, any new knowledge about motorbikes will be stored with existing 'motorbike knowledge'. When we need to recall it we will only need to search the 'man made', 'machine', 'transport', 'motorized', 'motorbike' hierarchy to find the information. If items were stored according to when we first discovered them we'd have to remember everything that happened to us for the last few years before finding the motorbike information. This would take ages, be completely uneconomical, and probably threatening to our survival.

In the early 1970s **Craik** and **Lockhart** proposed an alteration to the two process model for explaining memory. They see no particular need for separate systems of short and long term store, but rather see memory as the (almost accidental) by-product of the level to which information has been processed. Some stimuli that are barely or briefly perceived will hardly be processed at all. They will produce a faint memory trace which will soon decay as new information enters. They may be *attenuated*, or simply overwritten. Other information will be processed more deeply, depending on a number of factors, such as how important it is to the perceiver, how much time there is available before other stimuli are perceived, and the nature of the stimulation. The more deeply an item is processed, the more durable will be the memory trace it produces. The most durable traces last the longest time, and become longer lasting memories.

If you see a photograph of someone you know well, first your eyes recognize a two-dimensional form with a pattern of lines and colours on it. It has taken some *visual perceptual processing* of the structural

► Items stored in order would be stored sequentially (according to a sequence). Memory is said to be based on associations.

► Like Atkinson and Shiffrin, Craik and Lockhart are attempting to explain highly complicated physiological relationships in the human brain in terms of some relatively simple psychological principles.

► *Cognition* (knowing) means selectively attending to one stimulus rather than another. It results from *perception* (the senses responding to it in some way) and remembering (the memories and previous knowledge required to interpret it have been used). Cognition requires that information must have been deeply processed.

► To understand a sentence requires some deep cognitive processing, of each word, each phrase and each clause, until its whole meaning is understood. Yet we usually understand the whole sentence after one brief read.

parts of the picture to achieve this level of pattern recognition. (This is what Craik and Tulving describe as 'structural processing'.) An instant later further *cognitive processing* occurs and the lines and colours are interpreted as representing a human form. (If the stimulus was a word not a picture, this stage would involve phonetic processing – processing for sound.) Finally, memory processing occurs to find a match for the patterns in the picture, and we 'recognize' our friend. (The word would be processed semantically – for meaning.) Even this rather simple description of three levels of processing should give you an idea of just how complex and interrelated perception, cognition and memory are. And yet we recognize the person in the photograph, or know the meaning of a familiar word, in a fraction of a second.

Summary – Levels of processing

Craik and Lockhart identify at least three different stages in the depth to which stimuli will be processed. If the stimulus presented is the word 'octopus':

Level 1	Processing	Structural level	What does the shape or form of the word 'octopus' look like?
Level 2	Processing	Phonetic level	When spoken aloud, what does the word 'octopus' sound like?
Level 3	Processing	Semantic level	What is the meaning of the word 'octopus'?

Other skills also require increasingly complex levels of processing. Reading, for example, involves several stages of processing. First, to recognize the letters which make up a word requires limited sensory processing. Then follows recognizing the word itself. So far the level of processing required is small. The next stage involves registering the meaning of the word, and this requires much deeper processing. This must happen for each word in a sentence. Understanding, and being able to work out a response to each sentence you hear or read, requires very deep processing.

Craik's theory does not reject the possibility of a dynamic 'working memory' (which may be the same as 'consciousness' or 'attention'), but it only accounts for what we attend to, not for the type of active processing, especially rehearsal, which Atkinson and Shiffrin proposed.

An experiment by **Fergus Craik** and **Michael Watkins** supplies evidence for a levels of processing approach. According to the two process model, if information is to pass from short to long term storage it must be rehearsed. Craik and Watkins asked subjects to listen to a series of word lists and remember the last word beginning with a particular letter. For example, if the 'target letter' was 'l' then in the list 'grass, level, rejoin, potato, wolf, carpet, lady, launderette, legal, aim, stable, bungle, lurid, tadpole', the word 'lurid' should be

► Craik and Watkins' findings do not mean that rehearsal isn't important for things to be remembered for longer periods of time. If you wish to pass your exams, then you will need to remember the material, and one way to do this is to rehearse it.

easily remembered. It was.

Craik and Watkins also asked the subjects to recall as many of the other words beginning with 'l' as they could. If rehearsal was important they should have remembered 'level', and also 'legal' since there was time to rehearse them while 'non target' words were being heard. There wouldn't have been time to rehearse 'lady' or 'launderette' since these words were immediately followed by another target word which would be rehearsed. In fact Craik and Watkins found that all the target words were equally likely to be recalled. Rehearsal alone clearly does not explain what is remembered and what isn't.

 Summarize the role of rehearsal in memory.

Using your previous notes on memory compare and contrast the two process models and the levels of processing model with particular reference to the experimental evidence supporting and undermining each.

Comments on the two process model and levels of processing model of memory

Two process model Claims	Criticisms
Logical system of stores reflecting different functions of storage	Implies two separate locations for different memory functions. There is no reason or evidence for this.
Concentrates on explaining verbal memory	Memory has visual, non-auditory, spatial and other aspects too.
Suggests that memories are coded for particular features such as sound and meaning.	A rather simplistic view of the functions of memory. Cognitive processing is probably far more complex.

Level of processing model Claims	Criticisms
Memory is seen as an integrated part of the perceptual system.	Avoids considering the function of particular kinds of memory.
Has empirical psychological support, e.g. Craik and Watkins.	Studies of brain-damaged patients and patients with amnesia do not show evidence of a unified system, but rather of separate stores with different functions.
Shows how events which have most meaning will be best remembered.	Rather obvious, and doesn't prove the correctness of any theory.

► Some writers believe that after learning something new certain changes take place in the structure and chemical balances in those parts of the nervous system where the learning has occurred. The phrase 'metabolic consolidation' is used to mean the transfer of information between short and long term store.

► For a fuller discussion of Freudian ideas see Chapter 2, pages 25–32.

► A *defence mechanism* is an unconscious, and entirely normal, automatic response which we make to issues that might otherwise threaten our personality development.

WHY DO WE FORGET?

It is important not to confuse 'forgetting' with 'never knowing in the first place'. If you paid insufficient attention to something, such as learning about 'memory' for a psychology test, and you then fail the test, you can't claim that you 'just couldn't remember', or 'you forgot' the details. Information in the STS or the lower levels of processing may not be passed for further processing, in which case you wouldn't have known it, so couldn't have forgotten it. Some writers argue that some parts of the brain need a period for 'metabolic consolidation'. If it is interrupted then recall may become impossible.

Psychologists who believe in a particular perspective, such as psychoanalysis or behaviourism, have offered their explanations for why we forget. Those more interested in biological explanations for aspects of human behaviour advance neurophysiological explanations. Others are more interested in the practical implications for learning, remembering and forgetting.

Repression – the psychoanalytic view

Throughout life we all experience worries and upsets. Some will be serious enough to cause anxiety. Freud believed that the process of normal personality development created additional problems since it involves the erogenous zones and includes feelings of pre-genital sexuality, with associated fear and guilt. Anxieties which might threaten our personality could become repressed into our unconscious. Repression is said to be one of the more effective *defence mechanisms*.

According to Freud our unconscious mind eventually comprises two groups of impulses. One is those psychic urges that drive our thinking and behaviour, which were always unconscious and which have been there since birth. The other comprises all those fears, worries, memories, desires and wishes which produced too much anxiety when they were conscious, and so were repressed into the unconscious during development. Freud said 'forgetting, in all cases, is founded on a motive of displeasure'. We will have problems if we try to remember events which produced such anxiety for us.

It is probably true that it is easier to remember pleasant events in more detail than unpleasant ones. We may more easily forget things or people we do not like. However, Freud's explanation cannot be tested experimentally, doesn't explain why we do also forget pleasant things, and doesn't explain why we forget more as we grow older.

 How does 'motivated forgetting' fit in with Freudian theory?

Interference – the behaviourist view

Young people often have fantastic memories – sometimes to the embarrassment of their parents! As we grow older our memories start to fail. We say we can't remember. We suffer increasing retrieval failures. According to interference theory, as we gain more experience, more and more items will need to be stored. Some items will inevitably be similar to ones already stored. Occasionally the similar items will interfere with each other. We will become confused about the precise details, making accurate retrieval impossible. This is called *retroactive interference*. Sometimes the existence of some knowledge will distort the learning of some new, similar knowledge. We may confuse the new information with the old when we try to retrieve it. This is called *proactive interference*. Interference theory is based on the behaviourist view that memory consists of associations made between specific items – stimuli and responses.

Numerous experiments using lists of words and lists of nonsense syllables have demonstrated proactive and retroactive interference in the laboratory. However, they do not seem to be applicable to 'real life'. In fact just the opposite could occur. Having a fairly specialized knowledge of something which has built up over the past few years, e.g. a car enthusiast might know the specification of modern cars, shouldn't provide any problems for recalling relevant information, e.g. whether it's the Escort XR3i or the Astra SRi which has the higher torque or goes from 0 to 60 mph in the shortest time. If a new model is added to the range the enthusiast may enjoy increasing her or his knowledge. When it comes to learning about the new range of Golf GTis (which would be an example of proactive interference), the enthusiast's knowledge of the Escort and Astra might positively help because it provides points of reference to compare the Golf against. As Atkinson and Shiffrin claim, the concept of interference may be better at describing what can be shown to occur under particular laboratory conditions, rather than explaining what actually does occur in 'real life'.

(NM) Outline the behaviourist view of forgetting.

Trace decay and displacement – the physiological view

Neither of the previous explanations deals adequately with one of the most obvious features of forgetting – why does it increase with time? According to the physiological view, new experiences are coded into electro-chemical signals which are carried by groups of *neurons* in 'memory circuits'. Memories are a *neural trace*. With the passage of time metabolic processes in the brain cause the trace to decay until eventually the message it carried – the memory of that particular episode or meaning – is lost. Decay only occurs through disuse so the way to stop it is to recall the event.

▶ *Neurons* are individual nerve fibres which carry the signals around nervous systems. The brain is composed of millions of neurons, each being able to pass messages to an average of 60,000 other neurons.

This explanation has the attraction of being quite simple, but unfortunately it doesn't really fit the facts. Many elderly people can recall incidents from their youth in great detail. Unless they have recalled the instance many times throughout their lives the trace should have decayed. Skills learned in childhood, such as swimming or riding a bike, and not practised for many years, are often quickly re-learned by adults, for example when they come to teach their own children. If trace decay theory is correct, and you hadn't played the guitar for

► All our brain activity depends on electro-chemical and other messages being passed around extremely quickly to various locations in extremely complex systems. We do not fully understand how they all work, and any physiological explanation relies on much educated guesswork.

twenty years (the trace had decayed), then not only would you be unable to recall the chord sequence for a particular song, but it would also take you as long to learn the song the second time as it did the first. This simply isn't true. If you haven't ridden a bike since you were young (and the trace has decayed) could you not ride one now? Surely 'you never forget' to swim, ride a bike or play the piano once you've learned? People under hypnosis can often recall things that they haven't thought about for years, so their traces may still be there. Freud tried several techniques to encourage his patients to recall their earliest memories, presumably with some success.

Perhaps the biggest problem for trace decay theory is that it can't explain why some people seem to have poor recall of even recent events while others have incredible memories going back for decades. Such physiological processes must be fairly similar in most people, so why such huge individual differences?

(NM) Outline the trace decay explanation for forgetting.

Retrieval failure – the tip of the tongue phenomenon

The theories outlined so far are called *trace dependent* since they see the memory trace as the main cause for forgetting. If our memories are difficult to recall because of their unpleasant associations, or are 'interfered with' by new information entering memory, or are decaying with time, then some traces must still be there, but we can't gain access to them. Have you ever put something down, then forgotten where you put it, and tried to visualize where you were when you had it last? This visualization provides you with information to help you find the object. Something similar happens in memory. We have *retrieval cues* which are either stored with the information, or applied later, which help us find the memory. This is called *cue dependent theory* (after Tulving). It doesn't so much explain 'forgetting', but rather 'how not to forget'!

► While other explanations for memory loss look for problems in storage, cue dependent theory looks for problems in how we try to remember the information. Just because we can't find it doesn't mean it isn't there!

► Cues such as similarities of physical state and location are aids to remembering.

Numerous studies have found that recall is better if the physical state of the person is the same when recall occurs as it was when the learning first occurred. For example, **Overton** found that subjects who had drunk a large amount of alcohol could recall what had happened to them the last time they were drunk rather better than they could when they were sober! Another cue to remembering is where we were when we did the learning. **D.R. Godden** and **Alan Baddeley** had 16 divers learn lists of 40 (unrelated) words under two experimental conditions. They were either on shore or 10 feet under the sea when the learning occurred. Later the divers were asked to recall each list either in the context where it was learned or in the other context. Recall was better in the situation in which the learning had occurred.

Having category names for groups of items to be recalled is another cue. **Tulving** and **Pearlstone** asked two groups of subjects to learn lists of items in named categories, e.g. a category name could be ANIMAL, and the list would contain one, two, or four words such as

---

Improve your memory

To make your learning more efficient, here are a few simple rules.

1   Have confidence that you can learn the material and that you will not blame others for stopping you or blame yourself for not being bright enough.
2   Try to understand the whole topic in general, and where it fits into other, related items before trying to learn the details.
3   Learn the details, but always relate them to the whole topic, rather than seeing the details as ends in themselves.
4   Use rhymes and mnemonics to group related items together. Try to see the topic as a picture.
5   Use the information in another way as soon as you can afterwards, e.g. if you've read it, then talk about it, if you've heard it, write it down in your own words.
6   Having learned it, test yourself on it. For example, relate to yourself the major theories of forgetting, explaining how they fit into our understanding of the functioning of human memory.

'monkey', 'grass snake', 'ostrich', 'starling'. One group was given the category name when asked to recall the lists, the other was not. Predictably, those who were given the category name remembered far more of their lists. The group who weren't cued by hearing the category name missed out entire categories. Later the two groups were tested again. This time both groups heard the category name cue. The second group now performed almost as well as the first. This shows that retrieval cues are very useful to recall.

 Name some cues which could improve recall.

Using your previous notes on forgetting construct a table of contrasts showing the differences between the major explanations of forgetting. Note the major shortcomings of each.

Chapter summary

Sensations are decoded by the perceptual system to provide information about our environment. We selectively attend to some stimuli in order to gather enough information about them to be able to make some judgement. The position of the filter or other mechanism which allows certain information to be processed while inhibiting other data has been described as early or late, although the precise nature of this mechanism is unknown and seems more sophisticated than early research has been able to reveal. Cognitions that are rehearsed, vivid, personal, or in any other way important, will become a part of memory.

Memory may be organized into separate stages or processes. Short term storage lasts for less than 20 seconds, by which time new information will 'overwrite' existing information. Up to around seven items can be held at one time in STS. Information from STS can pass into LTS for permanent storage, from where it may be recalled later.

Several explanations for retrieval failure have been advanced. Existing memories may not have been stored correctly; they may have been 'overwritten'; they may have been repressed because recall may produce excessive anxiety. The memory trace may simply have decayed with disuse, or it may have been interfered with by other, similar memories.

Exam questions – 60 minutes each

1 Discuss the experimental evidence which attempts to explain selective attention.

2 Discuss the evidence for the view that humans have more than one type of memory storage system.

3 Why do humans forget?

Further Reading: Chapter 6

The most useful original source is probably

Bower G.H. 1977. *Human Memory*. London: Academic Press. This also contains Atkinson & Shiffrin's 'Human Memory: A proposed system and its control processes'.

A highly interesting and user friendly book is

Baddeley A. 1983. *Your Memory: a Users Guide*. Harmondsworth: Penguin.

A rather more serious, but no less informative is

Cohen G. *et al*. 1986. *Memory: a Cognitive Approach*. Milton Keynes: Open University Press.

A fairly comprehensive summary is

Norman D. 1976. *Memory and Attention* (2nd Edition). Chichester: John Wiley.

7 Language and thought

Introduction

If thinking separates humans from other animals, then the ability to communicate our thoughts through language sets us very far apart indeed. Whether thinking preceded language in evolution and whether thinking precedes language or vice versa in individual development have been subjects of considerable debate. In this chapter we will review the major contributors to the debate and note more recent attempts to invent 'thinking machines'.

WHAT IS THINKING?

Thinking is the process of mentally manipulating ideas, words, knowledge, beliefs, intentions, etc. According to *The Penguin Dictionary of Psychology*, thinking 'includes the mental activities associated with concept formation, problem solving, intellectual functioning, creativity, complex learning, memory, symbolic processing, imagery, etc.'. Ebbinghaus's scientific attempt to study the relationship between learning and thinking was the forerunner to research by such people as Carmichael, Hogan, Walter, Gordon Bower, Collins and Quillian, and many others into understanding various aspects of thinking (see Chapter 6). By no means all aspects of thinking have been equally studied by psychologists since it's impossible to know which everyday experiences contribute to which mental processes. Instead psychologists have concentrated on the reasoning processes which go into problem solving and the organization of thoughts into categories. This allows more scientific, standardized control of the material being presented and the measurement of responses.

 (ACT) Look again at *The Penguin Dictionary of Psychology* definition of 'thinking', then use the dictionary to look up the meaning of any of the terms in the definition which you do not know.

► It isn't possible to study all aspects of thinking. The main areas that have been studied are the processes of problem solving and mental organization.

> **REVIEW – Thinking**
> Thinking is a complex set of mental processes which develop throughout our lives. It derives from the combinations of experiences each person has during his/her lifetime of socialization. It is the putting together of ideas from perceptions and memory in order to achieve cognition, solve problems, reach decisions and many other mental skills.

THE RELATIONSHIP BETWEEN LANGUAGE AND THOUGHT

► Language is *species specific* to humans. Other animals have some communication skills, such as the signs and signals used in mating, or at the approach of a predator, or in territorial defence.

If thinking involves the mental manipulation of thoughts and ideas, then language is the device by which they are communicated. Language is a *species specific* system of sounds, signs or signals which allows humans to communicate their meanings to each other. There are thousands of different languages in the world, each with its own system of rules and concepts. In Chapter 4 we examined the major theories of language acquisition. Here we are interested in the relationship between language as a 'tool of thought' and the process of thinking. Since different languages have different rules and concepts a useful way to discover this relationship is cross-cultural research

There are three possible relationships between language and thought:

► Language determines thought
or

► thought determines language
or

► language and thought become related only after early development.

1 We could say that the rules and concepts of the particular language we speak determine the way we think. For example, if our culture's language doesn't contain words for speed, haste or quickly, then we won't be able to think in terms of doing something faster than someone else.

2 Reversing the previous possibility, we might say that the way we think determines the language style we use. If you are brought up in a culture which puts great emphasis on cooperation and sharing, then your language is likely to contain many such words as help, support, aid, assist, benefit, nurture, etc.

3 Language and thought may not be closely related at all during early development. They do not start to become related until the child is at least two years old and has some idea that objects exist independently of it, that it has labels to describe them and some ideas of their form and function.

Does language determine thought?

The linguistic relativity hypothesis

Benjamin Lee Whorf and **Edward Sapir** have studied the languages of people from different cultures and have concluded that what you can say determines what you can think. Their idea has become known as the 'Sapir–Whorf Linguistic Relativity Hypothesis'. It states that as we grow our language will help us learn what the world is like; how we can 'cut up nature'. Practice with crayons and paints could help Western children discriminate between fine shades of colour. Pink, red, crimson, ruby, scarlet and vermilion can be differentiated from each other, as might emerald, jade and chartreuse green. According to Whorf, people who could not *describe* the difference between vermilion and crimson or chartreuse and jade green could not actually *perceive* any differences between them. Whorf studied several groups of American Indians and claimed that those who described aspects of their world differently actually perceived it differently.

(NM) What is meant by the linguistic relativity hypothesis?

Whorf compared the language of Hopi Indians with American and other European languages, which he called SAE (Standard Average European), to see if there were any differences in the ways time, space and matter were regarded. He found various differences. For example, the sense of time is not expressed in the same way by all people. While Europeans can think of 'three weeks' as a period of time whose meaning they understand, Hopi Indians can't. They do not have the words which describe time as though it could be marked off in units of measurement in the same way that objects can. We can imagine five trees or ten feathers. So can the Hopi. They are 'real things'. Time is not a 'real thing' in this sense. The Hopi are able to say 'I left on the third day' since one day is 'real', and three of them which have been experienced have been real. They could not say 'I stayed for three days' since 'three days' is a period of time for which they do not have the words.

The Sapir–Whorf hypothesis was first proposed in its 'strong' version, which says that the whole of one's thinking is determined by one's language. **Carroll** and **Casagrande** noted that some languages put greater emphasis on some features than others. The Navaho tribe of American Indians, for example, put great stress on form and shape, rigidity and the material from which the object is constructed. These Indians have many words which can describe objects and events so that other people who haven't seen them can have a clear impression of what they are like.

Carroll and Casagrande gave three groups of children, two Navaho and one English/American, various objects such as a green stick, a length of green rope and a length of blue rope – and asked them which objects 'went together'. One group of Indians spoke only the Navaho language, the other group was bilingual so could speak both languages. The third group spoke only English.

The Navaho-only speakers said the objects with the same form, i.e. the ropes, went together. This confirms the linguistic relativity hypothesis. American children, who categorize by colour rather than form, were predicted to be more likely to say that the same coloured objects 'went together'. However, when the Boston schoolchildren were tested later, it was found that they also categorized by form rather than colour, so the results are far from convincing.

► *Benjamin Whorf* was an amateur anthropologist who studied the languages of North American Indian tribes as a hobby. He was trained as a chemical engineer, and worked for the Hartford Fire Insurance Company.

► According to the Sapir–Whorf hypothesis, if you can't describe a difference between two things, then you probably can't perceive any difference.

► Whorf conducted many studies of aspects of Hopi Indian language, looking for evidence that their language was determining their thought processes. His claims to have found it would be thought of as rather over-optimistic now.

► As each culture has developed it has found that some features of objects and events are more significant to its way of life than others. The languages of cultures reflect this.

► In its 'strong' version the Sapir–Whorf hypothesis claims that we cannot perceive what we do not have words to describe.

► Presumably the way children categorize objects depends on their previous experiences of such objects, or perhaps their categorization is influenced by the fact of being asked to categorize. Many children wouldn't necessarily think in terms of things like ropes and sticks 'going together' until someone asked them.

Comments on the linguistic relativity hypothesis

Dan Slobin reviewed the evidence for the linguistic relativity hypothesis. He found:

1 Many languages have words which express ideas that cannot be translated into other languages. So some ideas or meanings must be 'language specific', and people who speak those languages must have those ideas, and people who do not speak the language may not be able to comprehend the meaning.

However, there are over 5000 living languages in the world and it is inevitable that they will express best those meanings and ideas that are relevant to them. That is not to say that the ideas of one language cannot be expressed or understood by speakers of another if a serious attempt is made to explain them.

2 Languages vary in how precisely words are used to label certain things. For example, Eskimos have over 20 words which describe snow. English has about five (snow, sleet, hail, ice, slush). Eskimos are much more exact in their thinking about snow. The Hopi Indian uses one word to describe 'all objects which fly' (except birds), so an aeroplane, its pilot and a fly are all described by the same word. English speakers think more precisely about flight than do the Hopi.

However, this doesn't mean that the Hopi couldn't perceive pilots and planes as being different from each other. Since their cultural experience didn't include many planes and pilots why should their language contain different words for them?

3 The grammar of a language affects how people think about the objects being addressed. When you address a female in French you have to make a decision about her age relative to yours before calling her Madame or Mademoiselle. You show the intimacy of your relationship when you call someone 'vous' or 'tu'. Such grammatical rules automatically predispose one to think of people, objects and events in certain ways.

However, addressing a female as 'madame' doesn't prove that the grammatical structure of a language determines how the speaker will perceive that female, or other females they call 'madame'. They must already have made the perception and decision before using the word, so you could argue that the thought is determining the language.

The evidence to support Whorf's linguistic relativity hypothesis is criticized as being rather superficial and rather circular. Whorf claimed that people's language determined their thinking, not by studying their thinking, but rather by studying their language!

 What evidence is there to support the linguistic relativity hypothesis?

In its 'weak' version the linguistic relativity hypothesis states that certain perceptions are influenced by the language used. This is a much more realistic proposition. In English we put great emphasis on nouns for identifying things and on verbs for describing the actions associated with them. Other languages put their emphases on different things. Each will influence the way we perceive certain things. Also, there is evidence that far from being unique, each language has elements in common, which suggests a universality of linguistic structures.

► The weak version of the linguistic relativity hypothesis states that the structure of the language we use will influence the way we regard things.

How people perceive and describe colour has been extensively studied. According to two anthropologists, Berlin and Kay, there are 11 basic (focal) categories of colour. Some languages, such as English, use all 11. Others use less. The colours named form a hierarchy:

black		yellow		purple
	red	green	brown	pink
white		blue		orange
				grey

► Colours to the left are superior in this hierarchy.

Languages such as that spoken by the Dani, an agricultural people living in Indonesian New Guinea, use only two colour categories: *mili* (dark, cold colours such as black) and *mola* (warm, bright colours such as white). Languages with three words would have black, white and red. Those with four would have black, white, red and yellow, and so on. According to Whorf, since language determines thinking, the Dani would be unable to perceive yellow, grey, purple, etc. This has been shown to be untrue. When **Eleanor Rosch** presented people from 23 different language groups with names for the 11 focal colours, she found that they could learn to use them without difficulty. They must be able to perceive a difference, even if their native language doesn't have a word to describe it.

► Rosch's work with the Dani showed that they can perceive different colours for which their language has no word, and they could learn to use a word for them.

The 11 focal colours represent the major changes in the radiation of the visual spectrum, i.e. those light waves that the human eye can detect. The human eye may be better able to distinguish them from non focal colours such as mauve, cerise, scarlet and other combinations of the focal colours. The reason why people can see these focal colours may simply be that the physiology of the human visual system is more sensitive to them. This may offer a better explanation for people's perception of colour than the language they speak.

► On balance the evidence does not support the linguistic relativity hypothesis, at least in its strong form. It is possible to perceive something without necessarily knowing the word for it. After all, babies and young children do it all the time!

(NM) How does Rosch's research affect the linguistic relativity hypothesis?

The behaviourist view on language and thought

In a very different way from Sapir and Whorf, behaviourists have also claimed that language determines thought. In Chapter 2 we referred to the pioneering work of the American researcher J. B. Watson, who used the techniques of classical conditioning to elicit a fear response from 'Little Albert'. Watson was an early behaviourist who believed that all 'mental events' could be explained in terms of learned associations producing conditioned responses. In the first decades of this century psychologists studied 'mental events'. Watson was trying to counter this bias by emphasizing the central role of behaviour. Ultimately he would dismiss the role of thinking altogether.

Watson claimed: 'The behaviourist advances the view that what the psychologists have hitherto called thought is, in short, nothing but talking to ourselves.' This is another way of saying that 'thinking is merely subvocal speech', i.e. that 'mental activity' doesn't occur in your brain, but rather at a behavioural level in your windpipe and throat! (The idea that central mental events occur in the parts of the body which will enact them is known as *peripheralism*.) Research found that some subjects, under certain conditions, did show involuntary movements of their vocal apparatus when they were thinking.

Unfortunately for Watson, many people did not show such movement. His response was to say that the behaviour that some people call thinking could also operate at the level of our limbs. The thought 'I will pick up this book' could be nothing more than tiny electrochemical changes in nervous or muscular activity in the arm! This explained why some subjects' vocal apparatus didn't move when they were thinking.

 How do peripheralist theorists explain thinking?

In a decisive experiment in 1947 **Smith**, **Brown**, **Toman** and **Goodman** finally disproved Watson's claim. Smith allowed all the muscles in his body to be paralysed by an injection of the drug curare. Since breathing requires muscles this ceased too and he was kept alive on a respirator. According to Watson he should have been unable to 'think' since he was unable to move. In fact Smith could clearly recall his thoughts, feelings and experiences during his paralysis when the effects of the drug wore off. (Some patients have 'come round' while under anaesthetic and are aware of what is going on, but are quite unable to communicate.)

 What is the fundamental principle that dominates behaviourist psychology?

Bernstein's linguistic codes

Basil Bernstein is an English sociologist who 30 years ago began studying the differences in types of language used by members of the same society, and the implications this has for education in particular. After analysing the vocabulary, grammar and type of communication used by children of different ages and from different backgrounds, Bernstein identified two linguistic codes used in different social circumstances.

By the term *restricted code* Bernstein refers to the use of short, and often unfinished sentences, assembled in an ungrammatical way. The understanding of restricted code relies on the listener sharing common understandings with the speaker. Restricted code is the usual mode of speech both between people who know each other

▶ Structuralists believed that all mental activity was made up of combinations of basic elements of sensation and feeling, and these elements could be discovered by *introspection*. Psychoanalysts explained personality in terms of mental processing of experiences involving conscious and unconscious forces.

▶ If mental activity actually occurs at the part of the body that's going to respond, you might wonder what Watson thought the human brain was for at all.

▶ As with all areas of knowledge, particularly fairly new ones like academic psychology, there will be disagreement over the nature of the topic being examined. As more research is conducted the old idea gradually gives way to the new.

▶ Language cannot determine thought if thought can exist without language.

▶ *Restricted code* users employ short, ungrammatical sentences, relying on other people sharing the same basis of understanding.

intimately, such as husbands and wives or close friends, and between strangers who use off-the-peg cliches to interact with each other, such as clichés about the weather. Bernstein says that restricted code carries as much or more information about the relationships between speakers as it does about the topic of the conversation. For example the very fact that a husband can speak to his wife in ill-formed, incomplete sentences, and that she understands him, conveys that they are intimates with a common understanding.

By the term *elaborated code* Bernstein means the use of a more formal language: the kind this book is written in. Elaborated code employs a rich vocabulary, a complex grammar and is capable of conveying complex ideas.

Bernstein's ideas about the relationship between thought and language are a weak form of the Sapir–Whorf hypothesis. He believes that people who cannot use elaborated code will not be able to develop complex patterns of thought.

Bernstein notes that competence in linguistic code usage is socially distributed. Nearly everyone is capable of, and uses restricted codes, but some lower working-class people in Britain are unable to use elaborated code. This implies that they are unable to think in an abstract or complex way.

► *Elaborated code* users employ precise, grammatical forms to communicate their wide experiences.

An imaginary example of linguistic codes

A 10-year-old boy knocks on his friend's door. He is holding a football in his hand. It is half past four and they have finished school. Neither boy has tea until six pm. The door opens and his young friend is standing there. The visitor speaks.

The restricted code user, 'Foota?' The elaborated code user, 'Would you like to come out to play football?'

The boys run off towards the park.

Obviously the elaborated code user is grammatically correct. But if the point of language is to convey meaning, does it convey its meaning any more precisely than does the restricted code user? Bernstein has been accused of being rather critical of the restricted code. However, there are many ideas which may not be so easily

Features of restricted and elaborated codes

Restricted code	*Elaborated code*
Limited vocabulary.	Broad vocabulary.
Frequent pauses and lack of fluency in speech.	Fluent, confident communication.
Many grammatical errors.	Few grammatical errors.
Meanings are often implicit.	Meanings are usually explicit.
References are usually specific to one thing at a time.	References are more likely to be general taking more features into account.
More likely to be used between intimates in informal setting	More likely to be used in formal settings such as education, broadcasting, meetings, etc.

expressed using a restricted code.

Since teachers are middle-class people who mostly have middle-class values expressed through an elaborated code, middle-class children are likely to be at an advantage in school. They 'speak the same language'. Restricted code users are more likely to be seen as rude, assertive, deviant or lacking in ability. They are less likely to be allowed to attempt the more academic work, and may be less well equipped to understand it. People with academic qualifications are more likely to find employment which will allow them to enjoy a better quality of life than those without qualifications. So education becomes a *self-fulfilling prophecy* by promoting middle-class children to obtain middle-class jobs to have middle-class children who will benefit from middle-class education and obtain middle-class jobs ... . Those unable to use elaborated code are condemned to a worse quality of life, and their children and their children's children in turn.

 Outline Bernstein's thinking on linguistic codes.

Bernstein's analysis of children's speech was the result of asking them questions and encouraging them to make statements. However, those not skilled in elaborated code are also more reticent to speak in such a formal situation as being questioned by someone they know to be conducting research. In a more relaxed setting such people may be excellent communicators, even if not in grammatically correct forms. Bernstein's methodology may have been responsible for him identifying two linguistic codes. (Anyway why assume there are only two? Why not three or four or ten?)

This issue was investigated by **W. Labov** in America 20 years ago. Labov claimed that Black children in America have a shared use of non-standard English which disadvantages them in the same way as the restricted code is supposed to do in Britain. He claims that the environment in which the communication occurs is also important. Leon, an eight-year-old Black boy, was largely silent and unimaginative when questioned about a toy plane by an interviewer in school. It might have been concluded that Leon was linguistically incompetent. But when the interviewer shared a bag of crisps, sitting on the floor in the child's home environment, and using the child's non-standard English 'slang', Leon turned out to be imaginative and articulate.

Bernstein was accused of implying that the elaborated code is *qualitatively* better than the restricted code. His accusers said he claimed that meanings are best conveyed if everyone around could share them, they could be applied to a variety of situations, and they are grammatically correct. But Labov would argue that so long as the people who were intended to receive the messages could understand and communicate with each other, then the precise formulations of their speech were less important. Labov claimed that black American children are actually bilingual. They have their own non-standard English at home, and a more formal English at school. Bernstein

► A *self-fulfilling prophecy* arises when one person predicts another's characteristics and behaviour on the basis of some prior assumption, and then acts towards them according to this prediction. This produces a response from the other person which tends to confirm the original prediction. For example, if a teacher believes that a particular child lacks ability, then he or she may give the child less opportunities or encouragement to succeed, so that the child eventually fails.

► Bernstein sees social status and differential socialisation as explaining differences in language usage, thought patterns and educational achievement. Labov sees the problem lying with those who make value judgements about the quality of alternative forms of traditional, conventional, standard English.

► So long as the people you are talking to understand what you mean, does it matter that those you are not talking to do not understand? Why should their speech be 'better than' yours?

himself has made it clear that he did not claim that non-standard English was a form of restricted code.

Does thought determine language?

If language determines thought, then language must precede thought. It does not. Even quite young, pre-linguistic babies can 'think'. They indulge in intentional behaviour such as exchange games, and are quite capable of expressing such thoughts as happiness, displeasure, pain and discomfort (see Chapter 3). Neither do all mental events necessarily involve language. Some aspects of remembering and problem solving are probably non-linguistic.

The Earth has existed for something like two and a half thousand million years. Humans have been on the planet for a relatively short time, about two and a half million years. One reason why humans have come to dominate the planet and the other forms of life on it is that they can think, and this allows them to organize and to plan. The ability to think would have evolved long before the ability to use language. Language must then be seen as a tool of thought. If a society such as the Lapps developed in the frozen wastes of the far North, surrounded by snow, it is hardly surprising that its people need to describe different qualities of snow. They may well need their 27 words which describe it. Their language will be a tool to convey their familiar experiences. Pygmies have no words for snow. Guess why!

Further evidence for the 'language reflecting thought' argument comes from studies of non-human animals, notably primates. Primates cannot speak. The only attempts to teach them (Kellogg and Kellogg, Hayes and Hayes) were complete failures. They do not have the necessary physiology to produce actual speech. However speech isn't the only form of language. **Allen** and **Beatrice Gardner** trained a female chimp called Washoe to use some American Sign Language (ASL) by moulding her hands into the correct shapes and reinforcing her with food, tickles and other stimulation. Altogether she learned about 160 signs, and seemed able to combine them into short sentences. Washoe appears capable of some thought processes. Other studies have also shown that animals are capable of limited thoughts, and could express them through some kind of communication systems.

The structure of all human brains is much the same, and all brains probably work in much the same way. The way they work, combined with the particular experiences each person has, will influence the type of language structures they need. In the process of cognition, perception starts with a subject, e.g. I see a cup, which is followed by some action, e.g. I *reach for, grasp, lift* and *drink from* the cup. In almost every language in the West known to scientists the subject comes first, the object comes second. Jean Piaget has explained how language is used at first egocentrically, as 'spoken thoughts', and later as a way of expressing and extending schemas.

▶ Washoe lived with the Gardners from the age of 10 months. At five she was sexually mature so was returned to a zoo where she was mated.

▶ ASL is used mostly by deaf American people to communicate with each other and with hearing people. Washoe was observed trying to teach her own offspring to communicate with her and their keepers by ASL.

▶ Language can't determine thought if animals which don't naturally use a language can be taught to communicate by using one.

▶ The way the brain works probably has implications for the structure of language.

Outline the evidence so far which suggests that thought determines language.

▶ Piaget sees cognitive development passing through four universal stages, from *egocentric*, self-obsessed thought to the gradual acquisition of the rules of formal, operational thinking some time after puberty.

▶ *Symbolization* is a major feature of human thinking and communicating. It is another of the skills that marks humans off from other animals.

▶ According to Piaget language skills cannot develop until the child is cognitively mature enough to be understood. Language thus reflects thought.

▶ Vygotsky was born in 1896, the same year as Jean Piaget. He died tragically in 1934, at the age of 38, with many years of potentially promising research before him.

▶ Pre-linguistic thought appears long before language skills emerge. Observe any baby of around four to ten months, and you'll see signs which suggest that the child is capable of thought.

Piaget's view of language

In Chapter 4 we discussed Piaget's view of the cognitive development of the child. He believed that all children's cognitive development will be much the same, and so was seeking universal stages of development. Unlike Whorf, he was not therefore interested in differences between speakers of particular languages.

For the first few years the child's thinking is *egocentric*. Its language will be dominated by ideas about itself, often used for reassurance and as an aid to understanding. Providing its parents with a running commentary on its activities will help the child *assimilate* and *accommodate* them into the appropriate schemas. Consequently most of a child's early language will concern itself. Language is said to have a *symbolic function*, i.e. it helps the child understand that real, concrete objects do not always have to be present in order to be discussed. The label 'Daddy' will enable a child to maintain an image of its father, even when he is absent. Language isn't the only symbolic system the child uses of course. Play is used to aid symbolic understanding too.

Piaget investigated how language reflects thought by asking children questions such as 'What makes the clouds move?' and 'Why do some things float?' The answers he received indicated the child's progress towards operational thought. Pre-operational children are unable to understand the real answers to questions such as these, and often provide an answer based on what things appear to be like. *Conservation skills* aren't usually acquired until some time after the age of five, so children will be unable to describe accurately that which they cannot understand. Teaching children the kind of words that they are likely to use in conservation skills does not appear to help them to conserve. If they aren't cognitively ready for conservation they will not be able to conserve. So, according to Piaget, language reflects cognition.

 Summarize Piaget's view of the relationship between thought and language.

Are language and thought independent?

So far we have been discussing the relationship between thought and speech in children and adults. **Lev Vygotsky** was a Russian psycholinguist who was more concerned with the origin of the two skills from birth. He was interested in Piaget's explanation for early sensory motor cognition, and the role of language in it. He did not agree that language was simply a tool of thought and that if thought is egocentric, then language must also be egocentric. Some animals appear to be capable of 'thought' as well as instinct; they are not capable of much 'language'.

Vygotsky claimed that language and thought are quite separate activities during the first two years of life. Children do not begin to use language until around their first birthday. But they do have thoughts before that. At four months infants are mastering what they can grasp, and what they can't. They turn to look, and can recognize certain people and things long before they know what the person or thing they are looking at is called. They have thought without speech or *pre-linguistic thought*.

The forerunner of language is babbling, which appears some time around five to six months. In the beginning babbles don't have any meaning, they're just vocal noises. Babbling certainly doesn't reflect any particular thought pattern. It is 'speech without thought' or *pre-intellectual language*.

Vygotsky claimed that when babies are about two years old pre-linguistic thought and pre-intellectual language come together. The child begins to use language to 'think in', and to communicate with. Between two and seven years language continues to direct the child's thinking and its communication. Since the child can't distinguish between its two uses of language it will 'speak its thoughts out loud' and in the next moment talk to someone and expect them to understand it. This is what Piaget described as *egocentric speech*. By about seven the child learns to keep its spoken language to social matters where communications to and from others is necessary. The 'private' language that was previously spoken out loud becomes 'internal speech'.

 How does Vygotsky explain the relationship between language and thought?

▶ According to Vygotsky, babies of up to the age of about two years have pre-linguistic thought and pre-intellectual language. These two functions are quite separate.

▶ Do you ever 'talk to yourself' without speaking out loud? Does it help you organise your activity, perhaps by making a list of what you need to do?

Summary: language and thought theories

Sapir and Whorf's linguistic relativity hypothesis claims that the words we use to describe objects and events determine how we perceive those happenings. There is a wealth of evidence against this claim and it is hardly credible now. Equally unbelievable is Watson's early behaviourist claim that thinking is subvocal speech and that many 'mental functions' are actually organized at the level of the sense receptor. Neither does language entirely determine thought since animals can display primitive thoughts without the use of language, and pre-linguistic humans appear to think.

For Piaget language reflects the level of cognitive reasoning the child has attained, and becomes a symbolic tool for enhancing reasoning later. Vygotsky proposed that thinking and language perform quite separate functions for the first few years of life, and are separate from each other. They only merge after the age of two years.

 Construct a table which outlines the evidence for the view that language determines thought, that thought determines language and that the two are independent but related.

COMPUTER MODELS OF THOUGHT

Since the Second World War the electrical and electronics industry has become one of the fastest growing throughout the world. How many electrical gadgets do you have in your home? TV, radio, stereo, CD, video recorder, washing machine, kettle, coffee maker, bedside lamp, electric blanket, electric shaver, hairdryer, and so on have all been provided by the electrical industry in the last 40 years or so. Ask your grandparents how many of these items they had when they were your age. Microchip technology and miniaturization have allowed many devices to have all kinds of facilities that we wouldn't have imagined possible only a few years ago.

Inevitably the question has been asked – how can machines be used to take the place of people? Robot welders work 24 hours a day in some car factories. Computer controlled lathes produce finished components from a bar of steel for the engineering industry in a few seconds. Optical readers are being developed to replace human sorters in the Post Office. Will people be replaced by machines? One major difference that has always been claimed between humans and machines is that humans can think and machines can't. However computers are being developed which come close to changing all this.

'Thinking machines' use 'artificial intelligence' (AI), that is, they apply mathematical principles to coded data and compute a correct response. Computer scientists and cognitive psychologists might work together to produce a machine that can imitate human thinking. The programmer in your cooker or video recorder is an 'intelligent machine' since it monitors some information (the time) and instructs the machine to perform some actions, such as start or stop when the time signal you have instructed it to wait for is reached. Computers are able to use rather more sophisticated electronics to perform a range of functions.

There are two elements in artificial intelligence. First, there is the *hardware*, i.e. the machinery itself. Devices that perform some 'human like' task such as waiting to turn a video tape on, or welding car panels, are parts of machines using AI. Second, there is the *software*. This is the program of instructions that the hardware follows.

At the moment my computer (hardware) is following the instructions contained in a word processor program (software), to produce the chapters of this book. I could run a chess program and have a game, or I could use wages and accounts software if I had a business, or database software if I needed to keep track of the details of a large number of people, or spreadsheet software if I wanted to forecast what would happen to a company's profits if interest rates went up, or wages went up, or productivity went up.

Present day computers can only follow the instructions in their software programs. For example, the computer I am using will wait for instructions entered from the keyboard or by running a program in a machine code language that it recognizes. Then it will follow instruction number one, followed by the instruction which follows from the outcome of the first, followed by the next which follows the outcome of the previous one, and so on. Humans are rather different. You don't wait for instructions for your every move. You can think for yourself, behave according to your emotions, do something on the spur of the moment, or do things simply because they bring you pleasure.

 What is artificial intelligence?

▶ One of the problems in considering the question of whether machines can 'think' is that psychologists are not able to agree as to what exactly thinking is. Is it some form of 'sub-vocal speech' (the behaviourist's view), is it creative combinations of related and unrelated neural activity (the physiological view), or is it the systematic processing of coded sensory information according to previously stored experience (the information processing model)?

▶ As your cooker waits for the right time to start or stop working, is it 'thinking'?

▶ *Hardware* includes computers, printers, monitors, communications equipment etc. *Software* are the programs of instructions that make the hardware perform some function.

▶ Humans have several great advantages over computers. One is that they can think. Computers merely respond to precise instructions.

Some similarities and differences in human and machine processing

If computers are to be compared to the human brain then we might expect there to be similarities in their structure (how they are made up), their hierarchies (some parts will be more important than others), and their function (what they do). Let us see:

Structure

The human brain comprises many millions of tiny nerve fibres in various shapes, sizes and locations. Each nerve fibre – a neuron – can only carry one kind of specialized message. Neurons which are part of the visual pathways, for example, could not carry messages about what we hear. Each system of neurons has its own code which will be recognized by neurons in other parts of the same system, but not by neurons in other systems. The structure of neurons has been compared to the banks of wiring that you would find behind the control panels in any sophisticated machinery. There messages are sent along wires, switching other devices on or off. Each wire can carry one kind of message to one particular location.

Wires are put in place by electricians who decide, for example, which switch will connect with which motor. Once in place that wire cannot switch on any other motor. Neurons, on the other hand, can send their messages along millions of different pathways. Each neuron can form connections with many others. In the brain each neuron can connect with an average of 60,000 other neurons. Brain messages can pass from one place to another in a much more dynamic way than messages carried by wires.

When the power is turned on, the whole electrical impulse flows down the wire. It isn't possible for only some of the power to be transmitted (unless a transformer is placed between the supply and the distribution). Something similar happens in the nervous system. The 'all or none rule' states that the neuron either carries the complete message or doesn't fire at all.

Unlike the human brain, machines aren't adaptive. A breakdown in one part of the machine cannot be compensated for by extra capacity in another. If my car's starter motor packs up it doesn't matter how charged the battery is, how much petrol is in the tank, or how many people I can squeeze onto the back seat! When a crucial part fails the whole thing fails. The brain works in a more adaptive way. Some structures can take over parts of other systems, or other systems may compensate for breakdowns in one area. Some blind people, for example, have very acutely developed hearing.

Hierarchy

Some parts of any control system carry messages which are much more important than others. On my computer the on/off system is important to the machine's functioning. If it is damaged I may not be able to turn the machine on or off. Important too is the system which allows me to save my work to a magnetic disk for storage. Other parts, such as the volume control that beeps when I press a wrong key, or the contrast controls on the monitor screen, are less important. In a car the

▶ Bundles of neurons are nerves. Bundles of wires are cables. Each neuron carries a specialized message to a particular part of the nervous system. Each wire carries electrical messages to one other part of its system.

▶ *Dynamic* means constantly changing and adapting to new information.

▶ Where one human sensory system doesn't work efficiently other systems may become more sensitive in order to compensate. Where one area of the brain becomes damaged other areas may sometimes take over some of its functioning. Machines cannot do this.

▶ Humans have a central nervous system, comprising the brain and spinal cord, and a peripheral nervous system, comprising all other systems such as the motor system, the sensory system, the autonomic system etc.. Machines have control systems which govern what the machine does.

ignition system is more important to the car's functioning than the heater or cassette player. Damage to the ignition system or the on/off control would mean the machine would probably not work.

Some parts of the brain are more important to our survival than others. The first part of the brain to evolve was the brain stem. It contains two major organs, the *medulla oblongata* and the *pons varolii*, which are responsible for primitive bodily functions such as breathing, heart rate, circulation of blood, some reflexes which help us stay upright and which co-ordinate other senses such as hearing, balance and sensations and movement of the face. Behind these two is the *reticular formation* which is concerned with levels of arousal or sleep. Damage to parts of the brain stem could cause serious injury, and probably death.

▶ Human behaviour can appear spontaneous, or be the result of a long deliberation. Either way we usually know what we're doing. Computers respond logically to the instructions they're given. If the instructions are illogical the program will crash.

At the centre of the psychological hierarchy are *cognitive centres* which ultimately decide whether we do something or not. We may 'have a good think about it', then decide what to do. Or we might allow ourselves to be persuaded by others if we aren't willing to think for ourselves. We might even behave on the spur of the moment. Cognitive centres are involved in all of these decisions about behaviour. Computers can't do any of these things. They operate on a system of absolute logic. They can be programmed to behave erratically, if that is what the program demands, but the behaviour isn't spontaneous, it is a result of a random choice that has been generated logically. Computers can't be persuaded by others, they simply respond rationally, according to what would be the mathematically most probable outcome.

Construction

Most of the discussion so far has suggested that humans think and machines operate with logic. But the designers of a car or a computer would never have intended that it should be compared to a human brain. If we want to answer the question of whether a machine could think then we must try to devise a model of how we think the brain works, and then construct a computer and a program to operate in some of the ways in which humans think they operate. This is called *computer simulation*, and it refers to the attempts which have been made to programme computers to operate in ways which mimic human thinking. **Newell** and **Simon** made the first serious attempt to do this with two computer programs, the 'Logic Theorist' and later the 'General Problem Solver' (GPS), starting over 30 years ago.

▶ The human brain uses *heuristic logic* to provide a best guess based on seemingly logical principles. They may not always lead to the correct solution, but if they do they can save much time and effort.

Newell and Simon argued that human thinking involves taking a certain view, then making a series of educated guesses, or using a principle that has been found to work in similar circumstances. This is known as *heuristic logic*. It can save a lot of time, but there is no guarantee that it will be correct. Imagine that you are lost in hilly country and very thirsty. You know that ('take a certain view that') rivers, with water to drink, often flow through valleys which lie at the bottom of hills. This principle may even have worked for you in the past. Heuristic logic suggests you find a route which takes you down hills rather than up them. Since rivers flow into lakes or seas, and people (called fishermen?) often live near lakes and seas, then more heuristic logic tells you to follow a river downstream in order to find people.

The only way to be certain of being right is to check every possible answer until you find the correct one, or at least the one most likely to be correct. Imagine that you know that the country in which you are lost contains people within 10 miles of you. Walking in a large circle half a mile around your present position might find them. If not, move a further half mile out and walk another circle. And another until you eventually come across them. Repeating some procedure until a desired result is found is called an *algorithm*. It will eventually produce the desired outcome, but at what effort! Computers tend to use algorithms.

Newell, Shaw and Simon's 'Logic Theorist' program could use heuristic mathematical principles and procedures. It was provided with 52 complex mathematical theorems from Whitehead and Russell's *Principia Mathematica*, and was able to solve 38 of them, many in less than one minute. (It would have taken a human a great deal longer!) When given more advanced theorems to solve, where it wasn't able to use the principles it had employed for easier theorems, it failed. The more advanced 'General Problem Solver' programe could play chess to a high standard and could solve a range of other problems for which humans would need to employ heuristic logic.

Newell *et al*'s research suggests two things. Firstly, human problem solving is hierarchical in structure, with some principles being more likely to be applied than others, e.g. that water flows downwards and not upwards. The outcome of the first principles will influence the choice of the next principles and so on, e.g. finding a manageable route downwards. Second, human thinking appears to rely on previous experiences to provide information for later strategies, e.g. in the past we have noted where fishermen often live. The 'General Problem Solver' could do both of these things.

(NM) Draw up a table to show what differences and similarities exist between computers and humans.

Functioning

In Chapter 6 we described the brain as the centre for information processing in humans. It receives, attends to, filters, encodes, stores, retrieves and uses information from each of its sensory systems to guide the body's responses to objects and events in its environment. Each sensory system provides information about different aspects of the environment, e.g. what it looks like, sounds like, smells like, feels like. The human brain works at speeds which give the appearance of being instantaneous. (Neural messages travel at somewhere between 2 and 200 miles an hour.)

Computers work extremely quickly too. They can't take data in on their own, but have to be fed data, which they can then manipulate and store, retrieve and use in a similar sequence to the brain. The information is in the form of small amounts of electricity which it

► Children of three and four use trial and error. By seven and eight they use their own version of *algorithms*. Teenagers are able to apply heuristic principles.

► Newell *et al*'s programs were designed to mimic human thinking in the use of heuristic principles to solve problems.

► In order to construct a machine to mimic human thinking we must first have some idea about what thinking is like. Not everyone agrees with what thinking is, so Newell and Simon's 'General Problem Solver' is only one of several possible thinking machines.

► The information processing approach is concerned with the nature of consciousness. It identifies selective attention, sensory, short and long term storage, retrieval and non-retrieval as the main features.

► Computers use logic and are incapable of feelings so their decisions cannot be influenced by emotions.

► *Cybernetics* comes from the Greek word for the person who steers a vessel. It was developed originally by Norbert Weiner in America during the 1940s.

► Positive and negative feedback are feedback are used by cybernetic machines to control their functioning. Humans also use feedback to monitor and adapt their functioning.

► TOTE stands for
   Test, **O**perate, **T**est, **E**xit.

► Miller's rather mechanistic view of humankind suggests that we operate rather like robots. Most social psychologists would see human interaction being influenced by many factors apart from 'try something and see what happens, then try something else'.

receives from an external power source such as the electric mains or batteries. The brain is provided with energy by its blood stream.

What computers can't do however, is anything which is original or spontaneous. Since they operate on logic and have no emotion they are incapable of feeling, speculating, imagining, dreaming, hoping and all the other emotions and motivations that direct and influence human behaviour.

One important aspect of information processing is the use made of *feedback*. When some feature of your behaviour is approved of by those around you, then you may feel good about yourself and may try to repeat the action or maintain that image. Part of your behaviour is the result of feedback from others. If you sit with your arms folded for a long time, and one of your arms starts to feel cramped, then you will unfold them. Feedback from your arm muscles triggers your behaviour. After rushing for the bus you may become breathless. Your heart and respiratory system are sending you feedback. You need to flop in a seat until you 'get your breath back'. Much of our behaviour, both social and physical, is the result of feedback.

Computers also require feedback from those who interact with them. The first attempts to apply feedback theory to 'thinking' (or at least 'responding') machines were called *cybernetics*. Cybernetics applies three processes of human functioning to the machine: taking information in, processing it in some way, and responding to it. In terms of the machine this is called 'input', 'processing' and 'output'. For example, the central heating system or air conditioning system at home may be cybernetically controlled. The programmer instructs the boiler that it is time to switch on, and the thermostat controls the amount of time the boiler needs to be on to heat your rooms. The programmer and thermostat provide input. The water is being processed by the boiler. The response is that your radiators start to warm up. The thermostat is constantly monitoring the temperature. So long as your room is below the temperature set on the thermostat the boiler receives instructions to continue working. This is positive feedback. When the desired temperature in the room is reached, the processor ceases functioning. This is negative feedback.

According to **G.A. Miller** human behaviour follows a certain sequence. First we do something and observe what its effects are. If they are satisfactory then we perform some further action. We check to see that the consequences of this are acceptable. If so we repeat the procedure until such time as the consequences are unacceptable, or we decide to do something else. This is called a TOTE system, and reflects the way that human behaviour relies on feedback.

Miller suggests that human functioning is also based on *plans*. A plan is 'any hierarchical process in the organism that can control the order in which a sequence of operations is to be performed'. A high-level plan would be a general strategy, e.g. taking a fortnight's holiday in August next year. Lower-order plans involve specific strategies, e.g. finding the phone book to look up the number of the travel agent, or preparing for a family conference to discuss possible destinations.

Machines can operate on TOTE's and plans too. A word processor waits for someone to press a key. It scans the keyboard as often as 60 times a second to see if a key has been pressed. This is the Test. If a key has been pressed then it reads what that key is and instructs the screen to display it. That is the Operation. It then Tests the keyboard again. Finally the operator will tell the program that she or he wants to Exit, and it will hand control back to the hardware.

What computers can do is solve complex mathematical problems with minimal use of energy and time. Anything which can be reduced to mathematical principles and probabilities can be dealt with by a computer. They can apply an almost infinite number of principles to manipulate their data, so long as someone has instructed them about which order or under which circumstances each of the principles is to be applied. They can perform a limited number of tasks at the same time, although that time isn't very long!

If thinking is the logical application of principles which will produce the correct answer in a short time, then computers can think. If it comprises those abilities we outlined at the beginning of this chapter – mentally manipulating ideas, words, knowledge, beliefs, intentions, concept formation, problem solving, intellectual functioning, creativity, complex learning, memory, symbolic processing, imagery – then computers can't think. Yet . . . .

So can machines think or can't they?

Alan Turing was a mathematician who was fascinated by the idea of the thinking machine. One of the simplest features of human thinking is imitation, so Turing asked, 'Can machines imitate?' He argued that humans solve problems by logical thought processes involving rational deduction. If a machine could imitate these processes, then the machine must also be able to think.

He imagined a game whereby an interrogator had to discover the sex of a man and a woman whom he couldn't see but whose answers to his questions he could read. Just to make it difficult one of them, e.g. the woman, had to tell lies, while the other had to tell the truth. Turing thought that it would be impossible for an interrogator to discover the truth by using logical reasoning. (Since there was only one man and one woman being questioned, there's a 50–50 chance of guessing correctly anyway.) Turing believed that if a machine was to replace the woman, and the interrogator still could not tell 'which sex it was', then the machine was imitating human thought and so could be described as a thinking machine.

Many people disagree with Turing's assumption that a machine which could imitate human responses, even in good English, is actually thinking at all. It is behaving in an observable, uninventive way. Human thinking is unobservable and inventive. Many machines already exist which can perform actions that humans might otherwise perform. Thinking clearly isn't necessary for these kinds of processes. A chess computer that can beat its programmer doesn't use thinking to plan its strategies, it uses mathematically consistent probabilities deployed heuristically.

► Computers come in all sizes and with all kinds of specialized functions. Because they are able to perform their specialized tasks so well, some humans have been tempted to ask whether they can think. This isn't a fair question. Let computers compute, it's what they do best. And let humans do what they do best, let them think.

► Turing's assumption is that, since the simplest type of human thinking is imitation, then if machines can imitate they must be able to think. This is rather like saying that the simplest thing a goldfish can do is swim, so if you can swim you must be a goldfish.

► By today's standards Turing's 'identity game' seems rather naive. A computer that must say the opposite of what it has been programmed to accept as true and thus fool a human being seems a strange way of 'proving' that a machine can 'think'.

Can computers think?

No	*Maybe*
Computers are simply machines for performing calculations.	Computers can perform many tasks which do not involve calculation at all, e.g. storing data, retrieving it, comparing and sorting it, finding particular occurrences of specified items, etc. These processes resemble human 'thinking'.
Computers can only do what their programs instruct them to do.	True, but not all programs are simply lists of instructions whose results can be known in advance. Many a games program has beaten its programmer! Many computer programs perform actions that humans would take a very long time to do, and could easily make errors in, or couldn't do at all.
Machines can't learn from their past mistakes and so improve their performance.	Not true. The latest breed of computers can apply principles learned previously to new situations.
Machines apply rules of logic and cannot be guided by intuition or emotion.	The latest computers mimic intuition and could possibly be programmed to use some kind of artificial emotion (if there was any reason to programme them to do so).

(NM) To what extent can computers be said to think?

Chapter summary

Thinking is mentally manipulating ideas. This may be performed according to some logic, or may obey pre-operational rules. Its relationship with language has been hotly contested, and is very complex. The way we think both influences, and is influenced by, the language we use.

The comparison between human thinking and mechanical/electrical computing has centred on comparing the structure and functioning of the mechanisms of the brain to that of the machine. So far machines cannot 'think' in the same way that humans can. Nor do they allow irrational emotions to interfere with their reasoning. They can use similar procedures of deduction to humans, but we are still some way from the thinking machine.

Exam questions – 60 minutes each

1 Critically examine the theories that attempt to explain the relationship between language and thought.

2 Do you think that computer models of thought help to explain human thinking?

Further Reading: Chapter 7

Probably the best original sources here are

Skinner B.F. 1957. *Verbal Behaviour*. Appleton Century Crofts.

Bernstein B. 1972. 'Social Class, Language and Socialisation' in Giglioli P.P., (ed.). *Language and Social Context*. Harmondsworth: Penguin.

Vygotsky L. 1962. *Thought and Language*. Cambridge: M.I.T. Press.

Vygotsky L. 1978. *Mind in Society*. Harvard: Harvard University Press.

Useful summaries of the nature of language and thought are found in

Miller G.A. 1981. *Language and Speech*. Oxford: W.H. Freeman.

Greene J. 1987. *Memory, Thinking and Language*. London: Methuen.

Mayer R.E. 1983. *Thinking, Problem Solving and Cognition*. Oxford: W.H. Freeman.

8 *Social and interpersonal perception*

Chapter objectives

By the end of this chapter you should:

■ be able to review the intuitive and the inference models of how people form impressions of others

■ be able to describe how we attribute causes to people's behaviour, including our own

■ be able to review and evaluate the major theories of the self-concept

■ be able to describe the process of impression-management and how people manage impressions of themselves in every day life

■ be able to review the factors which attract people to each other and the experimental evidence on attraction and affiliation.

Introduction

Humans have developed very complicated social relationships. Children have to learn what they should say and do in all kinds of social situations. We have self-awareness and can judge the effects that our appearance or behaviour can have on other people, and we sometimes deliberately manage that impression for some end, e.g. to try to obtain a job at an interview or to attract a member of the opposite sex at a party. In this chapter we will be reviewing that area of social psychology that deals with such interpersonal perception.

FORMING IMPRESSIONS

► Interpersonal perception is 'the study of how the lay person uses theory and data in understanding people' (Gahagan).
Or
'the study of the ways people react and respond to others, in thought, feeling, and action' (Cook).

Most people are fairly sociable. We generally want to get on with others. We want to make and maintain relationships with some people (our friends), while avoiding relationships with others (people we don't like). Whenever we see people, we form impressions about what they are like, and we modify the impressions we have already formed as we find out more about them. We do this without much conscious awareness or effort. When someone asks you 'What is Leanne like?' or 'What is Harriet like?' you will probably be only too happy to pass on your impressions. If you have decided that Leanne is pleasant and likeable, then you will say complimentary things about her. If your impression of Harriet is that she is awful then you will be uncomplimentary. Social psychologists are interested in how we form our impressions of others.

Impression formation refers to the process by which we select certain features of someone's behaviour to observe – their sex, uniform, posture, actions, etc. – and interpret that feature in terms of our previous knowledge or prejudices about it, thus confirming or challenging our cognition. For example Stephen notices a woman driver pulling out from the kerb. He has selected the driver's sex. He could have selected the colour of her hair, how attractive he thinks she is, her age, the car she was driving or several other things. His previous, prejudiced, knowledge of 'women drivers' is that they are careless and incompetent. If her driving away from the kerb causes another car to swerve or brake this will confirm his 'women drivers' prejudice. If it does not he might say to himself 'She was lucky no one was coming'. No matter what she does Stephen's stereotype will be confirmed.

 What is impression formation?

M. Cook suggests that the research findings for explaining impression formation can be divided into two groupings. One suggests that we all share a scale of attitudes about certain characteristics, e.g. that cruelty and deceit are bad. If we see someone behaving cruelly or telling lies, then our impression of them will be that they are 'bad people' who we will dislike. This scale of attitudes is a part of everyone's way of making sense of other people. Cook calls this the *intuitive model*. Alternatively Cook suggests the *inference model*, which includes those explanations which suggest that we make individual judgements based on our own perceptions. We will review both models below.

 What factors do you take into account when you form your first impressions of someone?

The intuitive model

One theory within the intuitive model suggests that the ability to 'read' other people's 'body language', such as their facial expressions and posture, and make judgements about their intentions and personalities is innate. This is highly unlikely. Psychologists are much more cautious now about what they claim to be innate. Although we are learning more about the structure and specialized function of genetic material, we are still speculating about which more general skills are innately given or socially acquired.

We do not regard all characteristics as equally desirable or undesirable. Would you rather have as a friend someone who is untidy or someone who is a liar (assuming that they are the same in all other respects)? Nearly 50 years ago **Solomon Asch** hypothesized that there are certain 'central' personality characteristics which we use to evaluate others. Knowing whether someone is likeable or unlikable, trustworthy or treacherous, honest or deceitful, etc., is more important to us than knowing what someone looks like (whether they are tall or short, fat or thin, dark or blond) or knowing about their background (whether they are rich or poor, from town or country, Italian or Aborigine). According to Asch *evaluative traits* are more central to us than *descriptive traits*.

► A *trait* is a long-lasting, hypothetical characteristic which can help explain why a person usually behaves in a particular way under specific circumstances.

To test this, Asch gave a list of adjectives that referred to an imaginary character to a group of his students. Half of them had the attributes of the following list: 'intelligent, skilful, industrious, warm, determined, practical, cautious'. The other half had the same list except that the word 'warm' was replaced by 'cold'. Asch believed that 'warm' and 'cold' were two of the more influential evaluative traits, and that each group would have quite a different picture of what the imaginary character was like. Asch asked the students to write a paragraph describing what the person was like. He also gave all of the subjects a list of 18 personality traits and asked them to choose which adjectives from the second list would also describe the imaginary character.

▶ There's nothing surprising in Asch's claim that some traits are more important for our evaluation of people than others. Most people would agree that truthfulness and a sense of humour are more important traits than generosity and tidiness.

As Asch predicted, the 'warm' group rated the character more favourably then the 'cold' group. For example, 90 per cent of the warm group described him as generous, happy and good-natured, compared to only 10 per cent, 35 per cent and 25 per cent of the 'cold' group for those three characteristics; and 65 per cent of the 'warm' group said he was wise, compared to just over 30 per cent of the 'cold' group. The cold group saw him as mean, humourless, miserable, unfriendly and unliked. Both groups described him as reliable, good looking, persistent, serious, restrained, strong, honest and important. Asch believed that 'warm' and 'cold' are central traits. Other less important traits, such as competitiveness, tidiness and punctuality, are called peripheral traits.

(**ACT**) Repeat Asch's experimental demonstration of the existence of central and peripheral traits on your friends.

Not everyone agrees with Asch's insistence on the central–peripheral distinction. **Wishner** gave Asch's 'stimulus' and 'response' lists in various combinations to his psychology students. He obtained similar results to Asch, regardless of the combination of terms, and even when warm and cold weren't included in the stimulus list at all. Wishner does not believe that evaluative traits are more 'central' than descriptive traits. There are other explanations for how we form our impressions of others.

In 'real life' people aren't easily defined as 'all bad' or 'all good'. They each have their good points and bad points. We do, however, tend to generalize from what we do know about someone, e.g. that they are attractive, to other characteristics which we do not know, such as that they're kind and caring. Usually we will need to know more about the combination of their central and peripheral traits if we are to form an overall impression of what they are like. But few of us are like the judges of the ice skating championships who watch the skater's whole programme before making their judgement. We judge people on the basis of the first things we find out about them. Within the first few minutes we may have decided what we think, long before we could know all of someone's qualities. First impressions are important.

▶ Do you make quick judgements about whether you are going to 'get on with' someone within the first few minutes of meeting them? Or do you prefer to 'get to know' them a little before deciding if you're going to like them or not?

This was established by **Luchins** over 30 years ago. He compiled two

---

Luchins' story about Jim (1957)

Jim the extrovert

Jim left the house to get some stationery. He walked out into the sun-filled street with two of his friends, basking in the sun as he walked. Jim entered the stationery store, which was full of people. Jim talked with an acquaintance while he tried to catch the clerk's eye. On his way out he stopped to chat with a school friend who was just coming into the store. Leaving the store he walked towards school. On his way he met the girl to whom he had been introduced the night before. They talked for a short while, and then Jim left for school.

Jim the introvert

After school Jim left the classroom alone. Leaving the school he started on his long walk home. The street was brilliantly filled with sunshine. Jim walked down the street on the shady side. Coming down the street toward him, Jim saw the pretty girl whom he had met on the previous evening. Jim crossed the street and entered a candy store. The store was crowded with students and he noticed a few familiar faces. Jim waited quietly until he caught the counterman's eye and then gave his order. Taking his drink, he sat down at a side table. When he had finished his drink he went home.

---

paragraphs about an imaginary student named Jim. One paragraph described Jim as a sociable, friendly person (an extrovert), the other depicted him as a shy, solitary person (an introvert). His subjects were read the two paragraphs, but half would hear the paragraph which described Jim as an extrovert first, the other half would hear Jim described as an introvert first. Luchins used a matched subjects design to allocate subjects to four groups so that each group contained people with similar personalities. The first two groups were 'controls'. They simply heard the extrovert paragraph or the introvert paragraph, and could identify Jim as an extrovert or introvert. Seventy-six per cent of the subjects in the groups described it accurately so Luchins could be reasonably sure that most of his subjects were familiar with the concepts of introversion and extroversion.

Of the experimental group who heard Jim described as an extrovert first and an introvert second (EI), 52 per cent said he was an extrovert. A further 12 per cent said they didn't know. Of the 'introvert first' experimental group (IE), 56 per cent said Jim was an introvert. Another 10 per cent didn't know. A *primacy effect* appeared to be operating. (See Chapter 6 for a discussion of primacy and recency effects.) It seems that first impressions are important.

(ACT) Repeat Luchins' experiment on your friends.

(NM) What evidence is there that first impressions are important?

► The *primacy effect* says that the first things we find out about someone or something will make the greatest impression on us. The recency effect says that the last thing we heard has the most influence.

► Inference is very important in social exchanges. It increases our ability to predict what will happen if we do or say one thing as opposed to another.

► *Stereotypes* are simple, overgeneralized ideas about the psychological characteristics of whole groups of people.

► We may sometimes see people we don't know as 'things' having a particular sex, job, status, colour, dress, etc. These physical characteristics allow us to place the person into particular groups, such as 'women drivers'. There are many related stereotypes.

► Responding to individuals in terms of a stereotype can have damaging effects, if those in authority (e.g. doctors, police and teachers) respond to a member of a group according to a negative stereotype which they hold of the group, rather than to that person as an individual.

The inference model

Inference is a cognitive process we all use by which we draw a conclusion based on some previous experience or knowledge. If your previous experience of dentists is that they hurt you, then you will infer that the next time you go to the dentist the treatment is going to hurt. So you might avoid having regular check ups. Two major explanations contribute to the inference model, stereotyping and attribution theory.

Stereotyping

It would be impossible to take every person we come across and study them in detail as an individual – much as we may like to think that this is just what we do. We would spend all of our lives studying people and never have time to do anything else. Instead, we build up ideas about groups of people based on a very limited contact with them, or on things we have heard during our socialization. We build up pictures in our minds about people in groups such as 'mothers', 'hooligans', 'policemen', 'the Irish' and 'children'. These ideas are *stereotypes*. They are a shorthand way of categorizing people and organizing our perceptions. They also make our responses more predictable. (Is it surprising that many people's driving changes when they see a police car?)

Stereotypes are simple, overgeneralized ideas about the psychological characteristics, such as the attitudes, beliefs and behaviour, of a whole group of people. They are 'snap judgements' and so must be triggered by some characteristic that can be perceived instantly, such as what someone looks like. The easier some characteristic of a group of people can be recognized, the more likely it is that a stereotype will exist about them. Stereotypes are usually based on obvious visual characteristics such as skin colour, accent, size, sex or dress.

NM Why do humans use stereotyped ideas about other groups of people?

One important source of information on which we base our impressions is what we think we know about someone before we meet them. For example some people believe that students are basically lazy, and are always looking for an excuse to avoid tests or exams. (I wonder if many teachers share this view?) If a doctor believes this student stereotype her or his reaction towards you as a student might be less sympathetic than it could be. If you want something to treat a migraine, which makes it ok for you miss a test, the doctor might see this as you 'looking for an excuse to get out of a test', and tell you there's nothing wrong with you.

Stereotypes can become *self-fulfilling*. Sociologists talk about 'labelling theory', which suggests that people tend to behave in ways which they know are expected of them. (This is a major criticism of modern psychiatry too, as we shall see in Chapter 10.) If your teachers labelled and treated you as though you were a trouble-maker, then other people would start to see you that way too. They may become

> ### Some common stereotypes
> Men are supposed to be unemotional, strong, brave and skilful. Women are supposed to be emotional, weak, passive and helpless. Age is also a characteristic on which stereotypes are based. Teenagers are supposed to be assertive, radical, discontented and adventurous. The middle aged are supposed to be conventional, unexciting, cautious and boring. Ethnic origin is another observable characteristic. Jewish people are supposed to be mean, Asians are supposed to be good business people, the Chinese to be inscrutable, and Arabs are supposed to have all the oil!

more suspicious of you, and watch you more closely. Anything you did which could be interpreted as trouble-making would be labelled as such, and you would be more severely punished for it. Eventually you would probably start behaving more like a trouble-maker. Throughout childhood, adolescence and even adulthood, we form and maintain our perceptions about ourselves from the ways other people treat us.

Stereotypes can also affect our explanations for other people's behaviour. **Kay Deaux** showed a sample of subjects a group of men and women attempting a particular task. Some succeeded and others failed to solve it. She asked her sample to explain the outcome. She found that both women and men attributed men's success to their skill, while women's success was explained as 'good luck' or the result of trying harder. After studying the findings of many research projects on sex role stereotyping Deaux concluded: 'It is far more common for the female to explain her performance on the basis of luck, whether the outcome is a good or a bad one. Males, on the other hand, are much more likely to claim that ability was responsible for their successes.'

 What are the possible disadvantages of using stereotypes?

Once formed, stereotypes tend to be long lasting. They may be based on an element of truth, and many people go to considerable lengths to distance themselves from their stereotype. The bank manager who wears jeans in her spare time to appear less conventional and formal than she has to in the bank may be trying to modify the stereotype we have that 'all bank managers are stuffy'. The famous rock star who assures us that fame hasn't changed him and that he is quiet and modest may not want us to think that he is loud and destructive like 'all rockstars are'. The teacher who likes you to call her by her first name, or the yuppie who plays football rather than squash, may be trying to stop us responding to them as 'typical' members of the group whose behaviour we can predict from our stereotype.

Since most people are aware that stereotypes exist, and many realize that they may be a member of a group about whom an unflattering stereotype exists, they may try to do something which contradicts the stereotype, as if to say 'Look, I'm not really like that at all.'

► Some critics of psychiatry say that the diagnoses used do not actually reflect the true nature of mental illness, since we do not really understand it. Psychiatrists merely label someone as 'a neurotic', 'a schizophrenic', 'an obsessive compulsive', etc., and then everyone else treats them according to the label.

► If we keep on telling girls they are less capable than boys, they will eventually see themselves that way too. They may well behave in a 'less capable way'. But does that mean that girls *are* less capable than boys?

► Attribution is the process by which we draw conclusions about the causes of someone else's behaviour.

► *Attribution theory* says that in everyday life we act as naive psychologists attributing personality characteristics to others in order to explain their behaviour.

Attribution theory

We often do 'read more' into some of the things we see than are actually there. *Implicit personality theory* suggests that we group together perceptions that we believe are similar. For example, someone smiling would probably also be seen as capable and intelligent. Someone looking sad would also probably be described as unsure and less skilled.

Deciding a reason for someone else's behaviour is called *attribution*. If I see you being chased by a wild dog I can be pretty certain that I know the cause of your 'running away' behaviour: you are running in order to escape from a dangerous encounter which could cause you pain. If you are looking bleary-eyed and yawning in a Monday morning lesson your teacher could attribute your behaviour to a hectic weekend. Not all behaviour is so easily explained. If I see you being chased by your best friend, then I won't know exactly why you are running away. Are you really running away, or are you really hoping to be caught? Is it a huge joke you're having? In order to make an attribution, I might draw inferences from other aspects of the situation – are you laughing your head off, are you running quickly, how do you look? If you're laughing you must be having a bit of fun. If you are looking serious and running quickly, I will conclude that you're in trouble with your friend.

Previously made attributions also help us to predict future events. If I know that you often run away from people while having fun, then the next time I see you running away from someone I might reason that you are 'having fun'.

If Andrea is pleasant and helpful towards Val, then Val might conclude that Andrea likes her. It's important to Val to know whether Andrea really does like her, or whether Andrea is merely after something from Val? Is Andrea being genuine, or is she being cunning? If Val makes a mistake she could either be made to look foolish or, worse, she could lose a potential friend. These are the kinds of problems that people try to solve by making attributions.

 What is meant by attribution?

► Heider says that we usually assume the cause of someone else's behaviour is the result of personal factors such as their mood or intelligence, rather than environmental or situational factors. This is called *Fundamental Attribution Error*.

Fundamental Attribution Error

Over 30 years ago **Fritz Heider** suggested a theory for how we interpret the causes of other people's behaviour. As we mentioned earlier, there are two sources of clues – personal and environmental. If someone treads on your foot in a shop during the January sales, you might attribute the cause of their behaviour to environmental factors – the crowds in the shop – or to personal factors – someone intended to hurt you. How you respond will be influenced by whether you think it was accidental or intentional. Heider says that we tend to operate as 'naive psychologists', and we usually attribute to personal rather than environmental factors. This is called *Fundamental Attribution Error*, and often leads to us making mistakes. In the crowded shop we are more likely to think that the person who trod on our foot was at fault, if not for deliberately hurting us, then at least for being careless.

Ten years after Heider's introductory work, **Harold Kelley** provided experimental data which extended Heider's basic theory by reference to 'central personality traits' (see the discussion of Solomon Asch, page 168). He gave a group of students a brief written description of a visiting lecturer. They all had the same description, except that half of them read that the guest was 'very warm', while the other half read that he was 'rather cold'. The lecture began without the students knowing that their descriptions differed in any way. After the lecture the students were asked to say what they thought of the guest. Those who had read that he was 'very warm' said they thought he was better informed, more considerate, more sociable and popular, better natured, funnier and more humane than those who had read that he was 'rather cold'.

Kelley also recorded the students' interactions with the lecturer in a question and answer session. He hypothesized that the different perceptions people have of others will influence their desire for interaction with them. Of the students who were told that the lecturer was 'warm', 56 per cent participated in the class discussion, compared to 32 per cent of the 'cold' group. Are these differences necessarily the result of the list Kelley gave them at the beginning? This is far from proven.

According to Kelley most people prefer simple explanations for things they see or hear. He suggests a 'discounting principle' operates. If we know one explanation for the behaviour we observe we may well ignore alternative explanations. For example, knowing that Susan wants to be a doctor may be all the explanation we need for why she works so hard in school. However there are almost certainly other reasons for her hard work.

If we do have any explanation for our social perceptions Kelley proposes his co-variation model.

Kelley's co-variation model
In the late 1960s Harold Kelley proposed a three-part model for attribution, i.e. he claims that we use three sources of information, in making an attribution. Firstly, we look for clues in someone's behaviour which suggest it is caused by the individual themselves. Secondly, we seek clues from the behaviour of other people who are also involved to see whether their behaviour is similar or different from that of the individual we're interested in. Thirdly, we look for clues which suggest that the situation is responsible for their behaviour.

In order to qualify as a social situation there must be more than one person involved. Kelley identifies *the actor* (the person we see) and anyone else who is the 'target' of the actor's behaviour called *the entity*. The lecturer would have been the actor in Kelley's experiment.

Let's say that we want to understand why Lucy did not hand in her psychology homework. Kelley described the three sources of data as consensus, distinctiveness and consistency.

Consensus refers to how other actors behave in the same situation. Do the other students not hand their psychology assignments in, or is

▶ Harold Kelley offered the first complete and detailed explanation of how people assign or attribute cause to other people's behaviour. He suggested that people make attributions partly on the basis of their previous knowledge.

▶ Kelley identifies three sources of clues which we seek and combine in order to assist in the attribution of cause to people's behaviour. He adds the behaviour of others in the same situation as a source of data in making an attribution.

▶ Where all the people in the same situation agree on what is the appropriate thing to do, and the subject's behaviour is the same as everyone else's, then there is high *consensus*.

► The behaviour is *consistent* if it usually occurs in the particular situation.

► If the subject behaves in the same way in similar situations then the cause must be personal.

► When we do not know the status of *consensus, distinctiveness* or *consistency*, we may either guess them, and make an attribution that supports some prejudice of ours, or we may seek further information.

it just Lucy? If others don't hand work in either, then there is a high consensus of not handing work in. Lucy's behaviour isn't so special. If there is a low consensus of not handing work in, i.e. most students hand their work in, then Lucy's behaviour will stand out. Then she appears to be responsible for her own actions.

Distinctiveness refers to whether the behaviour is specific to one situation, or would be true of other situations too. Does Lucy hand her work in for her other subjects? If she does, then not handing in psychology work has high distinctiveness. She is responsible for her own actions, so again we attribute to dispositional (personal) factors. If she doesn't hand work in for anyone else either, then not handing it in for psychology has low distinctiveness.

Consistency refers to whether the behaviour observed would be repeated in similar situations. Does Lucy generally hand her psychology work in, or is this another in a series of failures to do the work? Is Lucy always missing things, like buses; is she a generally disorganized person? If consistency is low (Lucy misses one assignment), we aren't likely to make much of an attribution at all. Consistency must be high (Lucy doesn't seem to do any work in psychology) for an attribution to personal or environmental factors to be made.

With the help of these three sources of data an attribution to personal or environmental factors should be easy. If one of these causes consistently varies with Lucy's behaviour – they *co-vary* – then we are likely to assume that the one factor causes the other.

 What does Kelley mean by consensus, distinctiveness and consistency?

Kelley claimed that where consensus and distinctiveness are low, but consistency is high, we attribute to the actor, i.e. we make a personal attribution. When all three are high, we blame the entity – in Lucy's case, the psychology teacher. We make an environmental attribution. Of course we don't always have these three sources of data. For example, we may not know whether Lucy hands in her work for English or history. We may not know whether she always hands in her psychology work, or we may not know what the other psychology students hand in.

In everyday life people do not respond equally to the three factors Kelley identifies. Nor do we all necessarily make attributions at all. We may keep an open mind unless or until more information becomes available. Kelley's model is a useful indicator of the kinds of processes involved in attribution.

Jones and Davis's correspondent inference theory

In the mid 1960s **E.E. Jones** and **Keith Davis** proposed their *correspondent inference theory*. They agreed with Heider that when we see strangers behaving in particular ways we may well think that their behaviour is a consequence of 'what they are like'. The sequence of events which may result in attribution is:

Disposition – Intention – Ability – Choice – Action – Effects.

► *Correspondent inference theory* suggests that people's behaviour is the result of their disposition and their intentions, which are modified by their abilities.

We will go through each stage, using an example.

Disposition: Some people are generally friendly, honest, generous, cruel, aggressive, polite, happy etc. This is their disposition. Disposition is used here as a collective name for a group of particular personality characteristics. I may have a generous disposition.

Intention: our disposition usually influences our intentions to behave in certain ways. I may intend to be as benevolent, kind, giving, altruistic and charitable (some of the characteristics that make up my generous disposition) as I can in all my dealings. I may be approached to help in a fund raising event for a local charity.

Ability: we can only behave in those ways in which we are able. I can only behave generously if I have the ability to be generous. Do I have the time, money or skills needed?

Choice: where we have more than one alternative we must choose what to do. I may have a choice of things which I can do to help the charity. I'm a pretty fair guitarist so I could do a gig to raise money, or I could help set the stalls out on the day, or I could just donate some money.

Action: having made a decision about what to do, we might do it. Whichever way I choose to help will lead to certain actions. I'll either be running my stall or playing my guitar, or spending some money I'll start rehearsing my act.

Consequences: most of our behaviour is likely to have some effect or other, quite often on other people as well as on ourselves. The consequences of my actions might be putting on a pretty good show, and raising a lot of money.

When it comes to someone making an attribution to our behaviour all they will have to go on will be these last two stages, action and consequence. If you were to attend my charity gig all you will be able to observe will be me playing, and collecting lots of money. You might infer from this that I have generous disposition.

Jones and Davis' theory suggests that observers don't just make inferences based on the actions (and its effects) that they observe, but take into account all the other things (and their effects) that the actor might have done. I could have set the tables out and organized a stall instead. You might still have thought that I had a generous disposition. Doing the stall or playing the gig have some common effects. They both involve giving up some time and making some effort. An observer won't learn much about someone's intentions (and therefore their disposition) from common effects.

But each activity also has some uncommon effects. Playing the gig may make me feel important, give me great satisfaction when people applaud, and might lead to offers of (paid) gigs. Running the stall has quite different effects. It would lead to my feet aching, being tired, and maybe feeling undervalued. According to correspondent inference theory an observer might well take these uncommon effects into account when forming impressions about other people's intentions. Am I really behaving generously when I appear on stage?

▶ *Disposition* is a result of our general personality, our socialization and our experiences.

▶ The features that all behaviour has in common are of no value in making attributions.

▶ According to Jones and Davis, knowing the differences in the consequences of doing two things will help us understand why one was chosen rather than another. We could infer your disposition from your behaviour, and this will allow us to make predictions about your behaviour in the future.

(NM) What is correspondent inference theory?

► *Fundamental attribution error* refers to the way that we explain other people's behaviour in terms of their own personalities rather than in terms of their situation.

► We often attribute other people's success to luck or skill. If we like them we may admire their skill, if we do not we may say they were just lucky.

► The *figure ground* explanation for attributional error derives from the Gestalt view that we tend to perceive things as wholes – the holistic view.

► Something very prominent may distract us and lead to some unintended consequence. We may blame this for our behaviour, thus excusing what we actually did.

Self-attribution and the fundamental attribution error

According to **Jones** and **Nisbett** there are differences in the way we make attributions about our own behaviour – *self-attribution* – and other people's behaviour – *other attribution*. This tendency involves the fundamental attribution error. Jones and Nisbett suggest that we like to think of ourselves as competent and skilful in most of the things we do. (They attribute this to human nature.) We imagine that we are good at judging what we observe. Most behaviour results from a combination of situational and personal factors, but the most obvious explanations for other people's behaviour lie in their personality, ability, intentions or disposition, so we refer to these to explain what they do.

When our own performance is good we often claim that it is a result of our skill. When we fail we assume that the failure must be caused by something in the situation (since we know that we are essentially competent). If someone else's behaviour is appropriate and successful (and we like them), we may suggest that they are skilful and have ability. If we don't like them we're more likely to say that they were lucky!

One possible explanation for this lies in the *figure ground* relationship. This suggests that we see ourselves as stable figures, whose behaviour is realistic and intended, against a background of our environment which is always changing. Where our behaviour is inappropriate we attribute this to the environment. You might say that it's not your fault that the video timer didn't work, you did exactly the same as you have always done. There must be something wrong with the machine. However we often see other people's behaviour as the background to a stable environment. Any mistakes they make are seen as resulting from their inadequacies. Your parents might say that the video machine is perfectly alright and that the only mistake was letting you set the timer. One exception to this view occurs with very depressed people. They tend to blame themselves for their failures and attribute their successes to the environment.

Another source of error or bias in the attribution process is the prominence of an object that may be involved in a person's behaviour. If one aspect of the person's personality or their environment is more obvious than anything else we are more likely to include it in the attribution process. For example, imagine that Rachel is walking down the road and is distracted by a 20-tonne lorry hurtling past. At the same moment she bumps into a stranger. We might easily involve the lorry in the attribution for Rachel's apparent clumsiness. If someone was riding past Rachel on a bicycle and she walked into the stranger, we wouldn't hold the rider responsible for her action. The lorry is much more eye-catching than the bike!

Shelley Taylor demonstrated this when she arranged for three groups of subjects to watch two actors (confederates of hers) having a discussion. One group could only see one actor, another group could only see the other, while the third group could see both actors. When asked to say who they thought had dominated the conversation, the members of the first two groups said the actor they had seen led most of the discussion. The third group said both had participated equally. We appear to exaggerate the things we are personally involved in, or know something about.

Finally, we do not always attribute cause at all. A great deal of behaviour may be going on around us and we may not think much about it. Sometimes we seek further information before making an attribution. We might, for example ask another observer if they have any information which might cast some light on the behaviour observed. Having made an attribution which we believe to be correct, we tend to seek other information which will confirm it, and ignore information which will not. This often involves drawing information from a stereotype – and, for example can be a major source of misinformation for the police gathering eyewitness testimony.

► Where we are involved in some way with someone or something, we tend to exaggerate its importance as a factor in attributing cause.

► Where there is insufficient information for an informed attribution to be made, we may either not make one, or make an uninformed one. Once made, we try to confirm or justify it with other 'evidence', and ignore anything which might contradict it.

 Outline some of the <u>main factors that can lead to errors in attributing cause to people's behaviour.</u> Illustrate this list from your own experience.

Summary – Impression formation

Impression formation refers to the way we choose and interpret some features of a person or situation to suit our knowledge, prejudices, beliefs etc. It involves the use of stereotyping and inference in accordance with our own personality. In order to gather impressions we often try to establish why people behave in certain ways. Kelley sees attributions resulting from consensus, distinctiveness and consistency. However there are several sources of bias in the attribution process. A major one is the selective way in which we view our own and other people's behaviour.

SELF-CONCEPT

Humans are the only animals to have much idea about what and who they are, as individuals. What makes you *different* from your best friend? How do *you* feel about important issues? How exactly would *you* define yourself? Your self-concept is simply the description that you would give of yourself if you wrote as many statements as you could beginning with 'I am ...'. Your self-concept comprises three major forces, self-image, self-esteem and ideal self.

Self-image is your knowledge of the kind of person you are, and whether you like that person or not. Are you the kind of person that you would like to be, or are there things about yourself that you don't like? How do you feel about your personality? Are you sociable or private, trustworthy or deceitful, honest or vain? How do you feel about your social roles, as a student, a daughter, a son, a friend, a shop assistant? And how about your physical appearance, or body image? Are you too fat, too thin, too pretty or too tall?

Self-esteem refers to how you value yourself. Do you think you are a valuable member of the human race with something useful to give to the rest of humanity, even if only in the humblest way? Or do you have a generally low opinion of yourself? No doubt some features of your behaviour, personality or appearance will be more acceptable to

► Humans are the only animals to have a high degree of awareness of themselves, their ideas and of the impression they make on others.

► Self-image is your knowledge of your own personality, roles and appearance.

► *Self-esteem* refers to the amount of value you put on yourself. In some areas you may consider yourself worthy, while in others your self-esteem may be low. No other animal has self-esteem.

you than others. One source of information about what you are like, on which your self-esteem will be based, is how other people respond to you. If you are popular and well liked, then your self-esteem may be higher than if people tend to avoid you.

Ideal self refers to what you would really like to be like. We have all met people who have characteristics we admire. We may have learned about what qualities constitute excellence at school. We may have read about people who have achieved things that we wish we were capable of doing. The image we develop in our head of what we would really like to be like is our ideal self. Maladjustment occurs when one's ideal self differs very sharply from one's actual self-image.

 What does the self-concept comprise of?

So far we have been describing our self-concept as though it was a thing which existed in reality and which could probably be measured in some way. But are we so consistent? Have you ever behaved in a way which was quite 'out of character'? Have you thought or said or done something which really wasn't 'you' at all? Is it possible that there is actually more than one 'you'? Could we have several 'selves' which exist side by side? This is not implying that each of us is a Jekyll and Hyde character, but simply that it is no less reasonable to assume that we have several selves than it is to assume that we have only one.

John Rowan has been gathering information from psychological experimental research, from clinical treatments and therapies, and from philosophy to contradict the view that we have a single personality. He says:

> It is an extraordinary thing that all personality theories assume that there is just one personality. The questions they then ask are – what is the structure of this personality, what are the functions of this personality, what are the origins of this personality, what can we predict about this personality?

> But these assumptions are just assumptions, and they are made largely because it is convenient to do so .... Personologists are lazy people, like the rest of us, and do not want the bother of considering that people might be multiple. And other psychologists studying questions like the self, identity and so forth, are only too pleased to fall in with this for their own particular purposes.

Instead, Rowan (and others) claims that humans have several *subpersonalities*. The exact nature and function of these subpersonalities is yet to be revealed, but Rowan calls for a radical re-think of our current understanding of the concept of personality.

 Do we have one personality, or many?

► For many years it has been assumed that we have one global personality which reflects and comprises our real self. Recently evidence appears to challenge this view, suggesting instead that we have several *subpersonalities*.

Three-year-old logic?

Mike and Ann Stevens had a daughter of three and a half called Rebecca when Ann gave birth to another daughter, Nicky. When Nicky was a few months old she and Rebecca were playing in the kitchen. Nicky was in her baby bouncer and Rebecca was playing with her child's 'kitchen equipment'. Ann and Mike were in the sitting room when they heard a piercing scream from the kitchen. They rushed in to find Nicky screaming, with a large bruise on her forehead. Rebecca was holding her toy rolling pin. Mike asked Rebecca if she had hit Nicky. She denied it at first but soon admitted that she had, with the justification, 'Nicky was crying and I asked her to stop and she wouldn't so I hit her.' Mike showed Rebecca Mummy's rolling pin and asked if she thought he should hit her with it when she cried.

Where does the self-concept come from?

The three components of the self-concept emerge during childhood. All children are egocentric for their first few years. Egocentric children do things which bring them pleasure, e.g. hitting your baby brother who has taken your place as the centre of attention. Sometimes this results in punishment, so the child has to learn when it can do what it wants, when it can't do what it wants, and what happens when it does do what it wants. A child who is always rewarded and encouraged for doing whatever it wants, or a child who is always discouraged and punished for doing anything original or enjoyable, will both develop very distorted views of their own worth.

The child's perceptions of how others react towards it is all important. As Bandura and others have shown (see Chapter 2) children learn much about themselves and about the world by observing and imitating important models such as parents and older siblings. The child's general behaviour and attitudes are being shaped by parents and its knowledge of itself is growing. When the child starts school there are more important role models in the form of teachers. They respond to the child's achievements even more than parents might. More dimensions to the self-concept are added.

Children need clear rules about the kind of behaviour which is acceptable to their caretakers. Limits which are placed on behaviour must be enforced. There's no point in punishing a child for bad behaviour, and then apologizing to it, or trying to 'buy' back into the child's favour by giving it some reward. Within the limits of what is allowed, however, there should be considerable tolerance of a broad range of behaviour from which the child can choose.

Children should be encouraged to achieve in all kinds of areas. Also children benefit from a regular routine of times to get up and go to bed, to have meals and baths. A world which is predictable, and filled with people whose behaviour is also predictable, aids confidence and can help a child develop a stable self-concept.

Girls have been found to have lower self-esteem than boys, and to

► Children need consistent models to learn from. Buying a child a toy to apologize for hitting it is unwise since the child learns that making you angry enough to hit it results in having a new toy. The child has an incentive for making you angry.

► Albert Bandura's 'social learning theory' stresses the importance of observational learning and modelling. As children grow they learn to adopt more social roles.

► One of the main 'rules' of parenthood is to aim to be as consistent in your treatment of your child as possible.

► See Chapter 5 for a discussion of female socialization in Western countries. Much research has shown that girls are discouraged from behaving in a more assertive way, and from competing with boys, despite being rather better at some mental activities than boys.

underperform deliberately so as not to compete with boys. In mixed classes they are less likely to offer answers to questions if boys are present. The answer to this is not necessarily to segregate boys and girls, but to encourage girls to participate fully, and to teach them that they are equal to boys.

Children learn much about themselves from the way adults and others treat them. Constantly telling a child that it is hopeless, or useless, or 'thick' will result in the child absorbing that message into its self-concept. It will have little incentive for trying to improve or achieve academically, in sport or competitions, or even in social or personal relationships. A child who has been told that it is brilliant at everything is equally likely to have some unfortunate surprises in store as it adopts more social roles.

A realistic appraisal of a child's skills, and valid comparisons against other people in the same age group or same class or category, are more likely to assist in developing an adequate self-concept.

 Outline some of the factors which help develop a stable self-concept during childhood.

ACT Write a brief summary of who you are by writing ten sentences which begin 'I am ...'

Theories of self

Charles H. Cooley was an early American sociologist writing at the turn of this century. He claimed that we derive our knowledge about ourself from what we observe from other people's behaviour towards us. He said, 'The self that is most important is a reflection, largely from the minds of others'. He calls it a 'looking glass self'. We use others to see an image of ourselves. This image is important to us. Cooley describes what happens when we realize that people do not regard us in the same way that we regard ourselves:

► The *looking glass theory* suggests that children and adults develop and modify their ideas about their self-image and self-esteem by the way other people react towards them.

> We live on, cheerful and self-confident ... until in some rude hour we learn that we do not stand as well as we thought we did, that the image of us is tarnished. Perhaps we do something ... that we find the social order is set against, or perhaps it is the ordinary course of our life that is not so well regarded as we supposed. At any rate we find, with a chill of terror, that the world is cold and strange, and our self-esteem, self-confidence, and hope, being chiefly founded upon the opinions [of] others, go down in the crash.

Thirty years later **George Herbert Mead** claimed that 'self' was a dynamic process which was constantly adapting to new impressions of us formed from new people. It consists of all the ideas we have of how all people respond to us, and so isn't a 'thing' at all. It is completely bound up with general socialization and expanding cognition. It is simply a part of our understanding about the world.

According to Mead we are capable of responding to ourselves and changing our attitudes and behaviour as well as we might when

► According to George Herbert Mead 'self' is all the ideas we have about ourselves gathered from other people and from within. It is in a constant state of change as we adapt our ideas and behaviour.

responding to other people. This self interaction develops through the early and middle parts of our lives, as our self-concept is forming. As we grow older and become less concerned with other people's approval, it is of less importance.

In the 1950s and 1960s a number of psychiatrists and psychologists were rejecting the previous dominant psychoanalytic and behaviourist views of personality, learning and therapy. (They were sometimes thought of as being 'anti-psychiatry'.) **Carl Rogers** was an American humanistic psychiatrist and therapist who was among this group. He saw people as largely rational, sensible creatures, who usually have some reasonable understanding about their 'self'. According to Rogers every person is a unique individual who is different from every other individual. He saw the 'self' as the very centre of the individual.

Like Cooley and Mead, Rogers thought that the 'self' develops from interactions with all others. It can change with experience from those interactions, and it aims for consistency. Problems can arise when consistency is denied. If you think you are likeable and popular, but you don't think that anyone seems to like you, then a gap develops between your self-concept and reality. This could result in a personality problem which may need discussing with a therapist.

Like Rogers, **Gordon Allport** disagreed with many of the ideas about personality that were current in the 1950s. He had two main objections. Firstly, he rejected those theories which seek to describe and account for the similarities in people's personalities. Instead he argued that each individual is unique, and has a unique set of experiences which mould his understanding of the world and his part in it. Allport thus took an *idiographic* viewpoint. As such, he relied heavily on many case studies for his understanding of the role of self in personality development.

Secondly Allport regarded the concept of 'self' as far too vague and confused since it has had so many different uses in psychology. For example, it was used to identify a part of the psyche which controlled or directed some aspects of personality in both Jung and Adler's psychodynamic theories. It has also meant an inner 'guardian' monitoring and correcting our behaviour. Allport preferred to think of 'self' as our conscious awareness of ourselves. To avoid confusion he invented the term *proprium*, which comprised seven distinct but inter-related components. These include a sense of our own body, a sense of identity, self-enhancement (wanting to survive well), ego extension (things which 'belong' to the person), self-image, propriate striving (trying to improve, do better and achieve) and 'the knower' (the 'executive' which knows about all the other parts of self).

► Rogers described himself as a humanistic psychologist. See Chapter 1 for a discussion of the major early perspectives in psychology.

► *Idiographic* research relates to that which is individual, actual and unique.

► *Nomothetic* research relates to things which are general, common to all, or abstract.

► Allport is a humanist psychologist who proposes the term *proprium* be used instead of the rather vague term 'self'.

(NM) How have psychologists explained the emergence of the self-concept?

Summary – Self-concept

Self-concept is thought to be species-specific to humans and comprises self-image, self-esteem and ideal self. The closer the fit between what you know you are like and what you would like to be like, the higher self-esteem will be. Some psychologists argue that we have several subpersonalities rather than one 'self'. They develop during childhood socialization and continue developing throughout life.

The major theories of the origin of self include the idea of a looking glass, self-interaction, and the proprium view of self.

 Look back at your 'I am ...' statements. Can you identify where any of the characteristics you've described came from?

IMPRESSION MANAGEMENT

When you are being interviewed for a job you will be trying to create 'a good impression'. You will want to appear smart, so you'll wear a suit or something similarly formal. You will want to appear bright, so you will look attentive and have some clever questions prepared. You will want to appear relaxed and at ease, so you will try to convince yourself that there's nothing to worry about and just stay calm.

Or perhaps you see a member of the opposite sex who you find enormously attractive and who you would like to get to know better. You will want to appear intelligent, humorous and generous, without being gushing, silly or clumsy. In just about every social encounter we make, we try to manage the impression that we are giving of ourselves and what we are like.

Generally we try to promote our strengths and hide our shortcomings in the presence of people we like or want to impress. This is perfectly normal. In its extreme form it can become ingratiation and we might employ flattery, deceit and deliberate lying in order to achieve some particular end.

E.E. Jones suggests several forms of ingratiation. One is controlled self-presentation, where someone is careful only to allow favourable aspects of their personality to be seen. Another is flattery. We might like to think that flattery is insincere and wouldn't work with us. However, flattery often does work in influencing someone, even when they know that they are being flattered. If you're trying to borrow £5 from your mother you might like to tell her that she's the kindest, most loving, most generous and best mum in all the world. When you think you've softened her up you can ask for the loan. Perhaps your mum would like to believe that the flattery is true, and that by allowing the flatterer to influence her it makes the flattery more true. When your mum passes the fiver over she may be thinking to herself, 'You're only saying that because you want to borrow some money, but I must be generous and kind to be lending it to you'. This way mum has made the flattery more like the truth.

► *Ingratiation* means trying to become in favour with someone ('to creep') so that you may be able to obtain something from them.

► Impression management comprises making our own behaviour similar to the target's behaviour, conformity, showing appreciation and being consistent.

Processes in impression management

According to Fiske and Taylor five processes are involved in impression management. First, we try to make our own behaviour appear similar to the behaviour of the person we are trying to impress – the target person. Second, we make sure that we conform to the norms of the situation and do not say or do anything out of place.

Third, we use sincere appreciation, and sometimes flattery, to help make us appear desirable. Fourth, we avoid being seen doing or saying anything which contradicts our previous statements. Finally, we avoid saying one thing and doing something different. Consistency is important if someone is to have the idea that they know us, and that we are worthy of their friendship, respect, love, etc.

Self-disclosure

The amount of truthful information we give away about ourselves varies with the relationship. We tell strangers little about ourselves, but tell our best friends or lovers much more. This is called *self-disclosure*. It also increases if two people are forced to be together and away from anyone else, e.g. cell mates in prison. If one person tells another something quite intimate, the other is likely to respond by revealing something of their own intimacies.

Trust is the essential feature of self-disclosure. We are more likely to tell someone whom we trust deeply our most intimate secrets, knowing that they won't make fun of us or pass our secrets on, than we are someone who we are unsure about. This is the principle of *reciprocity*. If Harriet trusts Karen enough to tell her a small secret, Karen might tell Harriet one back. This shows Harriet can trust Karen, so Harriet tells Karen a bigger secret, Karen tells Harriet one back. And so it goes on.

The research suggests that more self-disclosure occurs between females than between males. Female friends will reveal intimate things to each other to a much greater extent than males. Males might exaggerate some aspect of their past experience in order to sound more impressive, or to make fun of themselves, but the events are unlikely to be described in detail.

► There is a gender difference in self-disclosure. Can you offer any explanation for this?

Self-disclosure includes non-verbal cues (NVC) as well as verbal cues. Body language can say a great deal about what you are thinking. Since it is easier to control what we say than what we think, people tend to put more importance on NVC than on verbal cues. If you are talking to someone who starts to 'look bored' you would be wise to shut up!

► How could someone 'look bored'? How do you know when someone else wants to say something? How could you tell that someone was lying to you? These are all examples of *body language* or NVC.

Self-monitoring

Finally we may want to ensure that our behaviour always stays appropriate to the situation, since people may not like a rebel, an individualist, or an anti-conformist. This is called *self-monitoring*, and some people are more concerned by it than others. High self-monitors are constantly striving to make their behaviour ideally suited to the needs of the situation. At the same time they are on the look out for how other people are behaving, and if anyone else is behaving more appropriately than them. Low self-monitors have little concern for the situational norms and remain 'themselves'. They are more interested in their own needs than those of others. High self-monitors are generally better socially adjusted than low self-monitors, and can learn how to behave in new situations more quickly than low self-monitors.

► High self-monitors ensure that their behaviour always matches that required by the environment.

► Low self-monitors are more concerned with their own needs than with the needs of others.

REVIEW – Impression management

Impression management is species-specific and perfectly normal in humans. Flattery can be an excessive form of impression management, although it can sometimes work. Self-disclosure concerns the amount of truthful information we are prepared to share about ourselves. There are gender differences in self-disclosure. Self-monitoring refers to the extent to which we stay aware of the needs of the situation and how quickly we adapt our behaviour to it.

(NM) What is meant by impression management?

Outline some of the main features of impression management.

INTERPERSONAL ATTRACTION

Interpersonal attraction covers that area of social psychology concerning how we are attracted to other people enough to want to become friends with. The depth and duration of that friendship will inevitably depend on psychological factors, such as whether the characteristics that first attracted you to the other person continue to be there, and whether you continue to value those characteristics. Social factors such as whether you maintain contact with them will also be important. 'Absence does not necessarily make the heart grow fonder', since 'while the cat's away the mice might well play'!

Research suggests that some of the most likeable characteristics of people are sincerity, honesty, understanding, loyalty and truthfulness. However, we do not choose our friends only from people with these characteristics, otherwise such people would have everyone wanting to be their friend, while other people would have no one. Most of us try to be sincere and honest most of the time. Most of us try to be understanding towards other people's needs. No doubt we usually try to be loyal and tell the truth. But there are bound to be occasions when we fall short of these targets, so while these characteristics might be amongst the most likable, it would be rare to find someone who embodied them all the time.

Apart from sincerity, honesty, understanding, loyalty and truthfulness several other factors influence the likelihood that we will want to become friends with someone. Some of the main factors that will determine whether two people will like each other, become friends, or even lovers, are described below.

Familiarity

Friendships include sharing knowledge, time and intimacy. Sharing details about yourself that you wouldn't want everyone to know requires trust. According to **Bramel** we are more likely to trust people who are familiar to us, and are more likely to be able to predict their responses. This makes us feel more secure. **Zajonc** suggests that we

► What sort of factors would you find desirable in a friend?

► *Affiliation* refers to the way in which we form ourselves into social groups.

► If sincerity, honesty, understanding, loyalty and truthfulness are the most desired characteristics, what do you think are the least desired?

► We are more likely to establish a relationship with people we see often than with people we see rarely. This is largely because increased exposure to someone gives increased chances for establishing any kind of a relationship at all.

are more likely to like people we see most often because we have a more complete idea of 'what they are like'. He conducted numerous studies in which people were asked to express their feelings about all kinds of things from photographs of strangers to groups of nonsense syllables. In each case they were more likely to say they liked the items they saw more than once. Whether this sort of evidence ought to be generalized to explaining interpersonal attraction is open to question.

 Why should familiarity play a part in interpersonal attraction?

Similarity

Generally we like people who are similar to us, and maybe even think the same way that we do. **Don Byrne** has shown that the closer someone's attitudes, values, beliefs, etc. are to your own, the more likely you are to say that you will like that person. A similar social class background, place of origin, status and occupational background, educational experiences and so on are also influential. Similarities of personality seem rather less important.

If two undergraduates meet early in their university course and find that they are both from Liverpool, the family of one has a fish and chip shop and the other's father is a plumber, they are quite likely to get on. Even if one is quite introverted and passive, and the other is quite extroverted with lots of hobbies, they are still likely to become friends.

If someone else shares your attitudes, beliefs, values, norms and behaviour it tends to reinforce your belief that you are right. That person could become a trusted friend whose reactions and responses you can understand and predict. This makes you feel more comfortable and secure. That person could also be someone you could share activities with, such as visiting the cinema, sharing records, attending football matches. You don't always have to agree with your friends, but when you disagree more than you agree, the friendship will suffer.

Newcomb tested 17 of one year's intake of male college students to discover their attitudes, likes and dislikes. He then assigned them to their study bedrooms. He matched some of them so that their room-mate had similar attitudes to themselves, and of these, 58 per cent developed close friendships. Some others were given room-mates who had quite different ideas and attitudes to themselves. Surprisingly, 25 per cent of them still managed to become good friends; 75 per cent did not!

It isn't only people who are similar to each other who can attract each other, however. Opposites can also attract. A dominant male may have a lasting relationship with a passive female. If both were similar, e.g. if both were dominant, then the relationship would be very stormy indeed! This shows a complementarity of relationships.

Relationships that last often depend on a complementary and mutually benefiting companionship. 'Romantic love' is impossible to

▶ People who are quite unlike us, but who we are forced to be close to, can still become our friends.

define precisely but is characterized by a strong liking for and a wish to be with someone who we care deeply for. Some writers include references to a variety of relationships those 'in love' may desire with each other.

 Why should similarity affect our feelings towards someone?

Reciprocal liking

Reciprocity means equality, give and take, cooperating among a group who are mutually benefiting. If someone who is similar to you likes you, you may feel you want to like them. The consequence is that people tend to like people who like them. Further, if we know our friend likes someone whom we have never met, we are prepared to like that person too. When we do meet the person we may of course find that we don't like them! Equally, we are prepared to dislike someone whom we know our friends dislike, and this too could change after meeting them – as is summed up in the proverb 'my enemy's enemy is my friend'.

Thus if you know that someone likes you, you will be more likely to like them (after all they must have excellent taste). If their NVC (non-verbal communication) and other signals confirm that they like you, then you may be more closely drawn to them. They may know some of your ideas or attitudes, and agree with them. They may have similar ideas or abilities to you, and want to pool resources and get together. When we find out more about them, as they become our friend, we may learn from them, and we may moderate some of our opinions in line with theirs. After all imitation is said to be the sincerest form of flattery.

 How are reciprocal liking and similarity linked in interpersonal attraction?

Physical proximity

As we have said, we are most likely to like people we are most familiar with, and we are most likely to become familiar with people we see most often. And we see most often the people who are physically closest to us. However, you do not automatically like those people you are physically closest to most of the time. You could quite dislike someone you are forced to be close to, for example, in the armed services, in prison or at boarding school. For two people to be drawn to each other, they usually need to be of similar status. A duchess is less likely to be attracted towards a butler than she is to a duke. People we like are often members of the same organization such as a club, college course or workplace, and they are usually pursuing similar goals.

Byrne and **Buehler** had their students sit in class in alphabetical order for the first term of their course. At the outset less than 10 per cent of the students knew each others' names. By the end of the term over 20 per cent knew all the other's names, but nearly 75 per cent

---

► We tend to like people who are similar to us, and the act of liking increases the similarity.

► One NVC cue: when someone (usually of the opposite sex) who likes you very much is near to you, the pupils of their eyes dilate. You may find this knowledge of some use!

► Being physically close to someone is not essential to attraction. You may have been attracted to a pop star when you were younger, but never been close to the star at all. However, we do usually draw our friends from the people we are closest to.

knew the names of the people they sat near to. Numerous neighbourhood studies have shown that people know, and often like, the people living nearest to them. The further away they lived the less likely they were to know each other. For example, people living nearest the stairs or lifts in apartment blocks have been found to know more of their neighbours compared to those living in the middle of a hallway, who knew only those living next door.

(NM) How is physical proximity involved in interpersonal attraction?

Physical attraction

If you asked all your friends how important good looks are to their choice of partner, compared to personality, sincerity, honesty etc., most would probably say 'not very'. However, this is not what most research suggests. Indeed attractive people are seen as being more likeable, modest, sociable and sexually responsive than unattractive people. We are more likely to be drawn to attractive people as a friend in the first place. This also works the other way round. If I describe someone very positively, suggesting that they have all kinds of qualities, then when you meet them you may see them as being more attractive than you might otherwise have done.

In the mid 1960s **Walster** arranged a 'computer dating dance' for 18-year-olds at the beginning of a term at the University of Minnesota. The first 376 boys and girls who applied for tickets were told that their partners would be chosen for them by computer on the basis of their interests. After they had bought their tickets they went into another room to fill out their questionnaires. They provided information about what they, and other people, thought about themselves, their expectations from their date, their interests, etc. While doing this, experimenters rated each of them as 'attractive', 'average' and 'ugly'.

The subjects were then randomly allocated a partner. Two and a half hours into the dance, during an intermission, the subjects were asked to fill out an 'anonymous' questionnaire asking such things as how they felt about their date, how attractive they found the date, how they thought the date felt about them, how similar their attitudes and beliefs were, and whether they were likely to have another date. Of course the questionnaire wasn't anonymous at all. The researchers knew which person filled in which questionnaire.

Generally, the more physically attractive the date was, the more highly their partner rated them, and the more they wanted to be dated again. Attractiveness was seen as more important than personality, intelligence, social skills, etc. About half of the 'ugly' males and females said they would date their partner again; the more attractive their dates were, the more they wanted another date. 'Average' males and females preferred the 'attractive' partners, but most of those who had 'average' partners were reasonably happy to date them again. Most 'average' subjects with 'ugly' partners did not rate their partners highly, and did not want another date. 'Attractive' subjects with 'attractive' partners were most likely to have another date.

► Attractive people are imagined to possess all kinds of other qualities too. Knowing that someone has these qualities before we meet them, we assume that they must be attractive too.

► Subjects were allocated partners randomly, except that no female was given a partner who was shorter than she was. This is an example of modified random sampling.

► Walster's conclusions were drawn from questionnaires filled in after only two and a half hours of meeting someone for the first time. (Follow-ups were conducted in six months to see if any partners had dated.) Can we really 'know' someone in this time? If not, these responses could only result from how physically attractive they appeared to be.

► The subjects in Walster's 'computer dance' genuinely believed that they were being matched on the basis of their interests while they were actually being experimented upon on the basis of their level of physical attraction. Do you feel that this is ethically acceptable? Would it bother you if you discovered that you had been experimented upon in this way?

► Can we generalize to all young people from this research? Do you think there is any reason why these findings would be any different in your country today?

Walster's experiment, conducted over 20 years ago, concludes that physical attractiveness is of considerable importance in deciding who 18-year-old American college students wanted to 'go out with' and that the more attractive they were the more they would be sought after. Equally, the uglier they were the less would attractive people want to date them.

People who are of similar levels of attractiveness tend to go together. Walster and others have found a slight sex difference in that physical attractiveness plays a greater part for men than for women. Women tend to include men's personality, intelligence and social skills as well as their looks in their choice of partner.

► Being attractive means that your 'looking glass' (note Cooley) will usually reflect a desirable self-image, encourage a high self-esteem and develop a close fit between actual and ideal-self image.

Levels of physical attractiveness have implications for other areas of our lives, apart from choosing a partner. For example, some evidence suggests that attractive criminals, especially females, are less likely to be convicted or sent to prison than unattractive ones, unless they used their good looks to further the crime. Attractive children are often treated favourably, compared with unattractive ones, both by adults (even parents) and other children. Attractive students are more likely to be encouraged by staff and other students. On the whole, being born 'good looking' can have a major impact on someone's self-concept and on one's whole life.

 Describe one piece of evidence which suggests that physical appearance is important to interpersonal attraction.

Gain and loss of esteem

Earlier we mentioned that one of the factors involved in self-disclosure was the reciprocity principle – if you tell your friend a secret they should feel safe to share one with you. If someone likes you, you are more likely to like them and if someone dislikes you, you are more likely to dislike them.

Some 25 years ago **Elliot Aronson** and **Darwyn Linder** demonstrated the reciprocity principle in an experiment. They wanted to show the effects on people of hearing someone's differing opinion of them. Two female subjects were asked to take part in an experiment on 'verbal conditioning' which comprised a series of seven conversations. The whole thing was prearranged by the experimenters. One of the female 'subjects' was actually an assistant (called a confederate) of the researchers who played the part of the 'learner'. The other was a genuine subject (called a naive subject), who was told that she was to help the researchers by monitoring the learner's performance.

► A naive subject is one who does not know the true purpose or nature of the research. A confederate is an assistant of the researcher's who has been trained to respond in particular ways.

After each conversation the confederate learner would be asked to go into another room, where she would evaluate the naive subject, saying how much she liked her. The naive subject was to 'overhear' this evaluation. After the conversations the actual naive subject was asked to describe her feelings about the learner.

Aronson and Linder ran four experimental conditions. In one the subject heard the confederate learner consistently evaluate her highly. This is the *positive condition*. Many positive things were said about her. When her turn came she was quite complimentary about her partner too. In the second condition the confederate started by being fairly uncomplimentary, but as the conversations progressed she made more and more complimentary comments about the naive. Aronson and Linder called this the *gain condition*. The naive then rated the confederate even more highly than the naive in the positive condition. It seems that if someone starts off by not liking us, and then improves their opinion until they do like us, this is even more a cause for liking them than if they simply liked us all along.

In the *negative condition* the naive subjects consistently heard uncomplimentary things said about them, and they were uncomplimentary about the confederate in return. Finally, in the *loss condition*, naives heard the confederate saying complimentary things about them to begin with, but as the conversations went on her opinion worsened. The confederate was then evaluated even more harshly than when in the negative condition. Losing someone's favour if they liked you to begin with seems worse than never being in favour with someone in the first place.

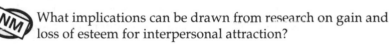 What implications can be drawn from research on gain and loss of esteem for interpersonal attraction?

Social competence

We usually prefer people who are socially competent, that is, people who are not excessively timid or inexperienced and who are familiar with the usual norms and values of the particular culture. However sometimes, under specific circumstances, social incompetence can be attractive.

Some 20 years ago **J. Cooper** explained to some subjects that they would be working in pairs to solve various problems. If both members of the pair could each contribute to the solution they would both be paid. He then told some of the subjects individually that the actual partner they had been assigned wasn't very bright and was unlikely to be able to help much with the problems. They were offered the opportunity to change to a different partner. None of them did. Some of the pairs then did so badly that neither of them were paid, yet the bright subject still said they liked their partner well enough.

When we make a decision which takes account of the abilities of other people, we are particularly prone to like them when their behaviour lives up to our expectations of it. If we know that they will behave in a certain way we feel quite happy when they do. Since they make us happy by confirming our predictions, and thus make us feel more secure, we are prepared to like them.

Clumsiness can be annoying and embarrassing, and it's hard to imagine any circumstances when you could actually like someone for their clumsiness. If someone you expect to be clumsy drops something, knocks something over, or walks into something, their behaviour confirms your expectations, just as in Cooper's research. However, the result is not usually the same. We are more likely to find it annoying than a source of endearment. If, however, a rather superior person, and someone we do not expect to be clumsy, does something

► In Aronson and Linder's experiment the naive subject thought that she and the other subject were both naive subjects, and that she was actually going to play the part of a confederate of the researcher. Is this level of deception acceptable from social psychologists?

► In the *positive condition* the subject would have heard a greater number of positive statements being made about her than in the *gain condition*. Those in the gain condition still rated the confederate more highly than those in the positive condition.

► In the *negative condition* the subject would have heard more uncomplimentary things about her than when in the loss condition. The confederate was still evaluated more harshly in the *loss condition.*

► When partners who were expected to do badly did so, they were liked even more than when some of them did better than expected!

► One cognitive theory suggests that we prefer to live in a state of *cognitive consonence,* where things are what we think they should be. *Cognitive dissonance* occurs when things are not what they seem, and this creates tension.

Summary – Interpersonal attraction

The main factors that influence whether friendships will be formed or broken are familiarity, similarity, reciprocal liking, physical proximity, physical attraction, gain and loss of esteem, and social competence. These apply to most people, most of the time, but as always when dealing with people, 'there's no accounting for taste', and it's sometimes

► Clumsiness is attractive only when it comes from someone who is obviously superior in most other ways, and even then when it is infrequent.

similar, this can increase their attractiveness. The clumsy person is frequently clumsy for a number of reasons, such as lack of attention or lack of thought. They are likely to be clumsy. The superior person is usually competent at paying attention and thinking ahead. Their mistake merely shows that they are human, like the rest of us.

Stupidity can be a source of attraction. A stupid person can be respected, pitied or appear appealing. But a clumsy person usually creates problems that other people have to clear up, and thus increase their work. This is not a source of attraction!

In the mid 1960s **Aronson** conducted research into the relationship between clumsiness and attraction. He let four groups of subjects listen to, but not see, one of two interviews. (If subjects could have seen the interviewees they may have been distracted by their visible levels of physical attraction.) Two groups heard an interviewee who wasn't terribly bright and didn't show much ability to think about what he was saying. Two of the groups heard an apparently intelligent and perceptive interviewee. One of the groups who heard the 'intelligent' interviewee and one of the groups who heard the 'unintelligent' interviewees additionally heard their interviewee spilling coffee towards the end of the interview.

Subjects were then asked to rate the level of attractiveness (before and after the coffee spillage) of the interviewee they had heard. The intelligent one was rated more highly by both groups who heard him but after the incident with the spilt coffee the intelligent interviewee's score increased. The unintelligent interviewee's score declined further for those who heard him spill coffee.

Perhaps the accident increased the listeners' sympathy for the 'superior' person since it would be rare for him to have had such an accident, while increasing their dislike of the other person for being 'typical' of his incompetence.

 From your own experience, do you find social incompetence appealing or unappealing?

Chapter summary

We form impressions of other people based on our perceptions of them, and our general state of knowledge in terms of previous experience, stereotyping and prejudice. We like predictability and understanding the things we see around us, so we attribute causes to other people's behaviour and judge how effective we think they are.

Forming these impressions of others depends in part on our own self-concept. What we know and feel about ourselves can affect how we respond to others. Our self-concept has derived, in part, from how other people have treated us, and this depends on the impressions of what we are like that we have allowed them to see.

We can manage the impressions we give to others, and modify our behaviour according to the needs of the situation.

Several factors are involved in whether people are likely to become attracted to us. These include familiarity, similarity, reciprocal liking, physical proximity, physical attraction, gain and loss of esteem, and social competence.

Essay questions – 60 minutes each

1 Assess the impact of some social factors on the development and maintenance of the self-concept.

2 In what ways have psychological studies helped us to understand how people attribute causes to human action?

3 What have psychologists learned about the processes of interpersonal perception?

4 What factors have been shown to attract people to each other?

Further Reading: Chapter 8

For those who like original sources

Cook M. 1971. *Interpersonal Perception*. Harmondsworth: Penguin.

Asch S. 1946. 'Forming Impressions of Personality', *Journal of Abnormal and Social Psychology*, Vol. 41, pages 258–90.

Asch S. 1956. 'Studies of Independence and Submission to Group Pressure', *Psychological Monographs* 70(9) (Whole no. 416).

Heider F. 1958. *The Psychology of Interpersonal Relations*. Oxford: John Wiley.

The most useful general texts are

Pennington D. 1986. *Essential Social Psychology*. London: Edward Arnold.

Argyle M. 1983. *The Psychology of Interpersonal Behaviour* (4th Edition). Harmondsworth: Penguin.

Wrightsman L. 1988. *Social Psychology* (5th Edition). Brooks-Cole.

9 Social influences in interaction

Introduction

In this chapter we will be looking at some of the research which helps to explain the way people's behaviour differs when in the company of others, and offers explanations for why this is so.

People tend to behave differently when in the company of others. As was said in Chapter 8, we draw information about ourselves, and so build our self-concept, from the way other people seem to treat us. We need them to be models for us to imitate, and to guide, approve of and discipline us. At the same time we try to create the right impression of ourselves. Most of us want other people to think highly of us. Children, and many adults, sometimes 'show off' in order to gain approval.

Most humans are concerned with what other people think about them, and the presence of other people can have a major impact on their behaviour, conformity to group pressures and obedience to authority.

SOCIAL FACILITATION: THE PRESENCE OF OTHERS

Some people work better on their own, away from distractions. Others work better in a public place such as a library. Many say it depends on what task they are supposed to be doing. Something requiring deep concentration may need a different environment from something requiring only repetition of some action. Whatever the task, the presence of other people can have some effect on the worker's thoughts, feelings, and actions. It may be a beneficial effect, helping motivation. Or it could be an inhibiting effect, distracting

► When alone you might well scratch an itch on parts of your body that you are unlikely to scratch in public!

attention. These effects are known as *social facilitation* or *social inhibition*. Social facilitation comprises the 'audience effect', where performance in a task varies if there are others present who are not performing the task, and 'co-action effect', where others present are performing the same tasks.

 In your own words describe what is meant by social facilitation and give an example of how social facilitation affects you.

Social facilitation was discovered in one of the first experiments in social psychology, performed by **Norman Triplett** in 1898. As a keen cyclist he had noticed that other cyclists rode faster when they were with others than they did when alone. He believed that the element of competition would emerge whenever the opportunity for it occurred. To test this he asked children to wind a fishing reel 150 turns. He did not ask them to do it quickly and imposed no time limit for the task to be completed. He did, of course, time them. Some of the children were tested when alone, others in pairs. When in pairs the children wound their reels faster. Triplett said that the presence of others speeds up performance — hence 'facilitation', which usually means 'to make things easier'.

Twenty-five years after Triplett's claims **Floyd Allport** found what he called a *co-action effect*. A co-action group is one where the members work side by side, often performing the same or a similar task, but without interacting with each other over it. Writing a timed essay in class or filling in a test questionnaire are examples of co-action. Knowing that other people are performing the same task (even when they are not actually physically present) is usually enough to improve a subject's performance on the same task.

Allport instructed his subjects not to compete with each other but to solve a series of tasks at their own pace. Some of the tasks were simple, requiring little concentration, such as crossing out all the vowels in a newspaper article. Others demanded more attention such as finding the logical flaw in a series of arguments. He still found that his subjects worked faster when in groups than when alone. 'Working quickly' is a co-action effect of the presence of others.

However, Allport also found that in working co-actively people make more errors in the more difficult tasks, possibly because of the distraction of having other people around. We might say that quantity increases but quality decreases. Allport concluded: 'It is the overt responses such as writing which receive facilitation through the stimulus of co-workers. The intellectual or implicit responses of thought are hampered rather than facilitated.' Neither Allport nor other researchers were able to explain why easier tasks are facilitated while harder ones are inhibited, and the subject of social facilitation was rather ignored by social psychologists for about 30 years.

 List some activities which people do better or worse when alone, when with others doing the same thing, and when with an audience.

▶ *Social facilitation* refers to any effect that the presence of other people has on an individual's behaviour. It used to mean only beneficial effects, but now we know the presence of others can *inhibit* performance too.

▶ Triplett concluded that the presence of others speeds performance by triggering the desire to compete. Can you think of any other reason why the boys wound faster when in pairs?

▶ In Chapter 3 we said that children pass through a stage of parallel play around the age of two to three years when they may be playing the same game as another child but they are not playing together. This is early co-action.

▶ Most of us work with other people, who may be doing very similar things to us. Many people work in co-action groups.

▶ It is customary in all areas of science that when some insoluble problem occurs it will be left aside while research in other areas proceeds, with the hope that one day implications from other research might suggest alternative solutions.

► Zajonc interprets *drive* rather loosely to mean *arousal*, which is simply an increase in some kind of brain, hormone and glandular activity that prepares an organism for some activity.

► If the job is easy the presence of others is likely to improve your performance. If it is difficult then having other people around will distract you and make achievement more difficult.

► Zajonc's claim implies a rather determinist, mechanistic view of human behaviour but humans interpret their experience so it's not merely the presence of others which is important, but what they are doing and how you feel about them.

 What is a co-action effect and what effect did Allport find?

After many years of studying social facilitation in various species of animals, and in humans, during the 1950s and 1960s, **R.B. Zajonc** suggested an answer to why the presence of others produces co-action effects, based on the **Hull-Spence** version of learning theory. This says that 'increasing drive leads to an increase in dominant responses'. Let's *operationalize* – define – our terms. *Drive* is a psychological term which means a state of motivation resulting from the deprivation of something one needs, such as food, or the presence of something one does not need, such as poisonous fumes or chemicals. Deprivation of food, for example, produces a drive called hunger which produces behaviour such as finding and eating food, which will reduce the drive. A 'dominant response' is simply one that is thoroughly learned and practised so that it will be produced almost effortlessly whenever the need arises. Making a sandwich if you're hungry, walking, using a knife and fork, possibly driving a car, can all become dominant responses.

Zajonc claims that if the task is simple, well practised or learned, and the worker is likely to obtain the correct answers or achieve the goals, then the presence of other people improves or enhances performance. If the task is poorly learned or complex and requires the utmost concentration, and the likelihood is that the worker will not be successful, then the presence of other people will reduce the chances of success even further.

The implications of Zajonc's claim are that you should not try to learn new material in large groups since their very presence is distracting, and that you shouldn't take exams in large groups if you're not certain of the answers!

 How does Zajonc explain social facilitation?

Not everyone agrees with Zajonc's claim. The presence of others does not always improve the performance of even well-rehearsed material. Their presence will only help if they are also performing some similar task themselves. If they are not paying any attention to the person performing the task, her or his performance isn't likely to be improved. Also some people tend to get nervous whenever they know they are being watched by anyone, regardless of how well they

---

Zajonc's claim about social facilitation
Zajonc claims that the presence of others leads to an increase in arousal which triggers the successful completion of easy or well learned responses. Equally, increased arousal inhibits performance of poorly learned material. 'Getting nervous' about doing something you're not very certain about in the company of others is an example of inhibition. He also claims that the presence of others inhibits the learning of new material.

know the task.

Summary – Social facilitation

Some people generally work better on their own, others generally prefer company. Social facilitation refers to how one's performance is affected by the presence of others. Zajonc claims that the presence of others increases physiological arousal which promotes ability. This isn't necessarily true; the opposite sometimes holds. The mere presence of others may have no effect if they are not paying attention to the worker.

CONFORMITY AND NON-CONFORMITY

Conformity

According to **Leon Mann** conformity means 'yielding to group pressures'. Specifically, conformity has three distinct areas of meaning. Firstly it concerns one's _behaviour_: whether or not to behave in ways that other members of the group would think appropriate to the group. Everyone is a member of one group or another. You might be a 'student', 'housewife', 'shop assistant', 'punk', 'yuppie', or anything else. Everyone expects members of these groups to behave in certain ways. If you are a member of an identifiable group we will expect you to behave appropriately to it. So will the other members. If you do not conform you are likely to be rejected by the group.

The second meaning refers to _attitudes_. Many people express attitudes which conform to those we would expect from a member of their group. We might expect a student to have certain attitudes towards sex, music, dancing and dress. If our mother expressed the same attitudes we might be rather surprised!

There isn't necessarily a correlation between the attitudes people express and their actual behaviour. We say all kinds of things which we don't actually mean, and wouldn't actually do.

The third area of meaning concerns _personality traits_. We could describe you as a conformist to the behaviour or attitudes (or both) of the group to which you belong. However, whether you conform every time you have the opportunity to do so depends on the situation, your mood, your cognition, your state of arousal and other things, so psychologists do not generally think in terms of a 'conforming personality'.

In general, there's nothing wrong with conformity. It allows us to 'know where we stand', what to think and how to behave. Like stereotypes, conforming and expecting others to conform maintains _cognitive balance_. The problem comes when someone's own personality starts to become obscured by their need to conform. If you become permanently frightened to say anything for fear of appearing ignorant or inexperienced, but always agree with whatever the last person said, then the desire to conform has gone too far and has become a personality problem.

▶ When was the last time you told someone to drop dead? Did you mean it? When was the last time you told someone you were going to kill them? Are you?

▶ There are times when you want to do things which would be expected of a member of your group, and other times when you would not. Humans are not always consistent in their responses. This makes them rather unpredictable ... but very human.

▶ Different groups require different kinds of conformity. They each may put different amounts and kinds of pressure on people to conform to their ideals.

▶ Perpetual conformity in humans is a 'weakness' of personality that is rarely admired by others. It suggests incompetence and inexperience, neither of which are likely to be found desirable in a friend. We prefer people who appear competent and to know what to do.

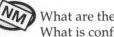 What are the three dimensions of conformity?
What is conformity? What is meant by cognitive balance?

During the course of our lives we become associated with many groups, each of which has certain responses expected of it. As a bus passenger you are expected to behave in certain ways, although your attitudes are not important. As a football fan your attitude towards the team is important, your behaviour is less so. As a mother your attitudes towards your children are expected to include encouragement, and you are also expected to show protective and helpful behaviour. Each of us spends some time with other members of our group so it is beneficial to try to achieve some common goal, and to do this we often need to conform. Psychologists have been interested in why we conform, and whether conformity can be increased or decreased by altering the kinds of pressures on us to conform.

► There are a number of reasons why people conform to the behaviour they see around them. They may publicly agree because disagreeing would be inconvenient; they may genuinely come to agree; and they may be seen to be agreeing because membership of the group could be useful to them.

There are several kinds of conformity, and we will be reviewing the major studies of the subject, most of which were conducted in the 1950s. They led Kelman to distinguish between *compliance* (where the subject goes along with the group view, but privately disagrees with it), *internalization* (where the subject comes to accept, and eventually believes, the group's view) and *identification* (where the subject accepts and believes the group view, because he wants to become associated with the group).

► *Normative conformity* comprises *compliance* (seeming to agree) and *true conformity* (actually agreeing).

Leon Mann identifies *normative conformity* which 'occurs when direct group pressure forces the individual to yield under the threat of rejection or the promise of reward'. This can only occur if someone wants to be a member of the group, or the group's attitudes or behaviour are important to the individual in some way. Mann identifies two kinds of normative conformity. One is *compliance*, the other is *true conformity* (similar to Kelman's internalization). According to Mann, 'True conformity occurs when the person both privately and publicly is in agreement with the group.'

► *Informational conformity* occurs when someone copies the behaviour or attitudes of the group in order to appear to be competent as a member. Making errors in informational conformity can lead to great embarrassment on the part of the conformist, and great amusement on the part of the competent group members.

Apart from normative conformity there is *informational conformity* which 'occurs where the situation is vague or ambiguous and because the person is uncertain he turns to others for evidence of the appropriate response'. If you're not sure which cutlery to use in a posh restaurant you may copy what someone who seems more experienced than you uses. Otherwise you may appear inexperienced or foolish, and not be welcomed in the group.

► According to Mann there is normative, informational and ingratiational conformity. Mann and Kelman are not disagreeing about the nature of conformity, just offering slightly different variations on its forms.

Thirdly, Mann identifies *ingratiational conformity* which occurs where 'a person tries to do whatever he thinks the other will approve in order to gain acceptance'. If you make yourself appear to be similar to someone else, they might come to like you. (Imitation may be a form of flattery, and flattery does sometimes work.) However we are usually very aware of ingratiational conformists. As Mann says, 'People are ... reluctant to overdo the conformity technique in case it should rebound against them, promoting dislike rather than acceptance.'

What are the main reasons for conforming?

Non-conformity

Non-conformity refers to behaviour which is different from that which appears appropriate or which would be expected. **R.H. Willis** identifies three possible ways of behaving when someone is faced with a situation in which other people's responses can be seen. Firstly, one can *conform* to others' behaviour. Secondly, one can be neutral, conforming if we genuinely believe that it is best, and doing something else if we do not. This is *independent behaviour*. And thirdly one can deliberately do the opposite of what is expected, which is termed *anti-conformity*. Anti-conformity is generally thought of as unnecessary and unpleasant, a way of drawing attention to oneself whereas independence is usually thought of as desirable and mature.

According to Willis, whether our response in one situation is conformist, independent or even anti-conformist, will depend largely on our perception of the situation rather than on whether we have a conformist personality. A person who behaves in a mostly conformist way in some situations or on some occasions may well behave in a more independent way on others.

► Those who behave independently are most likely to be admired, conformers are likely to be accepted, anti-conformers are likely to be rejected.

 Why is it inadequate to talk about the conformist personality?

Conformity studies

Sherif's research

The first major research in conformity was conducted in 1935 by **Muzafer Sherif**, who used a visual illusion known as the *autokinetic effect*.

Sherif told his subjects that a spot of light which they were about to see in a darkened room was going to move, and he wanted them to say the direction and distance of the movement. (We judge move-

---

The autokinetic effect

The function of the rods and cones, the light receptors on the retina of the eye, is to receive and respond to light. If they are to function correctly, keeping us informed of what's going on around us, they need constantly changing stimulation. Each individual rod or cone needs a changing pattern of light if it is not to become saturated and fatigued. Retinal fatigue would mean that we couldn't see anything distinctly at all. To ensure that the cells don't become fatigued the eyes are constantly making tiny movements. This is called nystagmus. One consequence of nystagmus is that a stationary spot of light in a darkened room will appear to move.

► Nystagmus is the tiny movements of the eyes which change the pattern of light stimulating individual retinal cells and keeping them from becoming fatigued.

ment by reference to things which are stationary, or whose movement is known. These are 'cues to movement'.)

In the first experimental condition the subjects were tested individually. Some said the distance of movement wasn't very far in any direction, others said it was several inches. Sherif recorded each subject's response. This would depend on their own level of physiological nystagmus.

 Why did Sherif's subjects in the first experimental condition report various distance and direction movements for a stationary spot of light?

In the second experimental condition Sherif gathered his subjects into groups, usually of three people, and asked them to describe verbally the movement of the light. He gave them no instructions about whether they needed to reach any kind of agreement among themselves, but simply asked them to give their own reports, while being aware of the reports that the other members gave (they could hear but could not see each other).

During the group sessions it became apparent that the subjects' reports started to converge much nearer to an average of what their individual reports had been. If a subject who had said that the light didn't move very far when tested individually said 'I think it is moving about two inches to the left', then another who had reported movements of four inches or more when tested individually might say 'I think it may have been three inches'. As the number of reported movements continued, the more the members of the groups conformed to each other's reports. Sherif asked if they felt their responses were being influenced by the scores of the other members, and they all said absolutely not!

So why were they conforming? Remember this spot of light was in fact stationary, so whatever reports were made were the consequence of the subjects imagining they saw something happen. The key is that they were not certain about the movement they observed, and so would not feel confident about insisting that their observations were wholly correct. When they heard other reported judgements they may have decided to 'go along' with them. It isn't worth demanding that you're correct if you're not positive that you are! Few people would enjoy being the 'odd one out', being regarded as extreme, dogmatic, selfish, drawing attention to themselves, inexperienced or just plain stupid! It is also possible that there is some psychological benefit in agreeing. It may confirm our self-concept, and make us feel secure that we are in the majority and must therefore be 'right'. It may strengthen our ego and make us more positive in our other attitudes.

 Why did Sherif's subjects in his second experimental condition conform to a group norm?

In a third experimental condition the subjects were re-tested individually. Their reports should presumably have resembled the scores they had given in the first experimental condition. They were alone,

▶ The three people in each group would previously have reported quite different extents of movement in the stationary light. Would they now conform to some kind of group norm, or would their reports be quite independent of what the others were saying?

▶ If one group's members had reported average movements of five inches, three inches and one inch when tested individually, their average group score would be near three inches.

▶ Despite claiming that they were not being influenced by hearing other group members' reports, each subject conformed nearer to an average of the members' individual scores.

▶ If you express an opinion, and you're not certain of the facts, you tend to look for signs of agreement from the others. If someone else expresses an opinion similar to yours, or partly agrees with you, you are usually quite happy to modify your ideas to make a compromise. Perhaps being in agreement and having our ideas confirmed fulfils some psychological need.

▶ When re-tested individually the subjects' scores more closely resembled their group's average scores than their own scores from the previous condition.

and whatever perceptions made them report the distances they did previously were operating again now. If, as seems likely, their perceptions were affected by their degree of nystagmus, then those effects would be felt again in this 'individual' experimental condition. However, this didn't happen. The subjects reported movements much more in line with their average group scores. For example, a subject who had reported an average of five inches movement in experimental condition one (alone), and three inches in condition two (group), would report three inches in condition three (alone).

Why should this happen? Nystagmus is a physiological reflex and so the subject's perception of movement would have been similar in each condition of this experiment. It was their reports, not their perceptions, which showed consensus. If they benefited from the consensus in condition two, there is no benefit to be gained by agreement in condition three since there's no one to agree with. They probably imagined that a group score was likely to be nearer the correct answer than their own individual perception since they weren't sure of the movement they saw. Perhaps three heads are better than one when the one doesn't really know!

The problem with this study for our understanding of conformity as one aspect of social psychology is that it is a totally artificial experimental situation. There isn't even a 'right' answer. Requested 'reports of imaginary movements of a stationary spot of light in a darkened room when alone or with two others' hardly reflect situations we come across in our everyday lives! Generalizing from its conclusions to 'real life' might be dangerous, although some of them do have a common sense appeal.

▶ Have you ever been on a car journey with other people and none of you was certain of the route? Did you discuss it and come to a best guess, or did you follow the directions of one who was most convinced they knew the way?

(NM) What have we learned from Sherif's 1930s studies of conformity?

Asch's research

Solomon Asch was a harsh critic of Sherif's experimental design and claimed that it showed little about conformity since there was no 'right answer' to conform to. Asch designed an experiment where there could be absolutely no doubt about whether subjects would be conforming or not, and it was absolutely clear what they were conforming to. He wanted to be able to put an individual under various amounts of group pressure that he could control and manipulate, and measure their willingness to conform to the group's response to something which was clearly wrong.

In the late 1940s and early 1950s Asch conducted what are now described as classic experiments in conformity. That is not to say that they aren't criticized today, or that his conclusions are wholly acceptable now. But they were masterpieces of design and statistical analysis at the time. They showed the rigorous application of the scientific method to social psychology and were used as models of how to conduct psychological research. With the benefit of hindsight Asch's experiments would probably not be conducted now since they have certain flaws, but that is not to detract from Solomon Asch's reply to

▶ All science proceeds by one scientist finding flaws in previous research and attempting to correct them and improve the accuracy of existing knowledge.

▶ Psychology as an academic subject is barely over a century old. Much of the pioneering work of Hermann Ebbinghaus, Herman von Helmholtz, William James, Edward Titchener, Sigmund Freud, Ivan Pavlov, J. B. Watson, Wilhelm Wundt and others was conducted in the 19th century. The application of science to investigating psychological matters has developed steadily since then. Asch's research reflected the state of scientific awareness at the time.

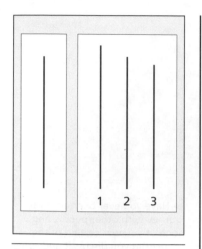

Asch's conformity cards

► A *naive subject* does not know what the research is actually about but is told that it concerns something else. The naive's responses form the data from which the research's conclusions are drawn. Some people have questioned the ethics of this kind of research. Do psychologists have the right to fool people in this way?

► Asch's experiment is another example of psychological research being conducted on American college students. In what ways are they not necessarily representative of the whole population?

► There were 1476 trials altogether, 861 of them 'rigged'. Over 30 per cent of the sample of 123 conformed on all 861. Only about 20 per cent didn't conform at all.

what he saw as the shortcomings of Sherif's research.

In an early experiment Asch gathered a group of seven university students in a classroom. They sat around one side of a large table facing the blackboard. On the left side of the board there was a white card with a single, black line drawn vertically on it. On the right of the board there was another white card with three vertical lines of differing lengths. The following instructions were given to the subjects:

This is a task which involves the discrimination of the length of lines. You see the pair of white cards in front. On the left is a single line; on the right there are three lines differing in length. They are numbered 1, 2 and 3 in order. One of the three lines at the right is equal to the standard line at the left – you will decide in each case which is the equal line. You will state your judgement in terms of the corresponding number. There will be 12 such comparisons. As the number of lines is few and the group small I shall call on each of you in turn to announce your judgement, which I shall record here on a prepared form. Please be as accurate as possible. Suppose that we start at the right and proceed to the left.

Two of the lines on the card on the right were longer or shorter than the target line. Matching the target line to the comparison line shouldn't have been a difficult task. However, as you may have guessed, of these seven students all but one was a *confederate* of Asch, and they had been instructed to give incorrect responses on seven of the 12 trials. The one *naive* subject was seated either at the extreme left or next to the extreme left of the line of students, so that he would always be last or next to last to answer. He would have heard most of the others give their 'judgements' about which comparison line matched the target line before he spoke.

The naive subject was a member of a group he didn't know and might never see again, who suddenly, and for no apparent reason, started saying something which directly contradicted the evidence of his own eyes. Would he stick to his own judgement, and regard the six other people as poor judges, inconsistent, or just plain odd? Or would he allow himself to be swayed by the others opinion, doubt his own senses, and conform to the group's judgement?

In subsequent experiments Asch used between seven and nine subjects, using the experimental procedure just outlined. In the first series of experiments he tested 123 naives on 12 'critical tests' (matching the lines) where seven were going to be incorrect. Each naive therefore had seven opportunities to conform to something they could see to be wrong. One third of the naives conformed on all seven occasions. About three quarters of them conformed on at least one occasion. Only about one-fifth refused to conform at all.

Just to be certain that the result was due to the influence of the confederates responses, and not the difficulty of the task, Asch used a control group. Each control subject was asked to make a judgement individually. There were no pressures at all. Over 90 per cent gave correct responses.

Some comments by Asch's non-conforming subjects

'Despite everything there was a lurking fear that in some way I did not understand I might be wrong: fear of exposing myself as inferior in some way. It is more pleasant if one is really in agreement.'

'I don't deny that at times I had the feeling, to heck with it, I'll go along with the rest.'

'I felt awfully funny, everything was going against me.'

'I felt disturbed, puzzled, separated, like an outcast from the rest.'

'Every time I disagreed I was beginning to wonder if I wasn't beginning to look funny.'

► Is there any difference between agreeing with a majority view when you are not in a position to judge for yourself, and being in a position where you can make a judgement and you still accept the majority view? Are they both 'conformity'?

NM How did Asch measure conformity in his 1950s experiments?

Asch also interviewed each naive after the experiment, explaining what had been happening and reassuring them that their judgement wasn't faulty. During this 'debriefing' interview he asked each subject why they had conformed. They admitted that the opinion of the others was a factor, but not the only one. Some blamed their own judgement and were content to believe that the others were better judges. Some had thought that a conforming response was what the experimenter wanted, and they were happy to oblige. Some thought some mistake had been made when drawing the cards and the answer they gave referred to the line that 'should have been' correct. Some claimed that they didn't want to be the odd one out in case they looked foolish or inferior to the rest.

Asch claimed to have found in this research some of the reasons for conformity, at least conformity to an unimportant task like matching the length of lines in a small group. He conducted several variations of this research in the early 1950s to find exactly what factors are involved in conformity. For example, he found that when there was one naive and only one confederate, the naive did not conform. There was no group or majority decision to conform with. With two confederates conformity increased, and with three it increased further. Asch claimed that increasing the number of confederates beyond three made very little difference to the amount of conformity shown. Other research has not confirmed this; the rate of conformity has been found to increase with more confederates, up to seven.

According also to Asch's findings, if one other member of the group gave the correct answer rather than the wrong one offered by the confederates, then conformity to the majority wrong answer fell to around 5 per cent. Feeling isolated may increase our tendency to conform, but we need only to know that there is one other person on our side, and we refuse to conform to something we don't agree with.

Asch decided to see if the difficulty of the task itself could contribute to levels of conformity. In one experiment he made the three

► 'Debriefing' is often necessary after research in social psychology, both for ethical and practical reasons. If a subject did something which followed on in some way from the research, then the researcher would be responsible. Some of the subjects here may have incurred charges for eye tests or visits to a psychiatrist which they didn't need!

► In Asch's experiments the naives did not know the confederates, so why would so many of the responses conform to the opinion of just three strangers when the naive can plainly see that the response is wrong?

► If you see two people having an argument, as soon as a third person supports one of them, that one becomes more determined.

comparison lines very similar in length so that it was difficult to tell which one truly did match the target line. The naives would have been less certain. Where there was a majority view expressed by the confederates, conformity by the naive subjects rose sharply. This suggests that the less able someone is to make an independent judgement confidently, the more likely they are to accept the judgements of others, either to solve a problem of uncertainty by believing that others are right – an example of informational conformity – or to avoid looking stupid or feeling isolated by going along with the majority judgement – an example of normative conformity or ingratiational conformity (see page 196).

 What factors did Asch find to be important in conforming?

▶ Conformity increases where the naives want to agree, don't know any better, regard themselves as less intelligent or competent, etc.

Asch's research has revealed two conditions which promote conformity. One is that individuals can be influenced to say something which they know to be wrong (at least under experimental conditions) when three or more others unanimously say it first. The second is that the presence of just one other person who disagrees with the incorrect decision of the majority is enough to massively reduce this conformity.

Further research has been conducted into why people conform to group norms. A few years after Asch published his findings **Deutsch** and **Gerard** suggested two reasons for the conformity Asch had observed. These are 'normative social influence' and 'informational social influence'. Normative social influence means that people conform in order to be socially accepted by those in the group. Informational social influence means accepting the group view if you have reason to believe that they have knowledge or evidence that you don't, and which you can't ignore. Other factors that increase the likelihood of conformity are if the naive is of a lower status, less

▶ The Sherif and the Asch experiments demonstrated only that people would conform by uttering agreements and not that they would conform by carrying out some action.

> ### Some criticisms of the early research on conformity
> **Hollander** and **Willis** have made the following four criticisms of the conformity studies of Sherif, Asch and other early research.
>
> 1 The studies do not identify the motive or type of conformity. Do the subjects conform in order to gain social approval? Are they simply complying? Do they really believe that their response is correct?
> 2 They do not identify whether the subjects are complying because they judge that it's not worth appearing to be different, or because they actually start to believe that the group's judgement is correct.
> 3 The studies cannot show whether those who do not conform do so because they are independent thinkers or because they are anti-conformists.
> 4 The studies seem to assume that independence has to be good and conformity has to be bad. As we found earlier, conformity is often beneficial.

experienced, less intelligent and more tired than the confederates.

There are certain problems with Asch's, and Deutsch and Gerard's studies and conclusions. Like Sherif, they used highly artificial laboratory procedures that do not reflect 'real life' at all. In real life we do not have to make judgements about such things as the length of two lines after having heard a group of strangers give the wrong answer. We could choose to say nothing, or we could ask for help if we weren't sure. In real life 'actions speak louder than words'. Asch's and Deutsch and Gerard's research concerns verbal conformity. Conformity of behaviour – being influenced to do something – is much more important than conformity of speech – being influenced to say something.

Asch assumes that conformity to experimental stimuli somehow represents 'real life' conformity. His measurements of the percentages of naive subjects who conformed under various circumstances says nothing about the frequency with which people conform to the opinions or behaviour of others in everyday life.

Another assumption of Asch's is that conformity is bad. He believed his subjects were wrong to conform. But in real life (and in his experiment) conformity is often very useful. We said earlier that agreement may have some positive benefits for us, so unless it's a matter of principle life may be more pleasant if we are generally agreeable. This is hardly bad. Those subjects who conformed avoided any stress that could have been associated with resisting the majority view. After all, it was only an experiment.

Finally, Asch's experiments do not identify whether the subjects were true conformists, independent thinkers or merely complying with the will of the majority. \l

(NM) Summarize the major criticisms of Asch's work.

Crutchfield's research

In 1954 **R.S. Crutchfield** published the findings of his study of military and business people who had been unwitting subjects in his experiment on the final day of their three-day assessment course. The men had been grouped into fives and seated, side by side, in individual booths. They could not see each other, and were forbidden to talk. Various multiple choice questions were projected onto the wall in front of the men, and they had to give their answers by pressing one of five switches which corresponded to the answer they favoured. For example if they thought the answer to one question was the fourth alternative, they would press switch number four.

Each subject was also told that he would see the responses that the others were making. A light on his panel of switches would illuminate to show what choice they had made. These 'responses' were in fact controlled by the experimenter from a master control panel behind the subjects. Each subject believed they were taking it in turns to be 'first', although this too was being controlled by Crutchfield.

On certain 'critical questions', when Crutchfield attempted to induce

► Conformity to some behaviour is demanded by law. We conform to driving on the same side of the road and stopping at red traffic lights too. Are these 'conformities' bad?

► Crutchfield used highly motivated subjects. They were on an assessment course that would have important consequences for their future and they would want to do as well as possible.

► Crutchfield's procedure is an improvement on that of both Asch and Sherif. He used professional adults rather than university students, and he didn't need any confederates. The type of stimuli presented is a great improvement on stationary lights and lines on cards. The 'responses' the other subjects were supposed to have made and the order in which the subjects 'answer' can be varied greatly.

► Crutchfield's experimental procedures were tightly controlled and little would be left to chance. Are you happy that these subjects should have been used, without their consent, in this research?

Conformity

R.D. Tuddenham followed up Crutchfield's research and found that some extreme conformist students would also agree with the following statements: '60 per cent to 70 per cent of Americans are aged 65 or over. Most must be women because the life expectancy of American male babies is only about 25 years. Males are on average eight or nine inches taller than females. Americans sleep four to five hours a night on average, and eat six meals a day. The average American family has five or six children. There is no overcrowding in America since it stretches 6000 miles from San Francisco to New York. Most people would be better off if they never went to school at all. There's no use doing things for people, they don't appreciate it. I cannot do anything well.'

It appears that some people will agree with almost anything at all!

---

some conformity, he made each man think he would be the last person to respond, and showed all of them the same (wrong) answer supposedly given by the others. During the course of a one-hour session up to 50 'critical questions' could be asked, mixed in with 'neutral' questions where the right answers were given. Some of these critical questions involved stating some fact, judgement or opinion.

Crutchfield found that on the judgement questions, such as asking whether one figure was larger than another, and on factual questions, such as asking for the next number in a given sequence, 30 per cent of his subjects would conform to the wrong answer when they thought that the others were giving the wrong response too. On matters of opinion one of his more celebrated findings was that 37 per cent of the army personnel he tested agreed with the statement, 'I doubt whether I would make a good leader.' When tested privately none of them had agreed with this statement.

Altogether Crutchfield and his colleagues tested over 600 subjects and found that around a third of their responses to 'critical questions' would conform to some response when informed that other people had given the same response.

► 30 per cent conformity is actually quite high in view of the nature of this sample. They were successful military officers and businessmen who were motivated to succeed and who we would expect to be individual thinkers.

 What have we learned from Crutchfield's studies?

Crutchfield had a mass of data about his subjects from the two days of assessment tasks they had completed before becoming involved in the conformity experiment. From this he was able to investigate the question, 'What is it that makes some people more likely to conform than others?' An obvious place to start was with the personalities, intelligence, social adjustment and other social factors of the conformers compared to the non-conformers. Here are his main conclusions:

► This description of conformers sounds as though the person possessing such a personality would be a poor creature indeed. However, moderation in all things. All of us have tendencies to be rather weaker than we would like.

1 Conformers tended to be less intellectually effective. By this Crutchfield meant that they lacked insight and were less able to apply

> **A comparison of Asch's and Crutchfield's techniques**
>
> *Asch* | *Crutchfield*
>
> Subjects can hear each other's responses. | Subjects are told how others respond.
>
> Subjects can see and read each other's NVCs. (non-verbal cues) | Subjects are isolated from each other.
>
> Subjects have personal contact, which produces a greater Pressure to Conform. | Subjects are anonymous and feel less pressure to conform.

logical principles to given data. Instead they were more cautious, following 'tried and tested' routes, or imitating other people's solutions.

2 They have less ego strength and are not self-sufficient. This means that they are less sure of themselves, lack confidence in their abilities and are less forceful in expressing opinions or ideas. They are less likely to be able to take care of themselves and need the support of others.

3 They have less leadership ability. Their cautious approach and general indecisiveness would not inspire confidence in their competence and would not inspire respect and loyalty.

4 They tend to have authoritarian views of what 'ought to happen', and what 'should be' done. Their ideas are narrow-minded, simplistic and mostly unworkable.

5 They tend to have inferiority feelings too, and are generally submissive. They know they lack confidence and competence, and so look to others to be strong and decisive. They will not defend their ideas with enthusiasm and tend to agree with whatever the most determined person in the group says. They are usually inhibited in their personal relationships.

6 They have rather limited friendship networks and their social relationships are often rather shallow.

7 They are not widely liked, although they may be widely tolerated. They can be relied upon to 'make the numbers up', but may not often be wanted for themselves.

► We are in danger of producing a circular argument if we say that there is such a thing as a 'conforming personality' and that people who possess it tend to conform. It is preferable to say that 'under certain circumstances some people who have certain personality characteristics are more likely to conform than others'.

(NM) What intellectual, personality and social characteristics did Crutchfield find correlations with those most likely to conform?

Whether this description constitutes a 'type of personality' which conformers have, and whether someone with such a personality could be relied upon to conform in all situations, is unclear. What can be demonstrated in experimental studies tends to rely on verbal or anonymous responses to fairly artificial stimuli. What might happen in 'real life' when actual decisive behaviour is required is much harder to demonstrate.

So why do we conform? In 1961 **Donald Campbell** noted that we gain our information about the world through personal, direct experience (our 'personal modes') and through what other people tell us (our 'social modes'). Usually these two confirm each other. If your mother told you to put your coat on before going out because it was pouring with rain, you would expect to see it raining if you looked through the window. Campbell suggested that conformity can be explained as a consequence of conflict between these two modes. If the naive subject sees (personal mode) that line 1 is the same length as the target line, but everyone else (social mode) says it's the same as line 2, then the naive has to decide whether to favour the personal mode or the social mode. All those factors which make it likely that the personal mode will be favoured, such as intelligence, independence, high status etc., increase the chances that the subject will not conform. All those which increase the chances that the social mode will be favoured, such as the group having higher status, higher intelligence, etc., increase the likelihood of conformity.

Strickland and **Crowne** suggest that some people have a higher need for social approval than others. They may be less confident for a variety of reasons. For example, their socialization may have discouraged their individuality, or their early emotional development may have made them unsure about themselves and needing constant reassurance (see Bowlby's work in Chapter 3). Conforming to a group's norms and values leads to being accepted by the group, and thus gaining social approval. In such cases conformity is actually fulfilling some psychological need in the individual conformer.

► Where a discrepancy occurs between what we know personally and what we find out from other sources, we have to decide which to believe. According to Campbell, the more confident and mature we are, the more likely we are to believe our own judgements.

► Rather than seeing conformity as a type of personality Strickland and Crowne see it fulfilling some psychological need. Conformity thus achieves a positively beneficial goal.

 What kind of people are least likely to conform?

Summary – Conformity and non-conformity

Conformity means yielding to group pressure and affects behaviour, or attitudes, or our wider personality, or all three. It comprises normative conformity, informational conformity and ingratiational conformity. Non-conformity comprises independent behaviour, which is usually admired, and anti-conformity, which is usually disliked.

Sherif, Asch and Crutchfield each conducted fairly artificial laboratory experiments which showed that about 30 per cent of responses can be explained by the need or desire of the subjects to conform. These experiments may not accurately reflect 'real life', when conformity might be beneficial and sometimes contribute to psychological well-being.

STUDIES OF OBEDIENCE

Obedience is a special form of compliance. Compliance simply means going along with the decisions, opinions, rules or conventions of a group. We may comply because it's easy, because we can't be bothered to act independently, or because we want to. Obedience is compliance where we generally do not want to comply. It also implies that someone is in power or authority over us giving us specific orders, requests or suggestions that require us to respond in some way. Obedience, like conformity, may be beneficial or destructive. It can contribute to the efficient achievement of some goal. It may also result in cruelty and evil.

The question has been asked – is there an 'obedient personality'? Are there some people who are willing to do the most wicked acts, such as those performed by some Nazis in extermination camps during the Second World War? Or are many or all of us capable of doing such things, if put into such a situation?

 What is obedience?

Milgram's experiments

The first major psychological research into obedience began in the late 1950s and early 1960s in a series of controversial experiments by **Stanley Milgram**. An American social psychologist at Yale University, Milgram had been working on various aspects of conformity, such as cross-cultural differences. He became especially interested in obedience since it was being suggested after the Second World War that the German people must have some national character defect which made them especially susceptible to obeying orders – and hence able to follow orders to exterminate people from other cultures. It was said that no other race could have performed such atrocities.

Milgram designed an experiment whereby pairs of male subjects would draw a piece of paper from a hat deciding who would be the 'teacher' and who the 'learner' in an experiment on learning. They were told that if the learner gave an incorrect answer to the teacher's question he would receive punishment in the form of an electric shock. This would be administered by the teacher pressing a switch on an electric shock-generating machine. With each incorrect answer the severity of the shock would increase, in 15 volt stages, up to 450 volts. If the teacher showed any reluctance or concern, the experimenter would give them a verbal instruction to continue: an order to obey.

Various groups of professionals were asked by Milgram what they thought the outcome of such an experiment might be. A group of psychiatrists suggested that most people would refuse to participate in such an experiment once they realized what was involved and that less than 1 per cent would continue administering shocks to the end. A group of psychology students agreed that most people would drop out by halfway, although a few might continue right to the end.

► Obedience is a special form of conformity, requiring some actual behaviour. A teacher telling a child to come here is a specific order from a known authority figure which requires some particular response.

► The 1950s saw the application of scientific techniques to social psychological issues. One of the first to be studied was conformity, and by the early 1960s Milgram had extended work on conformity to include the study of obedience.

► The obedience in Milgram's experiment was to a verbal request or statement from an unknown experimenter who had no legitimate authority over the subjects.

► This was a very controversial experiment. Can you identify any reasons why?

► Milgram wanted to compare the drop out rates of subjects in his experiments between people of different nationalities and different cultures to see if there are variations between people in their obedience to authority.

Milgram had intended to run this experiment among men and women from several nationalities, including German. If the historians were correct then the students' and psychiatrists' predictions for the high rates of early refusals among the American people would not be found among the Germans. If the Germans were more responsive to authority many more of them should continue to administer the shocks right to the end.

An advertisement was placed in local papers in New Haven, Connecticut, and a postal questionnaire also sent out, asking for men between 20 and 50, and from all walks of life, who would be paid $4.50 to take part in an experiment at Yale University, lasting for about one hour, 'to investigate the relationship between personality and learning'. Milgram selected 40 respondents, including engineers, teachers, salesmen, clerks and manual workers, and arranged appointments for the men to arrive at the Yale Interaction Laboratory.

► This is a self-selected sample and although all such samples may appear biased, Milgram was careful to select as representative a group from his respondents as possible.

 What is a self-selected sample, and why is it often biased?

On arrival each subject met the experimenter and the 'other subject', who was introduced as 'Mr Wallace'. He was a rather overweight, very mild and pleasant man in his late fifties. And he was, of course, a confederate of Milgram, although the other man believed he was a naive subject, just like himself. To decide who was to be the 'teacher' and who the 'learner', and make it appear authentic, the two men drew a slip of paper from a hat. Both slips had TEACHER written on them, but Mr Wallace claimed that his said LEARNER. Mr Wallace was strapped into a chair in the next room, in the presence of the naive 'teacher'. Electrodes were placed on his hands, at which point he told them that he had recently been in hospital for a heart condition and the doctors had told him to avoid stressful situations. The young, determined-looking experimenter told him that although the shocks may be painful, they would cause no lasting damage.

► A naive subject is being led to believe that someone is about to receive painful electric shocks as part of a psychology experiment. Any further thoughts about the controversial nature of this experiment? Any thoughts about ethics?

 Why was it necessary for both slips of paper in Milgram's experimental procedure to say TEACHER?

The naive 'teacher' was taken into another room where he could not see the learner and was seated in front of the electric shock generator, a rather intimidating machine with a row of 30 toggle switches along the front which were clearly marked in 15 volt steps. Above the switches were the following eight steps:

0–60	slight shock
75–120	moderate shock
135–180	strong shock
195–240	very strong shock
255–300	intense shock
315–360	intense to extreme shock
375–420	danger severe shock
435–450	XXX

The teacher was instructed to read out 10 words in five, unrelated pairs, e.g. 'Door – grass', 'book – carrot', 'brother – sky', 'radio –spoon', 'hill – sail'. After a pause the teacher would say one of the paired words, and then the five other words that formed the second word of the pairs. The learner would have to signal the first word's pair by pressing a switch which illuminated a light on the generator. If the answer was correct the teacher would pass on to the next set of paired words. If not, the teacher had to announce the intensity of the shock that was about to be delivered, and the appropriate switch was to be pressed.

The machine made a grinding sort of sound, as though it was working, although in fact the learner's electrodes weren't connected to it. The teacher heard a tape-recorded series of answers so that every naive teacher always heard the same answers in the same order. The next incorrect response would be punished by 30 volts, the next by 45 volts and so on.

Why did Milgram use a tape-recorded series of answers?

► After reading five pairs of words the teacher would say one of the words, and the learner had to signal its pair. Failure to do so resulted in a 15 volt shock the first time. The next mistake was 'punished' with 30 volts etc.

► The teacher believed he is to administer increasingly painful electric shocks to another human being. He received a 45 volt sample shock himself at the start of the experiment, just to convince him that the machine was working.

As the shocks grew more intense the learner started to complain. At 75 volts he began moaning and groaning. At 125 volts he shouted out, 'That really hurts'. At 150 volts he asked to be released from the experiment. At 180 volts he shouted, 'I can't stand the pain, don't do that.' At 195 volts he yelled, 'Let me out, my heart's starting to bother me now.' At 285 volts he screamed in agony. At 300 volts he kicked and hit the wall, and pleaded with them to let him out. At 315 volts he fell silent, and was not heard from again.

During this period most of the teachers became uncomfortable. Clearly they weren't happy at inflicting pain on someone they hardly knew. They looked to the experimenter for guidance. He had four responses which he could give. First he would say 'Please continue' or 'Please go on'. If the teacher still complained about what he was asking them to do, he would reply, more insistently, 'The experiment requires that you continue'. If that failed he would say, 'It's absolutely essential that you go on' and, finally, 'You have no choice, you must go on'. These were the 'special prods' to try to make the subjects obey, and continue giving the shocks. In addition the experimenter could accept responsibility for what was happening if the naive subject demanded it. After 315 volts, when the learner stopped responding, the subjects were to be told that no answer was to be treated as a wrong answer and that they must continue to administer the shocks.

Why were there four 'prods'?

► As the shocks grew more severe the learner made a series of protests, including begging to be released from the experiment. If anyone continued to administer shocks after 315 volts they heard nothing from the learner.

► The experimenter had four 'prods', each one more insistent than the previous one, to try to make the subject continue to obey the instruction to give the next set of words or the next shock.

To summarize, 40 ordinary American men, aged between 20 and 50, were being goaded into continuing to give electric shocks of up to 450 volts, marked as intense shock, dangerous shock, severe shock etc., to a mild and pleasant fellow subject who they knew to have had a heart

► The majority of Milgram's subjects continued to administer electric shocks to the learner, although most of them complained bitterly and showed physical distress at having to do it.

condition, beyond a point when they had reason to believe they may have killed him, in return for $4.50. And all because a 30-year-old, rather severe, unfriendly experimenter, dressed in a grey laboratory coat, told them, 'You have no choice, you must go on'. Surely no one would?

Milgram's conclusions

Of the 40 men in the first experiment, 26 continued to give the shocks, right up to the maximum of 450 volts. That is, 65 per cent of the sample allowed themselves to be bullied into (as they believed) causing pain, continuing to the point of possibly causing death, to a fellow human being. A man in a grey laboratory coat whom they had never met before and weren't likely to ever meet again, told them that they must continue, and 65 per cent of them did. None of the subjects refused to give shocks and all continued until 300 volts ('intense shock'), and even then only five finally refused. Nine more dropped out between 315 and 375 volts. The rest continued to 450 volts.

Lack of refusal to continue did not, however, mean lack of concern. Most subjects sweated, complained to and swore at the experimenter, several had seizures (one so violently that the experiment was terminated and medical assistance was sought). They trembled and stuttered, bit their lips and clenched their hands so tightly that they dug their nails into their flesh. But despite their distress most of them still continued to obey.

Milgram was amazed at his findings. His sample must surely be hopelessly biased? Could people so easily be made to inflict pain on others? He re-ran the experiments with a sample of 1000 residents of New Haven, whom he believed to be a typical cross-section of the male population. And he obtained similar results! There seemed little point in taking his apparatus to Germany – Germans couldn't be much more responsive to authority than Americans!

Milgram's findings suggest that the same is true of obedience as of conformity: there isn't an 'obedient personality character' any more than there is a 'conforming personality character'. Rather, there are circumstances under which most people can be made to obey and to conform. Milgram decided to investigate further the factors that promoted obedience, using variations of his experimental design.

 Summarize the conclusions from Milgram's first experiment on obedience.

Variations of Milgram's research

Some of Milgram's main conclusions about the situational factors involved in obedience are described below.

One factor in the likelihood of obedience seems to be the confidence the subject has in the institution in whose name the orders are given. If we believe that the orders come from a legitimate, trustworthy source, we are more likely to obey them. In debriefing sessions some of Milgram's subjects said that they continued giving shocks because

▶ All of the subjects continued to administer shocks until the learner begged to be released, screamed in agony and kicked the wall as the shock (supposedly) threw him across the room. Only five of the 40 refused at this point.

▶ Mantell re-ran Milgram's research in Germany and found an even higher percentage (85 per cent) of obedience. This isn't as significant as it might seem, and doesn't really support the idea that Germans are much more susceptible to authority than Americans.

▶ There seemed little point in contrasting other nations' willingness to obey since it became apparent that there wasn't an 'obedient personality type', but rather that situational factors were responsible.

they knew they were involved in research at a famous university where nothing bad would be allowed to happen. Milgram says 'A substantial proportion of people do what they are told to do, irrespective of the content of the act and without limitations of conscience, so long as they perceive that the command comes from a legitimate authority.'

Milgram rented some offices in a rather run down block in nearby Bridgeport, Connecticut, which he regarded as an 'average' American town. His newspaper adverts asked for volunteers to take part in some privately funded market research. Apart from that, the experimental procedure was identical. This time half of his sample refused to give shocks, but nearly 50 per cent still went on to the end.

▶ People still tend to obey if they see that the person giving the orders has the authority to do so, even though the organization doesn't appear to have any authority.

Showing subjects that other courses of action are possible also seems important. Milgram introduced a similar variation to that used by Asch 10 years previously. He arranged for the naive subject to associate with two other teachers (who were confederates) who refused to continue at 150 and 210 volts respectively. In this situation, only 10 per cent of the naives obeyed up to 450 volts. Having a model or someone to take the lead in non-obedience seems important. Many of the subjects said things like, 'I didn't realize I could refuse'.

▶ Where someone else behaves in a non-compliant manner, others may also refuse to obey.

Having someone else to blame for the consequences of one's obedience appears to be important too. In another variation there were two teachers, one being a confederate. The real naive read out the word pairs, and the confederate gave the shocks. 95 per cent of the naives now went to 450 volts. They reasoned that it wasn't their fault, they were only reading words. They argued that the guy who was giving the shocks (teacher) should have taken some action if he was worried about what he was doing to the other fellow.

▶ The nearer the person who gives the order is to the person who is expected to obey it, the more likely it is that it will be obeyed.

Another influential factor is having the authority figure close at hand to give the orders. In another variation, the experimenter left the room after explaining the procedure and issued all instructions by telephone. Considerably fewer subjects now obeyed the orders to give increasingly painful shocks. In a third variation the experimenter was never present, but left instructions on a tape recorder. Only about 20 per cent now obeyed, and many gave lower shocks than those required by the experiment. Why do something they found upsetting when no one could know if they obeyed fully or not?

▶ Being able to place responsibility for the consequences of our action elsewhere increases the likelihood that we will obey the orders for that action.

The distance between the teacher and the learner was varied in later experiments. It was found that the closer the learner was placed to the teacher the greater were the refusals to obey. Even so at 18 inches distance (half a metre), 40 per cent continued to give the maximum shock and when the teacher actually had to put the learner's hand onto an electric plate 30 per cent still continued to the end.

▶ The nearer the person whose obedience results in harmful effects is to those who suffer as a consequence of them, the less those orders will be obeyed.

How would Donald Campbell's theory explain why closing the distance between the teacher and the learner in Milgram's experiment decreases the likelihood of obedience?

What are the main social or situational factors affecting the likelihood of obedience?

If anything, Milgram's findings are even more disturbing than those of Asch. The percentage of ordinary men who could be made to behave in such an extreme way was higher than in Asch's experiments, and the consequences of their obedience were so much more serious. They protested and became disturbed, but only the minority refused to obey.

A cautionary note: Milgram tested over 1000 subjects, almost all of whom were male. Only in one of the variations did he test women, and then only 40 of them. Any conclusions we draw from Milgram's research ought therefore to be confined to males. When the experiments were repeated in Australia, 40 per cent of males obeyed, but less than 20 per cent of women did.

► Milgram explains the high levels of obedience in terms of the structure of society, and what we have learned during our socialization processes. Power is distributed hierarchically throughout society, and we are brought up to expect to obey and conform.

So why do people obey? According to Milgram we live in a hierarchical society where orders are always handed down to us. At first our parents, then teachers, older children, other adults, the police, and others have all laid down a structure of things we must do, things we may do, things we oughtn't to do, and things we must not do. These rules and conventions come to represent our culture. Harmonious and peaceful living demands cooperation and we have learned that obeying cultural rules and conventions leads to cooperation and harmony. We are 'programmed' to obey. Milgram notes how individual men and women (and members of other animal species) accept that they must subordinate their own individual wishes to the needs of the group.

(NM) How does Milgram explain the obedience he found?

Criticisms of Milgram's work

The usual criticisms of social psychological research concern the ethics of its conduct, the representativeness of its sample and its applicability to 'real life'.

Ethics

► Baumrind claims that Milgram's research should have been abandoned on the grounds of ethics, and the harm he was causing to his subjects.

Shortly after the publication of Milgram's research **Diane Baumrind** complained that Milgram's work was unethical. She says that the stress and discomfort clearly suffered by Milgram's subjects was not justifiable on any grounds, and that the research should have been stopped. Milgram wrote: 'In a large number of cases the degree of tension reached extremes that are rarely seen in sociopsychological laboratory studies. Subjects were observed to sweat, tremble, stutter, bite their lips, groan, and dig their fingernails into their flesh. These were characteristic rather than exceptional responses to the experiment ... on one occasion we observed a seizure so violently convulsive that it was necessary to call a halt to the experiment.'

► Milgram claimed that he never intended that his subjects should suffer and that they didn't come to any real harm in the long term. On the other hand he claims that we have learned a great deal about the nature of conformity from his studies.

Baumrind claims that research that can have these effects should not be conducted. Who can say what the long term effects of knowing that one is capable of such behaviour might be? Milgram made the following points in his defence.

Firstly he had not foreseen that so many subjects would obey to the end, or that those who refused would take so long to do so. He believed that most would have refused to obey the 'authority' long before 300 volts was administered. He did not intend his subjects to suffer such distress, and did not anticipate that they would. He also pointed out that subjects were free to stop at any time; all they had to do was refuse to obey the experimenter.

Milgram denied that any permanent harm would be caused to the subjects. They were all debriefed after the experiment, and reunited with the learner confederate. These were usually very emotional scenes, sometimes with the naive embracing the confederate as though he was a long unseen brother. Milgram also sent out a summary of the conclusions and a follow up questionnaire asking each subject for their feelings and opinions. He claimed that 80 per cent said they were pleased to have taken part in the research, and that more research of this nature should take place. Only 1 per cent said they were sorry to have been included.

Outline Baumrind's criticisms of Milgram's research, and the points Milgram makes in his defence.

Representativeness

Short of testing every member of the target population, any research with limited samples can be accused of being unrepresentative, particularly where the sample is self-selected. Although Milgram chose a cross-section of the population, they were male and some were volunteers. Some groups are less likely, however, to volunteer to take part in this research, for example, few wealthy people would volunteer. Further, even a representative cross-section of the population of one town may not be a valid measure of American behaviour since that town may not be typical of all American towns.

However Milgram used a relatively large sample and we have no reason to believe that the male residents of New Haven are much different from other American males: similar results have also been found by other researchers in other countries. Even if we reject Milgram's precise figures, we can't deny that a disturbingly large number of people were prepared to obey in a frightening way, on the instructions of a man who appeared to represent some kind of authority.

Generalizability

Laboratory studies such as Sherif's do not reflect 'real life'. Asch's methodology is also far removed from the normal processes of human interaction. In 'real life' people do not generally go around giving orders that could cause physical pain to others. Milgram argues that the processes involved in obeying the authority figure in his experiment are much the same as those involved in obeying people generally, and that there is a correspondence between his findings and 'real life'. He points out that the situation certainly felt 'real' to his subjects at the time.

► The target population for research into obedience among American adults would be 'all American adults' – clearly an impossible target to achieve. The solution is to find a representative sample which may not always be possible.

► Milgram's experimental situation may not have reflected real life, but he claims that it does reflect the processes involved in real life decisions about obedience.

► Both Asch and Milgram have dismissed the idea that certain people with certain personality characteristics will always conform or be obedient while others without such characteristics will not.

Whether you accept Milgram's justification or believe that Baumrind's first impressions are correct, Milgram's research has taught us a great deal about how humans perceive authority, and how willingly they obey it.

 List the ethical objections to Milgram's research and the benefits of doing the research. Do the benefits outweigh the objections?

Zimbardo's research

During the 1960s numerous stories appeared in the American press about alleged brutality in some American prisons. It was claimed that some prisoners had been robbed and humiliated, beaten and tortured, and even killed by some of their homicidal guards. Could it be that American prisons were staffed by sociopathic sadists? If so, why weren't masses of prisoners and ex-prisoners complaining to every possible civil rights and government organization? Are American criminals naturally submissive and accepting of injustice and hardship? In view of the claims so far that social and environmental factors are more influential than personality types in explaining conformity and obedience, could it be that the social environment, roles and relationships within prisons create the tendency for guards to be aggressive and prisoners to be submissive?

In 1972 **P.G. Zimbardo** published the findings from his experimental study of a 'mock prison'. It has become known as the *Stanford Prison experiment*. Zimbardo believed that the 'social psychological environment' of the prison experience would explain the dominant and submissive roles adopted by guards and prisoners. To test this he set up a mock prison, using paid volunteers, and he observed how their relationships changed.

► Zimbardo believes that social psychological pressures make people dominant and aggressive or submissive and dependent.

We will examine Zimbardo's experiment under three headings, representing the three stages: preparation, procedure and conclusions.

Preparation (the sample)

Zimbardo placed national newspaper advertisements for male university students to take part in a functional simulation of a prison. They would be required for eight hours a day and would be paid $15 a day for their trouble. The research was to take two weeks. Zimbardo received over 100 replies. He gave personality inventories and various tests and interviews to ensure these middle-class and well-educated people were psychologically 'normal', had no history of drug abuse or major convictions, were emotionally stable and physically healthy. From the original sample he chose 25 healthy, stable subjects. All said they would prefer to play the role of a prisoner, but they were randomly divided into prisoners and guards. There were therefore no differences between the students playing the part of guards or prisoners.

► Zimbardo went to great trouble to attract a group of talented, middle-class, emotionally stable and physically fit young men for his prison simulation. Exactly the 'same sort' of people are playing the part of guards as were playing the part of prisoners. Any differences between them later would not have been caused by individual differences in the two groups.

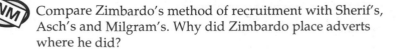 Compare Zimbardo's method of recruitment with Sherif's, Asch's and Milgram's. Why did Zimbardo place adverts where he did?

Procedure

Everything Zimbardo did was to enhance the subjects' impression that they were undergoing a 'real prison experience'. The students playing the part of 'prisoners' were arrested, without warning, by police on a Sunday morning (much to the surprise of their neighbours!). They were accused of some crime, read their rights, handcuffed and taken to the local police station. Here they were treated like every other criminal. They were fingerprinted, photographed and 'booked'. Then they were blindfolded and driven to the psychology department of Stanford University, where Zimbardo had had the basement set out as a prison, with barred doors and windows, bare walls and small cells. Here the *deindividuation* process began.

When the prisoners arrived at the prison they were stripped naked, deloused, had all their personal possessions removed and locked away, and were given prison clothes and bedding. Their clothes comprised a smock with their number written on it, but no underclothes. They also had a tight nylon cap, and a chain around one ankle.

They were only to be allowed visits from the chaplain and from their relations. They were to be locked in their cells all the time, except when let out for work, toilet privileges or head counts. Toilets were allowed only until 10 pm. After that the prisoners had to use buckets. There were no shower facilities. Each cell was two by three metres, and was to sleep three men. Apart from the cells there was 'the hole', a small, converted storage cupboard where men could be kept in solitary confinement for fairly short periods if they broke one of the prison 'rules'.

To assist in the deindividuation process, feelings of *dependency* on the guards were fostered. The prisoners needed a guard's permission for almost everything. They were not allowed to smoke, use the toilet or write a letter (which they could only do on prison notepaper) without a guard's permission. They had no knowledge of the time either. All clocks, radios, etc. were removed.

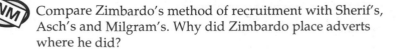 What is deindividuation?

Just as in a real prison, the guards were also deindividuated. They wore authentic khaki uniforms and had silver reflector sun-glasses (making eye contact and any kind of personal relationship that is facilitated by eye contact impossible). They also had short clubs, whistles, handcuffs, and the keys to cells and the main gate. The guards worked shifts and were allowed home in between. They had offices along the corridor.

When they first arrived the guards were instructed to maintain law and order in the prison, and to make the prisoners aware of the 16

► *Deindividuation* is the loss of one's sense of individuality as one becomes just another member of a group. Institutionalized mental patients, prisoners and people who work in prisons, or people who do things as part of a mob which they wouldn't do when alone, are said to be deindividuated.

► Removing their personal possessions and dressing these prisoners in identical clothes makes them more anonymous. Anonymity is an essential part of deindividuation.

► The conditions in Zimbardo's prison were primitive and unpleasant, and were thought to be fairly realistic.

► The guards were allowed to encourage prisoners who were slow to obey by pushing them, but any stronger physical violence was forbidden.

► Most prisons have lists of rules, many of them quite petty and probably unnecessary, which are often strictly enforced. They also have a role in deindividuation since they encourage prisoners to become dependent on the guards.

► Overall, Zimbardo's simulation bears a strong resemblance to a real prison and the relationships between prisoners and guards that exist there.

A non-conformist prisoner in the Stanford Prison experiment

One of the prisoners (416) began to become confused between his 'real identity' and that of prisoner 416. Starting as an act of independence or defiance he broke one of the prison rules by refusing to eat a meal. He also hoped to be regarded as ill in order to be released. He said: 'I began to feel I was losing my identity, the person I call myself, the person who put me into this place. The person who volunteered to go into this prison was distant from me, was remote, until finally I was not that. I was prisoner 416, I was really my number and 416 is going to have to decide what to do'.

The cruellest guard led the attack on 416 for disobeying prison rule number 2, which said that prisoners must eat at mealtimes. He kept

416 in solitary confinement for longer than was permitted, and made the other prisoners choose between keeping their blankets and having 416 released from solitary confinement. The majority sided with the guard against one of their own, and decided to keep their blankets. The guard finally decided that visiting privileges for all prisoners would be suspended if 416 continued to refuse to eat. Rather than protest at this injustice, the rest of the prisoners turned on 416.

Any prisoner who refuses to conform poses a potentially damaging threat to those who have most to lose by disruption (those in authority i.e. the guards). He must be made to conform before his behaviour is copied by others and those in authority face wider disruption.

▶ Within a few hours of the outset of the experiment both sides fell into their roles. The guards had expectations of their own superior, and of the prisoners' inferior role, which they soon exploited, and some guards began dehumanizing some of the prisoners. Yet all these people were educated, and emotionally stable, with perfectly 'normal' personalities, and had been randomly divided into playing the role of guard and prisoner.

▶ The result of the changing perceptions producing changing relationships was that the prisoners became depressed and began belittling themselves, which increased their feelings of hopelessness. A vicious circle was set up. The more the prisoners thought of themselves as useless and without hope, the more the guards despised them and increased their humiliation.

prison rules which they would enforce. For example, there must be silence after lights out, prisoners must eat at mealtimes and not eat at any other time. Tampering with walls was forbidden, and prisoners had to address each other by number only. Meanwhile they had to address a guard as 'Mr correctional officer, sir'. The final rule was that the failure to obey any of the rules might result in punishment!

Having explained the set up, the investigators left the prison and went into other areas from where they could observe and record what went on through spy holes and one-way mirrors.

Zimbardo's conclusions

Within a very short time both guards and prisoners were settling into their new roles, the guards adopting theirs quickly and easily. Within hours of beginning the experiment some guards began to harass prisoners. They behaved in a brutal and sadistic manner, apparently enjoying it. Other guards joined in, and other prisoners were also tormented. The prisoners were taunted with insults and petty orders, they were given pointless and boring tasks to accomplish, and they were generally dehumanized.

The prisoners soon adopted prisoner-like behaviour too. They talked about prison issues a great deal of the time. They 'told tales' on each other to the guards. They started taking the prison rules very seriously, as though they were there for the prisoners' benefit and infringement would spell disaster for all of them. Some even began siding with the guards against prisoners who did not conform to the rules.

 Why do you think a non-conforming prisoner would be attacked by the other prisoners?

Over the next few days the relationships between the guards and the prisoners changed, with a change in one leading to a change in the other. Remember that the guards were firmly in control and the prisoners were totally dependent on them.

As the prisoners became more dependent, the guards became more derisive towards them. They held the prisoners in contempt and let the prisoners know it. As the guards contempt for them grew, the prisoners became more submissive.

As the prisoners became more submissive, the guards became more aggressive and assertive. They demanded ever greater obedience from the prisoners. The prisoners were dependent on the guards for everything so tried to find ways to please the guards, such as telling tales on fellow prisoners.

As the prisoners were so dependent on the guards' good will, the guards sought more authority and new ways to degrade the prisoners. So the vicious circle went on.

► In a real prison with real prisoners and real guards (all of whom aren't intelligent and stable men) where people are together for years, the relationships and interpersonal behaviour between guards and prisoners will probably be worse.

 How did the social relationships between guard and prisoner change?

One prisoner had to be released after 36 hours because of uncontrollable bursts of screaming, crying and anger. His thinking became disorganized and he appeared to be entering the early stages of a deep depression. Within the next few days three others also had to leave after showing signs of emotional disorder that could have had lasting consequences. (These were people who had been pronounced stable and normal a short while before.)

Zimbardo had intended that the experiment should run for a fortnight, but on the sixth day he closed it down. There was real danger that someone might be physically or mentally damaged if it was allowed to run on. After some time for the researchers to gather their data the subjects were called back for a follow-up, debriefing session.

► Most of the guards found it difficult to believe that they had behaved in the brutalizing ways that they had. Many said they hadn't known this side of them existed or that they were capable of such things.

The follow-up
On the whole most of the participants said they had felt involved and committed. The research had felt 'real' to them. One guard said, 'I was surprised at myself. I made them call each other names and clean the toilets out with their bare hands. I practically considered the prisoners cattle and I kept thinking I had to watch out for them in case they tried something.'

Another guard said 'Acting authoritatively can be fun. Power can be a great pleasure.' And another: '... during the inspection I went to cell 2 to mess up a bed which a prisoner had just made and he grabbed me, screaming that he had just made it and that he was not going to let me mess it up. He grabbed me by the throat and although he was laughing I was pretty scared. I lashed out with my stick and hit him on the chin although not very hard, and when I freed myself I became angry.'

The prisoners too couldn't believe that they had responded in the submissive, cowering, dependent way they had. Several claimed to be assertive types normally. When asked about the guards they

► Since each person had been randomly assigned the role of prisoner or guard, any differences that existed between them must be the result of the situation (the roles they were playing), not their personalities.

► Zimbardo concludes that any social situation involves certain roles, e.g. prison guard, teacher, mother. When someone starts to play the roles their perceptions of what is the other's role – prisoners, pupils, children – becomes distorted.

described the usual three stereotypes which can be found in any prison: some guards were good, some were tough but fair, some were cruel.

Zimbardo was convinced that anyone was capable of the stereotyped behaviour of the guards. His subjects had been randomly allocated to play the part of guard or prisoner, so such differences in their perceptions of each other must be a function of the situation, and not of their personality.

In any situation where one group has power over another there is a tendency for the superior group to dominate the inferior group. The greater the gap between the two groups (as in this experiment), the greater will be the tendency to dominate. At the same time the inferior group will try to protect or improve its status by appeasing the dominant group, even including rejecting dissident members of its own group. Far from appeasing, however, this has the effect of making the dominant group more resentful of the inferior group, and more harshly disposed towards it.

 What is Zimbardo's explanation for how some people can behave with such brutality towards others?

 Identify the ethical objections which might be made of Zimbardo's research. How could the research be defended against these objections?

Summary – Studies of obedience

Milgram found that a large percentage of a sample of Americans would allow themselves to be bullied by someone who appeared to be an authority figure. The ethics of this experiment may not be justified by the lessons we have learned about those factors in any situation which allow people to dominate others.

Zimbardo's prison experiment also supports the idea that the situation, not the personality, is responsible for shaping the way in which people play their roles. The power of the dominant group leads to the dependency of the inferior group, which serves to increase the use of the power of the dominant group, and the submissiveness of the inferior group.

POWER AND LEADERSHIP

► Power is the ability to have your wishes obeyed. Authority is legalized power.

Power refers to the ability of a person or group to have their will obeyed. The various government departments have the power to decide on just about every aspect of our lives. The military or judicial system in some countries even has the power to end someone's life. If a criminal holds a gun to your head and demands that you hand over all your money, then that criminal has power.

Obviously there are different bases for power, such as the ability to reward the people who serve you, or the ability to punish them. They may follow you because you have the expert knowledge needed to run the organization, because you have a charismatic personality or

Leaders or leadership?

The usual way of defining a leader is 'the member of the group who has the most influence over the other members'. We may think of leaders as being the traditional heads of state, such as the queens and kings of some European countries, or the Emperor of Japan. An Italian sociologist, Mosca, claimed that there were two sort of leader, lions and foxes. Lions are strong and proud, assertive and dominant. They hold their position by strength and force. Foxes are cunning and sly. They use deceit and treachery, and hold their position by using their wits.

However leadership is a much more active, dynamic process since the members of the group inevitably exert influence on the leaders too. A good leader will be aware of the members' ideas and expectation, and be able to adapt leadership to the led. Also the actual leader of a group may not be the person who is its *official leader*. Quite a few headteachers (nominal leader) would be quite unfit to run their schools without their deputy heads (actual leader).

because you're the biggest bully! Authority is legalized power. When a policeman asks you to stop your car he has the authority of the law. When a criminal makes you stop he has the power of the gun and the threat that he might shoot you with it.

What power made the subjects in Milgram's research obey the 'prods' to continue? The experimenter had no legal status, no authority. They couldn't have thought that he was acting on behalf of any government agency. He wore a grey laboratory coat rather than a white one, to avoid any confusion that he represented the medical profession. He wasn't a physically powerful man, and no doubt many of the subjects were fitter and stronger. Yet 65 per cent of them still obeyed him when he said 'You must go on'. He had no weapon, except his rather stern personality and the tone of his voice. And the fact that we have learned that we must obey orders.

Why did the prisoners in Zimbardo's research obey and try to appease the guards? They were all university students who were each being paid the same amount of money to take part in an experiment. Zimbardo says that under the same circumstances most of us would have behaved in the same ways, since submissive or brutal behaviour is a function of our perceptions of the relationships in that social situation.

If we do as we are told, and there are circumstances under which we can behave in evil ways, then the question of leadership becomes particularly important. We need to know that our leaders are exercising their power in our best interests. To this end it is important that the best qualified people become leaders. Is leadership then, a personality characteristic or a function of the particular circumstances? Or to put it another way, are some people 'born leaders', who will always end up running whatever organization they are in, or are most people capable of being a leader of certain groups?

► Why did the naive subjects in Milgram's research continue to administer the shocks?

► According to social psychological research, under the right circumstances most of us would conform at least some of the time, and most of us would obey some orders.

► Whenever two or more people become a group one of them is likely to emerge as its leader. The one will be preferred to others, listened to more than others, and taken more notice of than others. As the group becomes more stable the role of its leader becomes more important.

> **Management: the Peter Principle**
> Here is one view of the process of management:
> • *I am a junior employee and I work hard and become good at my job. I can cope, and have more ability than the job needs. I am good at my job so I am promoted.*
>
> • *I am now a junior manager and I work hard and become good at my job. I can cope, and my ability is being fully used. I am good at my job so I am promoted.*
>
> • *I am now a senior manager and I work hard and try to do my job. I can't cope because I do not have the level of ability the job needs. I am bad at my job so I do not get promoted. Instead I get ulcers and a heart condition from worry and overwork.*
>
> Most managers therefore must be incompetent and inefficient, and suffering from stress!

The leadership characteristics approach

► What are the personal qualities which help the leader in any of the groups to which you belong? Are they the same for each leader?

► Be careful not to confuse personal characteristics such as height, sex, intelligence, etc., with personality traits. We are looking for any characteristics which correlate with leadership, not just personality characteristics.

Early psychology didn't reject the popular idea that there were 'born leaders' whose personality, skills, wealth or other personal qualities would always attract followers. This is sometimes called the 'Great man theory'. We said earlier (pages 185) how we become attracted to people who are good looking, truthful, sincere, honest and loyal. They may find themselves being regarded as the natural leader in some groups. But not all attractive, intelligent, sincere, loyal or honest people become 'great men'.

If there were identifiable personal characteristics or personality traits to leaders, then potential leaders could be spotted early and groomed for leadership. The future performance of their organizations could be predicted and measured. This might improve the efficiency of the whole management process.

 What could be the benefit of knowing the characteristics of the leader?

Of all the studies that have been conducted on leaders and leadership no particular personal characteristics have been found which explain why the person who possessed them became the leader. Some successful leaders are authoritarian, others attempt to see people as equals. Some are tall, others are short, some are old, others are young, some are extroverts, some are more introverted. Nor are leaders necessarily any more intelligent than the people they lead. In groups who have some task to accomplish, the best correlate of leadership is intelligence but the correlation isn't very high. (The tests for measuring leadership effectiveness and intelligence aren't always very accurate either!)

Different leaders use different styles of leadership, even if we cannot identify these styles as personality characteristics. Over 50 years ago **Kurt Lewin** directed **Ronald Lippit** and **Ralph White** in conducting an experiment to investigate the effects of different leadership styles on groups of children involved in making masks and other models. Three groups of 10-year-old boys were to make the models, and their performance and relationships were to be assessed. The number of models they made, and their quality, were also to be noted. Each group was to have a leader whose style was quite different. Any differences in the performance and behaviour of the three groups would be explained by the *independent variable*, the leadership style.

> ► The boys in the three groups were fairly similar, so presumably the average 'mask and model making' skill for each group would be similar. The difference between the groups was to be the leadership style employed.

One group had a *democratic* leader. He discussed his ideas and strategies for making the models with the boys and encouraged them to talk over their ideas with him. They chose their own workmates and who was to do what job. They were friendly and cooperative. They consulted the leader when necessary, and produced a reasonable number of models. When the democratic leader left the room the work continued cooperatively.

> ► *Democratic* leaders discuss and direct, they listen and judge, they encourage and praise.

Another group had an *authoritarian* leader. He was friendly enough, but unapproachable. He told each child exactly what to do and didn't welcome their comments. He divided them up into their groupings, without reference to who they wanted to be with. The children in some of the groupings were aggressive and unwilling to cooperate and share. Others couldn't be bothered and made little effort or progress. When the leader left the room most of the children stopped working. They still managed to produce much the same number of masks and models as the democratic group.

> ► *Authoritarian* leaders issue instructions and do not welcome questions or suggestions. They expect obedience and performance, and punish where this is not forthcoming.

In a third group there was a *laissez-faire* leader. (*Laissez-faire* is French for 'to leave to do'.) This leader left the children to get on with whatever they wanted, very much on their own. He didn't make suggestions, answer many questions, or offer much help. The boys didn't achieve much at all. They gave up at the first sign that something was going wrong. They were also fairly aggressive towards each other.

> ► *Laissez-faire* leadership lacks structure and discipline. It fails to provide a role model, a target, suggestions for achievement, or guidance and help with specific problems.

This study suggests that American children during the 1930s worked best with a democratic style of leadership. That is not to say that all children would necessarily work best with this kind of leadership. Children reared in countries where socialization is more authoritarian would no doubt produce more than groups with democratic leaders.

So far we have not found reliable personality traits or personal characteristics that consistently correlate with leadership. The studies have not always isolated all the variables, and some researchers may not have been sufficiently aware of the danger of cultural bias. Perhaps there are situational variables which correlate better with leadership style.

> ► One problem with interpreting psychological research is that we must be on guard against cultural biases. Because some result is found in the West does not mean that it would necessarily be found elsewhere. It may be a function of culture, not of human psychology.

 How successful have psychologists been in identifying the personality characteristics involved in leadership?

The situational approach

During the 1950s the emphasis in psychology was shifting away from the (nature) view that people were more the product of genetics and that when we had accumulated enough data everything could be understood in a deterministic way. Data inferred just from observation and tradition weren't enough. They had to be based on more scientifically approved methods and on a much more interactive view of human beings.

Successful leaders are popular with their followers, inspiring them to work well, at the same time as bringing success to the group. They are also influenced by their followers. They must be attentive to their followers' ideas and needs so that they can respond flexibly and with understanding to them.

Each group has different ideas and different needs from time to time. Thus leadership isn't a one-way communication system, with orders coming down from leader to led, but rather is a dynamic system with the effective leader being aware of and responding to the followers' changing ideas and needs as they occur. The ability to respond effectively and thus be a good leader may still be a personal characteristic that some people are better at than others, but their success will be modified by situational factors.

 What are the signs of the successful leader?

With this view of the dynamic nature of leadership in mind, attention can shift from what personal characteristics makes a good leader to what are the features of the particular situation that make this particular leader effective. This approach was partially adopted by **Fred Fiedler** in the mid 1960s. He doesn't reject the idea that leadership is a personality factor, but looks for the situational factors that make and maintain leadership.

Fiedler suggests a *contingency model. This* means that the most effective leader is the one whose leadership style best suits the needs of the organization she or he leads. Sympathetic and understanding leaders are most effective in running organizations that involve sympathy and understanding. Aggressive and competitive leaders thrive in organizations which have to compete to win. The contingency model suggests that a sympathetic and relaxed leader would be hopelessly ineffective in a competitive organization.

In his early writing Fiedler argued that an effective leader must be able to keep her or his 'psychological distance' from the co-workers. The leader 'must be willing to reject co-workers who do not adequately perform their jobs. This requires emotional independence and detachment from others. The person who readily forms deep emotional ties with his subordinates, who needs to be liked or supported by his men, will find it difficult to discipline or discharge them, since this may decrease his popularity or cause him to lose their friendship'. To do this requires psychological distance. Further research among many different kinds of groups, from farming cooperatives to

► Successful leaders must provide direction, but also be aware of the needs and feelings of the people they lead. Otherwise they become distant and unapproachable, and their popularity (and probably their influence) declines.

► Fiedler's *contingency model* stresses the important role of the particular circumstances in the organization which influence both 'leadership' and 'following' behaviour.

► *Psychological distance* is a vague concept which Fiedler needed to refine. There must be degrees of it, and it must vary over time and as conditions change.

aircraft bomber crews, revealed that there are grades of psychological distance.

Fiedler developed the 'Least Preferred Co-worker' (LPC) scale whereby leaders rate their most and least preferred co-workers. *Relationship oriented* leaders give a fairly high score, even to their least preferred co-workers, and tend to be more considerate, lenient and indulgent towards all their workers. *Task oriented* leaders (low LPC) were most successful in organizations where the leader was either highly regarded by his followers, or they thought very little of him indeed, where the tasks to be accomplished were either clearly structured or very unstructured, or where the leader occupied quite a powerful position, or had very little effective power (to give rewards to his followers). Where the situation was intermediate between those variables, relationship oriented (high LPC) leaders did best.

 How does Fiedler's contingency theory explain leadership?

Critics of Fiedler's model suggest that the LPC score method is too unreliable since it varies with time. As leaders mature, or are influenced externally, their perceptions of their task and their co-workers may change. Psychological distance alters with greater interaction. A subordinate who had never seemed very appealing may do something which makes her or him more highly favoured.

Rice reviewed Fiedler's and other studies which used the LPC and found inconsistencies and variations in what the LPC was supposed to be measuring. He also argued that Fiedler puts too much emphasis on the leader as a fixed personal characteristic and too little on the interactive nature of leadership.

Other correlates of leadership

Interaction

Leaders talk more than other people. (This is sometimes called the 'blabbermouth theory' of leadership!) So long as what they are saying is reasonably intelligent, those who talk the most are most likely to be perceived by other members of the group as being most intelligent. In an experiment conducted in the early 1960s **Bavelas** divided his subjects into discussion groups with four people in each, and asked them to discuss various topics. He noted how much each of them spoke. Some people dominated the conversation, others were more reticent. Most of the group members had more favourable impressions of those who spoke.

Bavelas wondered whether contributions to the discussion could be increased by feedback, and if so, whether this would alter the group's perception of the speakers. Bavelas told each group that the contribution of each of its members was to be evaluated by the experimenters, and the members were to receive feedback on their performance. A green light meant their contribution was valuable, a red one signalled that their contributions were unhelpful. The lights actually had

▶ *Relationship oriented* leaders are considerate towards the needs and feelings of co-workers and clients. They will be most effective in the caring professions.

▶ *Task oriented* leaders are more concerned with achieving targets and maintain the greatest psychological distance.

▶ Inevitably LPC will vary with time and experience and has been criticized for being unreliable.

▶ Bavelas found that increasing the amount of participation of a given member also increased the other group members' favourable perceptions of her or him.

REVIEW – Power and leadership

Early psychologists believed that some people were born leaders and that leadership was a personality characteristic that some people had more of than others. The evidence for this is highly inconclusive. Styles of leadership are influential in determining people's behaviour. Fiedler argues that those whose leadership styles reflect the needs of the organization which they lead are most likely to be effective. Other situational factors that can affect leadership include the amount of (intelligent) talking someone does, and such spatial characteristics as where they stand or sit.

nothing to do with the quality of the contribution at all.

Each time a previously reticent person spoke, the green light came on. They began to participate more. Their posture changed too. They sat more upright and looked more confident. After the session the other group members rated them higher on aspects of leadership such as ability and the quality of their ideas.

Spatial position

There are certain places that reflect leadership. The person who stands in front of the fire, with their back to it, may be assumed to be an important person. In offices the occupier usually sits in a slightly higher chair than that provided for visitors, looking down on them as they sit in front of him or her. Superiors are more likely to walk around their desk to stand beside and look down on them. Looking down on someone may give the leader some kind of psychological advantage.

In 1961 **Sommer** published the findings of an experiment in which five or six people were formed into groups and one was appointed leader. They were asked to enter a room in which there was a rectangular table, and take their seats. The leader usually chose to sit at one of the ends of the table. The position next to him was occupied by the next 'most important person'. This had implications for the choice of foreman of juries in criminal trials. A study by **Strodtheck** and **Hook** showed that the jury person sitting at the end position is over four times more likely to be elected foreman than anyone else.

▶ In interviews the interviewee may feel at a disadvantage since they are often looked down on by the interviewers, they have nowhere to look except at the interviewers while the interviewers can look at their notes, and the interviewers usually have the window behind them, giving them a slight advantage as the interviewee may have to look into the light.

 In view of the evidence, list the main points for and against the view that leaders are born not made.

Chapter summary

The presence of others may affect our performance if they are watching or competing with them, or simply pursuing the same task. This is social facilitation. Where their views are revealed, and ours aren't certain, we are more likely to conform to theirs. We might merely comply, or may actively internalize their views. In laboratory experiments some subjects have denied the evidence of their own senses in order to conform.

Where someone who appears to have authority states an order or request, rather than an opinion, the likelihood seems to increase that we will conform to their statement by obeying their command. Whether excessive willingness to conform, or excessive willingness to obey are personality characteristics is unproven. We know that situational factors can increase or decrease the likelihood that we will, or will not, conform or obey.

Essay questions – 60 minutes each

1 What have psychologists learned from their studies of audience and co-action effects?

2 To what extent may being a member of a group affect an individual's behaviour?

3 What have psychologists learned from the experimental study of conformity?

4 Critically evaluate psychological studies of conformity.

5 Why do people obey authority?

6 Discuss the major psychological research into obedience in humans and consider the implications of this type of research.

Further Reading: Chapter 9

For those who like original sources some of the most helpful are

Zajonc R.B. 1965. 'Social Facilitation'. *Science*, pages 269–74.

Sherif M. 1936. *The Psychology of Social Norms*. New York: Harper & Row.

Asch S. 1955. 'Opinions and Social Pressure'. *Scientific American* 193 (5), pages 31–5.

Crutchfield R.S. 1955. 'Conformity and Character'. *American Psychologist* 10, pages 191–8.

Milgram S. 1963. 'The Behavioural Study of Obedience'. *Journal of Abnormal and Social Psychology* 67, pages 371–8.

Milgram S. 1965. 'Some Conditions of Obedience and Obedience to Authority', *Human Relations* 16, pages 67–76.

Zimbardo P. 1972. 'The Pathology of Imprisonment'. *Society.*

Zimbardo P., Haney C., Banks W. 1973. 'A Pirandellian Prison'. *The New York Times Magazine*, April 8th, 1973, pages 38–60.

Fiedler F. 1968. 'A Contingency Model of Leadership Effectiveness', in Berkowitz, L. (ed.), *Advances in Experimental Psychology*. Vol 1. London: Academic Press.

In addition to the general texts mentioned in the further reading for Chapter 8, you might find the following summary of the nature of social interaction and the way we control our interactions with others useful.

Gahagan J. 1984. *Social Interaction and its Management*. London: Methuen.

Mann L. 1969. *Social Psychology*. Chichester: John Wiley.

Treatment and therapies

Introduction

As you now know from previous chapters different kinds of psychology explain normal behaviour in different ways. It is logical therefore that they should offer different explanations for abnormal, distressing or troublesome behaviour. For example, a psychologist who believes that most normal behaviour is greatly determined by genetic causes, will believe that odd behaviour is caused by unusual genes, and will look for the effects of these in the structure or chemistry of the brain. By contrast a psychologist who believes that most human behaviour is learned will believe that normal behaviour follows from a normal upbringing in a normal home, and abnormal behaviour results from abnormal socialization. Such different ideas about the causes of normal and abnormal behaviour lead to different prescriptions for how abnormal behaviour can be remedied.

There are hundreds of different treatments and therapies and no single treatment can be used to deal with all mental disturbances of behaviour problems but under the right circumstances and with receptive clients, most forms of treatment can be effective – although sometimes it is unclear as to whether they are effective for the reasons claimed by the therapist. This chapter deals with the therapies associated with medical, psychoanalytic, behaviourist, cognitive and humanistic approaches to abnormal behaviour.

Overleaf is a catalogue of some of the major therapies. I suggest you look at this now to get an overview before looking at each in more detail. Pay particular attention to the assumptions each kind of treatment makes about the causes of problematic behaviour. This is the key to understanding why different kinds of psychologist, psychiatrist and psychotherapist favour particular treatments.

► These are the two main positions adopted in the nature–nurture debate discussed on page 49.

► A psychologist studies human behaviour. Some called clinical psychologists have special training and are involved in treatment. Psychiatrists are medical doctors specializing in the treatment of mental illness. Psychotherapists also treat people with mental problems but there is no single recognized training for psychotherapists and anyone can call themselves a psychotherapist.

The major therapies

Therapies	Assumptions	Techniques
Medical therapies	Like physical illness, mental illness is caused by bodily malfunctions – in this case of the brain or nervous system.	—
Psychosurgery	Brain surgery can cure mental illness.	Remove or cut into brain structures.
ECT	Brain needs electrical stimulation.	Apply mild electric shock.
Chemotherapy	Chemical imbalance in the brain needs to be stabilized.	Giving drugs.
Psychoanalytically inspired therapies	Problem behaviour has an identifiable cause in previous experience.	—
Freudian psychoanalysis	Conflict between parts of personality can lead to repressed anxiety.	Analysis of early life through free association, dream analysis, Freudian slips, etc.
Adler's 'individual therapy'	Inferiority feelings develop during childhood because of inadequate relationships.	Reconstruct early experiences to build sense of worth.
Transactional analysis	Influence of 'parent' or 'child' state interferes with healthy 'adult' responses.	Games, contracts and other dealings within groups aid cognitive restructuring.
Primal therapy	Parents cause repressed childhood anxieties resulting in adult neuroses.	Expose true feelings by shouting and moving around.
Behaviour therapies	Problem behaviour results from unfortunate associations between stimuli and responses. Better patterns of behaviour can be learned.	—
Systematic de-sensitization	Treating symptoms will effect 'cure'.	Gradual exposure to feared object.
Implosion therapy	Prolonged exposure to a fear-inducing stimulus eliminates neurosis.	Full exposure to stimulus until neurosis subsides
Aversion therapy	Pairing undesired CS with an unpleasant CR eliminates the undesired CS.	Administer drugs to induce fear or nausea at the idea of the undesired CS.

Therapies	Assumptions	Techniques
Behaviour therapies (continued)		
Behaviour modification	Maladapted behaviour is learned by associating a reinforcer with a response.	Remove reinforcer from undesired response and positively reinforce desired response.
Modelling therapy	Irrational fear comes from lack of knowledge. Actual exposure eliminates fear.	Seeing someone else doing what scares us and then doing it ourselves removes anxiety.
Cognitive therapies	Problems arise from people having faulty ways of interpreting experience.	—
Rational emotive theory (RET)	Problems result from misinterpreting present events.	Replace incorrect interpretations with appropriate ones.
Cognitive restructuring	Depression is caused by mistaken beliefs about what we ought to be like.	Direct questioning and discussion to alter mistaken beliefs.
Self-instructional training (SIT)	Internal dialogues may be faulty leading to mistaken ideas about self worth and interpersonal relationships.	Make internal dialogues positive, and teach coping skills to help face problems.
Humanist therapies	Everyone is unique so it is nonsense to talk about normal and abnormal behaviour. People experience problems with living. Many of these problems arise from the way they treat each other.	—
Client-centred therapy	'Self' derives from unique experiences.	Therapist supports client, urging him towards self-actualization.
Gestalt therapy	Problems result from the client not being fully aware of their whole selves.	'Games' increase self-awareness.
Existential therapy	People are frustrated by the way other people treat them.	Therapeutic communities encourage freedom and responsibility.

THE MEDICAL MODEL

The medical model views mental illness as an illness like any physical disorder. Abnormal behaviour is seen as the result of some disease or disorder in the structure or chemicals of the brain. Faced with this problem what we need to do is to consult a doctor who is a specialist in the field of mental problems (called a *psychiatrist*), who will review the *symptoms*, arrive at a *diagnosis*, and suggest a course of treatment, possibly in a mental hospital.

The medical classification of abnormal behaviour

► A system of classification for organic illnesses is like a large encyclopedia with listings under various headings such as Skin, Respiratory system, Muscles, Stomach, etc. Doctors can look up the various symptoms and come to a diagnosis, which then suggests an appropriate treatment.

Those who hold to the medical model place a great emphasis on the precise classification of different kinds of mental disorder. Before identifying the cause or deciding on the treatment of an illness we must accurately define it. We need to discover which symptoms occur together so that our diagnosis and treatment will be correct. We need a system of classification of all the mental illnesses so that we can look up the symptoms a patient has and see what illness he or she is suffering from.

To be of any value, the classification must first be able to predict what will happen as the condition continues. Will it worsen, stabilize or improve? How and when will it change? Secondly, the classification must be a guide to possible treatments. As new drugs and therapies are developed and tested, those which prove effective with various conditions can be added to the classification. Thirdly, a good classification system must provide some guide to possible causes of the various conditions. As advances in psychosurgery and electronic body scanning are made new discoveries will be found about aspects of brain functioning. These may have relevance for treatments of certain kinds of mental illness.

► Any classification must take account of new discoveries as they are made, and so must be constantly evolving and changing.

The first system of classification for mental disorders was the *clinical classification*. It emerged as groups of psychiatrists such as Freud discussed the behaviour of their patients and came to agree on a name for their conditions, and then on names for subdivisions of them. For example, *psychotic disorders* became subdivided into *schizophrenia*, *paranoia*, *manic depression*, etc. Early this century a German psychiatrist, *Emil Kraepelin*, was one of the first to try to classify mental illnesses according to their symptoms. Systems of classifications were already advanced in some other areas of medicine. His system of classification is inevitably simplistic by today's standards.

► The clinical model for classification of mental or behavioural disorders is part of the medical model which sees such disorders as 'illnesses'.

Clinical classifications suggest four main groupings of disorders. It divides disorders into Neuroses, Personality Disorders, Functional Psychoses and Organic Psychoses. The first three of these were suggested by Freud's psychoanalytic model:

1 *Neuroses* such as 'free floating' (generalized) anxiety, phobias, obsessive-compulsive behaviour and mild depression are generally regarded as less serious, may be temporary, and often do not involve any kind of medical attention, though they may seriously effect the individual's day-to-day life.

Some major neuroses

Free floating neurosis	General anxiety, feeling restless, impatient, moody, jumpy and unable to concentrate. Sleeping problems, loss of appetite and other physical symptoms.
Phobias	Irrational fear of a (usually harmless) object or event. The most common is *agoraphobia* (fear of crowded places) comprising 60 per cent of all reported phobias. *Arachnophobia* (fear of spiders) is one of the *zoophobias* (fear of animals) which together comprise about 3 per cent.
Obsessive-Compulsive neuroses	Obsessions are irrational thoughts which are constantly 'on the sufferer's mind', and which they cannot control. Compulsions are actions which are driven by obsessions. An obsession with cleanliness may lead to compulsive hand washing.
Reactive depression	An intense sadness caused by some event in one's life from which it seems the sufferer loses the will to recover. 'Time (sympathy, understanding, encouragement and motivation) is a great healer.'
Hysterical neurosis	Physical symptoms of an 'illness' without any identifiable organic cause. *Amnesia* is an example; Anna O's (Freud's patient's) rigid arm was another.

2 *Personality disorders* are general patterns of reaction, such as anti-social behaviour, feelings of inadequacy about everything, being obsessive about everything. They are fixed and inflexible, and apply to the whole of a person's behaviour. They may well need psychiatric intervention and are resistant to change.

3 *Psychoses* such as schizophrenia, manic depression, and paranoia result in an inability to recognize and deal with reality. Symptoms include hallucinations, delusions, rapid changes of mood, incoherent speech and severe regressive behaviour (the person acting as though

► *Paranoia* is a delusion of being persecuted; that people are against you and that they seek your destruction.

► *Manic depression* refers to a state where a patient's moods swing wildly, from uncontrollably elated to being in deepest miserable depression.

Schizophrenia

Schizophrenia is one of the psychoses. The term covers a whole range of mental disorders, including *thought disorders*, where language and thinking are grossly disturbed; *delusions*, for example that some external force ('God', 'the government', etc.) is directing the person's behaviour; and *hallucinations*, where imaginary voices and figures are heard and seen.

Types of schizophrenia include:

Disorganized schizophrenia where behaviour is truly bizarre (laughing for no reason, bathing fully dressed, saying odd things to strangers in the street, etc.).

Catatonic schizophrenia where the patient displays strange physical activity such as physical contortions.

Paranoid schizophrenia where the person has bizarre delusions of being an extremely important person, or of being persecuted by 'others'.

Undifferentiated schizophrenics have many overlapping symptoms and can't be classified more precisely.

he or she was a child). Psychotic disorders can be serious and may require treatment in a mental hospital.

4 *Organic psychoses* (sometimes called *brain syndrome*) include those conditions resulting from genetic abnormalities, accidents, illnesses, addictions and diseases that have caused actual brain damage. They can be temporary, such as recovery from addiction to alcohol, or permanent, such as senile dementia. They are the kinds of conditions where medical intervention is least controversial.

Organic psychoses

Brain disorders can result from a genetically inherited condition, such as PKU (phenylketonuria), a head injury such as might result from a car crash or blow on the head, an illness or disease such as rubella (German measles) in the early stages of pregnancy, or they can be caused by a poison or withdrawal from a substance to which someone was addicted. They can be short term or permanent, and may be stable (staying the same) or progressive (getting worse). They are often associated with children or the elderly. For example, *delirium* results in an inability to process information clearly, repeating oneself and being unsure of where one is or what is going on. Delirium is usually temporary. *Dementia* is associated with old age and involves confused thinking, loss of memory, repeating oneself, and general confusion. It is usually permanent and progressive.

There are several systems of classification in use in different countries. In 1980 the American Psychiatric Association (APA) published the third edition of its *Diagnostic and Statistical Manual* (DSM III). (Numbers I and II appeared in 1952 and 1968.) Most American psychiatrists use it as the reference book to provide them with the guidelines for diagnosing mental illness. It lists 15 categories of mental disorders.

▶ The system of classification used in Britain is substantially different from DSM III, but this does not mean that the same patient would necessarily be diagnosed as having a different condition using the two systems, merely that the route to arriving at a diagnosis is rather different.

In Britain we use a system developed by the World Health Organization from the ninth edition of its *International Classification of Diseases* (ICD–9). This was also published in 1980, and is widely used throughout the world. It uses three major categories of mental disorders. First, 'mental illness', which contains neuroses and psychoses; second, 'personality disorders'; and third 'subnormality' or 'retardation'. Inevitably the likelihood of someone being defined as having one condition or another will be influenced by the norms and values of the culture in which the psychiatrists operate. For example British psychiatrists are more reluctant to diagnose people as suffering from schizophrenia than American psychiatrists.

Diagnostic and Statistical Manual (DSM III)

1 *Infant, childhood, or adolescent disorders.* These comprise mental retardation and any psychological problem that occurs during early development.

2 *Organic mental disorders,* such as senile dementia and psychoses with a known physical cause.

3 *Substance-use disorders,* e.g. glue sniffing.

4 *Schizophrenic disorders* of varying types but all featuring the inability to distinguish 'real' thoughts and feelings from fantasy.

5 *Paranoid disorders,* characterized by delusions. Paranoids have well worked out reasons why they are being persecuted and apart from this functional psychosis they are rational and logical.

6 *Psychotic disorders* not classified elsewhere, such as *brief reactive psychosis,* a confused mental state that lasts for no more than two weeks and has some identifiable cause.

7 *Affective disorders,* such as *depression* . 'Affective' refers to emotional states, so affective disorders result in distorted feelings such as manic depression.

8 *Anxiety disorders,* e.g. *phobias* characterized by irrational feelings about the importance, significance, or value of something. (Agoraphobics have an irrational fear of being alone in a public place. Obsessives have a permanent, irrational preoccupation with some person, object or event, such as washing their hands. Their obsession gives them no pleasure, except the anxiety it temporarily relieves when they give in to it.)

9 *Somatoform disorders,* such as *allergies,* where there are self-evident physical symptoms but no organic cause for them can be found. The cause is assumed to be psychological. (Freud's 'hysterical neurosis' is an example of a somatoform disorder.)

10 *Dissociative disorders,* e.g. multiple personality, where there is a breakdown in the person's knowledge about themselves, their consciousness, memories, self-concept, etc. They may take on another personality or suffer some memory lapse, as in amnesia.

11 *Psychosexual disorders,* these are failures to perform adequately sexually which are assumed to be caused by some psychological stimulus. Impotence, transvestitism (deriving sexual arousal from dressing up as a member of the opposite sex) and paedophilia (sexual drive towards children) are examples of psychosexual disorders.

12 *Factitious disorders,* i.e. those which are controlled by the person themselves, and which are referred to as pseudopsychoses. The person may pretend to have some pain or illness, or may take some drug to produce the symptoms of an illness or disease. People with factitious disorders do not 'put on' their symptoms for some benefit such as avoiding work, but seem to want to play the role of someone who is 'ill' for its own sake.

13 *Disorders of impulse control,* such as pathological gambling, habitual bed wetting, kleptomania and the inability to resist playing fruit machines.

14 *Adjustment disorder,* a change in one's life, such as losing one's savings, having children or changing jobs or homes can produce disruptions to normal behaviour and thinking, and an inability to adjust to the situation. School truancy is an example of adjustment disorder.

15 *Psychological factors affecting physical conditions,* e.g. a migraine. Where a physical condition already exists, such as a headache, serious concerns, anxieties, frustrations, etc. can make the condition worse.

▶ *Subnormality* means being below some widely accepted, culturally defined standard of what is 'normal'. To be of any use at all this standard needs to be defined quite precisely.

▶ Each society has expectations of 'normal' behaviour. These may be quite different from the standards set by other societies. Equally, what each society regards as 'subnormal' (and abnormal) will vary.

▶ Lack of stimulation in the early years can often be largely compensated for by intensive stimulation later.

▶ Intensive stimulation will often produce less dramatic results when the condition is biologically rather than socially based.

Retardation or subnormality

It is important not to confuse retardation or mental subnormality (or what is now often called 'learning difficulty') with mental illness. Subnormality implies that there is some socially recognized standard of intellectual functioning – or cleverness – which is 'normal'. Anyone who can't achieve this is 'subnormal'.

Let's take intelligence as an example. In the West, psychologists have IQ (Intelligence Quotient) tests which they may use to test children whose parents or teachers suspect them of not attaining the 'normal' standard. Anyone with an IQ of less than 70 used to be seen as retarded. Various psychometric tests measure reading, writing, mathematical, time and place relationships. Specific areas of difficulty can be identified and remedial teaching given. Someone who performs poorly on various psychometric tests may be described as being mentally retarded.

Being mentally retarded is usually the result of one of four possible causes. First, a lack of adequate stimulation during childhood may lead to retarded development. For the first few years, even of schooling, no obvious differences may be noticed between mildly subnormal and 'ordinary' children, but later attempts at education may prove difficult. Programmes of special stimulation and education can reduce the harsher effects of subnormality, even in severely deprived children, by training the child to use the capacity it does have. The Czech twins studied by Jarmila Koluchova (see Chapter 3) were severely retarded when discovered, and they made a full intellectual recovery.

Second, severe subnormality such as that found in *Down's Syndrome* is known to be caused by a fault in transmitting genetic material from parent to child; *infantile autism* is usually thought of as being caused by some genetically inherited condition. Intense stimulation can make some difference, but great improvement is unlikely.

The third cause of subnormality is the absence of essential vitamins and proteins during early childhood. Malnutrition is tragically widespread in parts of the Third World, and many of those children who survive it will never achieve their genotypical potential.

Finally, damage to the brain at birth can cause retardation. This used to be more common before obstetric practices improved.

 Giving examples distinguish between neuroses, personality disorders, functional psychoses, organic psychoses and retardation.

Medical or somatic treatments for mental illness

There are three types of medical intervention for dealing with disturbed thinking or behaviour. The oldest are psychosurgery and electroconvulsive therapy, both first used in the mid 1930s. Since the early 1950s drugs have been much more widely used and chemotherapy has largely replaced the earlier methods.

Psychosurgery

Psychosurgery involves cutting (making lesions) or removing (*ablating*) various parts of the brain. If we know, for example, that a certain part of the limbic system is responsible for levels of aggression, and if we have a patient with a pathologically aggressive personality, we could surgically remove all or some of that part of the system, and hopefully the aggression should be removed. Unfortunately, things are rarely so simple and patients who have had such operations have suffered all kinds of side-effects. Some have been made so docile that they are incapable of normal emotional responses. Other organs were sometimes damaged during surgery too, and many patients died. Whatever the effects of the psychosurgery, they will be permanent (unless offset by chemotherapy treatment) since we can't replace brain tissue once it has been destroyed.

The first psychosurgical operations were on people whose behaviour was severely disturbed. They involved making lesions in the white tissue (corpus callousum) which connects the brain's frontal lobes (where the major thought centres are found) with the major organs, the *thalamus* (the relay centre for co-ordinating sensory input) and the *hypothalamus* (which controls vital functions such as heart rate, feeding, sexual arousal, temperature and emotional state). Tens of thousands of such *prefrontal lobotomies* were performed. For most of the patients – mainly schizophrenics and acute depressives – their disturbed behaviour was removed, but so was much of their personalities. Many of them were made into little more than human cabbages. The general consensus is that the technique does not produce acceptable results, and it would be extremely unlikely to be used today.

Recent advances in the techniques used in psychosurgery include the ability to destroy precise and tiny pieces of brain tissue whose function is exactly known. Surgeons are aware of exactly what some brain centres do. This has increased the ability to treat specific symptoms such as severe (*grand mal*) epilepsy, and reduced the likelihood of undesired side effects, making it much more acceptable to perform brain surgery.

Electroconvulsive therapy (ECT)

Electroconvulsive or 'shock' therapy is highly controversial. It is used mainly with patients suffering severe depression. They are given a drug to relax their muscles and are anaesthetized, and an electric shock of between 80 and 150 volts (depending on the judgement of the psychiatrist in charge) is passed between their temples for about one tenth of a second. The patient has a minor convulsion, although in the past some patients have injured themselves during their semi-

▶ Psychosurgery is a physical intervention inside the skull. Such surgery is always dangerous and many patients have not survived it, or have suffered terrible side-effects.

▶ The prefrontal lobotomy was regarded as a major breakthrough in psychological treatment and in 1937 its inventor, Egas Moniz of Portugal, was awarded the Nobel Prize. One patient whom Moniz had operated on couldn't have agreed – he shot Moniz, causing him some paralysis.

▶ During an epileptic seizure the victim may have convulsions and may lose consciousness and control over motor functions. Excessive amounts of brain activity are often involved in the cause.

▶ ECT was first used because it was noticed that schizophrenics didn't have epilepsy. There might be something about epilepsy that inhibits schizophrenia, so some schizophrenics were given electric shock treatment to produce an epileptic type seizure.

epileptic convulsions. They usually lose their memories for the period of the treatment, although sometimes the amnesia can be more profound and the patients become quite disoriented. The treatment is usually repeated three or four times a week for about a month.

Studies suggest that ECT is generally effective. Between 60 per cent and 90 per cent of severely depressed patients show less depressed behaviour in the weeks following a series of ECT. No one knows why it works, and this has led some organizations which support and represent people with mental problems to call for its abolition.

Chemotherapy (drug treatment)
Until the 1950s psychiatrists used combinations of containment, psychoanalysis, behaviour therapy, psychosurgery and electroconvulsive therapy to 'treat' their patients. Since then increasing numbers of drugs have been refined which can control aspects of people's behaviour, and even their personality. Many perfectly 'normal' people buy drugs to relieve their headaches, help with their colds, reduce their travel sickness, give them energy and contain their allergies. Most homes have medical cupboards or drawers where drugs can be found. Psychiatrically prescribed drugs have largely replaced the use of strait-jackets and locked cells, and have allowed many people to live fairly normal lives who otherwise might have needed hospitalization.

There are three categories of psychiatrically prescribed drugs.

Anti-depressants, sometimes called *psychic energizers,* work either by stimulating the production of a 'neurotransmitter' substance in the brain called norepinephrine, or by inhibiting its destruction. Tofranil is a widely used anti-depressant that stimulates norepinephrine. Monoamine oxidase (MAO) inhibits its destruction, but this can have serious side-effects and is not widely used now.

Minor tranquillizers such as Valium and Librium reduce anxiety and cause drowsiness by inhibiting neural activity in parts of the brain. They can be useful in treating phobias, problems with sleeping and other somatoform disorders (somatoform refers to problems with the body). Valium is thought to be the most widely prescribed drug in many countries. The problem with such drugs is that people can sometimes become physically addicted to them or come to depend on them emotionally, and they may need to be weaned from them.

Major tranquillisers are anti-psychotic drugs. Chloropromazine (Largactil), for example, acts like a powerful sedative on severely disturbed psychotic patients. Such drugs reduce the general level of activity, stabilize mood, and reduce hallucinations and paranoid feelings. They have allowed many severely disturbed people to live in the community. However their effects wear off in a few days and they have to be administered frequently. They can also have the side-effects of blurred vision, fainting fits and a lack of energy.

► Many drugs are self-administered, many are prescribed by doctors. Concern is being expressed that people generally are becoming too dependent on drugs, including drugs prescribed by doctors.

► There are many drugs with specialized functions, but the minor and major tranquillisers and the anti-depressants are the main drug categories for treating psychiatric disorders.

 What is the medical model? How does it explain the causes of mental disturbance? What kinds of treatments does the medical model suggest?

Evaluation of the medical model

The medical model has been subjected to very intense criticism. Most of this criticism centres on the claim that it is inappropriate to regard abnormal behaviour as a kind of disease and that the very term 'mental illness' is misleading.

Criticism of the idea of 'mental illness'

In *The Myth of Mental Illness*, published in 1960, **Thomas Szasz** argues that the term 'illness' presupposes a precise definition of health. There are well-known and easily definable norms of physical health against which physical illness can be defined and measured: since we know what a healthy liver is like, there is little difficulty in diagnosing a diseased liver. By contrast Szasz says most of what is called 'mental illness' is a departure from social and moral norms. There is no scientifically precise way of deciding what kinds of beliefs or behaviour are socially healthy in a way that is equivalent to the definition of physical health. For example in the UK, until the 1930s and 1940s, unmarried mothers were sometimes put into mental hospitals and labelled as 'moral imbeciles', in the Soviet Union until recently those who dissented from the Communist Party line could find themselves diagnosed as schizophrenics, in the USA conscientious objectors to the Vietnam war often found themselves diagnosed as mentally ill. Increasingly children who are disruptive in school are treated as mentally ill. The norms against which all these people are defined as ill are little more than matters of opinion about good and bad behaviour. For Szasz abnormal behaviour is often nothing more than a 'problem with living'. For example if you are depressed about something, Szasz would describe you as deeply unhappy and having a problem with your life. You are not 'mentally ill'. The way to deal with your depression is not to prescribe anti-depressant drugs, but to find out what is causing your problem and help you to work it out for yourself.

Szasz acknowledges that there are some organic disorders which affect mental functioning – the organic psychoses (see page 240) but he would prefer to call these 'brain diseases' rather than 'mental illnesses'. For most so-called mental illnesses, he says, there are no obvious organic causes. Therefore since most so-called mental illness has no organic causes, treating it as if it were a physical illness is rather like calling in the television repair man because you don't like the programmes on your television.

 Why does Szasz say that mental illness is not an illness? Looking at the earlier classification of disorders which of them could be regarded as an illness by Szasz?

Criticism of the diagnostic system of the medical model

Although classifications such as DSM III may look precise and scientific, studies of the way in which psychiatric diagnoses are made in practice suggest that this is far from true. Again this relates to the fact that unlike physical illness which can be diagnosed in relation to

▶ Szasz argues that since there are no norms of mental *health* there can be no such thing as mental *illness*.

DSM 111 and the medical model controversy

When is an illness not an illness? Until quite recently homosexuality was regarded as a form of mental illness and was included in earlier classifications. Times and cultural values change, and homosexuality is no longer regarded in this way. How can we trust a model for diagnosing mental illnesses which can't discriminate an illness (psychosexual disorder) from a sexual preference?

---

well-defined norms of physical health, there are no well-defined norms of mental health in terms of which mental illness can be diagnosed.

In a classic study conducted 20 years ago **Rosenhan** investigated the validity of psychiatric diagnosis. In *On Being Sane in Insane Places* he describes how, over a three-year period, eight normal, healthy, 'sane' people turned up at various mental hospitals on the East and West coasts of America, complaining that they could hear voices in their heads which kept saying 'empty', 'hollow' or 'thud'. These 'patients' included a housewife, a painter, a graduate, three psychologists and a psychiatrist (Rosenhan himself). They all used invented names, and lied about their jobs (and their 'symptoms'). Otherwise, they answered every question they were asked as truthfully as they could.

Upon admission and during their stay they performed whatever tests they were asked to, to the best of their ability. Since they were not actually mentally disturbed their results must have reflected their sanity. The psychiatrists who saw them therefore had only the 'patient's' reported symptoms to base their judgements on. All the 'patients' should have been diagnosed as sane, but perhaps requiring some outpatient counselling for the 'voices'. Despite having no other evidence than the 'voices', all eight were admitted to the hospital, and all but one were diagnosed as being schizophrenic (a psychotic disorder).

Immediately after their admission they stopped 'hearing the voices', and started asking to be released from the hospital. None of the hospital staff suspected that they were actually sane, 'normal' human beings, despite the fact that they were behaving normally at all times. Several of the real patients however suspected the truth that these were sane people conducting a study, so the 'mentally ill' patients were able to make an accurate diagnosis even if the psychiatrically trained staff couldn't. On average the 'pseudo-patients' saw a member of the psychiatric staff for seven minutes each day.

One patient was released after seven days, another was kept in for 52 days. The average stay was 19 days. After release each 'patient' was diagnosed as suffering from 'schizophrenia in remission', i.e. the patient still had the condition but the symptoms had disappeared for the time being. It appears that once having labelled a condition by using a diagnosis the psychiatrists were determined to see the diagnosis confirmed.

The medical model: institutionalization and labelling

In more general terms the medical model has been criticized for leading to treatments which remove people from normal environments and place them in circumstances where it is very difficult to behave normally. Rosenhan's 'pseudo-patients' tried very hard to behave 'normally' but found that the routines of the mental hospital made this impossible. Moreover in their encounters with staff they were not treated as normal people. For example, when they asked staff questions they were frequently treated as if they did not exist, and even if staff responded to their questions they were rarely answered. Rosenhan comments that for ordinary patients who may have a problem with their sense of their own reality or their self-esteem this kind of treatment can hardly be therapeutic. This relates closely to the idea that we develop and maintain ideas about ourselves through the messages other people give us about ourselves which was discussed in Chapter 8.

Long-stay mental hospitals have been widely criticized for 'institutionalizing' patients: meaning that by organizing every aspect of the patients' lives they undermine their ability to organize their own lives, and make it more, rather than less difficult for them to cope independently when discharged.

In a series of studies of an American mental hospital **Braginski, Braginski and Ring** demonstrate that in addition to institutionalizing people, the mental hospital may teach people to be mentally ill, rather than assist them to be mentally healthy. In one of their studies they video-taped patients being interviewed either for discharge or for being granted additional privileges. They then showed the video-tapes to a panel of psychiatrists and asked them to rate the mental health of the patients. They found that long-stay patients being interviewed for discharge were likely to be rated as more mentally disturbed than long-stay patients being interviewed for additional privileges. They argue that this shows that in the mental hospital patients learn how to produce symptoms of mental illness when it is advantageous to them – in this case when they do not want to be discharged to a life of homelessness and poverty outside the hospital. And they learn how to behave normally when they want to improve their position within the hospital. Relatively recent arrivals did not show this ability.

The psychiatrists who rated the patients, and the psychiatrists who diagnosed Rosenhan's pseudo-patients were guilty of fundamental attribution error (see pages 180–5). This refers to the tendency to explain behaviour as being a reflection of the individual's personality, rather than being a response to their immediate situation. An alternative way of describing this is to use the idea of 'labelling'. For example, one of Rosenhan's pseudo-patients kept notes of his experience in the mental hospital. In his nursing record, day after day, nurses had written 'patient manifests writing behaviour'. Ordinary people 'write notes', mental patients 'manifest writing behaviour'. Once labelled as mentally ill anything the patient did could be regarded as a symptom of his 'mental illness'.

► *Institutionalization:* Patients who have been in an institution for a long time may come to depend on it to provide for them in most areas of their lives. Such patients may not be able to cope on their own outside the institution.

► Some critics of Western psychiatry claim that it is little more than a system of labelling behaviour which is considered objectionable and doesn't reflect any true underlying mental illness.

► Once people are labelled as having a particular mental illness others may feel justified in treating them very differently from 'normal' people.

Applying labelling theory to the medical model of mental illness gives rise to three kinds of criticism.

Firstly, it can be argued, by labelling someone as mentally ill, it becomes permissible to treat them differently from other people, sometimes to the extent of depriving them of their civil rights, or even of parts of their brains.

Secondly, the use of the label distorts the way in which the labelled person is perceived, so that everything about them comes to be seen as caused by a malfunction of the brain. What might be perfectly rational behaviour under the circumstances in which the patient exists is likely to be ignored or seen as another symptom.

Thirdly, treating those who are labelled as mentally ill differently from other people ensures that they really are different. Placing them in circumstances which are different from normal life does not help them cope with everyday problems. More importantly once someone is labelled as mentally ill they are likely to think of themselves and interpret their own behaviour in a different way. For example I might feel very unhappy, but encounters with psychiatrists may convince me that I am suffering from clinical depression. Instead of feeling unhappy and casting about for the reasons why and looking for strategies to make my life more bearable, I now experience myself as the victim of a chemical malfunction of the brain. In this sense labelling theory suggests that psychiatric diagnoses do not simply describe particular types of people, they actually help to create particular types of people. To use Szasz's term mental illness is 'manufactured'.

It is important to note that labelling theory does not claim that there is no such thing as distress, unhappiness, or unpredictable, dangerous or confused behaviour. What it does claim is that the medical model misunderstands the causes of these problems and that the medical treatments used may at best be irrelevant, and at worst damaging.

 How does Rosenhan's pseudo-patient experiment demonstrate the role of labelling in mental illness?

How do the studies by the Braginski's support Rosenhan's views?

Summary – The Medical Model

The medical model of mental illness assumes that abnormal behaviour is caused by malfunctions of the brain or nervous system. Therefore it should be dealt with in the same way as physical illnesses by treating the organic cause of the illness, or failing that, by alleviating the symptoms using drugs or surgery. Critics of the medical model claim that this kind of treatment is only appropriate where abnormal behaviour arises from an organic cause – as in the organic psychoses. Most abnormal behaviour, they say, has no organic causation and derives from unfortunate childhood experiences or current problems of living. In such cases treating the problem is if it had an organic cause is wrong and unlikely to effect a cure. Those who believe in the medical model respond to this criticism by claiming that eventually organic causes will be found for most mental illnesses, but only if we go on following the medical model of treatment.

 Write a paragraph summarizing the advantages of using a medical approach to 'mental illness'. Write another paragraph outlining its weaknesses.

PSYCHOANALYTIC APPROACHES

This is a convenient point at which to review what you have learned already about psychoanalytic (or psychodynamic) theories. You will find pages 26–38 in Chapter 2 very relevant.

Psychoanalysis was 'invented' or 'discovered' by Sigmund Freud during the last decade of the nineteenth century and developed during the first four decades of this century. It was enormously influential and became a paradigm for psychiatry, in the absence of any particularly credible alternative ideas about the origin of mental illnesses.

Psychoanalytic theories see the origins of problem behaviour as having been built into the patient's personality during their early formative development. Psychoanalytic treatments therefore tend to look backwards for the origin of a problem, rather than looking at the immediate circumstances of the patient. Psychoanalytic theories are sometimes called *insight theories* because they aim to give patients insight into the cause of their problems. Freud was mainly concerned with the emotional rather than the intellectual components of the cause of abnormal behaviour, so the patient's final understanding mustn't simply be theoretical. Patients have to 'feel' the cause of their problem. (Simply understanding it in theory is a *defence mechanism*). Psychoanalysis proposes that if we *feel* what is causing our problem we may be able to do something about it, and the problem should disappear.

Why should it be necessary for a person to feel rather than just understand the cause of his or her disorder?

Freudian psychoanalysis

Freud saw personality developing through the interaction between its three components: the *id*, which is the irrational, instinctive urge, the *ego*, which is the urge to be rational, and the *superego*, which is the learned, moral component of personality. This interaction would occasionally include conflict, which can produce anxiety. The rational ego reduces anxiety through a number of defence mechanisms, such as repression, identification, projection, rationalization, displacement, sublimation and many more. This uses a great deal of psychic energy.

The psychoanalyst has to uncover the original sources of the conflict, many of which will have a sexual element. The patient will often try to resist the therapist at first, by missing appointments, remaining

► Kuhn describes a *paradigm* as a set of ideas, attitudes, beliefs, procedures, techniques, etc. that form the majority view of the members of a particular discipline at a particular time. Until Freud there was no coherent paradigm for understanding the origin of mental illness. As you will guess from this chapter there are now at least five competing paradigms of mental illness.

► *Insight* means inner knowledge or understanding, and the aim of insight theories is to give people a better understanding of the causes of their own problems. Once they have insight they are likely to improve. Psychoanalytic and humanistic therapists rely on insight.

► The id, ego and superego are hypothetical components of the personality in psychoanalytic theory. Freud did not intend them to be thought of as real entities, any more than hypothetical concepts like time, justice or logic are real.

Freud's methods

Free association. The 'talking cure'. Patients relax and are prompted to recall any incidents they can from their childhood.

Hypnosis (in the early days). Patients might relive their most painful experiences. Hypnosis gave contradictory data, and Freud soon stopped using it.

Interpretation of dreams. Freud claimed that during dreams we sort through the events of the 'dream day' and live out our deepest wishes and fantasies.

Analysing slips of the tongue ('Freudian slips'). Minor errors in speech reveal what we really think as our unconscious thoughts are made conscious.

Analysing the sense of humour. What people find amusing reveals their true nature.

Freud would build up a picture of what he thought were significant aspects of traumatic events in order to make the unconscious conscious to the patient.

► *Defence mechanisms* are unconscious and entirely normal devices by which we protect and maintain our image of ourselves, and avoid the embarrassment of discovering that we are less valuable and infallible than we think.

► Psychoanalysis costs a great deal of money, and is therefore only really available to those who are wealthy enough to afford it.

► *Transference* is the process by which the patient projects and displaces (both defence mechanisms) his or her feelings onto the analyst.

silent during free talk, not recalling any slips of the tongue or what has made them laugh, or claiming to have no dreams to report. This resistance is considered to be a defence mechanism since the patient unconsciously avoids the anxiety which exposing their neuroses would create. The analyst explains the cause of the patient's behaviour until the patient finally gives in to the analyst and therapy can continue.

Freud used a variety of methods in his clinical therapy, but favoured free association, dream analysis and the analysis of common mistakes such as slips of the tongue. Therapy today often involves one-hour sessions, up to five times each week, sometimes for years. The analyst and patient slowly build up a picture of the dynamic workings and development of the patient's childhood and past and present experiences until they feel that they understand the causes of the patient's present conflicts.

The techniques of psychoanalysis are intended to lead to *transference*. Patients begin to recall early events in their childhood, and how they felt about them and the people involved. They express their attitudes and feelings towards these early experiences, which is sometimes like 'reliving' them. (The process of reliving early experiences is called *abreaction*.) The analyst remains neutral and aloof at all times. Slowly patients are encouraged to express their feelings to the analyst. If they felt anger, say, towards their father, they must say how they felt, almost as though the analyst *was* their father. Attitudes and feelings which could be the source of conflict and anxiety are thus *transferred* to the analyst. Present-day problems may be caused by repressed childhood emotions, and the analyst may also 'play the part' of the people – boss, spouse, lover, child – with whom the problem exists.

The analyst will explain the inappropriate nature of the transference until the patient eventually experiences *catharsis*. This is a great release of emotions as the patient realizes the nature of his or her relationships both with the therapist and with the people who had caused such emotional 'blockages'. The analyst and patient then work through the events that gave rise to these emotional blockages (repressions). This reduces the anxiety they produced originally, and removes the need for further repression. After sufficient working through of these problems the analysis can be stopped, although the symptoms may reappear at times of stress in the future, and will need further working through sessions.

► *Catharsis* refers to the release of anxiety and tension that occurs when past events are brought into consciousness. Catharsis is necessary if a patient and analyst are to work through the events that caused the repression.

(ACT) *Notes towards an essay*

Show how Freudian psychoanalysis as a treatment follows logically from Freud's view of the development of the personality.

What is the role of transference in Freudian therapy?

Alfred Adler's 'individual therapy'

Adler was a colleague of Freud's until they disagreed about the types of forces acting on early development. While Freud emphasized sexual motives lying behind many early anxieties, e.g. Oedipal conflicts, Adler emphasized social and interpersonal relationships as having more influence on self perception, and hence personality growth.

► Adler became quite a favourite of Freud's while attending his weekly session on psychoanalysis in Vienna. In 1910 Freud had him made president of the Psychoanalytic Society, but Adler criticized some of Freud's ideas and he was forced to resign in 1911.

According to Adler all people have a will to have power over others. When this can't be achieved we experience feelings of inferiority. Right from early childhood we will all experience inferiority feelings at some times. We may have the impression from others that we are too small, too big, too unattractive, too noisy, too greedy, etc. Later, feelings about the development of our genitals or breasts might give rise to inferiority feelings too. We must learn to cope with these inferiority feelings or we may develop an *inferiority complex*. Equally, overcompensation for feelings of inferiority can lead to a *superiority complex*.

► According to Adler a general *inferiority complex* develops out of feelings of inferiority about our bodies, or some of its organs.

Since these feelings which the child develops about itself are extremely important, so the main sources of information – parents, siblings, friends, etc. – are important influences on development. Adler isn't concerned with probing the unconscious mind, but rather seeks to discover how the patient feels about him or herself. The Adlerian therapist conducts intensive interviews to discover the early communications between the parents and their child, whether the child was first, second or third born, etc., the age of the other siblings, the lifestyle the child enjoyed, and anything else that could give an insight into the child's early feelings about itself. Having made these discoveries the therapist can begin to explain to the patient the background to his or her behaviour.

► Unlike Freud, Adler is not concerned with biological drives or unconscious forces. He sees the development of personality occurring as the result of conscious knowledge and feelings about ourselves.

Having explained where the patient's feelings came from in the past, the Adlerian therapist sets out to change the patient's future feelings by establishing a sense of worth, value, achievement and importance. The therapist establishes some areas in which patients have some

► Freud believed that a patient's symptoms would simply disappear after catharsis. Adler deliberately attempted to change the patient's future.

skill and builds on them, showing the patients that they can make a valuable contribution and that they have something they can feel good about. These two goals, understanding the negative aspects of past experiences and emphasizing a positive future, are the characteristics of Adlerian *individual therapy*.

 Contrast the aims of Freudian and Adlerian therapy.

Other therapies influenced by psychoanalysis

Such was the popularity of psychoanalysis that many therapies originating in its principles have been developed. They each have their supporters and critics. Only two are here because many failed to become popular or fell out of fashion quickly.

Transactional analysis

This is derived from **Eric Berne's** psychoanalytically inspired 1968 book *Games People Play*. Berne argues that most of our interactions with each other involve us in social games, competing, being assertive, cheating, losing, etc. In these games we are sometimes fun-loving, careless, immature and irresponsible. We are playing the role rather like an emotional *child*. This is similar to Freud's concept of the id. Sometimes we are more strict, severe and serious, exercising control and being critical, rather like the role of *parent*. This corresponds to Freud's superego function. And occasionally we are more rational, sensible and perceptive, more like an *adult*. This resembles Freud's concept of ego. The aim of transactional analysis is to make the person more aware of their three components and how they appear in their everyday lives.

People are encouraged, both alone and in group meetings, to be aware of the effect that their behaviour is having on others, to realize the influences that the id, ego and superego are having, and to try to make their behaviour more like an adult and less like a parent or child. The ego is to be made stronger, particularly at the expense of the id.

Primal therapy

From the mid 1960s there was something of a social revolution in the West. The 'hippy generation' flocked to the West coast of America to wear flowers in their hair, beads around their necks, and to practise their ideals of making love, not war. This spirit of liberation from the traditional values of seeking success, advancement and prosperity reflected itself in some academic areas too. In California **Arthur Janov** invented a 'pop therapy' called the *primal scream*.

Primal therapy accepts that we experience anxieties during childhood, which can become repressed. Every time parents fail to satisfy a child's wishes it suffers some anxiety. Repressed anxieties can appear as neurotic symptoms in adulthood. The neurotic symptoms will relieve some of the repressed anxieties, but the only way to eliminate them altogether is to *relive* the experiences that caused them in the first place – the withholding of parental love.

► Berne was a psychoanalytically trained therapist who believed he recognized the influence of the three hypothetical parts of the personality identified by Freud at work in our everyday social encounters.

► Transactional analysis uses several techniques to make people aware of the influence of their id, superego and ego, and lessen their more destructive elements.

► Apart from the emphasis on sexuality in Freud's early writing, primal therapy accepts that early childhood traumas produce adult neuroses.

► *Reliving* an emotional experience is called *abreaction* in psychoanalytic theory. It is supposed to produce catharsis. Whether it does or not depends on many factors, including the person's ability and desire to 'let it all hang out'.

People are encouraged to remember these occasions and to relive them, but this time letting their parents know what they want and need, what they think and feel. They must speak out loud, shout, scream, cry, rage, groan, moan, whimper, sob, howl, beg and generally expose their deepest feelings. They must run, jump, roll, writhe, twitch, kneel, crawl, wriggle and make any other movement which expresses the way they were feeling. These feelings are called 'primals'. This is supposed to produce *catharsis* by 'getting it out of the patient's system'.

Evaluation of psychoanalytic therapy

Most psychoanalytic therapies rely to varying extents on Freudian views about the structure and functioning of biological and social forces in development. Psychoanalytic approaches propose that emotional and personality disorders are caused by childhood experiences. If we reject this theory then techniques designed to relive childhood cannot produce a 'cure' for an 'adult' problem. It is sometimes argued that by always looking backwards for the origin of problems psychoanalysts may miss real causes of problems in the here and now. For example, if being trapped in a tower-block with two young children is what is making me miserable, there seems little point in analysing my early relationships with my mother. From the point of view of labelling theory then, psychoanalytic approaches can appear as ways of helping people *misunderstand* the true nature of their problems in the here and now. From the viewpoint of the medical model which assumes that there are organic causes for mental illness, psychoanalysis can appear equally worthless. As you will see in later sections of this chapter, behaviourist psychology, cognitive psychology and humanistic psychology also provide criticisms of the psychoanalytic approach.

Critics of psychoanalytic approaches have to face the fact that these therapies sometimes seem to work. However many neuroses are caused by a combination of mind and body experiences and if the condition is not too severe, then almost any therapy could be effective. Many problems show spontaneous remission: they get better irrespective of what treatment is applied. A neurotic symptom could easily be a cry for attention, so any therapy that provides attention could well remove the symptom. A placebo effect may be operating. Telling a patient who believes that there is something wrong with him or her, that a particular kind of treatment will be effective may be enough to eliminate the condition, regardless of any treatment which

(**ACT**) Complete the following chart summarizing Freud's main ideas.

2 instinctive urges	3 parts of personality	4 stages
a	a	a
b	b	b
	c	c
		d

is given. For lonely, depressed, anxious people with low self-esteem there can be something very gratifying about being listened to by a psychoanalyst, or being a valued member of a transactional analysis group. In this way psychoanalytic therapies may work by transforming the patient's life, rather than for the reasons therapists claim. Evaluation studies of these kinds of therapies have generally failed to come to any definite conclusion about their benefits.

BEHAVIOURIST APPROACHES

One of the major psychological alternatives to the medical model and the psychoanalytic approaches is derived from the learning theories of classical and operant conditioning which stress the importance of learning by association. This is a convenient point at which to review what you have learned so far about behaviourism and learning theory. You will find the discussions in Chapter 2 most relevant.

While the medical approach seeks to treat and even 'cure' problem behaviour by surgery, ECT, or chemotherapy, and while psychoanalytic theories try to put patients in touch with the cause of their problems, behaviourists believe that any maladapted behaviour is likely to be the result of an inappropriate association of an act and a reinforcer. According to behaviourists the cause of the maladapted behaviour is less important than its consequences.

▶ Behaviourists' only concern with the cause of maladapted behaviour is in the nature of the reinforcer that maintains it.

The cause of the act could be external, such as a broken relationship, the death of a friend or failing an exam. This external factor could induce an internal state of stress, conflict, anxiety or frustration and these emotional states could bring about behaviour which has the symptoms of depression, anxiety, obsession and so on. Other people's sympathetic or understanding reactions might provide reinforcement for the symptoms.

▶ According to the supporters of the behaviourist tradition, any learning (including maladapted learning) which has come about through association can be removed in the same way.

Three broad areas of learning theory have been applied to changing maladapted behaviour. These stem from classical conditioning with its concern for physiological explanations for behaviour. **Hans Eysenck** developed the applications of classical conditioning in the 1950s calling them 'behaviour therapy'. A year later **B.F. Skinner** also used this term to describe his techniques for modifying behaviour based on operant conditioning principles. Later the term 'behaviour modification' was used for operant techniques. These two approaches are discussed below. The third broad area of theories which have been applied to changing some problem behaviour are the social learning theories developed originally by **Albert Bandura** and his colleagues' modelling therapy.

▶ *Learning theory* covers a vast range of approaches in psychology, from those which seek a physiological explanation for learning to those which reject the influence of physiology altogether.

Classical conditioning and behaviour therapy

Many learned responses that both humans and animals make are *conditioned reflexes*. In Chapter 2 we described how conditioned reflexes are learned by being associated in time and place (and hence in the organism's awareness) with something that naturally elicits that response. Watson and Rayner showed in the 'Little Albert' case that very young babies can be conditioned to show a fear response. By

▶ Responses become conditioned to a neutral stimulus when the stimulus that naturally elicits them is associated with it. Animals need several "pairings".

the age of five you probably acquired a conditioned reflex to 'be hungry' when you heard the tune played by a passing ice cream van. As we grow we acquire many such associations, and by the time we are adult some neutral events, people, animals or objects may have become inappropriately associated with such emotional reflexes as fear and anxiety, pleasure and need.

Sometimes the association results in problem behaviour. For example, someone might have an irrational fear of cats because a cat was involved in some frightening previous experiences. This means they cannot visit friends who have cats and are constantly on guard against being near a cat. Or an alcoholic may have pleasant experiences associated with drinking. The addiction is a problem. This 'problem behaviour' needs 'treatment' either to change a negative behaviour (avoiding cats) to a neutral or positive one (accepting the presence of cats), or to change some positive behaviour (alcoholism) into a negative one (not being addicted). Each type of behaviour change requires a different type of therapy. The first requires *systematic desensitization* or *implosion therapy*, the second requires *aversion therapy* or *stimulus satiation*.

Systematic desensitization
Desensitization works by the therapist providing a stimulus which has a pleasant response. The stimulus is usually some kind of relaxation. The client's unpleasant response is gradually associated with it. The pleasantness of the first response must always have a more profound effect on the client than the unpleasantness of the second. The two responses are incompatible, and the weaker of them should disappear.

Let's take as an example a man who had several frightening encounters with birds as a child, and is now a zoophobic. The therapist provides a pleasant unconditioned stimulus (a relaxation technique), which will elicit in the client a pleasant unconditioned response (comfort). A second, unpleasant, conditioned response (the man's anxiety reaction to birds) is then gradually paired with the comfort he feels from the first. At all times the conditioned anxiety response must be weaker than the unconditioned comfort response. Since the two responses (comfort and anxiety) are incompatible, the weaker of them will fade away.

Systematic desensitization is an effective technique for treating people with minor phobias. They need to be able to allow themselves to imagine the anxiety-producing stimulus, and the therapeutic situation must be so controlled that they can tolerate the phobic object. They may also need to learn to use a relaxation technique. Such an approach couldn't be used with people whose behaviour is more deeply disturbed, such as those with psychotic disorders or severe personality disorders.

There is some disagreement about whether it is necessary to arrange the anxiety-producing stimuli in an 'anxiety hierarchy' from least distressing (the bird-like sketch in our example – see inset) to the most distressing (actually being close to the bird). There is also

► Humans are capable of learning after a single pairing. (How many times do you need to be bitten by a dog to become afraid of dogs?)

► Systematic desensitization and aversion therapy are examples of *counter conditioning*. This means taking a powerful conditioned stimulus which elicits a pleasant response and associating it with a less powerful (undesired) conditioned response.

► There are several kinds of relaxation and the techniques can be learned in a few hours. The stimulus to trigger the pleasant reaction response might be the sight or sound of the therapist, or simply entering the therapy room.

► It is impossible to feel two incompatible emotions at the same time. You may cry because you're happy, but this crying is not seen as a symptom of unhappiness. You can't feel relaxed and comfortable at the same time as feeling anxious and afraid.

Desensitization procedure with a zoophobic

Stage	Aim	Example
1 The therapist explores the thresholds of tolerance of the anxiety-producing stimulus.	To discover the shortest distance the phobic can tolerate between himself and a bird. What other bird-like stimuli cause anxiety?	20 metres Pictures, photographs
2 The most desirable outcome of the therapy is established: the 'target behaviour'.	To establish the distance the phobic would find acceptable. What other stimuli would the phobic want to tolerate?	Actual bird at 1 metre Pictures, photographs
3 Relax the client and make him imagine being in the presence of various bird-like objects, from least feared to most feared. (This is an 'anxiety hierarchy'.)	To achieve a relaxed state incompatible with being anxious.	Client can tolerate thoughts of birds.
4 Continue relaxation and introduce some simple bird-like sketches on the other side of the room.	Same as above	No anxiety in the presence of the sketches.
5 Bring the sketches nearer until the client shows some anxiety reaction, then stop.	As before	As before
6 Repeat the last stage until any anxiety reactions to the sketches have disappeared (been 'extinguished').	As before	As before
7 Replace the simple sketches with a more realistic drawing of a bird at some distance, and bring it closer as before.	As before	No anxiety in the presence of the drawings.
8 Replace the drawing with a photograph and repeat.	As before	No anxiety from a photograph.
9 Replace the photograph with a stuffed model of a bird and repeat.	As before	No anxiety from a model bird.
10 Replace the model with a small caged bird and repeat.	As before	No anxiety from a small bird.
11 Use a larger bird and repeat until the bird is 1 metre from the former zoophobic. He has now been desensitized to birds.	As before	No anxiety from a larger bird at 1 metre.

► In a faster working version desensitization called *graded exposure* clients are not taught relaxation but have to find their own way of coping with the phobic object.

disagreement about whether it is necessary to have the pleasant, unconditioned response at all. Merely exposing clients to the source of their anxiety may be enough to reduce the anxiety, particularly where clients are well motivated to want to reduce their anxiety reaction.

 Outline a systematic desensitization procedure for reducing an agoraphobic's fear of open spaces.

Implosion therapy and flooding

The idea behind *implosion therapy* is that no one can maintain any response indefinitely, including an anxiety response to a stimulus about which one is phobic. A fear of birds can only persist when the client generally avoids birds and is able to escape from them on the rare occasions that he comes into contact with them.

With implosion therapy the aim is to achieve extinction of the fear response very quickly. There are no relaxation exercises and phobic clients are not gently and systematically exposed to the source of their fear. Instead they are simply made to imagine that there are, for example, masses of birds all around them. The therapist describes the scene in great detail. Some of the birds touch the client, wings flap, beaks peck at the ground, and eggs are laid all over the place. This should be enough to produce a fair amount of anxiety! The therapist goes on and on, despite the client pleading with her or him to stop. After a time the client should no longer find the descriptions so frightening.

Clients can't escape from the descriptions of the birds and the theory is that they will eventually become exhausted, even bored, by them. When next confronted by a real bird it is hoped that the response in the therapy session will be generalized, and the client will not feel afraid of them. Similarly, someone who is afraid of heights will be shown photographs or videos taken from high places in an attempt to lessen the client's sensitivity to them. When next in a high place the person's anxieties should be lessened.

An even stronger version of implosion therapy is *flooding therapy*. Here the client is actually exposed to the objects themselves, rather than to hearing verbal descriptions of them. An arachnophobic could be shut in a room containing jars and glass-cases full of all kinds of spiders, with pictures of spiders lining the walls. The initial anxiety attack (assuming it doesn't provoke instant heart failure!) should, in theory, eventually subside. Someone who has a phobia about aeroplanes, perhaps having been involved in a plane crash, might be made to watch a few hours of films featuring planes, including war films, documentaries about aircraft, flight simulators, etc. An agoraphobic could be made to walk around a busy shopping precinct, buy things in the shops, have a coffee in a coffee bar, etc. Someone afraid of heights could be made to ride on elevators or lifts up and down tall buildings.

Implosion and flooding are successful with some clients, although there are ethical and practical implications. The client's motivation has to be very strong. An agoraphobic who would consent to spending some hours in a shopping precinct must be so well motivated to overcome his, or more usually her, phobia that the phobia can't be regarded as extreme, and the client may well have improved without therapy. Anyone who would willingly stay in a room full of feared spiders is unlikely to have that severe a phobia.

A further problem is that the therapy may backfire and make the client's phobia even worse. Exposure to the phobic object during flooding might confirm or reinforce the phobic response.

► Escape and avoidance behaviour are important sources of learning and allow us to maintain many of our normal daily routines.

► Compared to desensitization implosion therapy can be very speedy (and therefore cheaper), it can also have some dangers.

► Generalization means making an induction from examples of something, and applying the same principles or conclusions to other, similar objects. Having learned the principles of servicing one car engine you may generalize your knowledge to other car engines.

► In implosion therapy the client's experiences happen inside her of his own head (they implode). In flooding the experiences are real and exist outside the client.

▶ Unlike the other therapies described so far, aversion therapy pairs the undesired behaviour with an *unpleasant* response so that if the stimulus for repeating the behaviour occurs in the future the unpleasant response will be elicited.

▶ As with systematic desensitization, two opposing emotions cannot be felt simultaneously. The strongest will win. The fear or dread of vomiting should be greater than any enjoyment that one might have from a drink.

▶ Aversion therapy works on the principle that a positive response, e.g. sexual arousal, will be replaced by an incompatible, negative one, e.g. feeling sick, if several pairings are made.

(NM) Contrast implosion therapy with desensitization techniques.

Aversion therapy

Aversion therapy can be thought of as being the opposite of desensitization. It doesn't try to *eliminate* the fear response, it tries to *trigger* it. The behaviour which is to be eliminated is associated with an unpleasant response so that the unpleasant response will be elicited if the client begins the behaviour in the future.

A common problem that has been successfully treated by aversion therapy is alcoholism. Clients are given a drug that has an unpleasant effect when combined with alcohol, such as causing vomiting or eliciting a fear response. They are then asked to smell, sip, savour and finally swallow, the alcoholic drinks to which they are addicted. As they are enjoying their drink, the drug begins to make them feel ill or frightened. The pleasure soon disappears in the face of the effects of the drug. An association between drinking alcohol and being ill or frightened should be formed, and any time they think about having a drink in the future they should start to feel ill or scared.

Aversion therapy has also been found effective with sexual 'disorders', from sexual fetishes such as transvestitism, to homosexuals who feel uncomfortable with their sexuality and desire to be heterosexual. Transvestites (who derive sexual pleasure from dressing as a member of the opposite sex) will be asked, in the privacy of a room in a clinic, to dress up in their favourite female garments. As they do so they will probably experience some sexual arousal. Unknown to them, their dressing will be recorded on video. Later they will be given a nausea-inducing drug and shown the film. They should learn to associate the thought of themselves dressing in women's clothes with feeling sick. After several such pairings the association should be so strong that the mere thought of 'cross dressing' should induce nausea. Since it is impossible to feel sick and sexually aroused at the same time, the desire to achieve arousal through cross-sex dressing will, in theory, be eliminated. (The fear inducing drug would not be used in this treatment since fear and sexual arousal are not incompatible: fear can sometimes increase sexual arousal.)

There are problems with the aversion therapy approach too. A major ethical problem concerns deliberately giving someone a treatment (the drug) that is intended to make them ill. This goes against the whole of clinical practice, where drugs are administered to make people better.

Secondly there are problems with generalization. A former transvestite who feels sick at the thought of dressing in female clothes may generalize this to feeling sick whenever he is near to a female who is wearing clothes. This could severely limit his social life! Former alcoholics may generalize their fear or sickness response to being in any place where alcohol can be seen or smelt. Supermarkets, hotels, aeroplanes, restaurants and even other people's homes may all elicit their response. Some alcoholics have been known to drink themselves insensible to avoid feeling sick!

How does aversion therapy differ from the other behaviourist techniques?

ACT *Notes towards an essay*

Show how desensitization, implosion therapy and aversion therapy follow from the theory of classical conditioning.

Operant conditioning and behaviour modification

Operant conditioning (described in Chapter 2) is founded on the idea expressed by E.L. Thorndike's 'law of effect', which states that any action that has pleasant consequences is likely to be repeated, while any action that has unpleasant consequences will be avoided. These consequences are termed *positive* and *negative reinforcement*. This has obvious significance to therapy. In the early 1960s, for example, **Ayllon** and **Houghton** asked the attendants on a ward for psychotic patients to ignore the patient's descriptions of their hallucinations, delusions and erratic ramblings. Instead they were to reinforce (with attention, praise and any other appropriate reward), any of the more sociable or sensible utterances. The results were quite dramatic. The number of sensible comments increased, and the number of signs of disordered thinking decreased, quite markedly.

Before deciding on a course of therapy it is first necessary to establish exactly what the problem behaviour is, what are its consequences, and which circumstances in the client's environment trigger it. Behaviourists such as Skinner argue that *antecedents* (the situation, environment or circumstances in which people find themselves) provide stimuli which trigger certain *behaviour* (actually doing something in response to the stimuli). The behaviour will inevitably have some *consequences* (be they great or small, pleasant or unpleasant). It is the consequences of our behaviour which largely determine the likelihood of us repeating the action. For example, the smell of freshly baked cakes as you walk past the bread shop are antecedents to the behaviour 'buying and eating some cakes'. The consequences of your behaviour – your enjoyment in eating the cakes, your weight, your complexion, your bank balance – will influence whether you buy cakes again the next time you pass a bread shop.

In Ayllon and Houghton's experiment, the ward, the behaviour of the attendants and the other patients were all antecedents for each of the patients. Their disturbed behaviour occurred (partly at least) in response to those antecedents. The consequences (before the experiment) were that the most disturbed patients received the most attention. A behaviourist would claim that a 'vicious circle' has developed in which the most attention is paid to the patients whose behaviour is most disturbed, and the patient knows therefore that to obtain attention they must behave in a disturbed way. To put it simply, the caring behaviour of the attendants is actually *causing* some of the problem!

The therapist must discover exactly what each client would find positively and negatively reinforcing. People vary in their likes and dislikes, and what one would find reinforcing another might find

► A *positive reinforcer* is anything a person finds beneficial in some way. It could be primary (essentials like food and sleep) or secondary (anything, such as money, which can be exchanged for primary reinforcers).

► *Negative reinforcers* are either escaping from an unpleasant stimulus or avoiding it in the first place.

► Behaviourists identify ABC (*Antecedents, Behaviour and Consequences*). According to Skinner it is the consequences, not the antecedents, which determine behaviour.

► Some of the symptoms of some of the patients in Ayllon and Houghton's research appear to be caused by their treatment, i.e. they are social symptoms and not part of a medical condition or mental illness.

► Discovering precisely what each person finds reinforcing and what is reinforcing particular behaviour is not as easy as it might seem. If you don't buy a cake, can I infer that you do not find cakes reinforcing? A cake is only a positive reinforcer if you're hungry, or have some money, or are not off cakes, or not on a strict diet.

► No system of therapy will always be effective for treating the condition with which it is usually effective. Other variables will inevitably intervene.

distressing. For example, would you find smoking a cigarette positively reinforcing? Would all your friends? (Some of Ayllon and Houghton's patients stayed unnaturally quiet for most of the day, seemingly absorbed in their own pursuits. Attention was not a positive reinforcer for them.) Having found what is presently reinforcing the undesired behaviour, and what the client would find rewarding, the therapist must remove the reinforcer from the undesired behaviour and apply it to the desired behaviour.

Positive and negative reinforcement are most effective when used with specific symptoms rather than entire disorders. Eliminating specific, simple problems and then successively removing the next simplest until eventually the more complex symptoms have been extinguished is an ideal goal for behaviour modification therapy. It isn't, however, always possible because of the nature of the client's personality or condition, the antecedents or the therapy situation.

 How does behaviour modification based on operant conditioning differ from the methods employed in classical conditioning?

The following are some examples of problems where behaviour modification techniques have been used.

Infantile autism
Autistic children are generally preoccupied with their own perceptions and have no interest in other people. This makes them difficult to train in basic skills such as washing, dressing and using the appropriate utensils to eat with. In therapy they often appear to be ignoring the therapist, and do not make or keep eye contact with him or her. Chemotherapy cannot improve their condition, and insight theories are impractical when the subject cannot or will not cooperate.

Ivar Loovas adapted and applied a behaviour modification approach – specifically 'behaviour shaping by successive approximation' – to training some autistic children in California in the 1960s. It isn't necessary, or possible, to establish the antecedents of autistic behaviour and Loovas simply reinforced every aspect of any behaviour that was vaguely sociable, such as making eye contact, making sounds, imitating the therapist's actions, cuddling, etc. He used encouragement, praise and pieces of chocolate as reinforcers.

► The programme of reinforcement to be used with autistic children has to be much longer than with 'normal' children, and substitution of reinforcements must be made very gradually.

After a while the children had to make more speech like sounds and had to hold eye contact for longer, or imitate more complex action, in order to gain reinforcers. Cuddles were now a normal part of the child's repertoire of behaviour and could be used as a reinforcer. As the children's behaviour continued to become slightly more 'normal', verbal reinforcement, e.g. 'good boy' and 'well done', was all that was necessary to maintain progress. By now the children had learned to make combinations of sounds into words, although correctly applying them required immense patience, many months of training, and countless reinforcements.

► Many parents of autistic and other retarded or behaviourally disturbed children have been taught the principles of behaviour modification with considerable success.

Infantile autism

This is a rare pathological condition in which the child is severely socially withdrawn, fails to develop much language and appears to have little interest in communicating with others. Autistic children 'live in a world of their own'. They fail to make normal attachments (see Chapter 3) to people, but often become obsessed with an inanimate object such as a blanket or a soft toy, and they often indulge in repetitive behaviour such as rapid rocking backward and forward, sometimes for hours.

The cause is unknown, and not everyone agrees that infantile autism is a single disease since the individual's responses, recovery rates and incidence of brain damage vary so widely. Some specialists claim that what is sometimes diagnosed as infantile autism is actually a form of schizophrenia since some sufferers also have hallucinations, delusions and other schizophrenic symptoms.

Loovas found that considerable improvements could be made, with tremendous and constant effort on the part of the child's carers. Autistic children are unlikely ever to be able to compete with normal children in language, creative skills, co-ordination, etc. For a child who is completely isolated to become even slightly more sociable has to be seen as great progress. Luckily the principles of behaviour modification are not difficult for parents to understand, and they are usually the people most highly motivated to strive for improvements in the child.

Behaviour modification and children with behaviour problems

Children whose behaviour in school or at home causes acute problems for their carers, and indirectly for themselves, are sometimes treated by a 'time out' procedure. For example, a child may be uncontrollable, attention seeking, aggressive, or hyperactive. The frustration, anger or distress the child is causing its carers may be reinforcing the child's behaviour. In 'time out' the child is removed, forcibly if necessary (and it often is necessary), from the situation where it is behaving badly and placed in an unstimulating part of the classroom, away from anyone else, or in a separate, empty and bare room. The child is told what is happening, and that it will only be released when its behaviour has been acceptable for a period of, for example, five minutes.

▶ *Time out* is a quite extreme measure and is usually used only when other, less severe attempts at control have failed.

In most cases the child's behaviour becomes more extreme in the time out. The child may scream constantly, wreck the place, appear to hurt itself or do anything else that might tempt its carers to release it. This has to be resisted at all costs, despite the carer's urge to give in to the child who seems to be in such distress. After a while in time out the child's behaviour will usually subside for long enough for it to be returned to the company and activity of the class or family. The child is told that if its behaviour becomes unacceptable again it will be returned to time out.

▶ Time out was developed from operant conditioning and attempts to extinguish undesirable behaviour by removing the child from the situation which could be reinforcing the undesired behaviour.

▶ Do you think that the time out procedure used here is ethically acceptable for use with retarded children? Or do you think that the benefits they will gain from being more able to control themselves justify the use of this technique? A time out procedure called 'pin-down' used by Staffordshire Social Services was recently severely criticized and discontinued as cruel and arbitrary.

▶ There are several applications of operant conditioning which have been applied to children with various behavioural or mental problems. Most have been found effective. Dressing, eating and using the toilet, for example, are basic life skills which have been successfully taught to retarded children.

▶ Labelling theory suggests that we tend to behave in the ways that people around us expect us to behave. Our conforming behaviour results in a self-fulfilling prophecy.

▶ It would be nice to think that every time we did something good in real life we received some reward. But this is far from true!

▶ Most forms of treatment, even those based on the principles of conditioning, at least attempt to 'cure' the problem. The token economy has had some success in changing some aspects of behaviour, but never offered a 'cure'.

Severe retardation and behaviour modification

In 1971 **Azrin** and **Foxx** published the results of their procedure for toilet training severely retarded children. The children were given extra drinks, and taken to the toilet every half hour. When they used it successfully they were given sweets, biscuits, praise and lots of attention. When they 'had an accident' they were strapped into a chair for half an hour, away from the rest of the class. (This is a time out procedure.) On the whole the number of 'accidents per week' declined fairly dramatically.

Severely retarded children have been taught to dress using an application of operant conditioning called 'prompt and fade'. They were first taught to dress themselves in large, loose, elasticated smocks. As the children were helped to dress themselves, each operation was explained to them, and they were told what they would have to do. Each time the child had to get dressed, the helpers would tell the child what to do, but reduced the amount of help actually given. As each operation was mastered the child was praised and given reinforcers such as spoonfuls of chocolate pudding. When they could put on their loose smocks without any help, they were then taught how to dress in conventional clothes. This technique has worked with children with IQs of below 10.

Institutionalized adults with psychotic disorders

As **Ayllon** and **Houghton** and others have shown, some of the disturbed behaviour of psychotic mental patients may be a consequence of the routines of the institution, and the definitions, labels and expectations which the staff and others have of the patients. If everyone treats you in a certain way, and expects you to behave in a certain way, then the likelihood is that you will start to behave in that way.

An application of operant conditioning which was widely used in the 1960s to prepare some patients for life in the outside world was the 'token economy'. Patients had to start doing things for themselves, as one does in 'real life', in order to gain some tokens. For example, chores such as tidying, cleaning, washing up, dressing and helping to prepare food were all rewarded by tokens which could be exchanged for privileges. The more complex or demanding the task, the more tokens could be given.

There is no doubt that well-run token economies have led to improvements in the behaviour of even quite severely disturbed schizophrenics, but they have not led to anything which can be remotely thought of as a 'cure'. The patients remain schizophrenic right through the system of treatment. Although some patients have been able to cope with life outside the institution, for example in 'half-way houses', nearly all of them have needed great assistance and supervision. Once the token system is removed, improvements in behaviour tend to disappear. This shows that the token economy is treating the symptoms of maladapted behaviour and largely ignoring its cause.

Also, a number of problems have been found when running token economies. Some patients stole others' tokens, other patients hoarded

---

**A token economy programme
(based on Ayllon and Azrin 1968)**

Examples of how tokens can be earned:

Job	Reward
make own bed and clean area	1 token
brush teeth once a day	1 token
10 minutes waiting on table	2 tokens
10 minutes washing up	6 tokens
30 minutes writing names of other patients brushing teeth	3 tokens

Examples of what tokens can be exchanged for:

Cost	For
1 token per day	the use of a personal chair
1 token per day	the choice of a bedspread
2 tokens	a 20-minute walk in the grounds
3 tokens	choosing a TV programme
1-10 tokens	toiletries, e.g. toothpaste, comb, lipstick
10 tokens	attending a religious service off the ward
20 tokens	a private meeting with the ward psychologist
100 tokens	a private meeting with a social worker
12-400 tokens	clothes and accessories, such as slippers, skirt, handbag

---

them. Some were simply unable to understand the benefits of changing their behaviour, or unable to control their behaviour sufficiently to make it change.

Token economies are not widely used today in the West, partly because it is recognized that mental patients have the same human rights as anyone else. These rights (to see a psychologist or social worker, to sit in a chair, etc.) have been tested in the courts. In America legal action has been taken against institutions that denied patients the right to attend religious ceremonies unless they had enough tokens. Also there are legal limits on the minimum wages that can be paid for many of the duties which patients had to perform in order to earn tokens. The value of the work in dollars amounted to rather more than that to which the tokens would entitle a patient. A few psychiatric wards were run as token economies in Britain, but with limited success.

 Notes towards an essay

Explain how behaviour modification illustrates the principles of operant conditioning.

► Patients who were sufficiently aware of themselves to be able to control their behaviour and benefit from the tokens were often on the same ward with even more severely disturbed patients who were unable to earn any tokens. This seems like discrimination.

► Token economies bring some improvements in the behaviour, and the quality of life, of some patients (and staff) but possibly at the expense of some basic human rights.

Social learning theory and modelling therapy

Observational learning has been researched by **Albert Bandura** since the 1950s and is part of social learning theory. We saw in Chapter 2 (pages 44–5) and Chapter 5 (pages 103–5) how social learning theory contributes to an explanation of how children's personalities develop. As adults we often watch someone else and imitate their performance as a means of improving our own. We can learn appropriate behaviour by watching others who are more experienced than ourselves. If someone's responses (for example towards spiders) are maladapted (i.e. they have a phobic reaction), and he or she sees someone else behaving appropriately then the maladapted response could be replaced by an appropriate one. This technique is known as *modelling therapy*.

▶ *Modelling therapy* comprises showing the client someone behaving appropriately in a situation in which the client's responses are inappropriate. It has been used both to extinguish unwanted behaviours and to rebuild appropriate ones.

Eliminating inappropriate behaviours such as phobias by modelling someone without the phobia interacting with the phobic object has been demonstrated many times. The best known is Bandura's experiment with severe snake-phobic subjects. They were first tested by seeing how closely they would approach a glass tank containing a snake. Their attitudes towards snakes were also tested. They all had negative images of snakes and found snakes disgusting. Bandura then divided the subjects into three experimental and one control group.

▶ The live modelling group had some direct experience with the object of their fear, the snake.

The first experimental group, called the *live modelling* group, saw a therapist handle a live king snake without fear. The subjects were encouraged to touch the snake, first while wearing gloves, then with their bare hands and finally near to its head. Gradually each subject allowed him or herself to be touched by the snake's body, even allowing it to crawl over them.

▶ The symbolic modelling group saw others interacting with snakes, but had no personal experience.

The second experimental group, called the *symbolic modelling* group, watched a film of children and adults interacting with various snakes. In the film the stimuli were fairly mild to begin with and became progressively more frightening to the phobic viewers. In the early scenes the people played with plastic snake toys: later they touched and handled a live king snake without any fear; and in the final scenes the king snake slid across their shoulders and around their necks. The people on the film obviously enjoyed their experience with the snake. If the subjects became too aroused they could stop the film, rewind it and watch any parts of it again if they wanted to.

▶ The desensitization group were relaxed and were gradually exposed to images of snakes and eventually to a live snake.

The third experimental group, the *desensitization* group, had a systematic desensitization procedure as described earlier under classical conditioning. The control group received no therapy at all.

▶ The live modelling group had had direct experience of snakes as well as watching others handle the animals without any ill-effects.

After the modelling sessions all the subjects were asked to approach the snake in the tank again. Those in the control group were still unwilling to go very close and refused to touch the snake. More subjects in the desensitization group were now able to touch the snake, and many more still in the symbolic modelling group were now prepared to handle the snake. However the greatest change occurred in the live modelling group, many of whom were even able to have the snake placed in their laps while they sat with their hands down by their sides.

Each experimental group's attitude towards snakes had also changed in relation to their experience with the live modelling group now having quite positive attitudes towards snakes. Bandura claims that 90 per cent of snake phobias can be cured using a live modelling technique.

According to Bandura the explanation for the success of this and other cognitive therapies lies in *self-efficacy*. By this he means the change in our cognition which says 'I can do this'. Much maladapted behaviour is the result of negative views of what the sufferer can't do or what they are afraid of. The best way to achieve self-efficacy is to encourage people to come face to face with the object which frightens them and encourage some interaction with it. The more we know about some things, the less likely we are to fear them.

Social learning theory uses the principle of operant conditioning, but it gives the subject another person as a model to identify with and the main reward for showing a desirable behaviour is usually the subject's sense of achievement.

Evaluation of Behaviourist therapies

Behaviourist therapies have had considerable success in dealing with phobias. They have sometimes been successful in dealing with addictions and with psychosexual problems, but their use in this context sometimes has unfortunate side-effects. Behaviour modification has been used to shape and change the behaviour of autistic, retarded and psychotic patients. But in these contexts it cannot be said to offer a cure: rather it makes their behaviour more socially acceptable.

A common criticism of behaviourist therapies is that they are based on a grossly oversimplified picture of human behaviour. In the behaviourist model people react to stimuli and act because of learned associations. They do not seem to reason, think, or make sense of their experiences. This criticism is most telling with regard to the failure of behaviourist therapies to effect improvement in psychotic patients whose problems probably lie in thinking and interpreting things differently from other people.

In treating any conditions like phobias, a major limitation of behaviourist therapies is that they usually require a highly controlled environment if the improvement is to persist. It is easy to arrange things in a treatment room so that undesirable behaviour is followed by an unpleasant experience, or desirable behaviour is rewarded with a pleasant one, but once out in the real world it all too often happens that the alcoholic overcomes his nauseous association with alcohol and returns to drinking for pleasure, or the badly behaved child re-learns the joys of being naughty.

Another line of criticisms of behaviourist therapies is moral rather than practical. Humanistic psychologists in particular object to people being treated like laboratory animals.

► According to Bandura desensitization (classical conditioning) was not as effective as the live modelling therapy.

► Self-efficacy involves some cognitive restructuring from 'I can't do ...', to 'I can do ...'.

COGNITIVE APPROACHES TO THERAPY

During the last 30 years or so there has been a movement in psychology away from some of the more rigid ideas of behaviourism such as 'behaviour being the result of situational antecedents and previous consequences'. This is now seen as a rather narrow view of the causes of human behaviour. We do things for all kinds of reasons, including 'for the hell of it' and 'because I just felt like it'. These may not be logical reasons, but humans aren't the logical robots that some behaviourism implies.

In other areas of psychology there has been a trend towards seeing human cognition and human interaction as the key to a better understanding of human behaviour. Our thoughts, understanding, reasoning, memories, guesses, intuition, perception, imagination, motives, intelligence, abilities, self-concept and other mental processes all contribute to explaining human behaviour. This has relevance for therapies to deal with the 'mentally' (or 'behaviourally') 'disturbed'. If behaviour is the result of mental, cognitive processes, and behaviour is 'disturbed', then the mental processes must be 'disturbed'. What is needed is not behaviour shaping, but rather some cognitive restructuring. Some examples of cognitive therapies are described below.

Personal construct theory

During the 1950s **George Kelly** was among the first to reject both the medical and psychoanalytic models, with their assumptions of 'illness' which has a 'cause' and which can be 'cured'. He also rejects the behaviourist emphasis that the consequences of previous behaviour determine future behaviour. He regards each person as a unique 'scientist': we test our ideas each day, and adapt our behaviour accordingly. For example, you might express your ideas about some current item in the news, and others around you may give their response. You might learn something you hadn't realized before, and you may modify your ideas in the future. If you do something to achieve some aim which is ineffective, then you won't do it to achieve the same aim again. Kelly sees this as adaptive functioning. If most of your ideas about your world allow you to function effectively in it then you have an effective personal construct system.

If some of our personal constructs about ourselves, other people or our situation repeatedly appear to be wrong, we may consider that we have a problem. If I believe (have a personal construct) that birds are generally threatening and frightening, then I will try to arrange my life so that I do not come into contact with any birds. This might include not going near any trees. Since most birds are quite harmless, and I am not harmed in any way by any birds that I do come into contact with, my personal construct is clearly wrong, but I still believe it. I have a problem.

According to Kelly the aim of therapy is to reconstruct those ideas which are clearly producing an inadequate or inaccurate response. The client and therapist work together, using whatever therapeutic

► Every branch of science should be dynamic, with new ideas, new theories, even whole new perspectives emerging as knowledge leads to speculation.

► Disturbed does not mean ill. Ill implies a breakdown in structure which causes a breakdown in normal functioning. Disturbed means a breakdown in normal functioning for which there is no organic cause.

► A personal construct is a general term for each of the ways in which people try to understand, predict and control their situation.

Review – Personal construct theory

Kelly sees each individual as a 'scientist', who tests her or his 'theories' about what is going on in their own situation. Ideas which prove correct will lead to adaptive functioning.

Where our personal constructs about the world are incorrect our behaviour and thinking become distorted and we may need therapy to rebuild a more realistic view.

techniques seem appropriate (including those of Freud, Adler and Skinner among others). They seek out what clients think about themselves, others, and their environment which could explain their particular problem. They are then shown that it is possible to change their constructs.

Ellis' rational emotive therapy (RET)

In the early 1960s **Albert Ellis** suggested one of the first therapies which attempted to 'restructure' part of a person's cognition by emphasizing the rational, problem-solving aspects of cognition and the appropriate role of emotions in thinking. He believed that one of the main causes of maladaptive behaviour was that people developed some irrational ideas about themselves or their situation. For example people who have an obsession about cleanliness and a compulsion to keep washing their hands may have the idea, without ever admitting or even realizing it, that the environment is grubby and grimy, that their hands inevitably become dirty, and that filthy hands are a major threat to health. Ellis's aim was to make the person confront his or her 'irrational' ideas in order to replace them with more 'rational' ones. One's hands do not necessarily become filthy, and dirty hands do not necessarily pose a major threat to health.

People may also develop distorted views about relationships. For example, someone who is convinced that they should be the centre of everyone's attention may become very depressed when it appears that some people ignore them. They may begin to feel a failure, worthless and incompetent. The therapist has to make them recognize that they have an irrational idea; that no one should or could be the centre of attention all the time, that we are all ignored sometimes, and that they need to have a more optimistic, positive outlook on life.

> ► Ellis doesn't use the term 'irrational' literally. It isn't irrational to think that the environment is dirty or that washing hands isn't a good thing to do. It's the hand washing in response to the obsession that needs to be eliminated. The obsession is an irrational cognition that needs restructuring.

> ► *Rational emotive therapy* is highly directive and fairly aggressive: it tells the client what to think and do, and challenges them to do it. It emphasizes positive thinking such as 'be happy', 'pull yourself together', 'look on the bright side', 'you can do it'.

Some common irrational assumptions

Ellis identified 11 basic irrational beliefs which lead to disturbed behaviour. These include:

It is necessary to be loved by everyone.

It is necessary to be thoroughly competent in everything if one is not to be considered worthless.

Some people are essentially bad and should be punished.

Things should be the way one would like them to be.

Past history will always determine present events.

I am unable to control my emotions.

Unhappiness is always caused by other people.

We are each responsible for other people.

Beck's cognitive restructuring

At about the same time that Ellis was developing RET, **Aaron Beck** had abandoned his psychoanalytic training in favour of *cognitive social learning theory*. He adapted cognitive restructuring for use with depressives, believing that depression is often caused by people's faulty ('depressogenic') cognitions – beliefs, expectations, fantasies,

► Beck uses the depressed client to actively explore the client's cognitions both during therapy and between therapy sessions. He regards the client as a 'colleague' and they explore the client's cognitions together.

► Other research on depressives supports Beck's idea about how they see themselves, their world and their future.

► According to Meichenbaum faulty perception leads to a failure to *self instruct* and results in faulty cognition.

► Meichenbaum insists that people describe to themselves what the problems are and how they are going to overcome them in a positive, optimistic way. This is a deterministic, directive therapy.

► Familiarity with the situation helps take the anxiety out of anxiety-producing situations. This is achieved by role play and verbal descriptions of thoughts and feelings.

etc.– about themselves and their failings. These ideas dominate the clients' thinking about themselves (helpless and worthless), their world (insensitive, empty and unpleasant) and their future (hopeless and limited).

Beck's therapy involves asking specific questions about how clients feel about themselves and helping them to realize how wrong they actually are. Between therapy sessions Beck sets his clients homework which is intended to make them achieve something enjoyable and positive every day. Depressed people often deliberately avoid pleasant experiences. They have to keep a log of their feelings and anything which causes them to change their mood. Such things are explored further in therapy to see how they affect the client's cognition. In Beck's therapy, changing the cognition is all-important since if cognition changes behaviour will surely follow.

Meichenbaum's self-instructional training (SIT)

During the 1970s **Donald Meichenbaum** speculated that people hold 'internal dialogues' with themselves. We talk to ourselves, describing our thoughts and feelings. We tell ourselves what we should do next. These are *self instructions*. Sometimes these discussions can be very negative and by focusing on these negative thoughts, levels of arousal are increased. If this continues then various neuroses result.

Meichenbaum's therapy is even more directive than Beck's. He insists that people talk to themselves in a positive way, emphasizing the power of positive thinking in training sessions. Having been faced with their negative thoughts, clients are taught various practical coping skills such as relaxation techniques, breathing exercises for controlling heart rate and arousal, and planning strategies for adapting appropriate behaviour.

One coping strategy is *advance role play*. Here the client runs through the situation which will produce anxiety, talking out loud and describing what he or she is doing. If you know you will be anxious and

---

An internal dialogue

Imagine that you are about to sit your end of year exams. As you approach the first paper you are saying to yourself, 'I can't remember anything, my mind's gone blank, everyone else seems more confident than me, I can't do this, I didn't understand much of it anyway, it's a waste of time me trying this. But if I fail it badly I won't be able to continue next year and my parents will be furious. I'll have wasted a year of my life, and I'll never get on to college or the job I want.'

With this defeatist attitude you're increasing your chances of failing. Meichenbaum would insist that you replace your negative thoughts with more determined ones. Outside the exam room you must say, 'I'm going to do my best in this exam, I'll take my time to read each question carefully and when I've chosen the first one I'll take a deep breath and search my memory for relevant facts for the answer.'

nervous outside the exam room, then several days before the exam you could go to the exam room and familiarize yourself with it, saying out loud what you see and how you feel. Explain what you intend to do on the day of the exam, how you intend to relax, be fresh, be prepared, and be positive. If necessary do this several times on subsequent days.

 Summarize the main cognitive restructuring therapies. What kinds of problems can cognitive restructuring therapies work on?

Evaluation of cognitive therapies

If behaviour is the result of cognition, then changing the cognition will change the behaviour. Cognitive restructuring theories tend to direct the client's perceptions and cognitions wherever possible, and focus on positive rather than negative images. At first sight, whilst it may seem obvious that gaining a better understanding of ourselves is good, understanding our thoughts isn't the same as changing our actions. The emphasis in therapy must be on changing undesired behaviour into desired behaviour.

Thought influences behaviour, and behaviour influences thought. Since these two are inseparable, cognitive therapy should emphasize behaviour. Most modern therapies are better described as 'cognitive behaviour' therapies, and there is mounting evidence that they are successful in treating depressive and anxiety disorders, and those where low self-image and poor self-control lead to difficulties in coping with life.

HUMANISTIC THERAPIES

Humanistic psychology is an idiographic and deliberately non-scientific branch of psychology which rejects behaviourism as having an inhumane mechanistic view of human beings, and rejects psychoanalysis because it treats adults as the victims of their early childhood experience. Humanistic psychology places great emphasis on the uniqueness and creativity of each individual, their potential for self-improvement and for taking charge of their own lives. As with cognitive approaches humanistic psychology sees people as thinking and reasoning beings rather than as objects moved by biochemistry, by psychological complexes or by stimuli. It is central to humanistic psychology that the individual with problems – who is never called 'a patient' – should be treated with respect as a fellow human being, and however odd their way of thinking about the world may seem it should be treated seriously as an alternative, rather than as a faulty way of understanding.

Humanistic psychology is a rather diverse group of theories. One of the ways in which they vary is in the degree to which they are critical of society. Most other theories tend to take society for granted and see so-called 'abnormal behaviour' as a problem and conformity as desirable. Humanistic psychologies by contrast do not necessarily

► Humanism developed out of the work of such people as **Alfred Adler**, (see page 35) and **Abraham Maslow** (see page 46).

see normal behaviour as healthy behaviour, and in the case of existential psychology, as you will see, normal social life is sometimes regarded as 'mad'. Other humanistic psychologies make less radical criticisms of normality.

The circumstances and demands of 'normal' social life are often seen by humanistic psychologists as the cause of the kinds of personal problems which get called – or labelled as mental illness. Szasz who is an important critic of the very idea of 'mental illness' (see page 236), Rosenhan who conducted the pseudo-patient experiment (see page 236) and others use labelling theory to explain how the attitudes and responses of other people may be the cause of mental illness – people literally being driven mad by being treated as mad by others.

Humanistic psychology has generated many different therapies, some of them bordering on the mystical and spiritual. Here I will deal with the three more common humanistic therapies.

Gestalt therapy

Fritz Perls was a German psychoanalyst who rejected most of the traditional Freudian ideas. He developed and used *Gestalt therapy* in the 1960s in America, and after his death in 1970 the techniques were used and extended by others. There are three major differences of approach between Gestalt therapy and psychoanalysis. First, Gestalt therapy is not based on any particularly explicit theory, unlike Freud's (or Skinner's). It is a system of therapy rather than a doctrine of development. Second, it is not particularly concerned with the cause, origin or development of the condition or problem. Its primary concern is with the here and now. (It shares this view with the behaviourist theories.) Third, it does not rely on the therapist interpreting the clients' condition, but rather on the clients becoming aware for themselves.

The basic assumption that Perls made was that we sometimes erect emotional barriers to 'block out' things which we would find distressing. These barriers, which are like Freud's defence mechanisms, also stop us from really 'knowing' our 'true' selves. Gestalt therapy aims to remove the barriers by using techniques originally designed by Perls.

People are instructed to talk in the present tense. Everything must be about how they think or feel here and now, and they are sometimes asked to add the statement 'and I take responsibility for that'. If, for example, someone says 'I feel depressed', they might have to add that they were responsible for that feeling.

One of Perls' games or exercises is the 'empty chair'. Two chairs are placed opposite each other, and the client plays the role of herself or himself in one of the chairs, and imagines the person she or he has a problem with is in the other chair. The client may then swap chairs and take the role of the other person.

Imagine that you have a problem with your husband or wife, boyfriend or girlfriend. Perhaps you feel that you've been betrayed in some way by them. While you are sitting in one chair you are to say what you feel to your partner who you imagine is sitting in the other

► Gestalt therapy is much more about the here and now. It is less concerned with the origin of the condition than with its future.

► Perls invented his own techniques designed to remove emotional barriers to self-expression and to make people more aware of themselves as whole beings so that they could move towards self-actualization.

► Helping someone to take responsibility for their feelings and behaviour is a major step towards them becoming more aware of themselves.

► In the 'empty chair' exercise the client expresses their fears, hopes, anxieties, hatreds, loves, etc. to the person whose reaction to them is causing a problem in order to gain insight into themselves. As with all of these therapies, the technique could work for some people who want it to work for them.

chair. When you've complained about them, and expressed feelings that you haven't expressed before, or may not have realized you had, you swap to the other chair and reply, as though you were your partner. Try to imagine what they would say in defence, or what they may accuse you of. You continue to move from one chair to the other holding your conversation.

The client may later talk with the therapist about the experience, and the idea is that people gain insight from analysing how they interact with these 'important others'.

Carl Rogers' client-centred therapy

Rogers was a psychiatrist and psychotherapist who noted that his clients often referred to their symptoms as coming from within their sense of themselves, who they were, what they were like, how they saw the world, etc. Their actual feelings and behaviour often fell short of what they would like to be like. Like Freud, Rogers distinguishes between 'actual self' and 'ideal self'. The greater the distance between the clients' understanding of their own actual and ideal selves, the greater would be the problems they experienced.

Rogers concluded that the sense of self is the source of our knowledge about ourselves, and this knowledge contains evaluative as well as factual information – whether you are a 'nice' person, an 'arrogant' person, a 'superior' person, etc. According to Rogers, how people view themselves is the most important aspect of the functioning of the personality. His theory of personality is based on a set of principles which may be summarized thus:

1 Every individual can only see their particular world from their own point of view and each person is therefore the centre of their own world.

2 Each person's perception of the world is real to that person. Since each individual is unique, each one's perception is also different from anyone else's.

3 We all share the same basic desire to survive and get ahead and much of our behaviour will be an attempt to satisfy our various needs (ultimately for actualization: see Chapter 2).

4 Knowledge of our self is part of our view of the world and comes from interaction with the environment, particularly with other people in it. How they treat us is built into our knowledge of what we are like and how we value ourselves.

5 We tend to behave in ways that reflect what we know we are like. If we know we are generous (because people have told us so, and treated us as though we are generous), we tend to behave in a kind and giving way. If we know we are aggressive, we tend to act in an unpleasant, anti-social way.

6 We are each strong enough to understand our own perceptions if we can be helped to review them, and we can change our views if we can be encouraged to examine them.

► The ego ideal is part of what Freud called the superego and describes what a person would be like to be like and what they would like to achieve. It changes during our life as new experiences alter our perceptions.

A client-centred therapy session

Mary, a 32-year-old physician, is seeing Dr G., a client-centred therapist. She begins one of her sessions by explaining that she has been thinking of talking with him about sex but she isn't sure how to begin. Dr G. says,'You feel that you want to bring this up with me, but you're also feeling uncomfortable about how to proceed.'

A brief silence follows. Then Mary asks, 'Can't you help me with this somehow?'

'You are really feeling a bit helpless, unable to go ahead, and you're wishing that I will break the impasse for you. Is that how you're feeling?'

'Yes.' Mary feels tense, uneasy, then angry at Dr G. because he won't help her get started. She turns, looks him in the face pleading without saying anything.

Dr G.'s only reply is 'You're just feeling stuck and helpless.'

'Can't you help?'

'You're even mad at me, feeling that I'm deliberately holding out.'

Now Mary is frustrated. 'You're always leaving it up to me telling me that I can do it. Why do I always have to do everything by myself?'

'It's like everything is always your lonely, solitary burden, all your life long.'

This statement strikes home for Mary. She cries, and then says softly 'Oh damn it, damn it, damn it.' She glances up at Dr G. and sees him completely attentive to her, empathic, feeling what she feels. She cries, relaxes, and says 'You don't go away just because I'm hard to get along with. You're good to me.'

'You're always afraid that if you aren't nice the other person will go away. It's nice to be able to be a pain and a burden without having to be afraid of desertion.'

This statement from Dr G. seems to loosen Mary's tongue. She talks for 20 minutes about her sexual experiences and anxieties. She mentions her 'intense relations' with girl friends. Then she blurts out 'I'm afraid I'm queer.'

Dr G. replies with understanding. 'In the background now for some time you've been living with this fear that you are sexually abnormal ... just the way you say it, I can feel how very much of a haunting, spooky fear is connected with that for you.'

(From A. Barton, *Three Worlds of Therapy*, 1974, National Press Books, quoted in Morgan, King, Weiss and Schopler, *Introduction to Psychology*, 7th ed, McGraw Hill.)

► Rogers would have agreed with Cooley that we live in a 'looking glass' world, and with Guthrie that we see ourselves as other people see us.

► Client-centred therapy was a dramatic change for the medical profession. Many psychiatrists preferred to keep their distance from their patients and preserve their professional status. Rogers' ideas were met with considerable hostility.

7 If we are to understand each other we must first understand the other person's perception of his or her world. A good way to do this is through open and honest discussion. The first aim of *client-centred therapy* is to achieve this understanding so that re-orientation of a distorted self-perception can begin.

In client-centred therapy the first aim is to build a cooperative, trusting relationship between therapist and client (*not* patient). The therapist must appear supportive, emotionally receptive, and not judge the client in any way. He or she must genuinely regard the client as a valuable person, and not be interested only because the person *is* a client. The therapist must try to understand what the client is thinking and feeling, so must concentrate deeply on what the client says, asking for clarification where appropriate. Rogerian therapy is very demanding of the therapist.

The second goal of the therapy is to help the client think about their problem, which is encouraged by the therapist reflecting back what the client is saying, so that the client is enabled to see his problems differently.

In client-centred therapy the client takes the lead, the therapist simply supports and tries to be understanding, helping the client to come to terms with his or her own perceptions and feelings. The clients may then grow to 'know themselves better', as the woman in the extract grew to know herself better. Each client is quite unique. No two clients described the same set of perceptions as leading to their particular views. (This has led Rogers to reject all systems of classification of diagnoses since he sees everyone as unique.)

 Outline the principles upon which client-centred therapy is based.

What would a client-centred therapist aim to provide and why?

Existential therapy

Existential psychiatry represents the most radical wing of the humanistic psychology movement. Most other forms of psychology tend to see socially acceptable behaviour as desirable, and the person who deviates from it as being or having, a problem. Existential psychologists by contrast do not make this assumption. Psychiatrists such as **R.D. Laing** see madness as understandable responses to 'insane' social circumstances. Existential psychiatrists have taken a particular interest in schizophrenia. More orthodox psychiatry views the schizophrenic as someone who has a faulty grasp of reality. Laing by contrast argues that the schizophrenic may be someone who has a better grasp of reality than most people, and that this is the schizophrenic's problem. In a world in which most people behave inconsistently, lie to each other, fool themselves, and push unpleasantness under the carpet, the schizophrenic is someone who is unable to do this, and confronts the awfulness of the human condition directly. In a well-known book of case-studies R.D. Laing and **Aron Esterson** demonstrate that if you take the trouble to understand things as the schizophrenic understands them their beliefs and behaviour seem quite rational and reasonable responses to insane social situations. In *Sanity, Madness and the Family* they give a picture of the diagnosed schizophrenic as someone attempting to adjust to the contradictory messages about reality that others give them, especially contradictory messages about who they really are.

Most other therapies assume that there are 'normal' ways of thinking and behaving which are superior to those of the 'mad' person. Since existential psychiatry does not involve this belief, improvement does not necessarily mean becoming more like other people. Rather the task is for the mad person to find a personality and life-style for themselves with which they can live without undue distress. Since the problems experienced by the 'mad' person derive from normal society, it is logical that existential therapy often involves creating new and better societies for them to live in, in the form of therapeutic communities.

▶ The therapist aims to help the client come to terms with his or her feelings, and the first step might be to enable clients actually to face their emotions by stating them out loud.

▶ The two goals of client-centred therapy are to establish a supportive, caring relationship between therapist and client, and to help the client develop towards actualization as they realize their true feelings.

▶ Existentialism is an important school of philosophy which became very popular in the 1960s.

▶ Existentialists put most emphasis on free will, subjectivity and individuality. It is what people themselves think which is most important.

Laing and others claim that if you treat people with equality, dignity and respect, regarding them as important individuals with the right to exercise their free will within the framework of a caring community then most mental problems will resolve themselves. In the kind of therapeutic community in which this is supposed to happen all reasonable distinctions between staff and other residents are removed. They usually live in the same place, eat the same food, and are subject to the same general 'rules' which the community as a whole decides at regular meetings. At these meetings issues are discussed which are of concern to any of the members. No one is obviously 'in charge' and the aim is to make the whole atmosphere supportive and non-threatening.

► R.D. Laing has been accused of viewing the 'straight' world as mad, and the mentally ill as sane. He doesn't quite say this but he does query the sanity of a world dedicated to weapons of mass destruction, and environmental pollution.

Evaluation of humanistic therapies

Many people who have undergone Gestalt Therapy or Client-Centred Counselling claim that they have benefited from it. As with other

---

Schizophrenic families

In their book *Sanity, Madness and the Family*, R.D. Laing and Aron Esterson give case studies of the family circumstances of a number of people diagnosed as suffering from schizophrenia. These case studies were produced through interviewing the schizophrenic and members of their families, alone and together, building up a picture of the way each family member saw the others, and of how they often said different things in different company. The case studies give a picture of the schizophrenic as someone locked into a family which gives them contradictory messages so that they cannot gain a coherent picture of themselves. Looked at as an attempt to come to terms with the contradictions of their experience the behaviour of schizophrenics becomes understandable.

One case study for example, concerns Maya Abbott who feels that she is not in charge of herself and is driven by forces beyond her control so that she cannot understand her own behaviour. She says that she feels that her parents try to influence her every movement. Her parents say this is nonsense but they pray for her, and if they sit and think hard about her she will come into the room, and that they have to keep a close watch on her since she is unable to look after herself. She says her parents try to stop her reading. Her parents say this is nonsense and anyway she reads too much. She says she masturbates and has sexual fantasies. Her parents say she does not. When she says she feels well enough to do things for herself her parents say her attempts to act independently are symptoms of her condition deteriorating.

Like everyone else Maya Abbott has two sources of evidence about what is real and what is not: her own experience and other people. Her parents constantly invalidate her own experience – is it any wonder, say Laing and Esterson, that she has a 'reality problem'?

therapies there is always the possibility that they would have felt better irrespective of any therapy at all, and the vast majority of people who receive these kinds of therapies are not suffering from very serious complaints. However since the humanistic approach shows considerable respect for the opinions of clients, expressions of client satisfaction are regarded as important evidence of success.

Existential therapies are virtually impossible to evaluate in their own terms. This is because they reject the idea, and/or the desirability of 'normal behaviour' hence it is impossible to judge their success or otherwise in terms of whether or not they help someone to behave normally. For R.D. Laing, for example, 'madness' can be a valuable voyage of self-discovery, equivalent to a religious quest, so that whether or not existential therapies promote sanity is irrelevant. Other kinds of therapists who see the object of therapy as curing behaviour problems would not agree.

COMMUNITY AND OCCUPATIONAL PSYCHOLOGY

People generally live in social groups, and many psychological problems arise because of difficulties in social interactions. Rather than offer therapies for problems, community and occupational psychologists attempt to prevent problems arising in the first place. Psychologists are employed by many agencies that deal with people, from education departments, police forces, large employers and the military, to advise on the design of situations which will minimize the stress that can lead to problems.

Two aspects of any situation can promote or minimize stress. These are the physical characteristics, such as the areas in which activities take place, and the social relationships which exist between people. The layout of a workplace, the decoration of prison cells, the routines of school and army life, can all be analysed to discover areas of potential stress, and strategies may be suggested to reduce this. Also the way teams are organized and treated can influence the relationships between their members and the chances that they will work harmoniously together.

Re-arranging an organization to reduce stress and conflict is a possibility if resources can be found to do so. Re-organizing life in the community for the same purpose is much more difficult. Studies of the distribution of some kinds of mental problems suggest very strongly that social causes are to blame. For example **George Brown** has shown conclusively that depression is diagnosed much more frequently among young working class housewives with young children than among any other single group. If it is the social situation of these women which causes their depression, prevention may mean radically changing their lives in terms of income, housing, childcare facilities and marital relationships. Resources for such grand social engineering are rarely made available. However community psychologists can give advice on the design of housing estates, the provision of meeting places and other amenities for housebound mothers and other facilities to make their lives less depressing.

▶ Brown & Harris (1978) compared 458 working class women in England with 100 similar women being treated in psychiatric hospitals for depression. They found the same factors of little communication with their husband, having 3 or more young children at home, lack of a mother to help or confide in, and lack of outside employment to be common to most of those in hospital and many of the others.

Since community psychologists tend to see many problems arising from community life (or the lack of it), it is understandable that they usually favour treatment in the community rather than in hospitals or therapy rooms. There is not much point in curing someone in hospital and then returning them to the same situation which caused their problem in the first place. Community psychiatrists favour treatment in the community, often using half-way houses where patients can be supported by staff, while living as near a normal life as possible, or day-centres where people living in their own homes can visit during the week for support or treatment. Day-centres are sometimes organized so that groups of fellow-sufferers meet together to support each other.

NORMAL AND ABNORMAL BEHAVIOUR

The different kinds of psychology give different pictures of what is 'abnormal' about the abnormal person. In terms of the medical model, the abnormal person is someone whose brain doesn't work properly. In terms of psychoanalytic theory people who show abnormal behaviour have had problems embedded into their personalities during their early childhood experience. Much of the work done by social workers and child guidance clinics assumes that abnormal behaviour arises because children have been deprived of love or affection. Behaviourist psychologists see abnormal behaviour arising from unusual and mainly accidental associations being formed between particular stimuli and particular responses. Cognitive psychologists view abnormality in terms of having different ways of interpreting the world from other people or having unrealistic and damaging ways of viewing and judging the self. Humanistic psychologists are uncomfortable about using terms like 'abnormal' at all. They see human beings as being so diverse that the idea of 'normal behaviour' makes no sense at all. They would rather talk about people experiencing problems of living, and would draw attention to the way in which terms like abnormal are used as part of the way in which people try to control each other.

In reading about various therapies you will have gathered that there is no consensus about the nature of normal and abnormal behaviour. At first sight it might seem a simple statistical matter to define what is normal and what is abnormal. Isn't 'normal behaviour' what most people do most of the time, and normal thinking the way most people think?

▶ The statistical model may only take the 'usualness' of the single act, disregarding its social context.

In theory, sometimes in practice, it is possible to measure human behaviour and define statistical norms. For example, it is possible to say when the average English child begins to speak. It is possible to measure intelligence, and say what the average intelligence score is for a particular age group, and it is possible to take public opinion polls and make comments about the most usually held attitudes on some issue or other.

But this simple statistical approach will not take us very far. It is considerably rarer to compose symphonies like Beethoven or understand the finer points of nuclear physics than it is to sexually abuse a child or murder a spouse. We wouldn't want to say that great composers or scientists were more abnormal than child sex abusers or spouse murderers – indeed being a psychologist is more unusual than being child sex abuser. 'Abnormal' doesn't simply mean unusual.

Whatever the term 'normal' means, the term 'abnormal' implies a moral judgement that abnormal behaviour is behaviour which is undesirable or unfortunate. Since people disagree widely in their moral views, there is considerable room for disagreement in judging behaviour as abnormal. To clarify matters we could suggest four categories of behaviour. That which is common and desirable, common and undesirable, uncommon and desirable, uncommon and undesirable.

► We are usually in danger of making an attribution error when we try to explain any act when not taking its social context into account.

(ACT) Take the four categories provided above and provide your own examples.

We could probably reach some agreement about which behaviours were (statistically) common, but moral judgements and personal preferences would lead to considerable disagreements about which behaviours were undesirable whether commonly or uncommonly manifested.

Nor is the statistical definition of normal behaviour as simple as it might seem. Firstly to decide whether some behaviour or pattern of thought is statistically normal we have to classify it. For example if I encounter someone who is terrified of leaving her house I am tempted to classify her behaviour as 'agoraphobia': an unreasonable fear of open spaces. If I discover however that she is incontinent, I might then reclassify her behaviour as a much more normal fear of being publicly embarrassed in the street. Or again if she is someone who has been sexually or physically assaulted I might reclassify her behaviour as a more extreme form of a rather common fear among women of walking alone in the street. By changing the way in which I classify the case her behaviour can be made to seem either more or less unusual.

Secondly there is the problem of deciding whether the belief or behaviour in question is really unusual in itself, or merely a usual form of behaviour expressing itself in unusual circumstances. Take for example someone who seems excessively frightened of being burgled. The burglary statistics for her area show that the odds are overwhelmingly against. But she derives her information about burglaries from the popular press, the television news, crime thrillers and the television programme, *Crime Watch*. In these terms her fear of burglaries seems like a normal response to the evidence available to her.

Thirdly, we always have to ask 'normal for whom'? Statistical definitions about the commonness or uncommonness of some phenomenon depend on the population we are talking about. In the case above it would make a considerable difference if we measured the woman's fear of burglaries against the norms for all women, or against the norms of all women living alone in inner-city areas who are avid readers of popular newspapers. Similarly it makes a great deal of difference whether we judge the behaviour of a Downs' syndrome child living in a children's home against that of other children, against that of other Downs' syndrome children, or against that of Downs' syndrome children living in care.

'Normal for whom?' becomes a crucial question when we take into account the fact that we live in a very diverse society made up of groups of people who themselves have different ideas about normal and proper behaviour, reasonable and unreasonable beliefs. What can look like 'violence towards children' from one point of view, can look like 'good parental discipline' from another. Someone who believes that their every action is directed by God, may seem odd among atheists, but would be normal in many religious sects.

Lastly in talking about normal behaviour we are always talking about matters of degree. How unusual does behaviour have to be in order for us to call it 'abnormal'? There is really no statistical answer to this question. In fact it is the wrong question. The right question is 'How upsetting, and disturbing and objectionable does something have to be before we call it abnormal?' To define abnormal behaviour as opposed to unusual behaviour requires a moral judgement.

Whenever terms such as 'abnormal behaviour', 'behaviour disorder' or 'mental illness' are used, someone is saying in effect, 'this is undesirable and something should be done about it'. This raises in turn the question of who says this is undesirable, and what they say should be done about it. Terms like 'abnormal behaviour' then, tend to be used for behaviour which causes problems for other people. In any society everyone's behaviour has to be limited to some degree by the interests of everybody else, but whether people are designated as suitable cases for treatment and control depends greatly on how their behaviour affects others, and how tolerant other people are. On the first count, the unusual behaviour of a rich recluse who can indulge his eccentricities in isolation (and to the profit of others) are much less likely to be seen as a problem by others than the same behaviour by someone who has to earn a living working closely with other people, or shares a flat with other residents. On the second count it is noticeable how public tolerance for particular kinds of behaviour shifts from time to time. Opium addiction was common, and little fuss was made about it in 19th century England, compared with attitudes towards opiate addiction today. Male homosexuality, on the other hand, was regarded by the public, the law and the medical profession as a very severe form of mental aberration in the 1950s and by many people as merely a sexual preference today. The use of therapies to control or alter the behaviour of people because they are a problem to others raises acute ethical dilemmas. How should a psychiatrist choose between the interests of someone who wants to fill his council flat with rotting newspapers and empty cans, and the interests of his council landlord, and fellow tenants?

Sometimes these ethical issues are obscured by an unquestioning

► The opiate drugs include opium which was in common use in 19th century England, and more modern drugs such as morphine, codeine, heroin, pethidine and methadone. Today these drugs are very strictly controlled but their pleasurable effects and addictive qualities make for a huge and profitable illegal market. Some experts in illegal drug use believe that most of the problems associated with illegal drug-use are caused by the fact that the drugs are illegal.

assumption that 'normal' people must be right, and those they object to as 'abnormals' must be wrong. The use of the term 'mental illness' can have the same effect. Everybody knows that an illness is a bad thing, and by calling some pattern of behaviour 'mental illness' encourages us to side with health against illness. Labels such as 'abnormal', 'behaviourally disordered', 'mentally ill', or 'insane' are used to deprive people of their civil rights, lock them up, dose them with mind altering drugs, deny them employment, or subject them to brain surgery. Whether this is right or wrong it is not something which can be decided scientifically, but is a moral matter about who has the right to do what to whom.

One group who are often very important in defining the 'abnormal', are the people who suffer from the very real fears, anxiety, miseries, mood changes, and so on, that get defined as mental illness. 'Why can't I be more like other people? I need treatment' they say. At first sight there might seem to be no ethical dilemma in treating someone who themselves has asked for treatment. In all kinds of medicine it is usual to require the patient to give informed consent to medical treatment. Informed consent however means that the patient gives permission in the full knowledge of the likely consequences of the treatment. It is doubtful whether many patients treated for physical illnesses really have enough knowledge to make a fully informed judgement. With regard to mental illness, where patients may be confused, the idea of informed consent is even more tricky. Sometimes it is assumed that one of the symptoms of the mental illness is that the patient is unable to make rational judgements anyway. Mental health legislation and the laws on criminal insanity allow patients to be treated without or against their consent.

A less obvious ethical difficulty arises if the patient's problem derives largely from the attitudes and behaviour of others towards them. For example it can be a relatively unproblematic matter to be a transvestite in a society in which cross-dressing is tolerated, as it is in many parts of the world. But it can be a deeply distressing experience to be a transvestite where this behaviour is regarded as odd, wicked or mad. If a transvestite asks for aversion therapy, should the psychiatrist give it, or advise him to move to Amsterdam, Berlin or Bangkok? The issue is whether the person showing the problem behaviour should be changed to conform, or whether social attitudes should be changed to accommodate more diverse ways of behaving.

► Ethics is that branch of philosophy concerned with 'good' and 'bad', 'right' and 'wrong'. We must not allow ethical issues about who has the right to do what to whom to be ignored in psychiatric practices any more than we should in any other areas of social life (including the design of psychological experiments).

Further Reading: Chapter 10

A good British text outlining the orthodox view of mental illness is

Stafford Clark P. & Smith D. 1979. *Psychiatry for Students*. London: George Allen & Unwin.

For those who prefer original sources the best on Freud could be chosen from *The Pelican Freud Library*, which contains translations of all of Freud's major works.

Otherwise useful introductions to psychoanalytic theory and therapy are found in

Brown J.A.C. 1961. *Freud and the Post Freudians*. Harmondsworth: Penguin.

Kline P. 1981. *Fact and Fantasy in Freudian Theory*. London: Methuen.

The behaviourist view is well covered in

Walker S. 1984. *Learning Theory and Behaviour Modification*. London: Methuen.

Cognitive theories are explained in

Cochrane R. 1983. *The Social Creation of Mental Illness*. London: Longman.

Martin B. 1984. *Abnormal Psychology*. London: Holt Saunders.

The humanist and existential views are explained in

Laing R.D. 1960. *The Divided Self*. London: Tavistock.

Laing R.D. & Esterson A. 1970. *Sanity, Madness and the Family*. Harmondsworth: Penguin.

Rogers C. 1970. *Encounter Groups*. New York: Harper & Row.

An original, and still highly stimulating illustration of labelling and institutionalization theory is

Goffman E. 1968. *Asylums*. Harmondsworth: Penguin.

Szasz's alternative view is neatly summarized (in conversation with Jonathan Miller) in

Miller J. 1983. *States of Mind*. London: BBC Publications.

and in his own book

Szasz T. 1973. *The Manufacture of Madness*. London: Paladin.

Appendix: Study skills

Would you go sky-diving without first learning how to use a parachute? No. It would be stupid. You would be risking your life without bothering to learn the basic skills of your chosen activity.

And yet many people still try to follow programmes of study, and try to take exams, without learning the skills involved. Some students have said to me 'I haven't got time to do all that study skills stuff: I have to spend all my time learning the material.' This is not good thinking. The point about study skills, in every subject, is that, by spending time in developing them, you can then make better use of your learning time. It is like making a good financial investment: it costs you in the short term, but it pays off over and over again in the long term.

Any fool can jump out of an aeroplane. Only someone who has spent time training can do it safely and with enjoyment.

Anyone can enrol for a course, complete assignments and take an exam at the end. Someone who has spent time developing their study technique can do all this to the best of their ability and enjoy it as well.

That's why this Appendix is here. If you are tempted to ignore it, think about sky-divers.

Getting Organized

For 90 per cent of students, the difference between success and failure (or a low grade) is not a matter of how clever you are but of how organized you are.

What do you need to get organized for study? Answer:

(INFORMATION) (TIME) (PLACE) (EQUIPMENT)

Information

Find out, at the start of your course
- (i) how long it is, both in hours per week and in total;
- (ii) what the content (syllabus) is;
- (iii) what homework and coursework you will have to do;
- (iv) how you will be assessed;
- (v) when the final exams are. If your tutor doesn't tell you all this fairly early in the course (though not necessarily on the first day), then ask. When you know the answers, you can start to plan your ...

Question
► Why is a student like a sky-diver?

A sky-diver

► How much time will you need?

► Analyse how you use your time now. Identify the best times for study.

► How can you measure the effectiveness of your study?

► Set objectives for yourself when studying.

► Plan your week's study programme.

► Keep a 'things-to-do' list.

Time

(i) how much study time will you need?

- This varies from one course to another and between part-time and full-time students. A full-time student should think in terms of spending a forty-hour week, including lessons and lectures, on study. After all, that's the least that a full-time job means for most people. A part-time student needs to work out a suitable fraction of this.

(ii) how will you fit this in with your other commitments?

- We all have other commitments, family, social, financial and leisure, and they all have to be met. Unless your life has become very empty, you will have to find the study time by taking it from other areas or, more probably, by identifying all the in-between spaces which you are currently frittering away (we all do it!). You cannot simply add a course onto an already full life.

(iii) when should you study?

- At what time of the day do you work most effectively? (not 'prefer to work' but 'work *effectively*'; there's a difference).

- For how long can you study *effectively* at a stretch, once you are into the habit of study? Practise, and test your own learning, until you know the answer to this question. For most people, the answer is 'about an hour, then I need a short break'.

- Private study for two hours every day is much more effective than one ten-hour stretch on Sunday.

(iv) how can you use this precious time effectively?

- For each period of study, set yourself a realistic objective (e.g., 'I will have read and taken notes from this chapter', 'I will have made a rough draft of this diagram/essay'). Don't stop until you have achieved your objective, but then DO stop, and reward yourself. Phone someone; eat a chocolate biscuit; watch the news.

- Plan your study sessions and their objectives a week in advance. An assignment is much less daunting when you have broken it down into specific tasks with specific objectives. This also makes it easier to use short study periods effectively. Things may not go exactly according to your week's plan, but at least you will know what you have to do to make up the lost time.

- Keep lists of things to be done. These should be specific (e.g., 'Make notes from Chapter 3 of Psychology textbook' not 'Learn about attachment'). Give a realistic deadline to each and cross off items as you complete them.

Place

If you possibly can, identify a location in your home which is your study place and nothing else. Just a table will do. With practice, you will (I promise!) reach a point when the act of sitting in that chair, at that table, triggers the 'work response' in your head. This will *not* happen in relation to your bed or to the armchair from which you watch TV.

It should be a warm place (though not too warm), with a comfortable chair (though not too comfortable), and be well-ventilated. Your brain works on oxygen. Feed it regularly.

▶ Find a suitable place to study.

Equipment

The minimum you will need is:
- A4 size paper, bought in a pad with holes ready punched, lined and/or plain

▶ Paper

- ring-binder files, so that you can store your notes subject by subject, and add to them as you go along
- a good quality pen

▶ Pens

- pencil and rubber
- a ruler (in good condition!)
- possibly a set of drawing instruments
- your text book.

Other materials, such as highlight pens, wallet folders, a stapler and so on are optional. Don't spend more than you can afford, but don't skimp on the essentials.

Take one file to college as your 'current' file, and make regular transfers from it to your subject files, which you keep at home. In this way, you don't carry a huge file around with you, you don't risk losing all your material in one go, and you review your notes regularly.

▶ Files

I strongly recommend that you start a card-index at the beginning of your course. The cards are not too expensive, and the box can be improvised until you have some spare cash.

▶ Card indexes

What you put in your card index will vary from subject to subject, but might include:
- definitions of key words
- formulae
- quotations
- small diagrams
- references (books and articles) for key topics
- summaries of procedures, histories and arguments
- summaries of key ideas or theories
- summaries of books, articles, etc.

The act of summarizing onto a small card is an excellent learning technique, and you will have all your revision notes, organized and easily retrievable, when revision time comes round. Making a card index is easy as you go along, but it's a pain to make one up from scratch from a file full of A4 notes.

> **NB**
> It should be a serious offence for anyone to remove any of your study equipment from its place.

► Knowledge

- Find it
- Get at it
- Record it
- Recall it
- Use it

Catalogue
Index

► Really big libraries are amazing places. Why not arrange to visit one at a university or a polytechnic?

Learning

To be a successful student you have to acquire knowledge, understand it, and be able to use it.

So, you have to be able to:
- find out where you can get the information you need;
- develop the ability to understand this information;
- extract it from a book, lecture, practical exercise or whatever;
- record it in a useable form (on paper, in your head, or both);
- recall or retrieve it when you need it;
- use it skilfully in a variety of situations.

The library

The college library (or Learning Resource Centre) is at the centre of the learning process and is indispensable.

Many people think of libraries as stores of books, and that you use them by going to the shelves and seeing if they have anything of interest. This may be enough if you want just a good read from the fiction section, but it is hopeless as a way of making the most of the library as a learning tool. Modern college libraries have not only books (for lending and for reference) but journals, access to databases on computers and CD-ROMs, photocopying facilities, tapes, videos, word processors and other equipment. You must know how to make the most of all this material.

The catalogues and indexes are the heart of the library and the main skill you will require is using them effectively and efficiently. There is not the space here to tell you in detail how to do this, so follow the golden rule:

> WHEN IN DOUBT, ASK THE LIBRARIAN

Information retrieval is a science. Librarians know all about it and they like to share their knowledge and skill with others. Find out from your college librarian what arrangements they have for library induction and make a point of going. Learn how to use the catalogue. Get to know the library staff and use their expertise.

Remember that the inter Library Loans Scheme enables you to go into your college library, however small it is, and order any book from any library anywhere in the UK. Probably for a fee, you can also order copies of journal articles. Your college library is your route, via the catalogue, to all the knowledge in all the libraries in the country.

Reading

You have found the book or journal article that you wanted. And you can read. So what's the problem?

Many students find that the reading skills which are ok for a novel or the newspaper don't seem to work when reading an academic text. 'I read it four times, and it just didn't sink in.' Don't get upset by this: just recognize that this kind of reading requires different skills.

When you are reading a good story, you can rely on being drawn along by the story-line. When you are reading something which is explaining facts, procedures or arguments, you have to work at it. Sentences are longer. You have to look for the structure of a paragraph, a section or a chapter.

There are crucial linking words like 'therefore', 'however', 'since', and 'although'. In stories, we hardly notice these words. In reading for learning, you must pay attention to them.

▶ Learning to read and reading to learn.

You will need to develop and practise strategies for this kind of reading. These include *skimming* (to get a general idea), *scanning* (to search for particular facts or ideas), and *detailed reading*.

It is not helpful to take an academic book, open it at page one and read it to the end. Instead, you should build up your understanding in stages.

This is the basis of the often-recommended SQ3R method of reading

S   Make a quick SURVEY of the book (or chapter), just to get a general idea of its content and approach.

▶ SQ3R

Q   Identify and list some QUESTIONS, and have them in mind as you read. This will involve you in a dialogue with the text and make you an active reader.

R   Now, at stage 3, you READ the text. This may involve a quick skim, followed by a careful reading, or be just one thorough run- through.

R   Spend some time RECALLING what you have read, may be at the end of each chapter or long section. Don't just think about it: jot it down.

R   Check on your recall by going over the text again and REVIEWING your notes.

Making notes

Please notice that I've called this section 'making notes' rather than 'taking notes'. Notes are not there waiting to be taken: you have to make them. It's another skill to be developed.

Wherever you make notes from, the main purpose is to help you learn, but there are variations. Good notes from a lecture (which are made under pressure of time) mean that you have a permanent record of it. Good notes from a book (made at your own pace) mean that you don't have to read the book again to find out what it was about.

But the main purpose of making notes is that it helps you to RECORD what you read or heard, which helps you to RETAIN it in your memory, so that you can RETRIEVE it later. That adds up to LEARNING.

▶ Record + Retain + Retrieve = Learn

Notes should be notes. Don't write full sentences, but words and phrases. Leave lots of white space around your notes. You may find it helpful to use plain rather than lined paper, especially if you develop the skill of making pattern notes rather than linear ones. I much prefer pattern notes, where you jot down key words and

▶ Reinforcement helps you learn.

phrases and link them together, using circles and arrows, to show how the argument hangs together. If you have never used this technique, ask your librarian for a Study Skills book which explains it in more detail.

The acid test of good notes is whether you can make sense of them six months or a year later when revision time comes round. While you are developing your note-making skills, test yourself by using your notes as the basis of an explanation to a friend. This will reinforce both your learning so, if you take turns, you are doing each other a favour.

The diagram shows you notes taken in this way from pages 7–12 of Chapter 1. You will see that it is half way towards a plan for an essay on the different techniques of collecting data, and the limitations of each.

Presenting your work

You are aiming to communicate what you know, understand and can do. While you are preparing and delivering your work, think not of yourself but of your audience. What will they need to see, read or hear in order to recognize your achievement?

► Think of the reader.

Practise, practise, practise.

Writing, speaking, drawing, layout, making calculations, programming ... they all improve with *practice*.

Written assignments

Some students are perturbed by the fact that the proper style for written assignments varies from subject to subject. For example an English literature essay can be much more personal than a psychology essay, which should take a more detached and analytic stance. You can have opinions in psychology, but you must support them with evidence, and you must give a fair account of other views even if you don't agree with them. Learning the style required by the subject is important. Make sure you take note of your tutor's comments on your written work, and if you don't feel that the tutor's comments give adequate guidance, ask for more.

Planning and writing an assignment can be broken down into stages (*remember what I said about setting study objectives*).

► Study the title.

- The first stage is to study the title until you understand what it is you are being asked to do. If you are asked to 'describe' then do that. If you are asked to 'compare', do it. Pick the question to bits until you really understand it. I'll say some more about this in the next section (on exams) but, if you are not sure about what is wanted from a coursework essay, ask your tutor. But don't just say 'I don't understand': show how you have tried to understand the title, and ask for your ideas to be confirmed or corrected.

► Assemble your resources.

- When you know what the assignment is about, you can start to assemble your material. Look at your lecture notes and file-cards. Check the reading-list of books and articles. Look in the index of

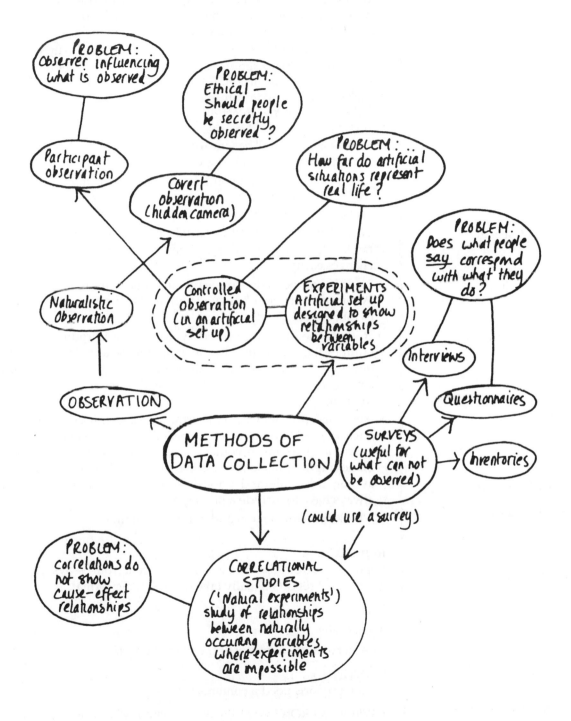

PROBLEM:
Observer influencing
what is observed

PROBLEM:
Ethical —
Should people
be secretly
observed?

PROBLEM:
How far do artificial
situations represent
real life?

PROBLEM:
Does what people
<u>say</u> correspond
with what they
do?

Participant
observation

Covert
observation
(hidden camera)

Naturalistic
Observation

Controlled
observation
(in an artificial
set up)

EXPERIMENTS
Artificial set up
designed to show
relationships
between
variables

Interviews

Questionnaires

OBSERVATION

METHODS OF
DATA COLLECTION

SURVEYS
(useful for
what can not
be observed)

Inventories

(could use a survey)

PROBLEM:
correlations do
not show
cause-effect
relationships

CORRELATIONAL
STUDIES
('Natural experiments')
study of relationships
between naturally
occurring variables,
where experiments
are impossible

► Make notes.

► Organize your notes.

► Check the title again.

► Write the first draft.

► Leave it a while.

► Write the second draft.

► The final draft.

► Check the final version.

► Meet the deadlines.

your textbooks. Since you know what you are looking for, you can read using the 'scan' technique described earlier. This means you read actively not just wandering vaguely about the printed pages. Make lots of notes, all the time, perhaps on half-size pieces of paper. As you do this, a structure will begin to emerge.

• Organize your notes into sections which correspond to the emerging structure. Every assignment must have an introduction, a middle section, and a conclusion. If you have made your notes on lots of pieces of paper, you can literally shuffle them about until it all hangs together. You may find it necessary to write additional notes that show how one idea or fact relates to another. Use lots of paper at this stage. It can all be scrap or recycled, and you can use the backs of the pieces when planning your next essay.

• Check that the resulting outline responds to the title of the assignment. There's a good chance that your first plan will have to be changed quite substantially.

• Now write the first draft, based on your organized notes. It is helpful to write this on every other line, so that you can make changes easily.

• Now if you possibly can, leave this first draft alone for a week. When you come back to it, you will see its strengths and weaknesses much more clearly.

• Rewrite the draft. Remember, you need an introduction (which outlines the key themes of the assignment), a main body (which develops the main points, quoting evidence and argument) and a conclusion (which draws the thing together and refers directly back to the title).

• Your final draft, which might be the second or third version, should be clearly written and correctly spelled and punctuated, and should have wide margins. If your tutor requires it, you should include a bibliography. This is a list of the books which you used, giving author, title, date and publisher. In higher education, you will always have to include a bibliography.

• Check the final version and hand it in on time.

Reports

Reports require a structure which is different from essays. Psychology practical reports usually take the following format:

TITLE

ABSTRACT
  A very short summary of the whole report.

CONTENTS
  Long reports need a contents list.

INTRODUCTION
  This starts with a brief review of the psychological literature relevant to the report and ends with a clear statement of the hypothesis which the research was designed to test.

METHOD
The design of the research.
Characteristics of the subjects and how they were chosen.
Description of the research instruments or apparatus used.
Procedures followed – how the research was done.

RESULTS
Summary of the results.
Analysis of the results.
Was the hypothesis confirmed or not?

DISCUSSION
How well did the research methods work/how could the research design or procedures have been improved?

CONCLUSIONS
You may have already given most of the conclusions in the results section. If not, complete the job here. End with a discussion of the implications of your results for psychological theories, i.e. tie the conclusion back to the relevant psychological literature discussed in the introduction.

REFERENCES
List only those books and articles you have actually mentioned in the report. List in alphabetical order. Follow the style used in this book.

APPENDICES
Write the report so that it is easy to follow. Use the appendices to store material which would interrupt the flow of your report, i.e. if you used a questionnaire, include it in the appendices. Don't put all your results in the report. Put them in the appendices and show them selectively in the report. But do refer to the appendices in the report.

Graphs and tables

Never be slapdash about this material. Graphs and tables should communicate as clearly as do the words in your assignment. Think about whether a table, a pie-chart, a bar-chart or a graph will best communicate what you want to say. Draw them carefully (NOT freehand). Be careful about scaling. Make sure you have labelled everything fully. Use colour imaginatively.

A note on extended assignments

You will be given weeks or even months for an extended assignment. It is essential to break the task down into its elements, to make a careful plan about what you will do when, and to set yourself a series of deadlines, the last one of which should be at least ten days before the assignment is due in. It is often helpful to keep a diary of your work as you go along.

Everything I have said about files, card-indexes, note-making, planning and drafting applies even more emphatically here.

And do write, all the time. Don't leave yourself with a mass of notes to 'write up' in the last fortnight.

Doing a substantial piece of research and writing it up should be the most satisfactory experience of your whole course. Without proper organization, it will be the most miserable.

Revision and exams

Many courses nowadays are assessed through a combination of coursework and exams, but very few have no exams at all so revision and exam skills are still needed by most students.

In an ideal world, you would be reviewing and revising your work from the second day of the course, but we don't live in an ideal world and most people leave revision until the last few weeks before the exams. Nevertheless, if you have taken some of the advice offered earlier, you will have been maintaining notes and file-cards throughout your course, so you are off to a flying start when revision time comes.

▶ Active revision.

You will (I hope) have noticed that, throughout this section, I have advised that you study actively rather than passively. Nowhere is this more important than in the revision period. Passive revision, i.e., sitting reading through notes and textbooks, is both boring and ineffective.

▶ What kind of examination?

- Make sure you know how you will be examined. How many exams? How long? Will you have a choice of questions? Will there be any compulsory questions? Short answer questions? Multiple choice questions? Essay questions? Data-response questions? Is there an oral exam? Is there a practical? Will you be allowed books or a calculator in the exam room? These all require different skills and different ways of revising.

- Establish, probably with the help of your tutor, just how much of the syllabus you should revise.

▶ What is being assessed?

- Check what are usually called the 'assessment objectives' which are printed in your syllabus document. In modern exams, most marks are given for applying and using the information you have, rather than just regurgitating it, so you must practise that skill.

▶ Revision objectives.

- Work out a revision schedule, with realistic learning objectives at each stage. You will find many of the Chapter objectives in this book helpful.

▶ Using past papers.

- Use past papers, but NOT to question-spot. Question-spotting is a bad mistake. Use past papers to identify which broad topics the examiner asks about and revise them carefully. What you must NOT do is revise actual questions or prepare model answers. See the 'golden rule' below.

- Read the Chief Examiner's Report for previous years. These are available from the Examination Board and should be in your college library.

▶ Notes about notes.

- Make notes and summaries, all the time. Make notes of your notes and summaries of your summaries. You can reduce the whole course to a series of trigger words and phrases!

- Ask yourself questions, and answer them.

- Write answers, do calculations, make plans, draw diagrams, under pressure of time. How much can you get down on paper in the time allowed? Practise writing answers of that length. Practise the skills you will use in the exam. You may be a terrific talker but, in a written exam, that is worth nothing.

- Work in regular sessions, with breaks every hour, but get used to working for three hours at a time.

- Revise with friends, discussing questions and trying to explain things to each other.

- Give yourself some time off, especially on the day before the exams start.

The examination

Think of the exam as an opportunity for you to give a performance, with an audience of one – the examiner. You are displaying your knowledge, understanding and skills to someone who wants to applaud them.

Examiners want you to do well. They are instructed to mark your work by giving credit for everything you do properly, not by penalising your mistakes. Your marks start at zero and go up whenever you do something right. The examiner is looking for opportunities to 'reward positive achievement'. So supply plenty of these opportunities and make it easy for the examiner to find them. Exam answers are vehicles for you to display your achievement.

Here are some key points about exams:

- Make sure you know exactly when and where the exam will be held.

- Make sure, the evening before, that you have all the pens, pencils, drawing instruments, calculator (spare battery?), etc. that you will need.

- Arrive in good time, but don't stand round chatting. Go for a walk to loosen up and to get the oxygen flowing to the brain.

- If you suffer badly from nerves, learn to relax through the use of deep breathing techniques. Don't take pills, except as a last resort and under medical supervision. Definitely, don't drink alcohol before an exam. It relaxes the wrong bits of your brain.

- When the exam starts, read through the whole paper (or those parts that relate to your options). Do NOT start writing straight away, but settle down, get the feel of the paper, check the instructions and find the questions you feel ok about. Take these first few minutes slowly and methodically.

- Choose your probable questions, but don't 'firm up' at this early stage.

- The marks allocated to each question are a rough guide to how much you should write on each. If two marks are allocated, make

► Questions.

► Answers.

► Revision syndicates.

► The exam as a performance.

► Help the examiner.

► Find out where and when the examination is being held.

► Get equipped.

► Dealing with stress.

► Take it easy.

► Write enough but not too much.

two good points and stop. You will get no more than two marks, however many brilliant points you make. Similarly, you won't get the marks on a ten-mark question if you only make two points.

- Start your first question. Now for the golden rule of all exams.

> ANSWER THE QUESTION SET:
> DO WHAT THE EXAMINER TELLS YOU TO DO

► The golden rule.

I have marked hundreds of exam papers. The most common reason for candidates failing to get the marks they should is not that they lack the knowledge but that they ignore this rule. They usually deal with the right topic but they don't 'discuss' or 'compare and contrast' or 'outline' or 'describe' or 'give three reasons why' or 'explain and account for' or they answer only the first part of a multi-part question.

- Unless only a very short answer is required, make a plan.

► Think of your audience.

- Presentation and layout are important, because they should help the examiner to find your good points easily. Use short sentences and paragraphs. Lay out diagrams, calculations and graphs clearly and make them as large as is reasonable.

- Think all the time about scoring marks. If what you are doing doesn't help score marks, it's worthless.

- In fact, THINK all the time. Don't just try to remember things, but think about how to use and apply what you know to the question set.

- Answer the number of questions required. You are guaranteeing a disappoint result if you don't.

- Don't overrun your time on a particular question. It takes much longer to get a few more marks at the end of one answer than to get the first few at the start of another.

- Take rests during the exam. Loosen up physically, breathe, stretch, shut your eyes while you are thinking.

Good luck!

- Leave time for checking and polishing your answers. A single additional mark could mean a higher grade.

Further Reading: General

Burns P. & Dobson C. 1984. *Introductory Psychology*. Cambridge: MIT Press.

Coolican H. 1990. *Research Methods and Statistics in Psychology*. London: Hodder & Stoughton.

Dobson C. Hardy M. & Heyes S. 1981. *Understanding Psychology*. London: Weidenfeld & Nicholson.

Gross R. 1987. *Psychology*. London: Hodder & Stoughton.

Gross R. 1990. *Key Studies in Psychology*. London: Hodder & Stoughton.

Hayes N. 1984. *A First Course in Psychology*. London: Nelson Harrap.

Hayes N. & Orrel S. 1987. *Psychology: an introduction*. London: Longman.

Lefrancois G. 1982. *Psychology*. London: Wadsworth.

Medcoff J. & Roth J. *Approaches to Psychology*. Milton Keynes: Open University Press.

Morgan C. & King R. *et al* 1986. *Introduction to Psychology (7th edition)*. Maidenhead: McGraw Hill.

Roediger M. & Rushton J. *et al* 1984. *Psychology*. London: Little, Brown & Co.

Wade C. & Tavris C. 1989. *Psychology*. New York: Harper & Row.

Index of proper names

index